Shojo Beat

O*T*O*MEN

Story & Art by
Aya Kanno

Volume
FOUR

OTOMEN CHARACTERS & STORY

What is an OTOMEN?

O•to•men *[OH-toe-men]*

1) A young man with girlish interests and thoughts.

2) A young man who has talent for cooking, needlework and general housework.

3) A manly young man with a girlish heart.

Asuka Masamune

The captain of Ginyuri Academy High School's kendo team. He is handsome, studious and (to the casual observer) the perfect high school student. But he is actually an *otomen*, a man with a girlish heart. He loves cute things ♥, and he has a natural talent for cooking, needlework and general housekeeping. He's even a big fan of the girls' comic *Love Chick*.

STORY

Asuka Masamune, the kendo captain, is actually an *otomen* (a girlish guy)— a man who likes cute things, housework and girls' comics. When he was young, his father left home to become a woman. His mother was traumatized, and ever since then, he has kept his girlish interests a secret. However, things change when he meets Juta, a guy who is using Asuka as the basis for the female character in the shojo comic he is writing (←top secret). Asuka also starts having feelings for a tomboy girl who is good at martial arts. Because of this, he's slowly reverting to his true *otomen* self!

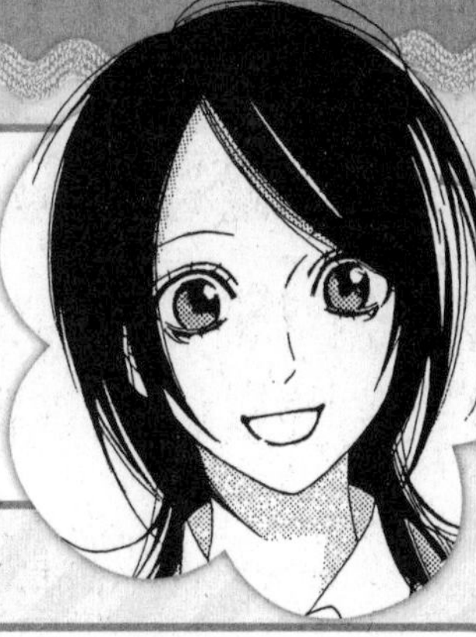

Ryo Miyakozuka

Asuka's classmate for whom he has feelings. She has studied martial arts under her father ever since she was little, and she is very good at it. On the other hand, her housekeeping skills are disastrous. She's a very eccentric beauty.

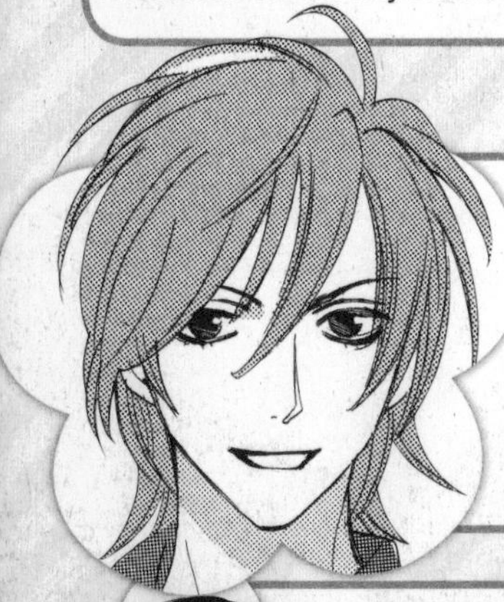

Juta Tachibana

Asuka's classmate. He's flirtatious, but he's actually the popular shojo manga artist Jewel Sachihana. He is using Asuka and Ryo as character concepts in his manga *Love Chick*, which is being published in the shojo magazine *Hana to Mame*. His personal life is a mystery!

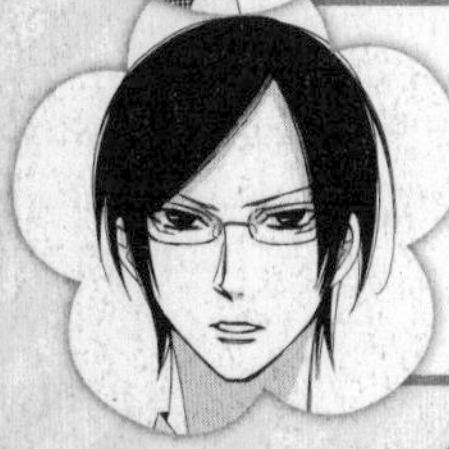

Hajime Tonomine

The captain of Kinbara High School's kendo team, he sees Asuka as his lifelong rival. He is the strong and silent type but is actually an *otomen* who is good with makeup. A *Tsun-sama*. ("Tsun-sama" © Juta Tachibana.)

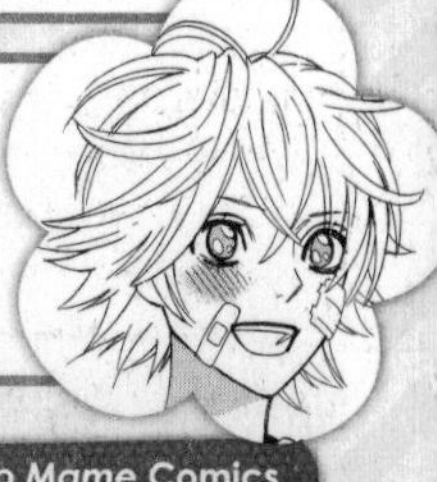

Yamato Ariake

Underclassman at Asuka's school. He looks like a girl, but he admires manliness and has long, delusional fantasies about being manly…

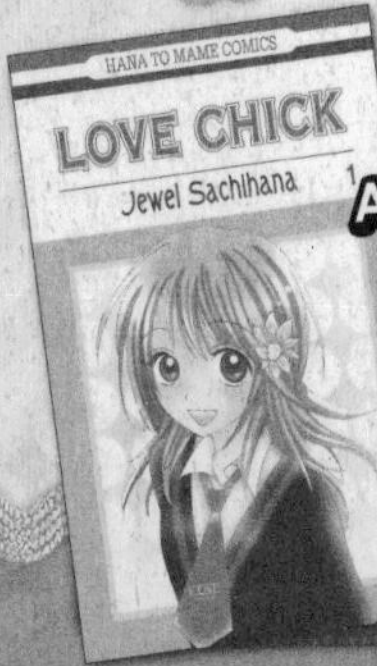

HANA TO MAME COMICS
LOVE CHICK
Jewel Sachihana 1

Asuka is also a BIG FAN!

Hana to Mame Comics

LOVE CHICK by Jewel Sachihana

(Now serialized in *Hana to Mame*)

The very popular shojo comic that Juta writes (under the pen name Jewel Sachihana). It is a pure-love story about Asuka, a tomboy girl who falls head over heels in love with a boy named Ryo!

OTOMEN

volume 4
CONTENTS

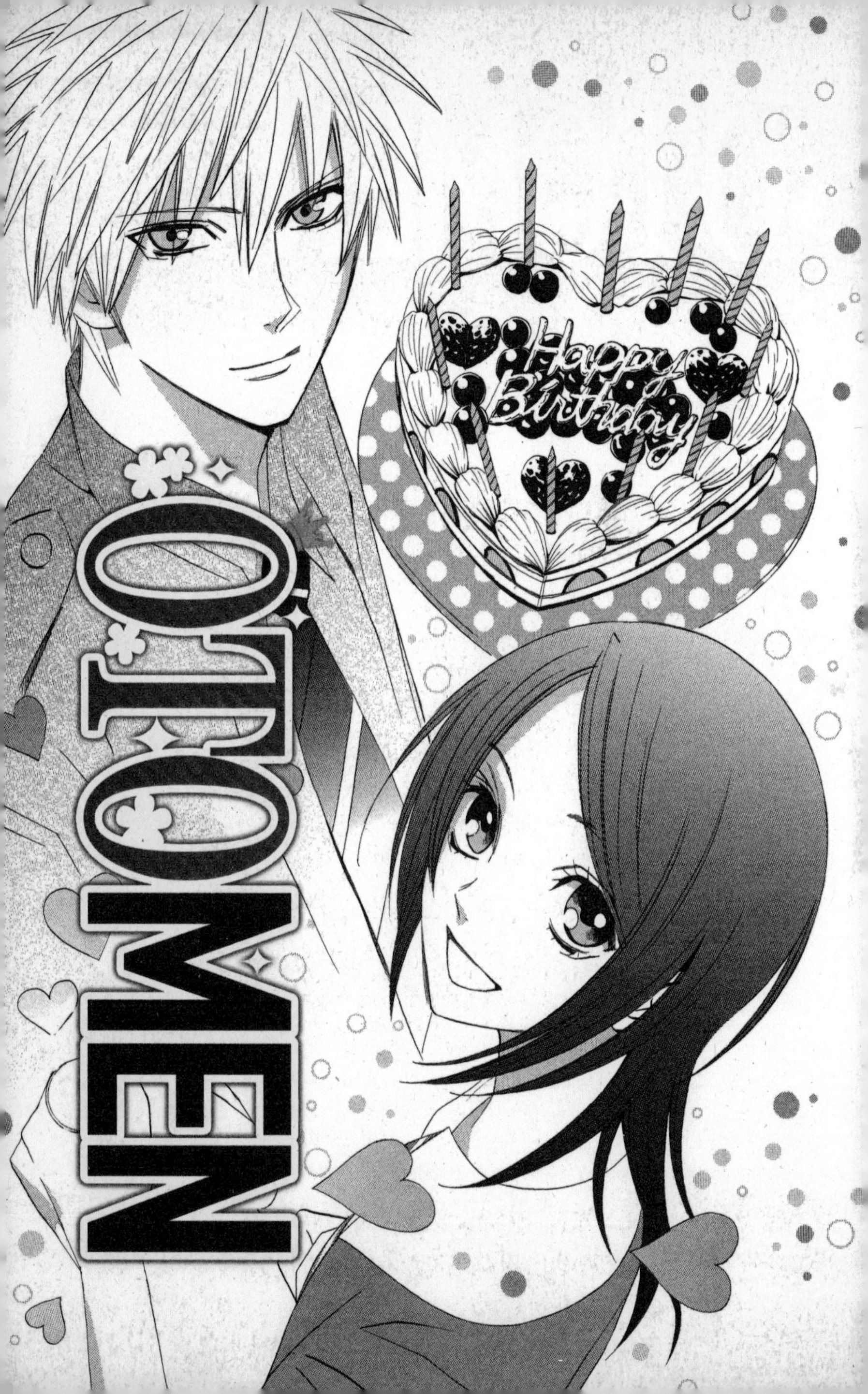
OTOMEN
Happy Birthday

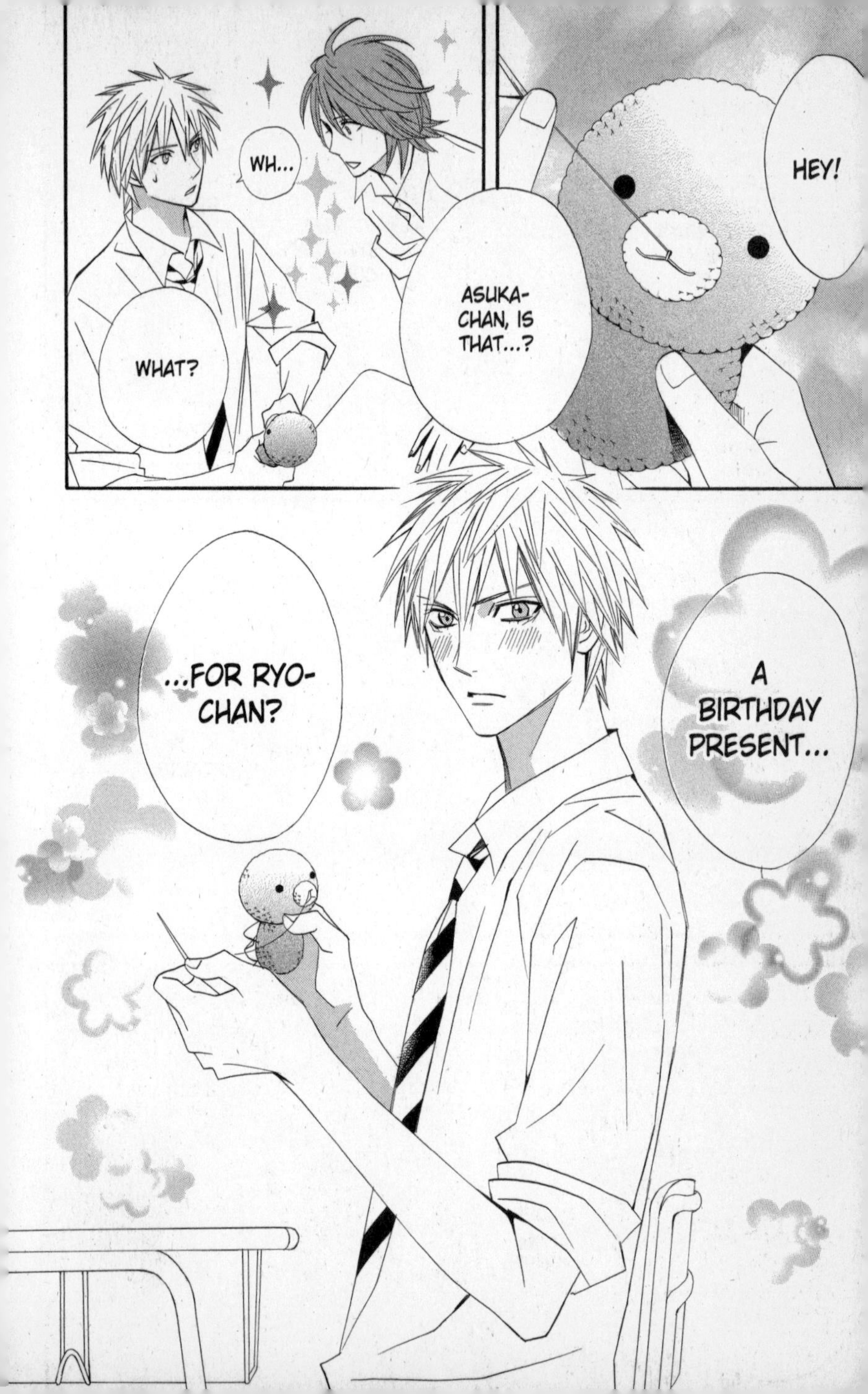
HEY!
ASUKA-CHAN, IS THAT...?
WH...
WHAT?
A BIRTHDAY PRESENT...
...FOR RYO-CHAN?

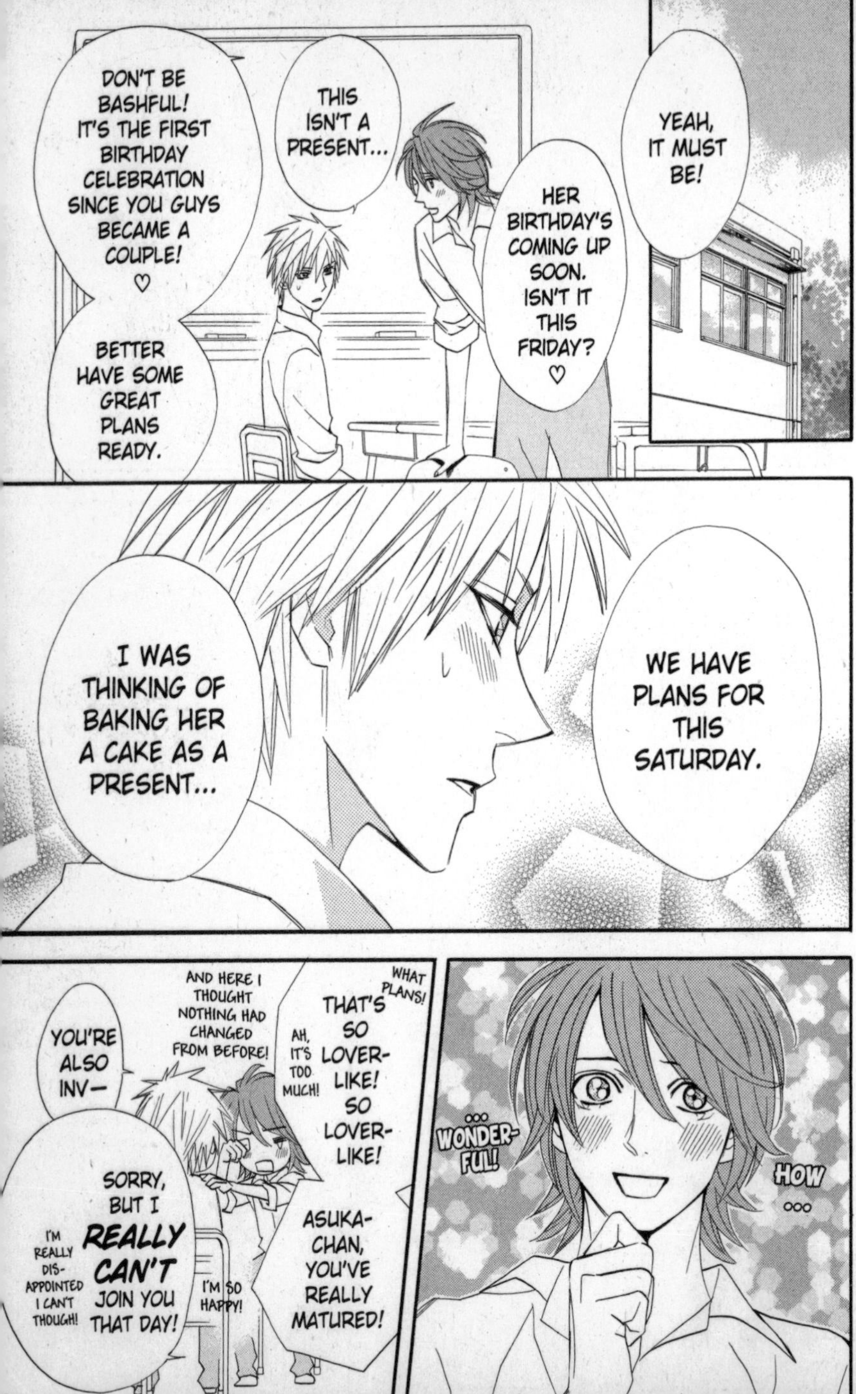
YEAH, IT MUST BE!
HER BIRTHDAY'S COMING UP SOON. ISN'T IT THIS FRIDAY? ♡
THIS ISN'T A PRESENT...
DON'T BE BASHFUL! IT'S THE FIRST BIRTHDAY CELEBRATION SINCE YOU GUYS BECAME A COUPLE! ♡
BETTER HAVE SOME GREAT PLANS READY.
WE HAVE PLANS FOR THIS SATURDAY.
I WAS THINKING OF BAKING HER A CAKE AS A PRESENT...
HOW ...
...WONDERFUL!
WHAT PLANS!
THAT'S SO LOVER-LIKE! SO LOVER-LIKE!
AH, IT'S TOO MUCH!
AND HERE I THOUGHT NOTHING HAD CHANGED FROM BEFORE!
ASUKA-CHAN, YOU'VE REALLY MATURED!
I'M SO HAPPY!
YOU'RE ALSO INV—
SORRY, BUT I **REALLY CAN'T** JOIN YOU THAT DAY!
I'M REALLY DIS-APPOINTED I CAN'T THOUGH!

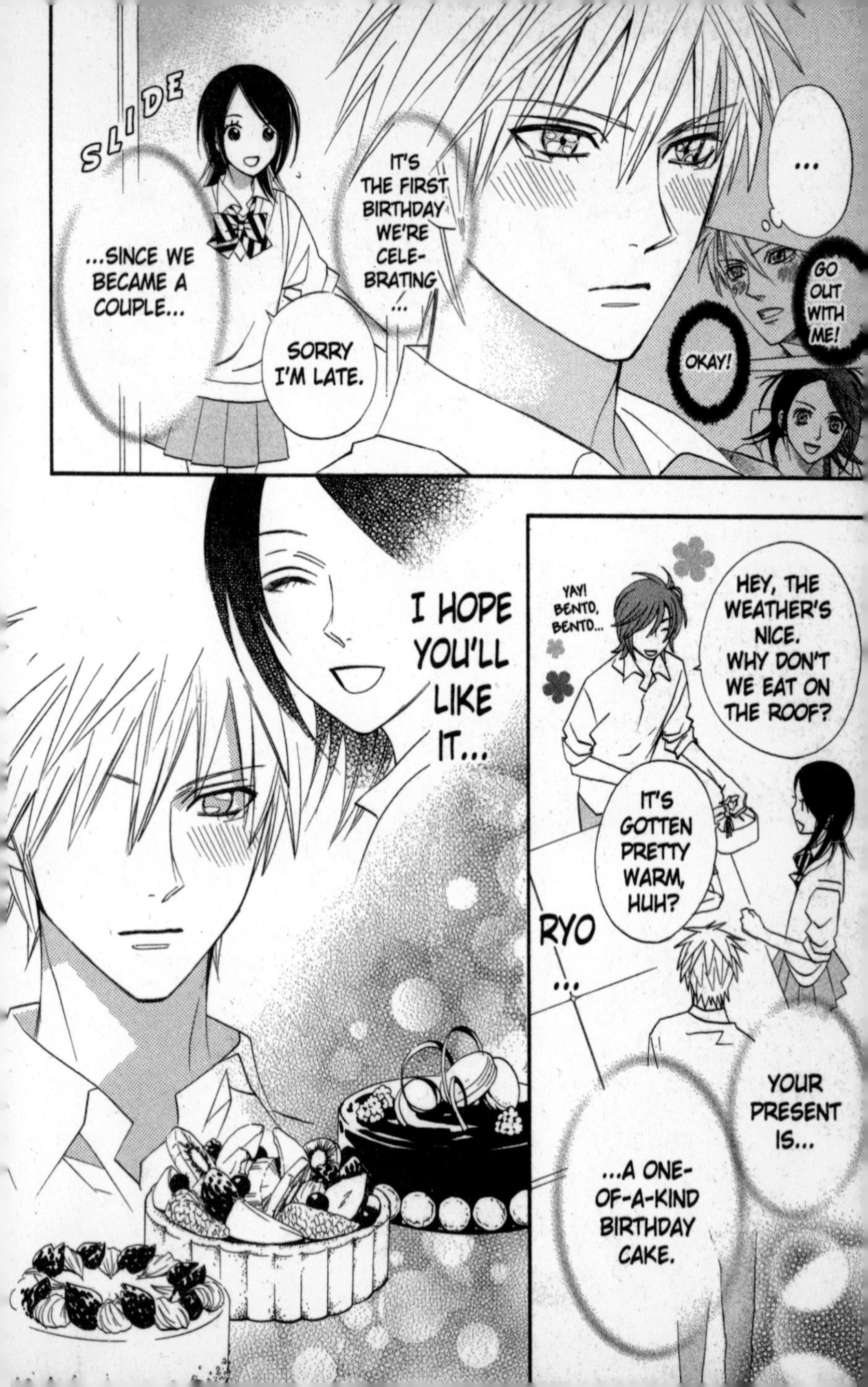
...
GO OUT WITH ME!
OKAY!
IT'S THE FIRST BIRTHDAY WE'RE CELE-BRATING...
SLIDE
...SINCE WE BECAME A COUPLE...
SORRY I'M LATE.
HEY, THE WEATHER'S NICE. WHY DON'T WE EAT ON THE ROOF?
YAY! BENTO, BENTO...
IT'S GOTTEN PRETTY WARM, HUH?
RYO...
YOUR PRESENT IS...
...A ONE-OF-A-KIND BIRTHDAY CAKE.
I HOPE YOU'LL LIKE IT...

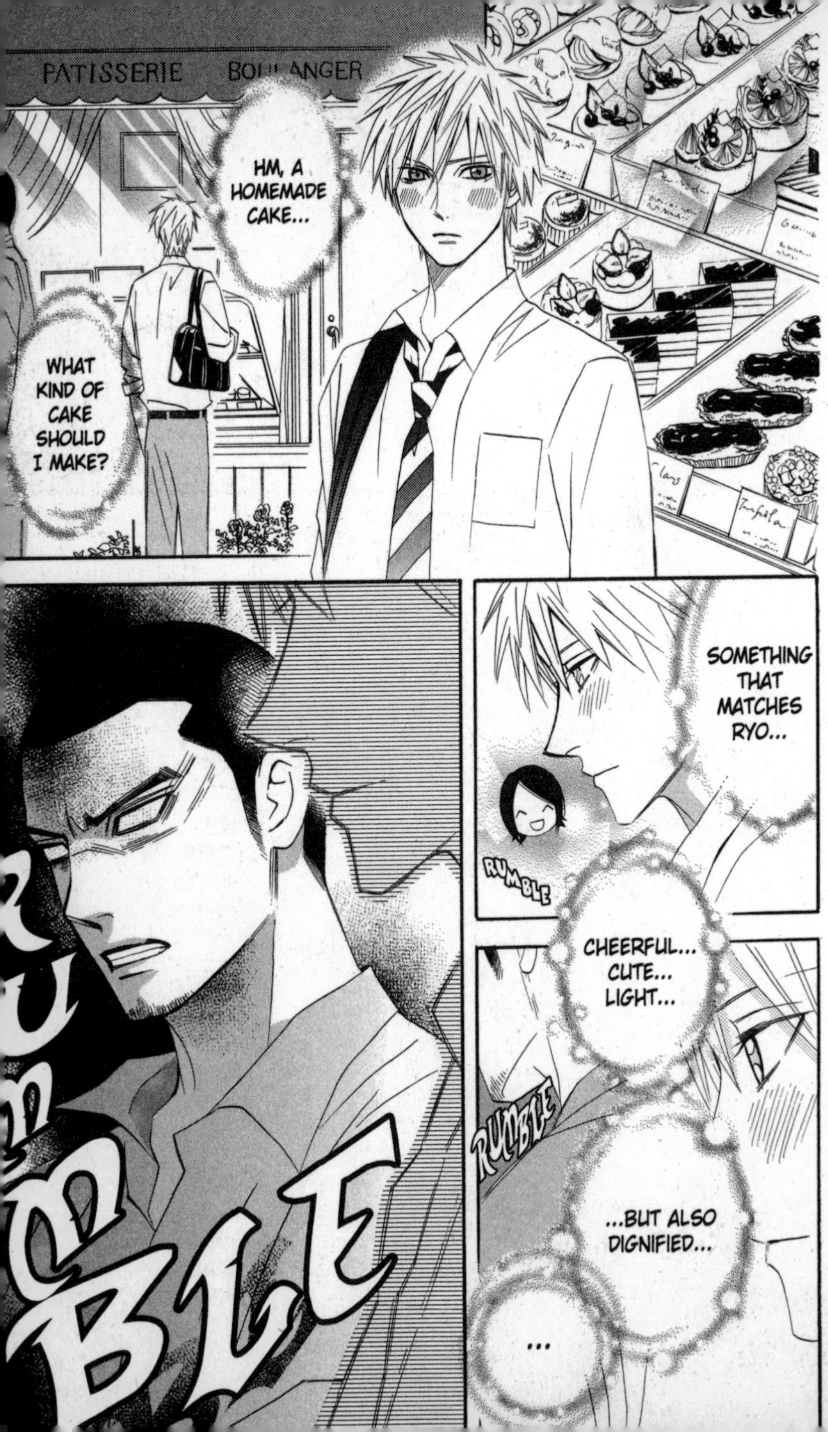
PATISSERIE BOULANGER
HM, A HOMEMADE CAKE...
WHAT KIND OF CAKE SHOULD I MAKE?
SOMETHING THAT MATCHES RYO...
RUMBLE
CHEERFUL... CUTE... LIGHT...
RUMBLE
...BUT ALSO DIGNIFIED...
...
RUMBLE

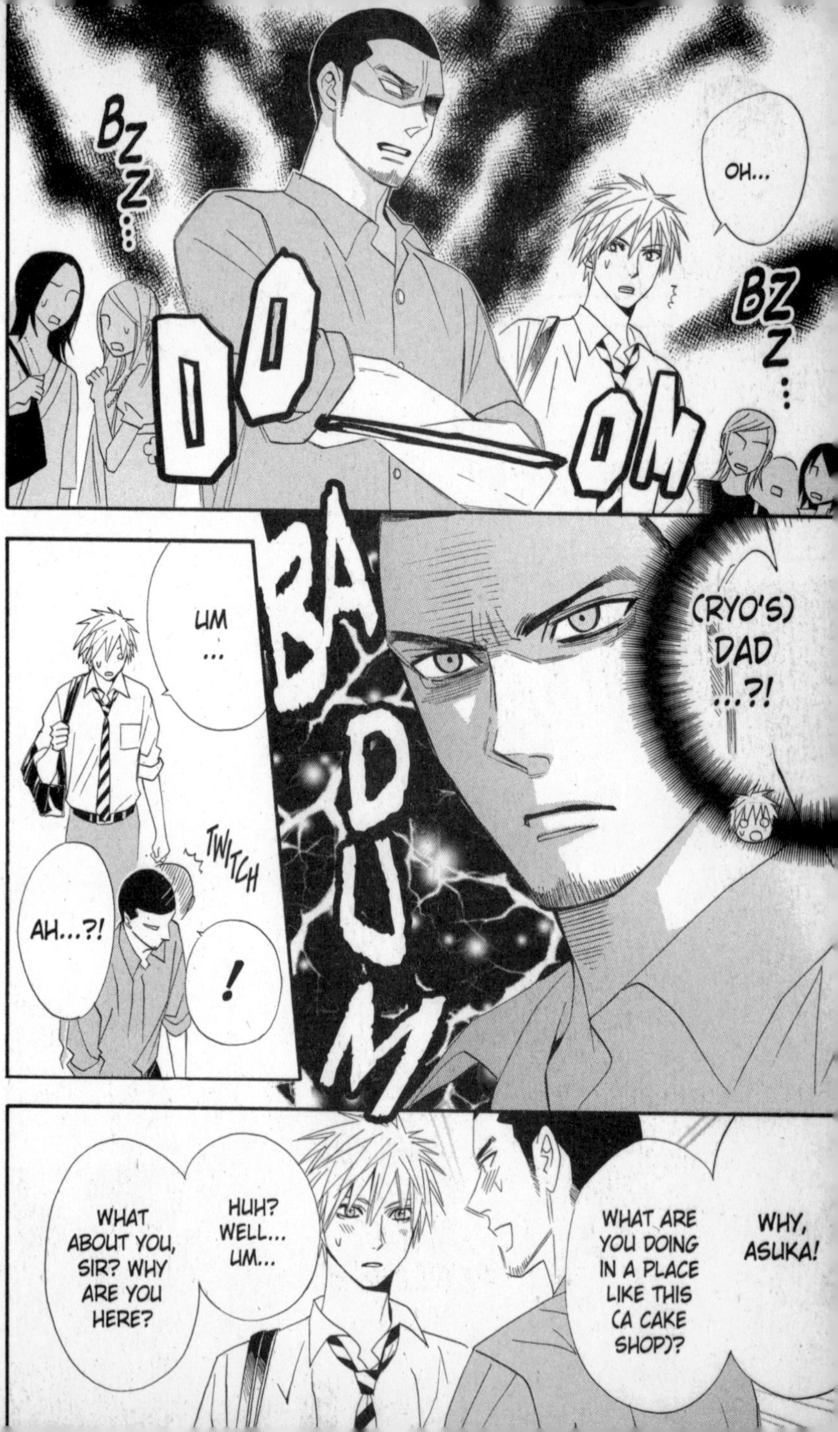
OH...
BZZZ...
DOOM
BZZZ...
(RYO'S) DAD...?!
BADUM
UM...
TWITCH
!
AH...?!
WHY, ASUKA!
WHAT ARE YOU DOING IN A PLACE LIKE THIS (A CAKE SHOP)?
HUH? WELL... UM...
WHAT ABOUT YOU, SIR? WHY ARE YOU HERE?

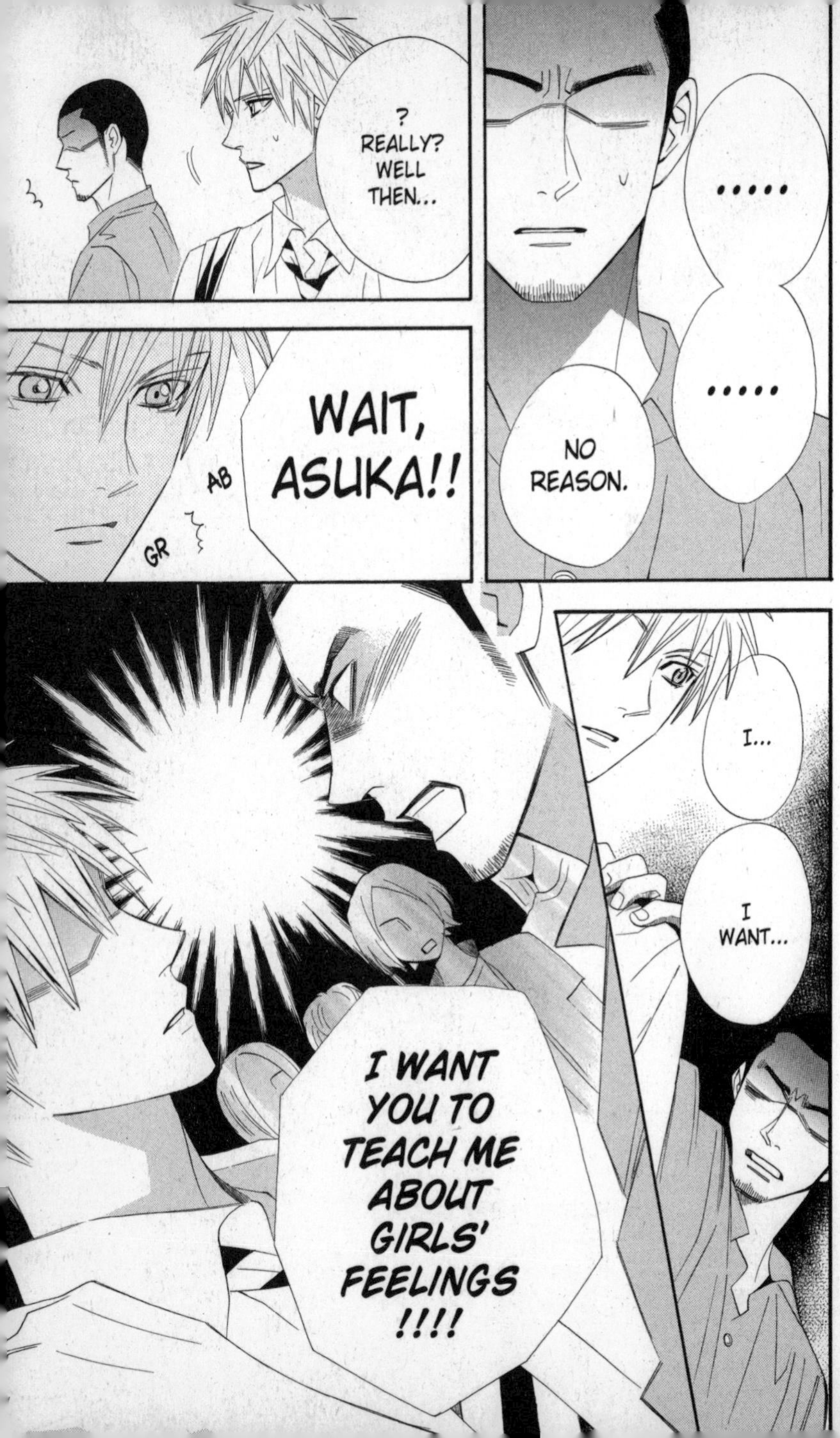
.....
.....
NO REASON.
? REALLY? WELL THEN...
WAIT, ASUKA!!
AB
GR
I...
I WANT...
I WANT YOU TO TEACH ME ABOUT GIRLS' FEELINGS !!!!

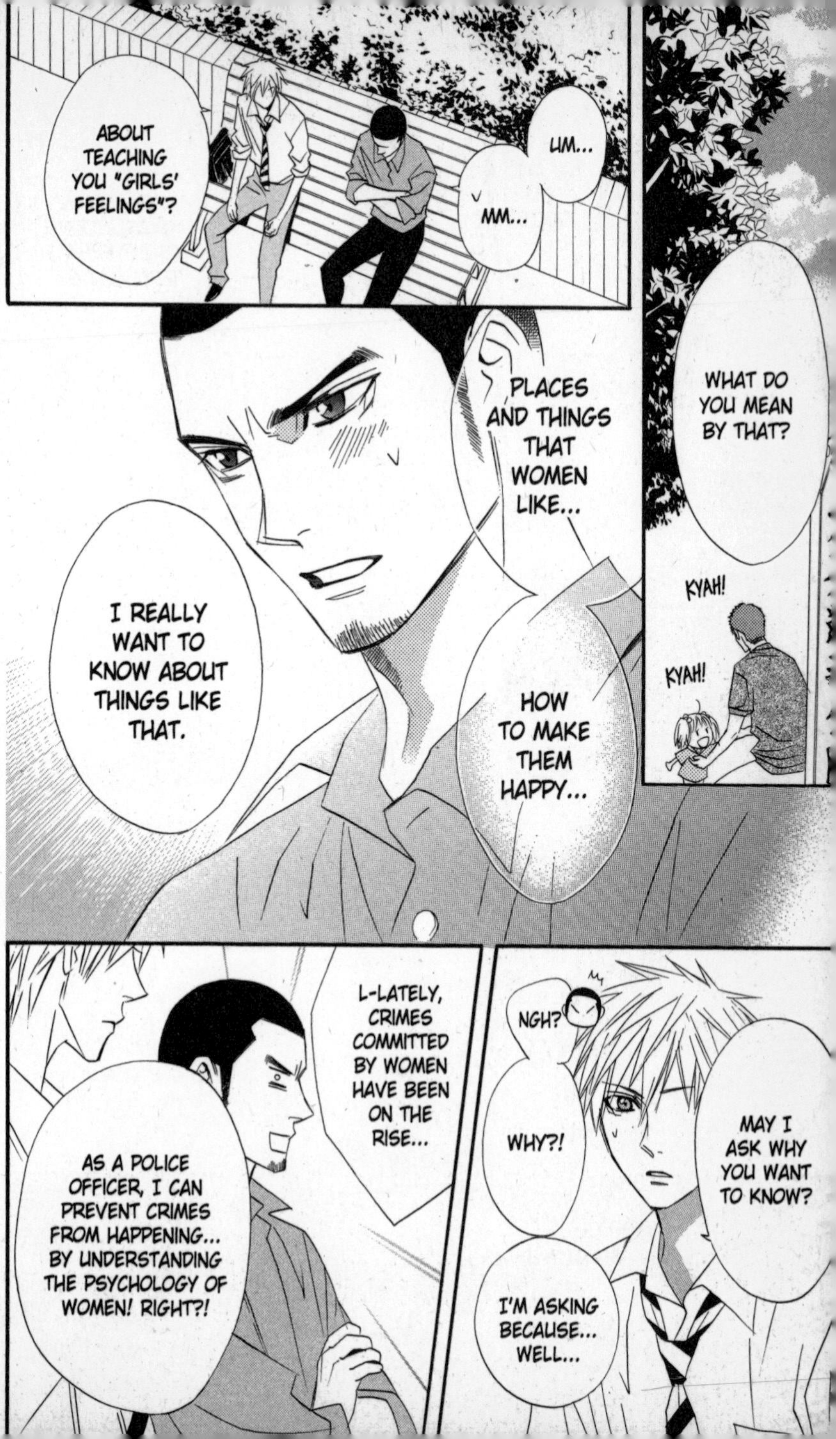
WHAT DO YOU MEAN BY THAT?
KYAH!
KYAH!
UM...
MM...
ABOUT TEACHING YOU "GIRLS' FEELINGS"?
PLACES AND THINGS THAT WOMEN LIKE...
HOW TO MAKE THEM HAPPY...
I REALLY WANT TO KNOW ABOUT THINGS LIKE THAT.
MAY I ASK WHY YOU WANT TO KNOW?
NGH?
WHY?!
I'M ASKING BECAUSE... WELL...
L-LATELY, CRIMES COMMITTED BY WOMEN HAVE BEEN ON THE RISE...
AS A POLICE OFFICER, I CAN PREVENT CRIMES FROM HAPPENING... BY UNDERSTANDING THE PSYCHOLOGY OF WOMEN! RIGHT?!

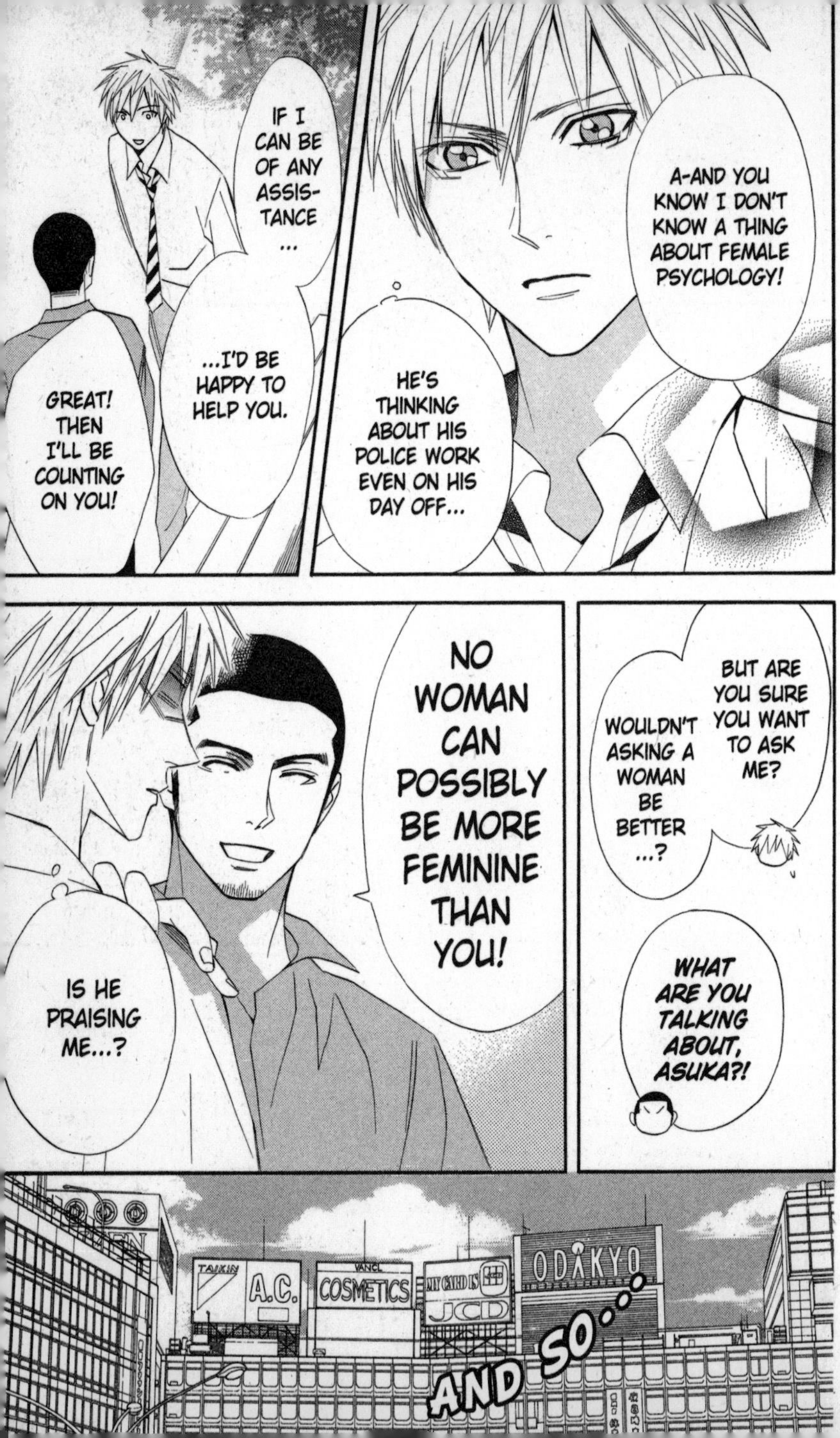
A-AND YOU KNOW I DON'T KNOW A THING ABOUT FEMALE PSYCHOLOGY!
HE'S THINKING ABOUT HIS POLICE WORK EVEN ON HIS DAY OFF...
IF I CAN BE OF ANY ASSIS-TANCE ...
...I'D BE HAPPY TO HELP YOU.
GREAT! THEN I'LL BE COUNTING ON YOU!
BUT ARE YOU SURE YOU WANT TO ASK ME?
WOULDN'T ASKING A WOMAN BE BETTER ...?
WHAT ARE YOU TALKING ABOUT, ASUKA?!
NO WOMAN CAN POSSIBLY BE MORE FEMININE THAN YOU!
IS HE PRAISING ME...?
ODAKYO
MY CARD IS
JCD
VANCL
COSMETICS
TAIKIN
A.C.
AND SO...

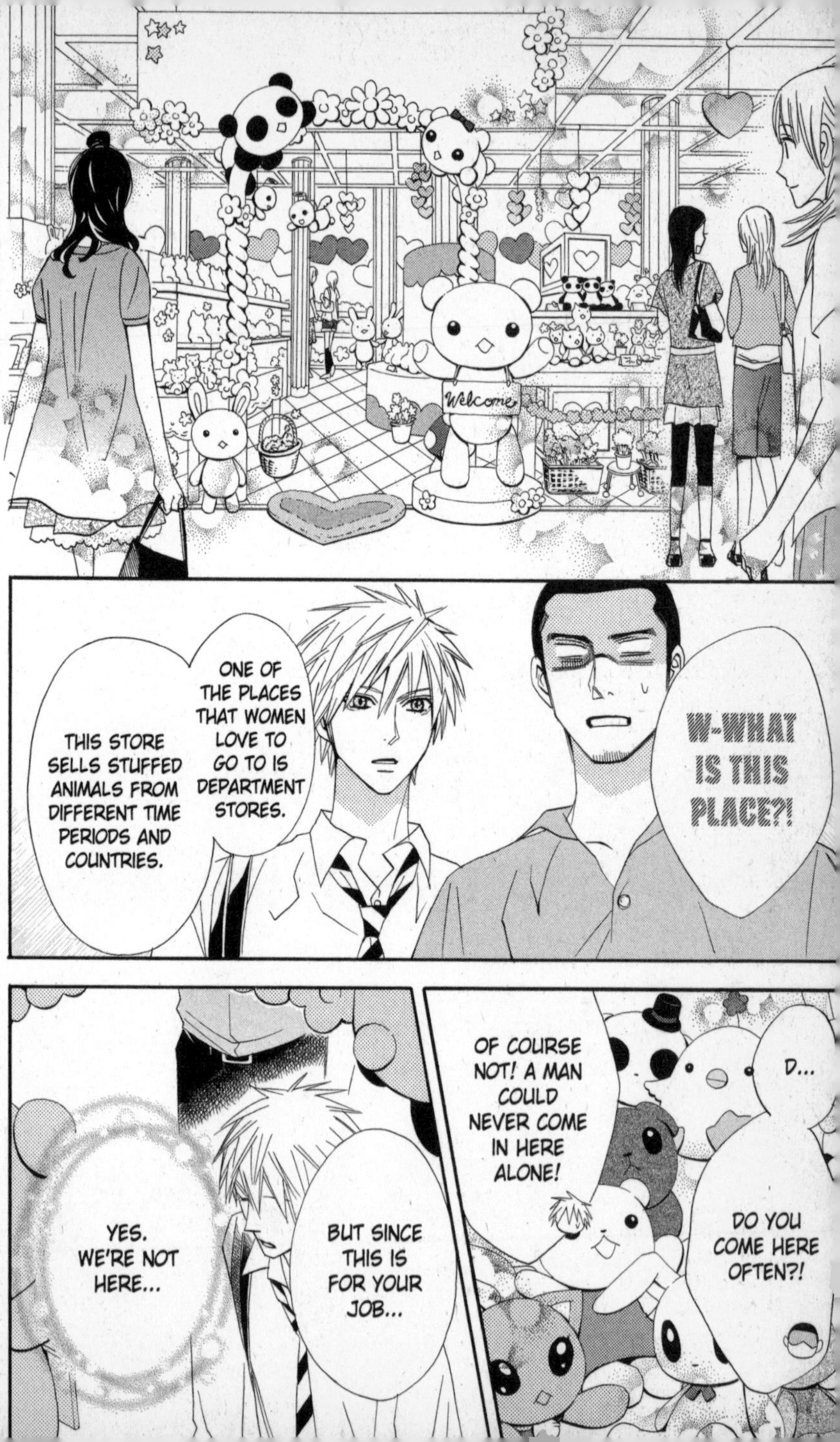
Welcome
W-WHAT IS THIS PLACE?!
ONE OF THE PLACES THAT WOMEN LOVE TO GO TO IS DEPARTMENT STORES.
THIS STORE SELLS STUFFED ANIMALS FROM DIFFERENT TIME PERIODS AND COUNTRIES.
D...
DO YOU COME HERE OFTEN?!
OF COURSE NOT! A MAN COULD NEVER COME IN HERE ALONE!
BUT SINCE THIS IS FOR YOUR JOB...
YES. WE'RE NOT HERE...

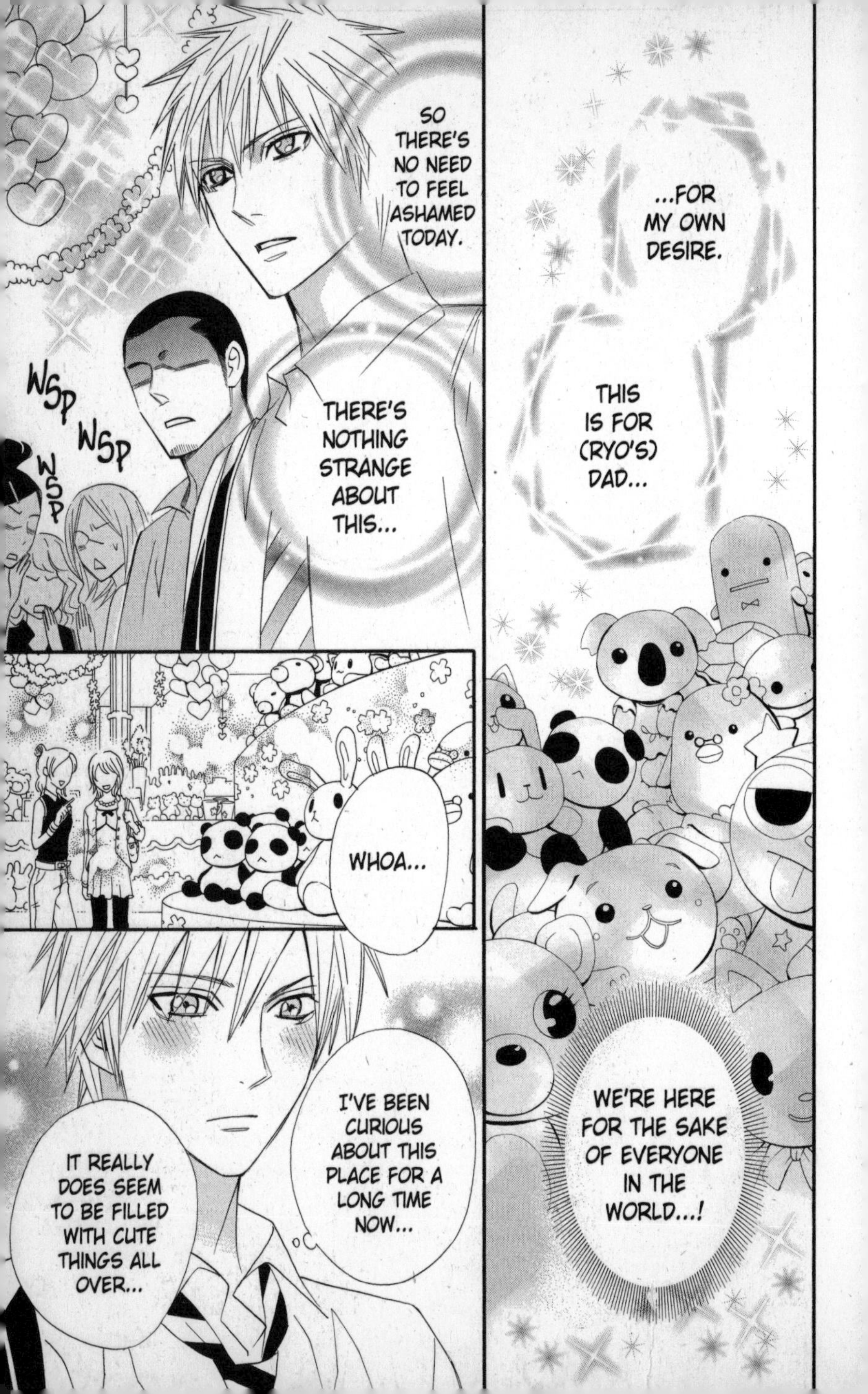
...FOR MY OWN DESIRE.
THIS IS FOR (RYO'S) DAD...
WE'RE HERE FOR THE SAKE OF EVERYONE IN THE WORLD...!
SO THERE'S NO NEED TO FEEL ASHAMED TODAY.
THERE'S NOTHING STRANGE ABOUT THIS...
WSP WSP WSP
WHOA...
I'VE BEEN CURIOUS ABOUT THIS PLACE FOR A LONG TIME NOW...
IT REALLY DOES SEEM TO BE FILLED WITH CUTE THINGS ALL OVER...

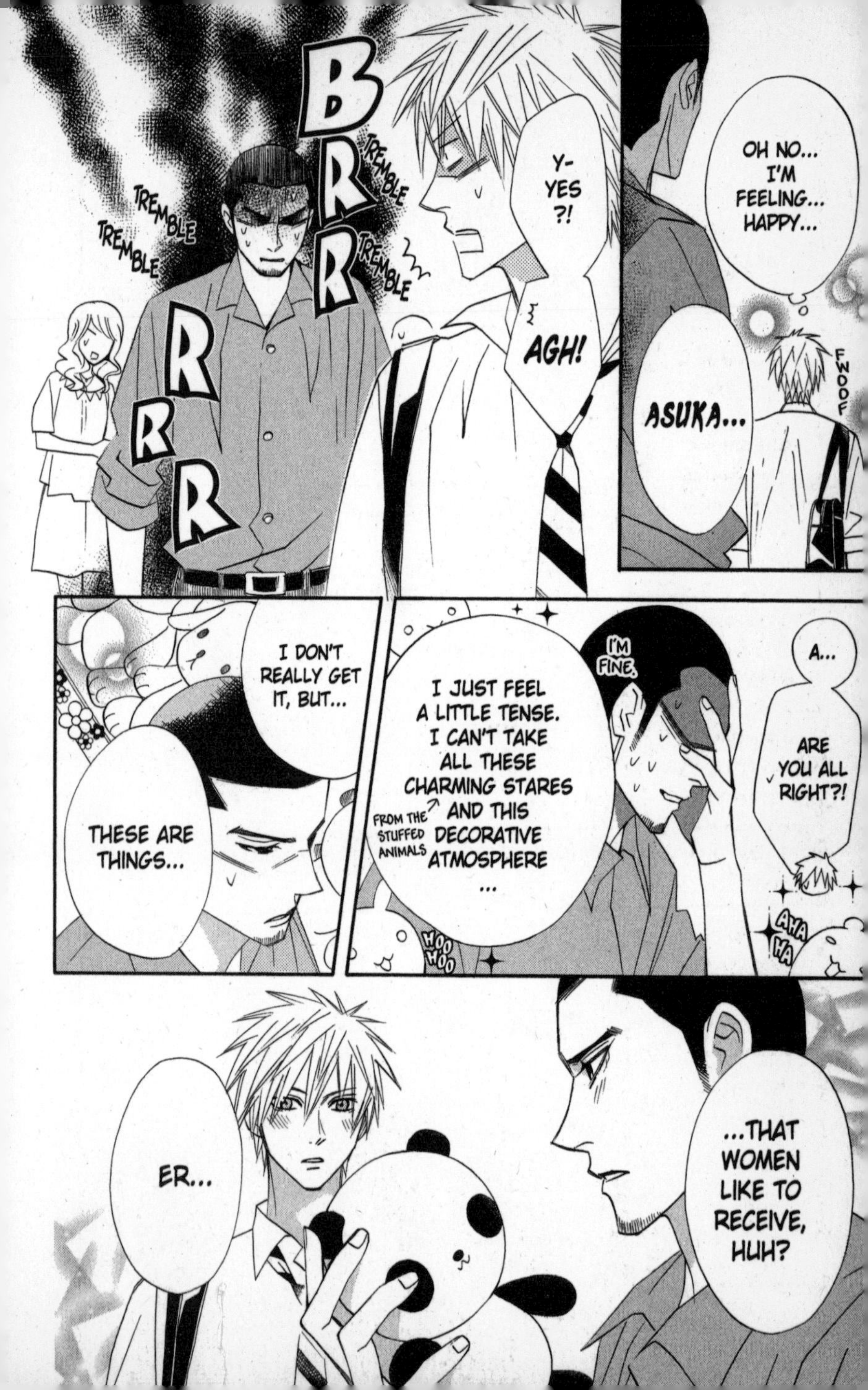
OH NO... I'M FEELING... HAPPY...
FWOOF
ASUKA...
Y-YES?!
AGH!
BRRRR
TREMBLE TREMBLE
TREMBLE TREMBLE
A... ARE YOU ALL RIGHT?!
AHA HA
I'M FINE.
I JUST FEEL A LITTLE TENSE. I CAN'T TAKE ALL THESE CHARMING STARES AND THIS DECORATIVE ATMOSPHERE...
FROM THE STUFFED ANIMALS
HOO HOO
I DON'T REALLY GET IT, BUT...
THESE ARE THINGS...
...THAT WOMEN LIKE TO RECEIVE, HUH?
ER...

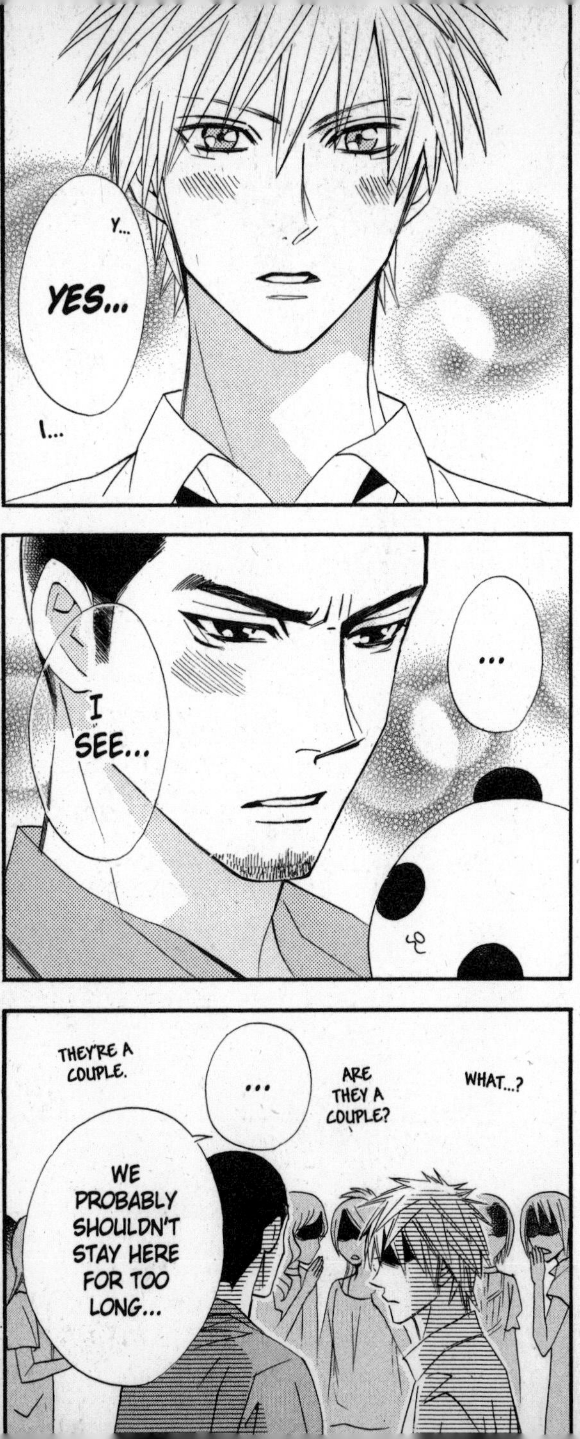
Y...
YES...
I...
...
I SEE...
WHAT...?
ARE THEY A COUPLE?
...
THEY'RE A COUPLE.
WE PROBABLY SHOULDN'T STAY HERE FOR TOO LONG...

Hello.
This is volume 4.

Ryo's father makes another appearance.

He's macho and has a shaved head, so I thought that he wouldn't be popular with girls. I'm pleased that my readers seem to have taken quite a liking to him though. I like shaved heads so much that I think all men should shave their heads. He's very fun to draw.

Ryo's father's feelings toward cute things in this chapter are about the same as my own...

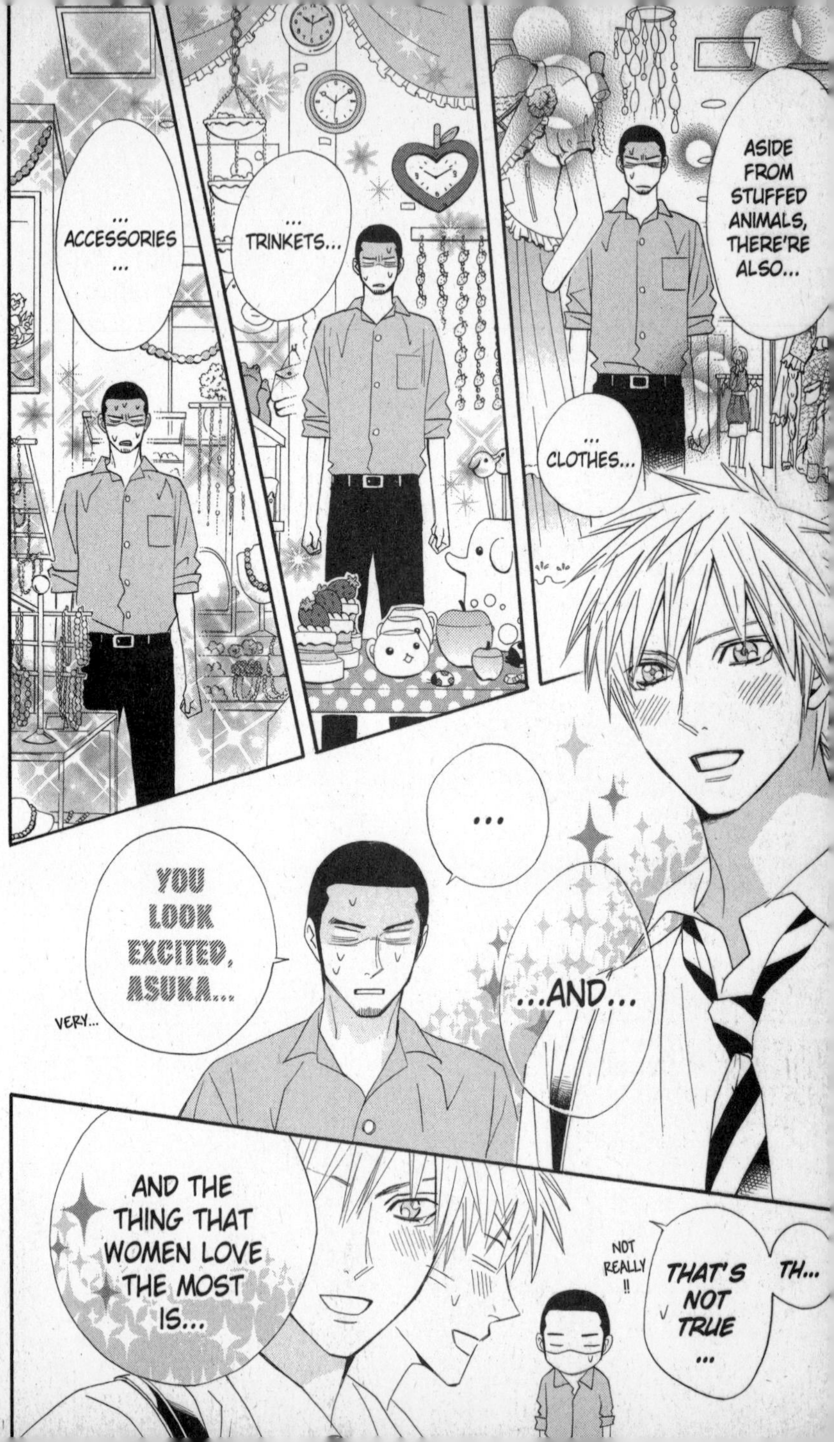
ASIDE FROM STUFFED ANIMALS, THERE'RE ALSO...
... CLOTHES...
... TRINKETS...
... ACCESSORIES ...
...AND...
...
YOU LOOK EXCITED, ASUKA...
VERY...
TH... THAT'S NOT TRUE ...
NOT REALLY !!
AND THE THING THAT WOMEN LOVE THE MOST IS...

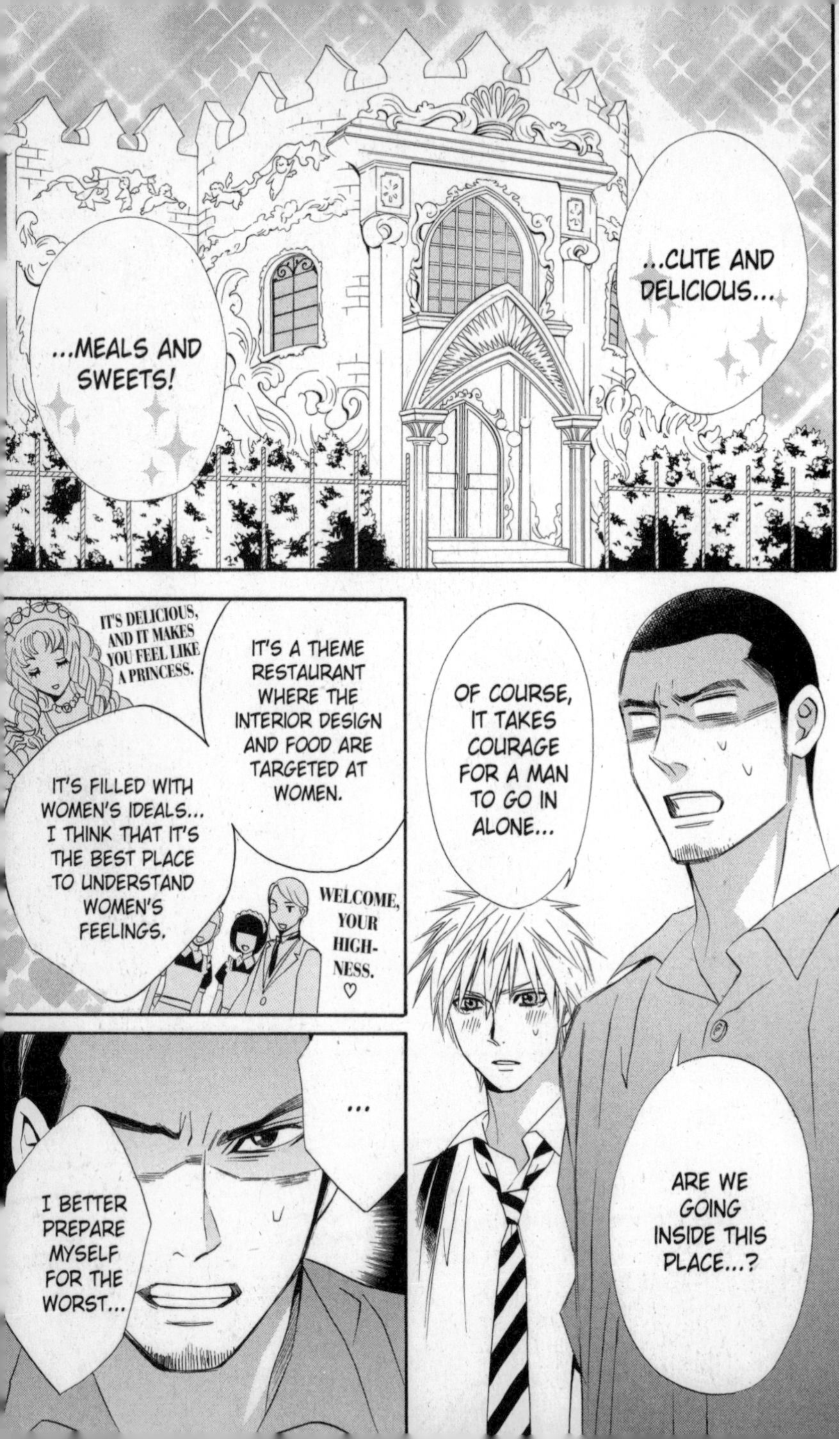
...CUTE AND DELICIOUS...
...MEALS AND SWEETS!
OF COURSE, IT TAKES COURAGE FOR A MAN TO GO IN ALONE...
ARE WE GOING INSIDE THIS PLACE...?
IT'S A THEME RESTAURANT WHERE THE INTERIOR DESIGN AND FOOD ARE TARGETED AT WOMEN.
IT'S DELICIOUS, AND IT MAKES YOU FEEL LIKE A PRINCESS.
WELCOME, YOUR HIGH-NESS. ♡
IT'S FILLED WITH WOMEN'S IDEALS... I THINK THAT IT'S THE BEST PLACE TO UNDERSTAND WOMEN'S FEELINGS.
...
I BETTER PREPARE MYSELF FOR THE WORST...

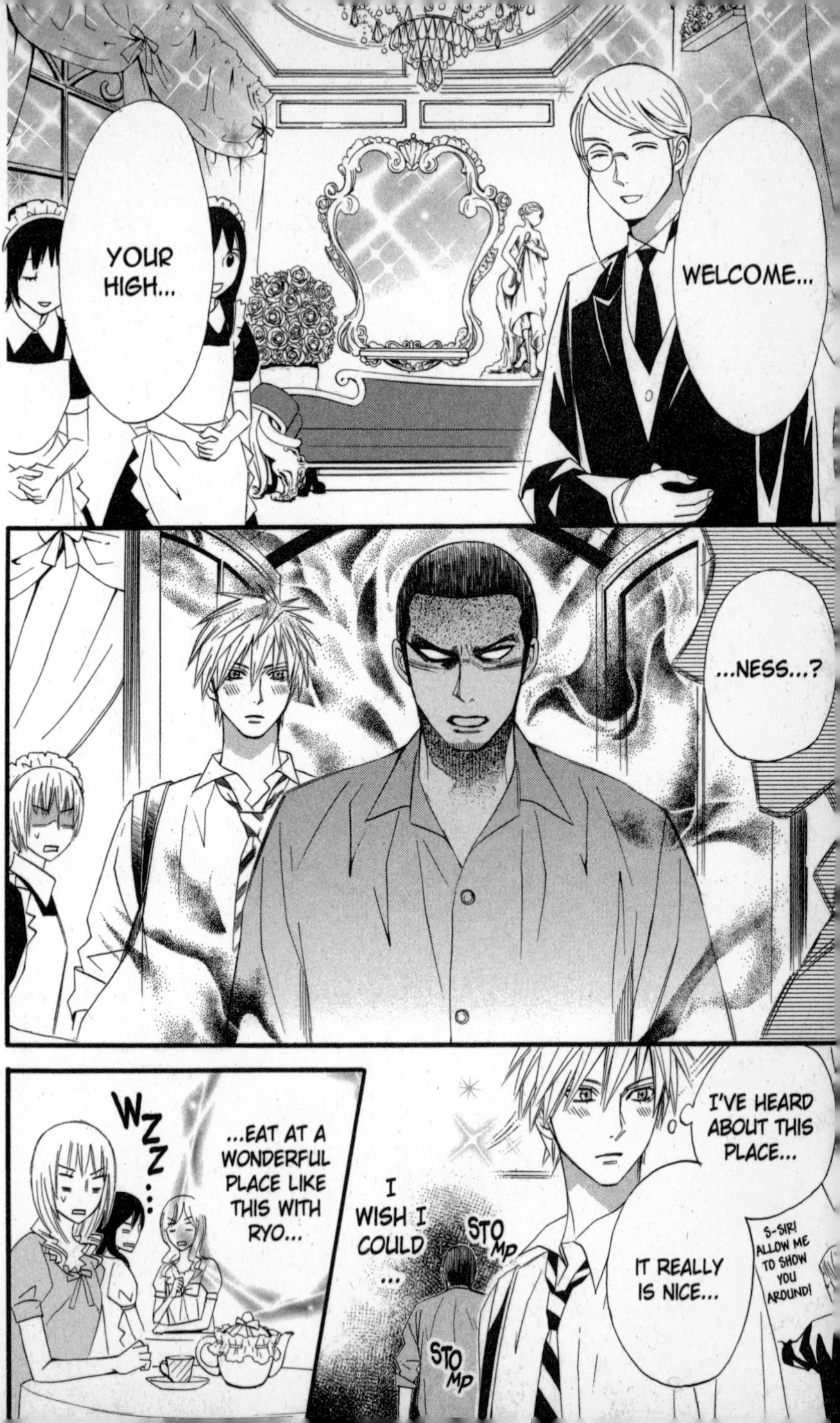
WELCOME...
YOUR HIGH...
...NESS...?
I'VE HEARD ABOUT THIS PLACE...
IT REALLY IS NICE...
S-SIR! ALLOW ME TO SHOW YOU AROUND!
STOMP
STOMP
I WISH I COULD ...
...EAT AT A WONDERFUL PLACE LIKE THIS WITH RYO...
WZZ...

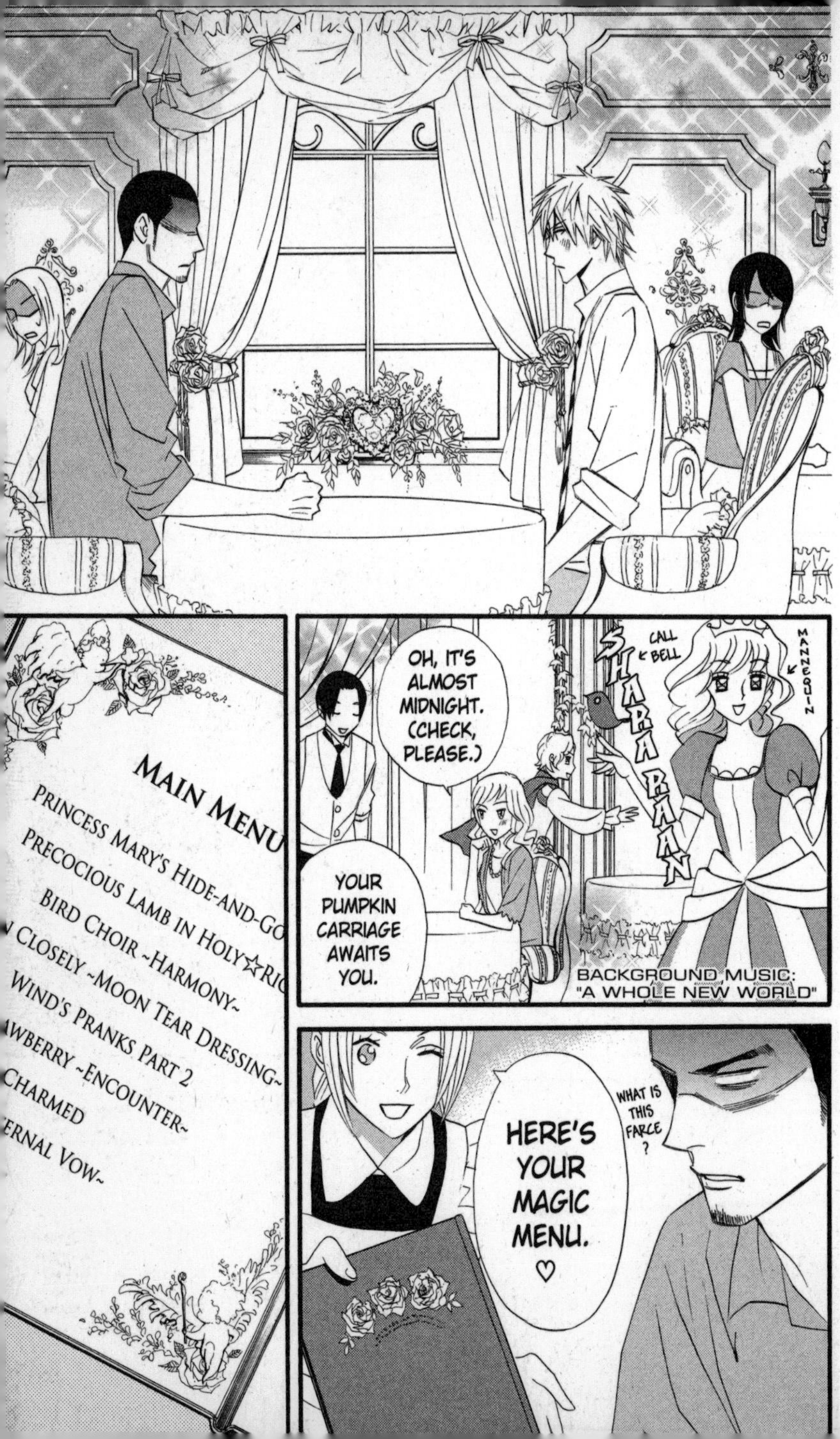
MANNEQUIN
CALL BELL
SHARARAAN
OH, IT'S ALMOST MIDNIGHT. (CHECK, PLEASE.)
YOUR PUMPKIN CARRIAGE AWAITS YOU.
BACKGROUND MUSIC: "A WHOLE NEW WORLD"
WHAT IS THIS FARCE?
HERE'S YOUR MAGIC MENU. ♡
MAIN MENU
PRINCESS MARY'S HIDE-AND-GO
PRECOCIOUS LAMB IN HOLY☆RIC
BIRD CHOIR ~HARMONY~
N CLOSELY ~MOON TEAR DRESSING~
WIND'S PRANKS PART 2
AWBERRY ~ENCOUNTER~
CHARMED
ERNAL VOW~

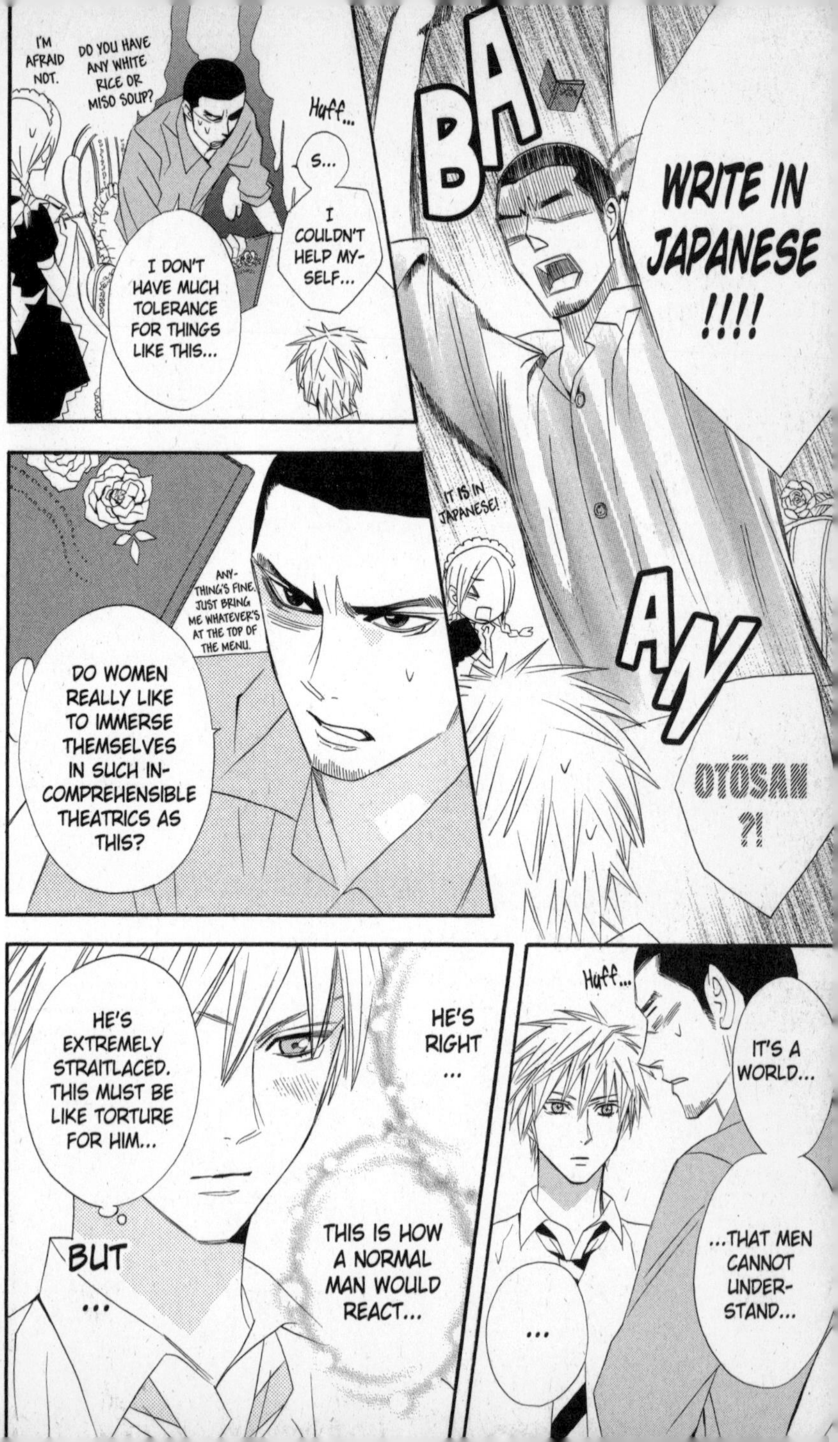
BA
WRITE IN JAPANESE !!!!
IT IS IN JAPANESE!
AN
OTŌSAN ?!
Huff...
S...
I COULDN'T HELP MY-SELF...
I DON'T HAVE MUCH TOLERANCE FOR THINGS LIKE THIS...
DO YOU HAVE ANY WHITE RICE OR MISO SOUP?
I'M AFRAID NOT.
ANY-THING'S FINE. JUST BRING ME WHATEVER'S AT THE TOP OF THE MENU.
DO WOMEN REALLY LIKE TO IMMERSE THEMSELVES IN SUCH IN-COMPREHENSIBLE THEATRICS AS THIS?
Huff...
IT'S A WORLD...
...THAT MEN CANNOT UNDER-STAND...
...
HE'S RIGHT ...
THIS IS HOW A NORMAL MAN WOULD REACT...
HE'S EXTREMELY STRAITLACED. THIS MUST BE LIKE TORTURE FOR HIM...
BUT ...

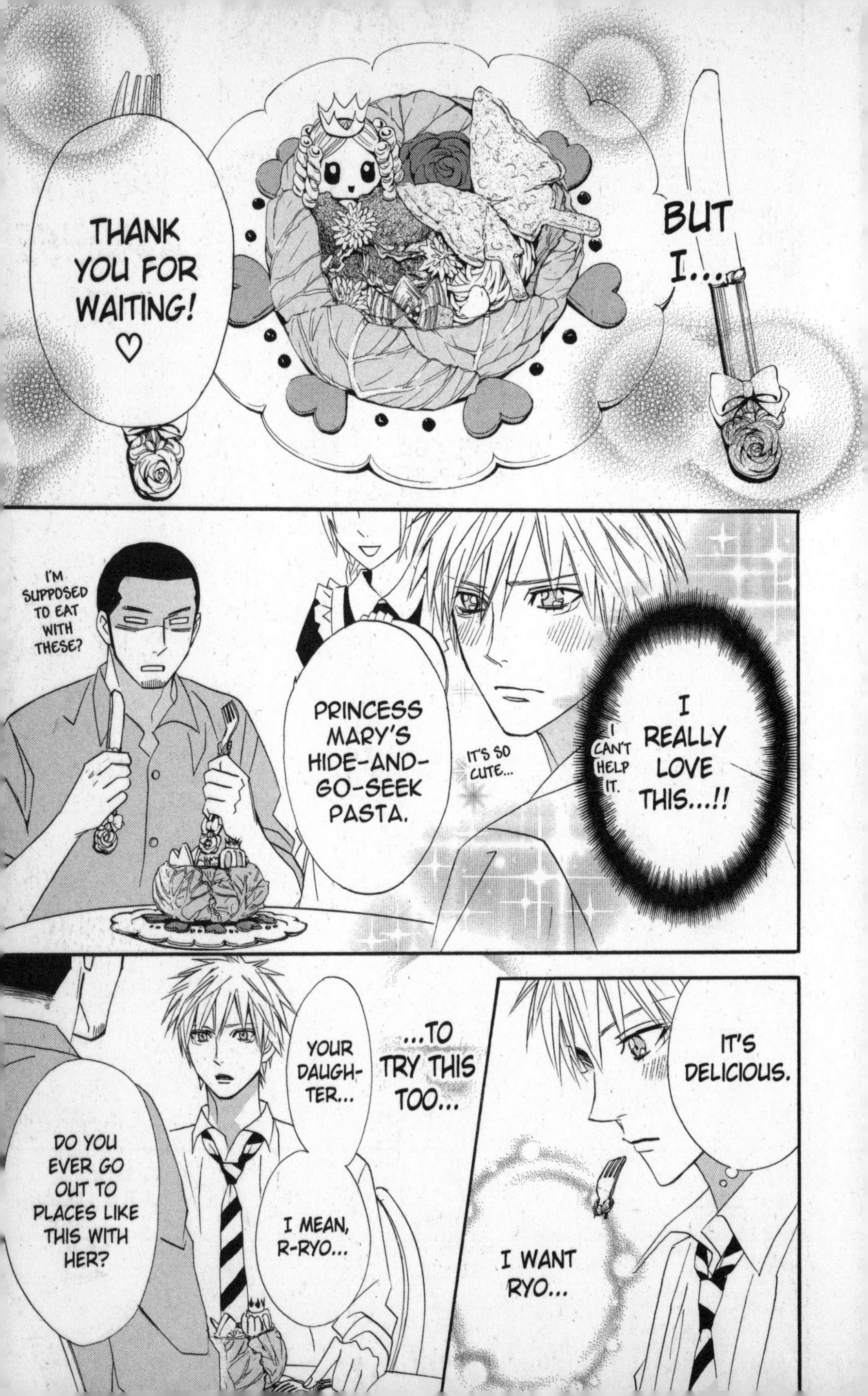
THANK YOU FOR WAITING! ♡
BUT I...
I REALLY LOVE THIS...!!
I CAN'T HELP IT.
IT'S SO CUTE...
PRINCESS MARY'S HIDE-AND-GO-SEEK PASTA.
I'M SUPPOSED TO EAT WITH THESE?
IT'S DELICIOUS.
I WANT RYO...
...TO TRY THIS TOO...
YOUR DAUGHTER...
I MEAN, R-RYO...
DO YOU EVER GO OUT TO PLACES LIKE THIS WITH HER?

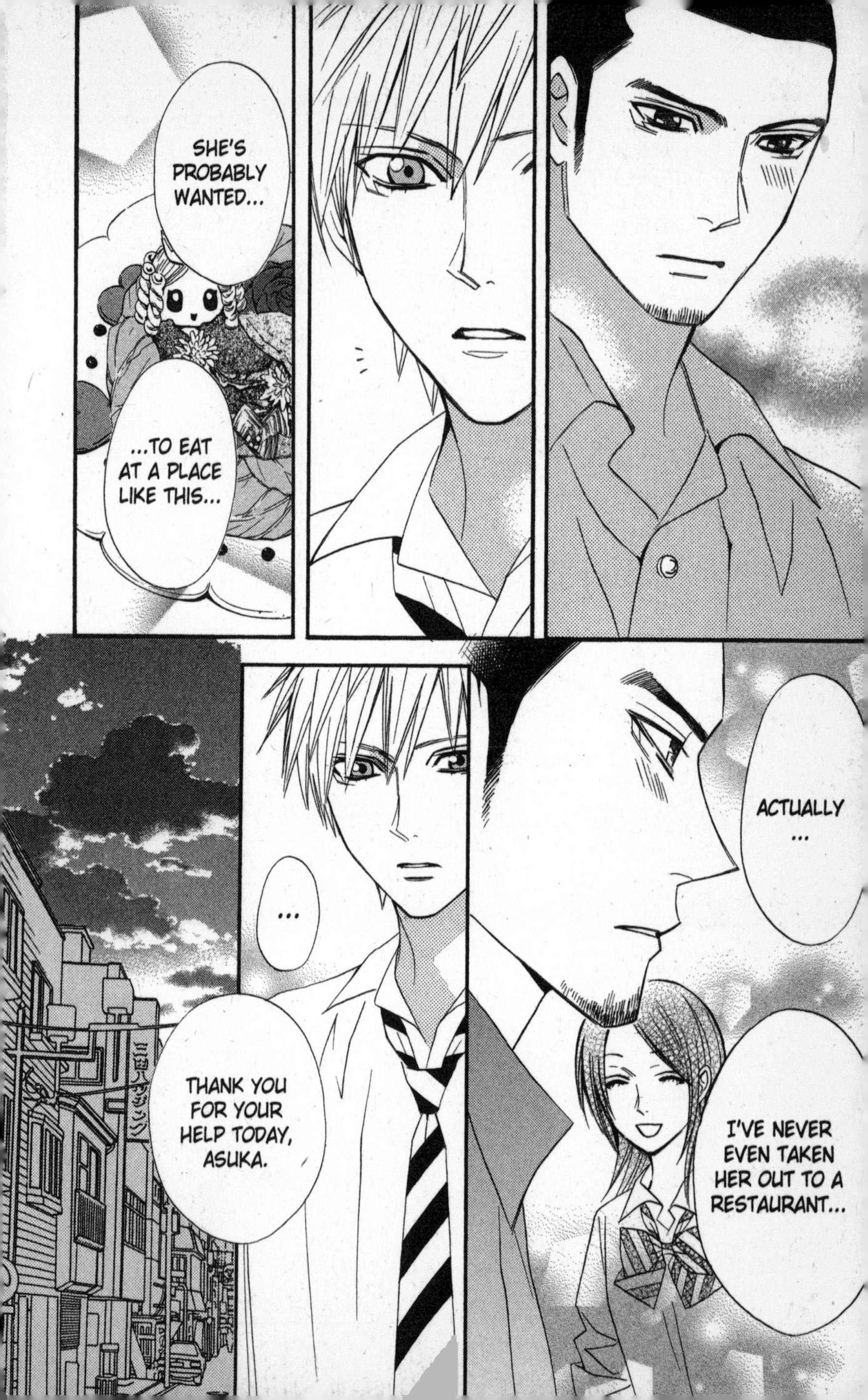
SHE'S PROBABLY WANTED...
...TO EAT AT A PLACE LIKE THIS...
ACTUALLY...
I'VE NEVER EVEN TAKEN HER OUT TO A RESTAURANT...
...
THANK YOU FOR YOUR HELP TODAY, ASUKA.

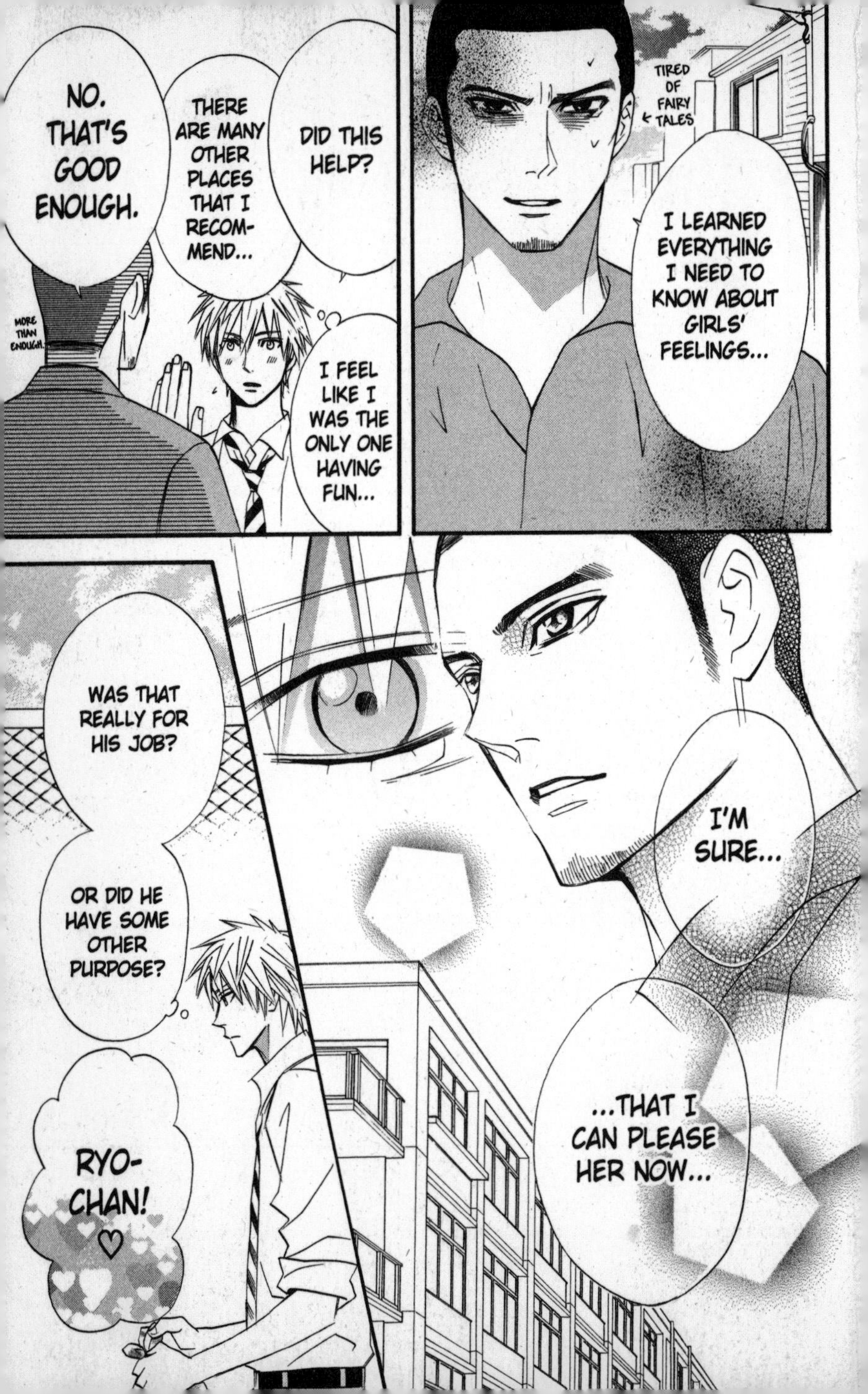
TIRED OF FAIRY TALES
I LEARNED EVERYTHING I NEED TO KNOW ABOUT GIRLS' FEELINGS...
DID THIS HELP?
THERE ARE MANY OTHER PLACES THAT I RECOMMEND...
NO. THAT'S GOOD ENOUGH.
MORE THAN ENOUGH.
I FEEL LIKE I WAS THE ONLY ONE HAVING FUN...
I'M SURE...
...THAT I CAN PLEASE HER NOW...
WAS THAT REALLY FOR HIS JOB?
OR DID HE HAVE SOME OTHER PURPOSE?
RYO-CHAN! ♥

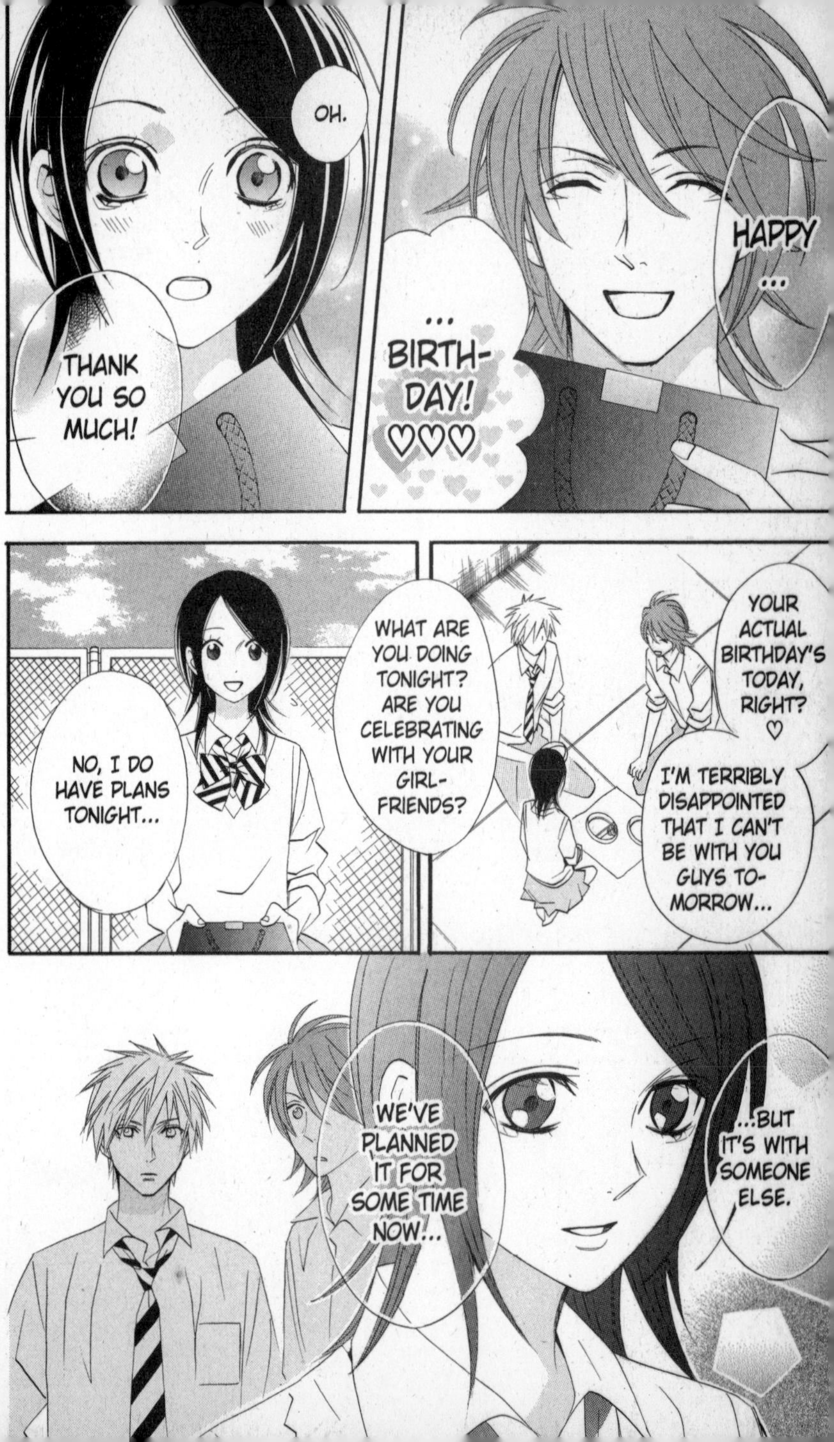
HAPPY...
...BIRTHDAY! ♡♡♡
OH.
THANK YOU SO MUCH!
YOUR ACTUAL BIRTHDAY'S TODAY, RIGHT? ♡
I'M TERRIBLY DISAPPOINTED THAT I CAN'T BE WITH YOU GUYS TOMORROW...
WHAT ARE YOU DOING TONIGHT? ARE YOU CELEBRATING WITH YOUR GIRLFRIENDS?
NO, I DO HAVE PLANS TONIGHT...
...BUT IT'S WITH SOMEONE ELSE.
WE'VE PLANNED IT FOR SOME TIME NOW...

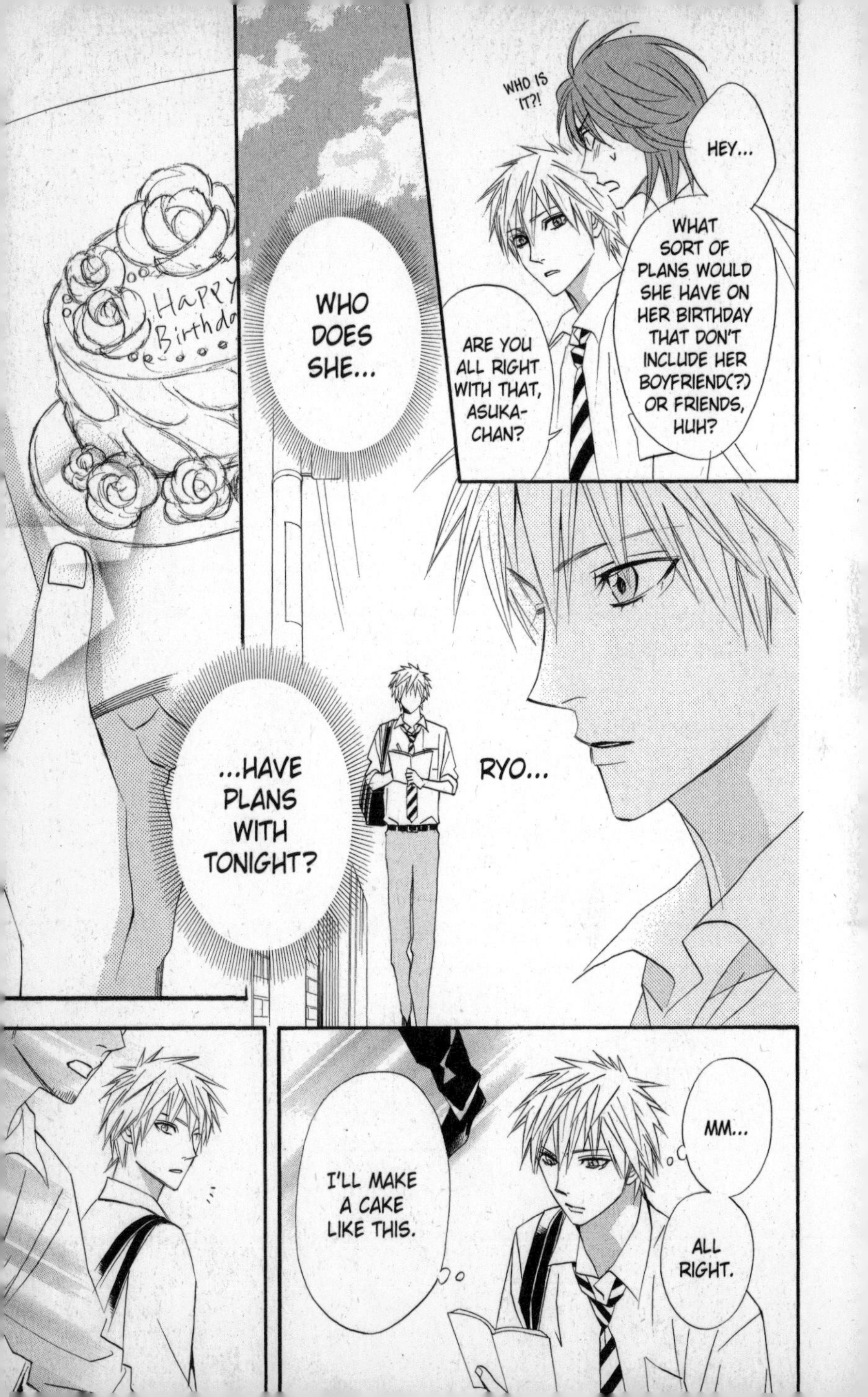
WHO IS IT?!
HEY...
WHAT SORT OF PLANS WOULD SHE HAVE ON HER BIRTHDAY THAT DON'T INCLUDE HER BOYFRIEND(?) OR FRIENDS, HUH?
ARE YOU ALL RIGHT WITH THAT, ASUKA-CHAN?
RYO...
WHO DOES SHE...
...HAVE PLANS WITH TONIGHT?
Happy Birthday
MM...
ALL RIGHT.
I'LL MAKE A CAKE LIKE THIS.

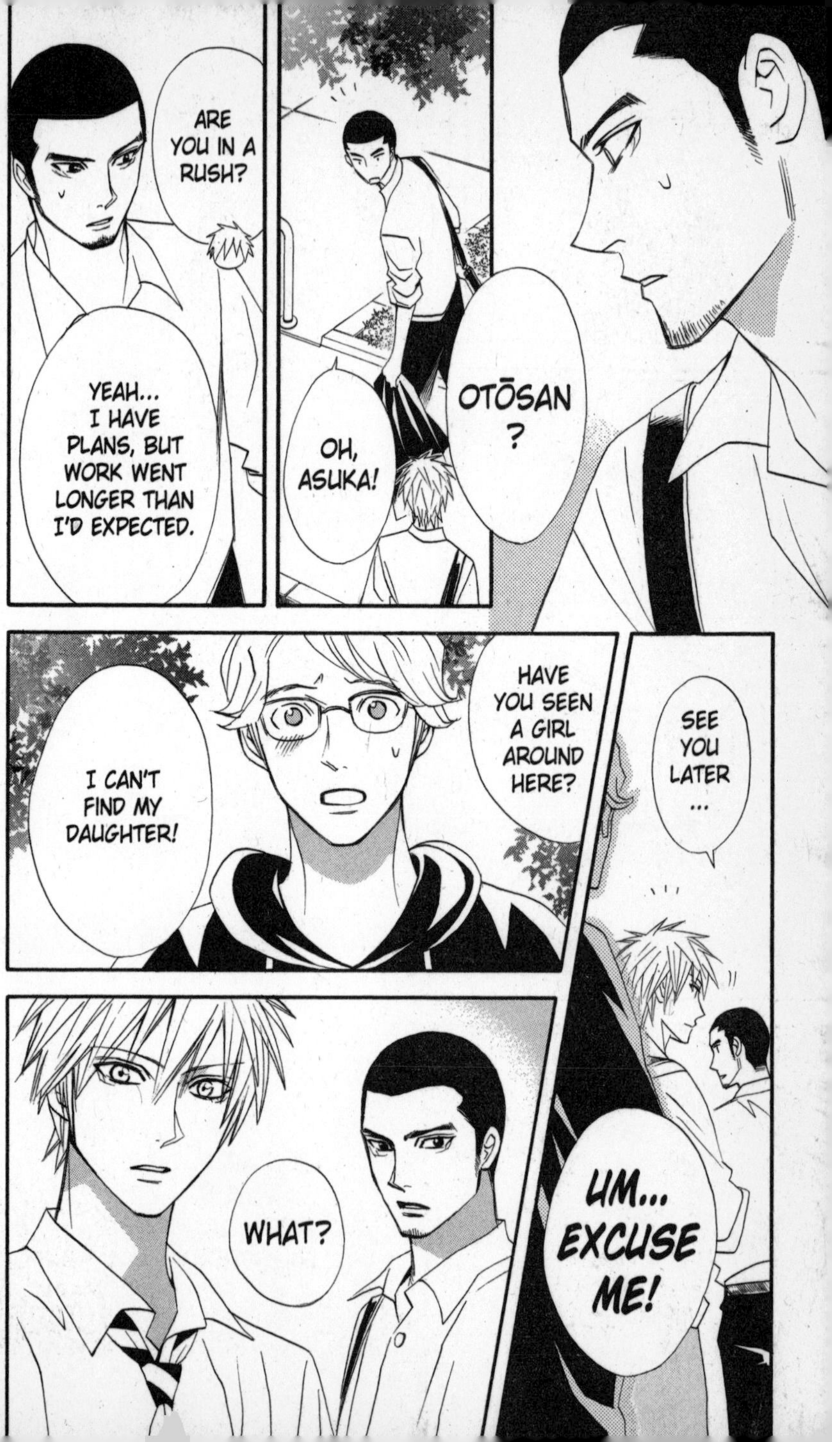
OTŌSAN?
OH, ASUKA!
ARE YOU IN A RUSH?
YEAH... I HAVE PLANS, BUT WORK WENT LONGER THAN I'D EXPECTED.
SEE YOU LATER...
UM... EXCUSE ME!
HAVE YOU SEEN A GIRL AROUND HERE?
I CAN'T FIND MY DAUGHTER!
WHAT?

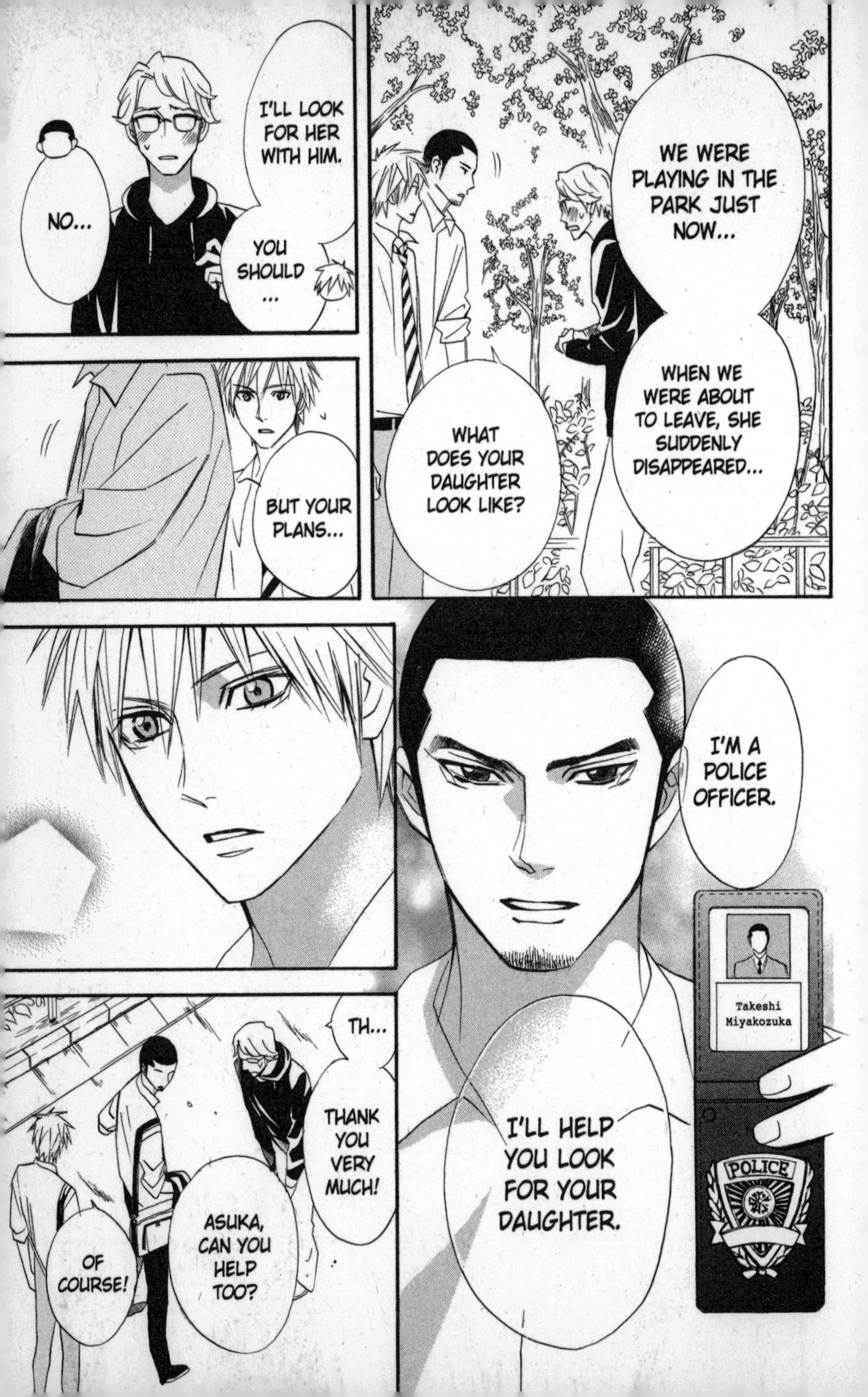
WE WERE PLAYING IN THE PARK JUST NOW...
WHEN WE WERE ABOUT TO LEAVE, SHE SUDDENLY DISAPPEARED...
WHAT DOES YOUR DAUGHTER LOOK LIKE?
I'LL LOOK FOR HER WITH HIM.
YOU SHOULD ...
NO...
BUT YOUR PLANS...
I'M A POLICE OFFICER.
Takeshi Miyakozuka
POLICE
I'LL HELP YOU LOOK FOR YOUR DAUGHTER.
TH...
THANK YOU VERY MUCH!
ASUKA, CAN YOU HELP TOO?
OF COURSE!

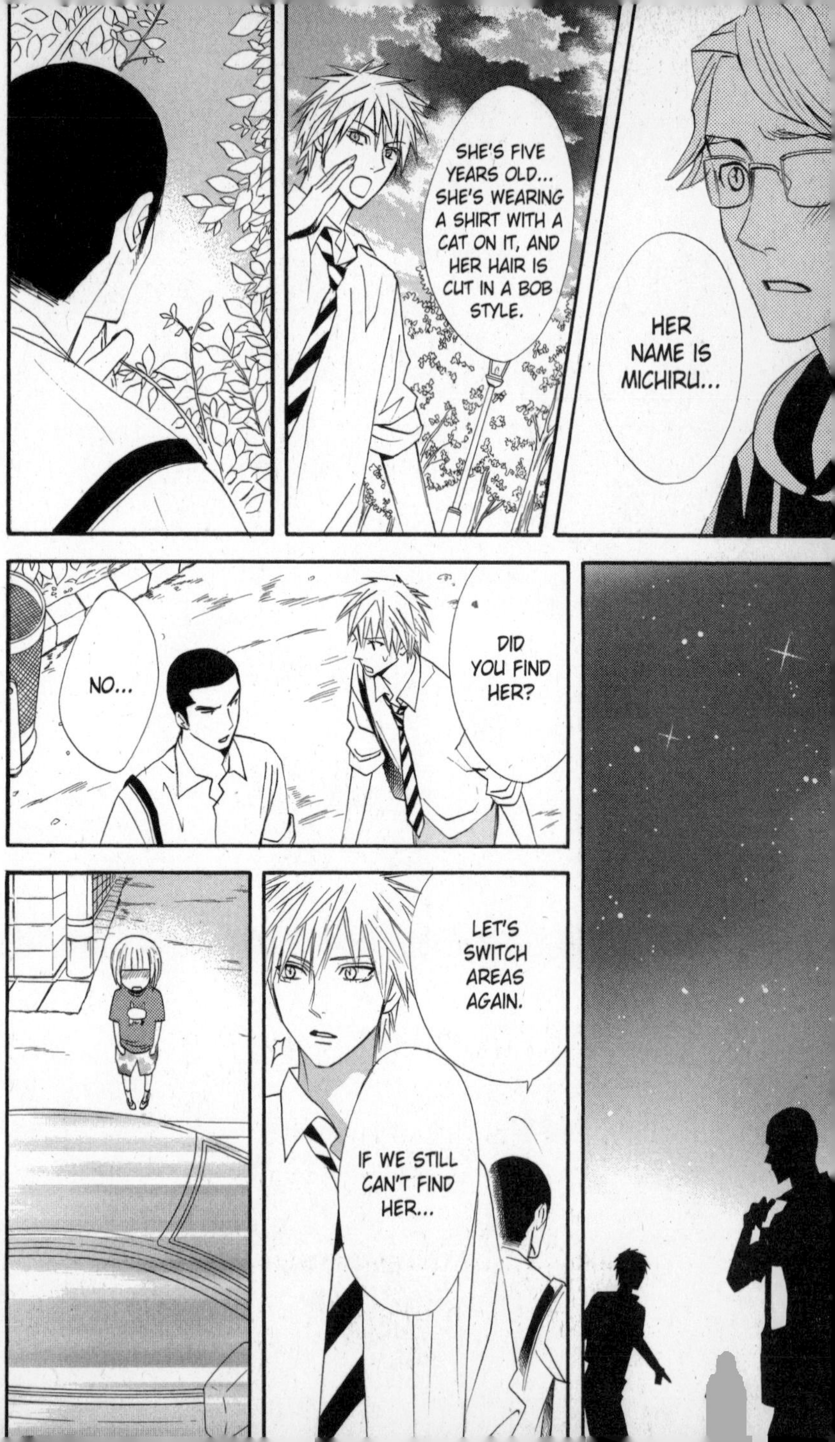
HER NAME IS MICHIRU...
SHE'S FIVE YEARS OLD... SHE'S WEARING A SHIRT WITH A CAT ON IT, AND HER HAIR IS CUT IN A BOB STYLE.
DID YOU FIND HER?
NO...
LET'S SWITCH AREAS AGAIN.
IF WE STILL CAN'T FIND HER...

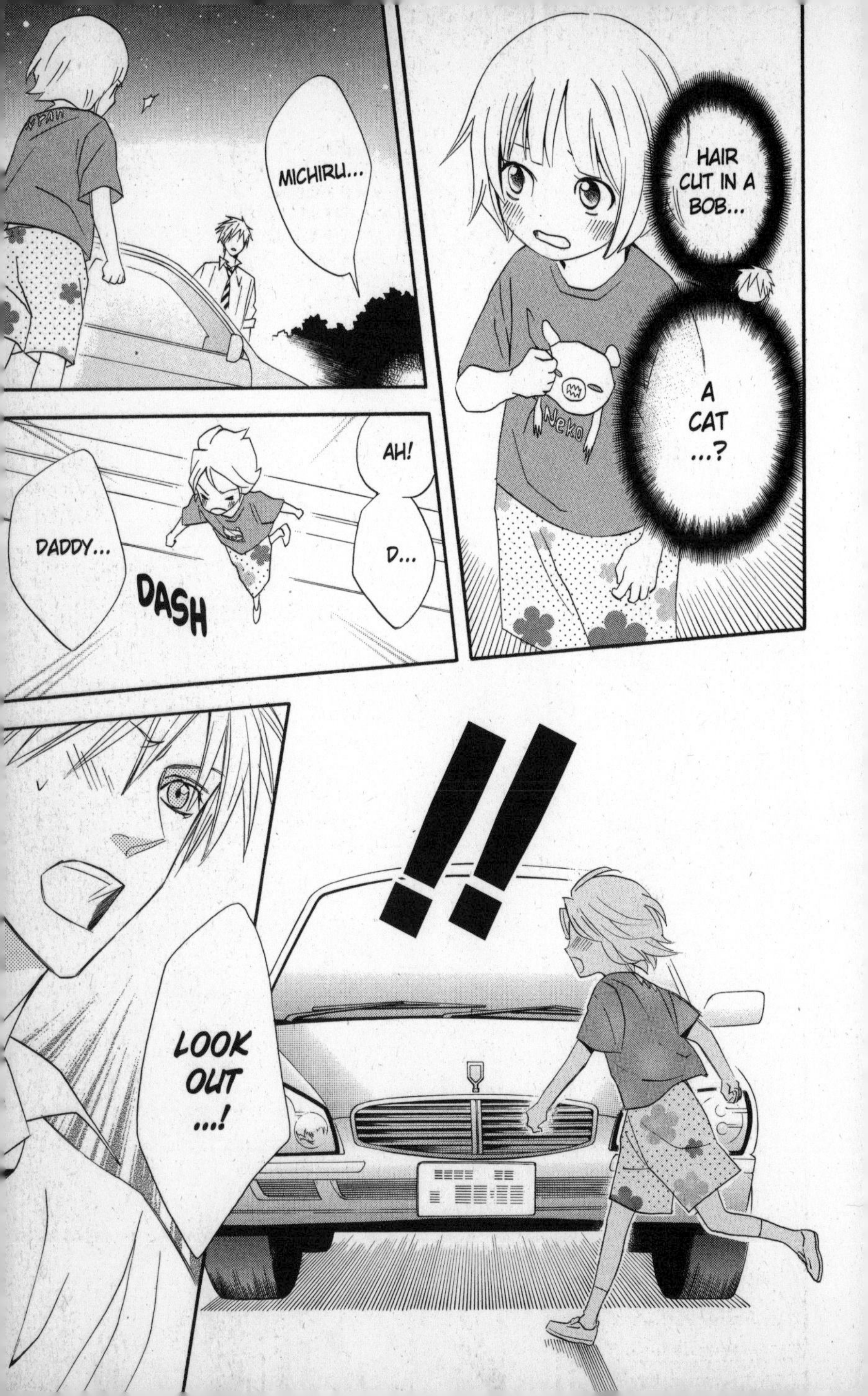
HAIR CUT IN A BOB...
A CAT ...?
MICHIRU...
AH!
D...
DADDY...
DASH
!!
LOOK OUT ...!

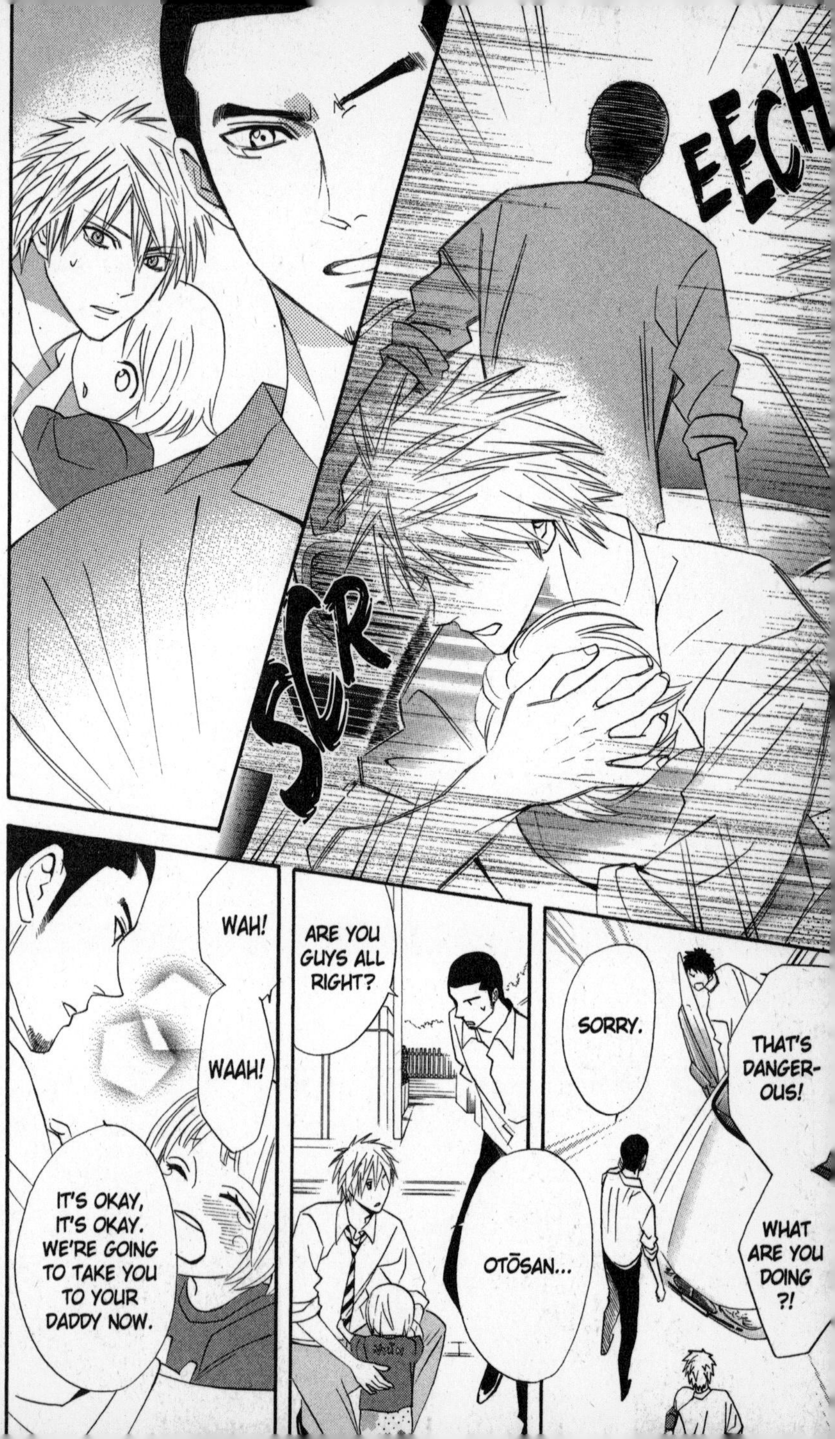
EECH
SCR
THAT'S DANGER-OUS!
WHAT ARE YOU DOING ?!
SORRY.
ARE YOU GUYS ALL RIGHT?
OTŌSAN...
WAH!
WAAH!
IT'S OKAY, IT'S OKAY. WE'RE GOING TO TAKE YOU TO YOUR DADDY NOW.

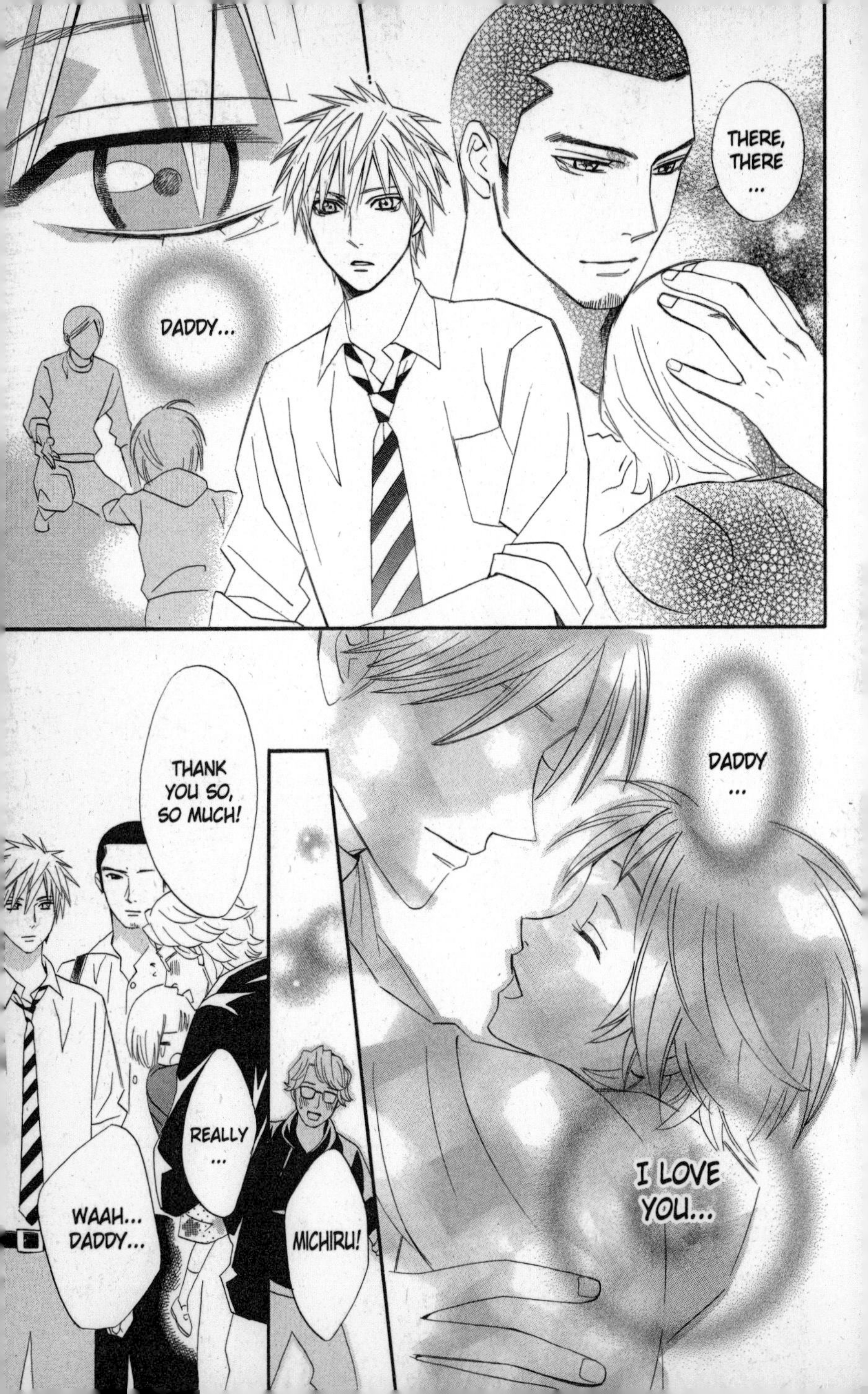
THERE, THERE ...
DADDY...
DADDY ...
I LOVE YOU...
THANK YOU SO, SO MUCH!
REALLY ...
MICHIRU!
WAAH... DADDY...

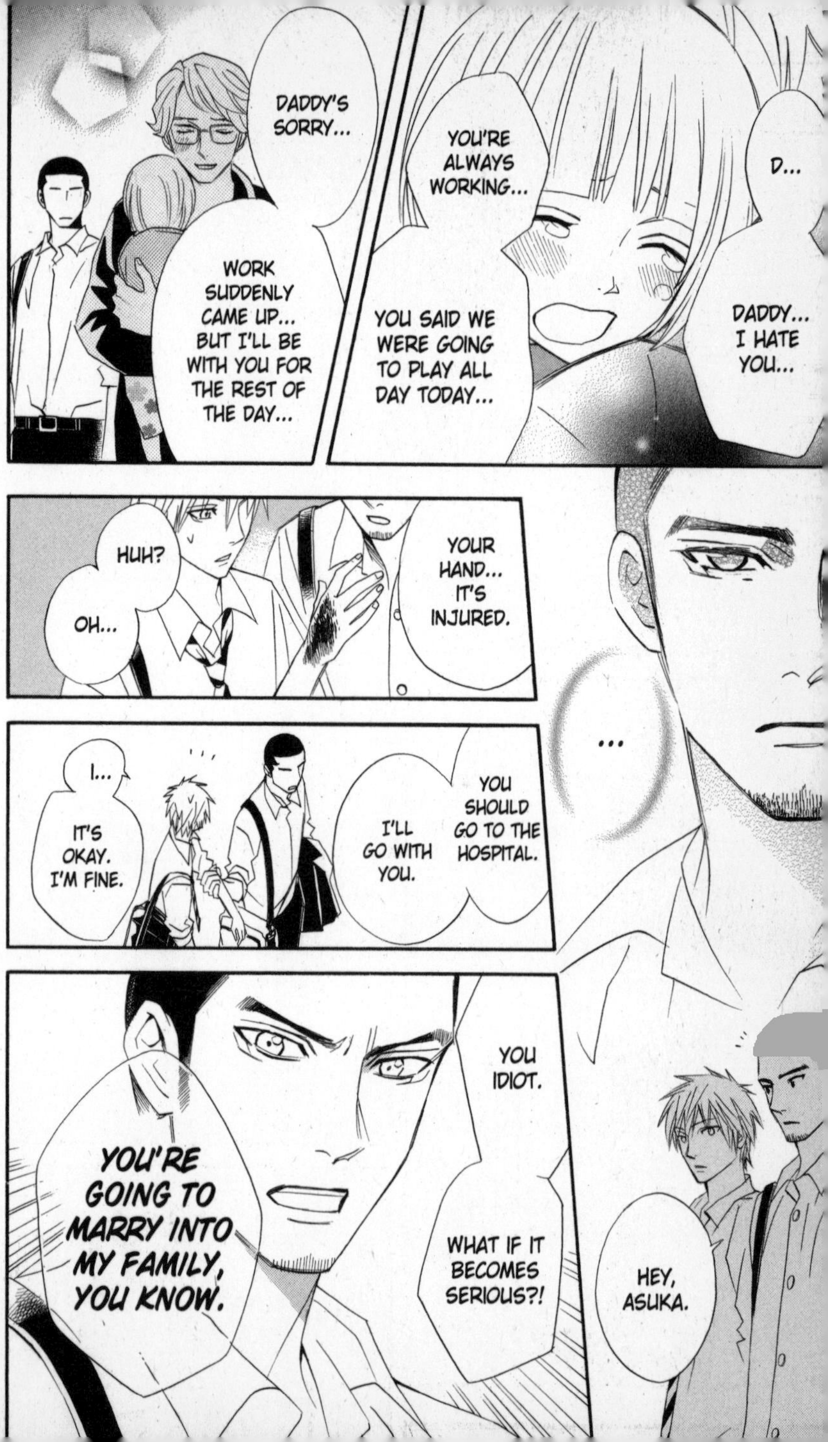
D...
DADDY... I HATE YOU...
YOU'RE ALWAYS WORKING...
YOU SAID WE WERE GOING TO PLAY ALL DAY TODAY...
DADDY'S SORRY...
WORK SUDDENLY CAME UP... BUT I'LL BE WITH YOU FOR THE REST OF THE DAY...
...
YOUR HAND... IT'S INJURED.
HUH?
OH...
YOU SHOULD GO TO THE HOSPITAL.
I'LL GO WITH YOU.
I...
IT'S OKAY. I'M FINE.
HEY, ASUKA.
YOU IDIOT.
WHAT IF IT BECOMES SERIOUS?!
YOU'RE GOING TO MARRY INTO MY FAMILY, YOU KNOW.

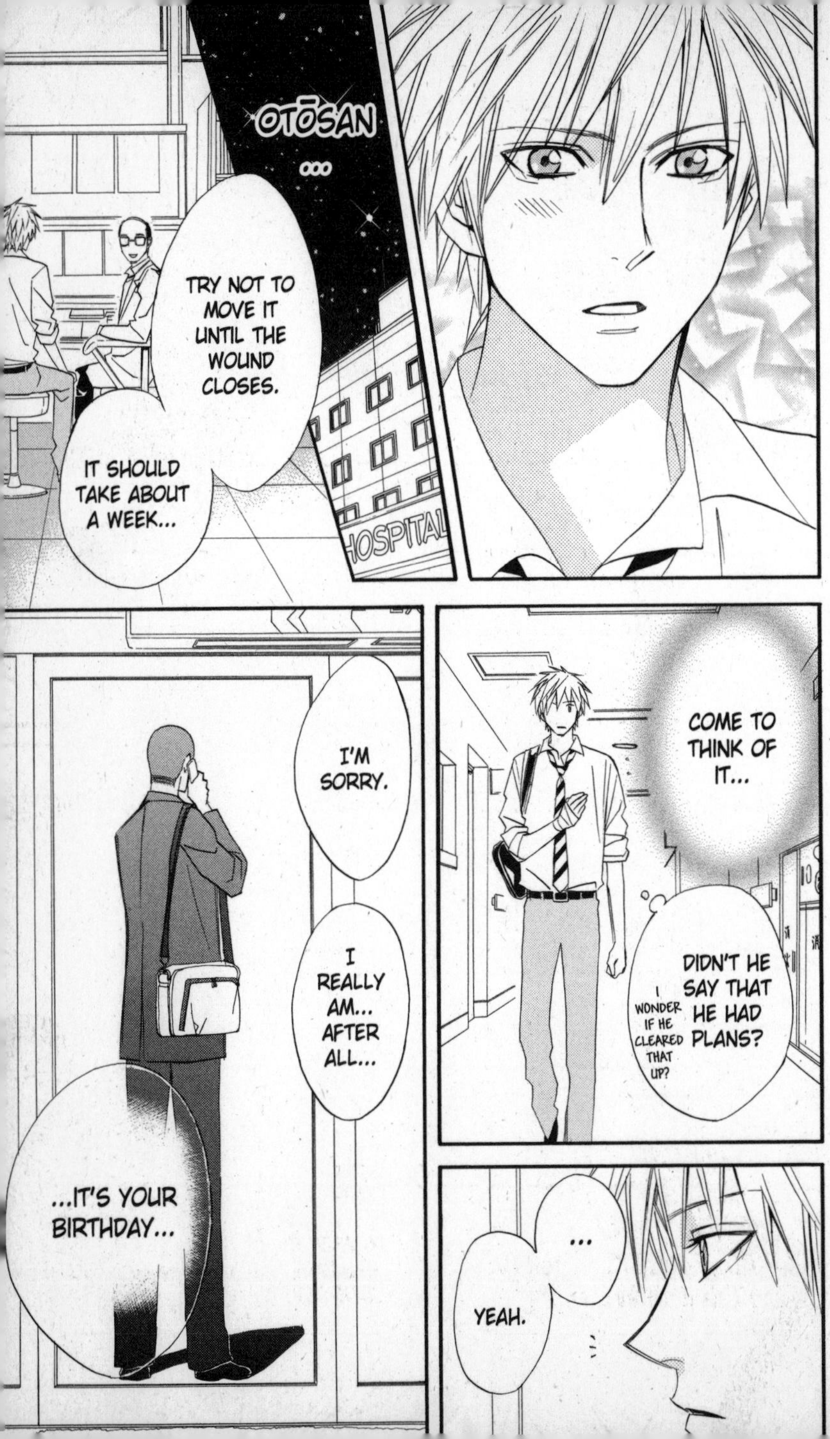
OTŌSAN ...
TRY NOT TO MOVE IT UNTIL THE WOUND CLOSES.
IT SHOULD TAKE ABOUT A WEEK...
COME TO THINK OF IT...
DIDN'T HE SAY THAT HE HAD PLANS?
I WONDER IF HE CLEARED THAT UP?
...
YEAH.
I'M SORRY.
I REALLY AM... AFTER ALL...
...IT'S YOUR BIRTHDAY...

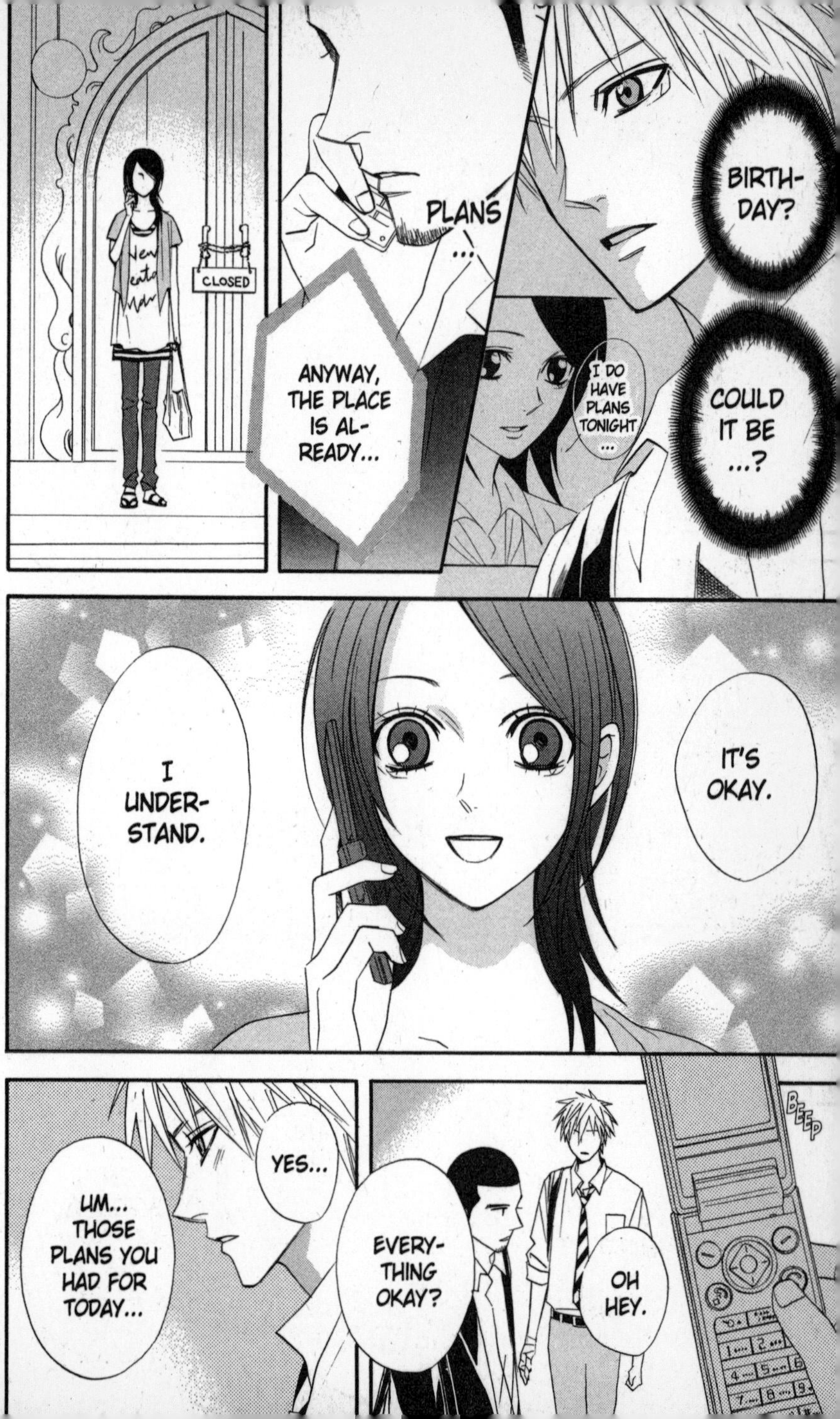
BIRTH-DAY?
COULD IT BE ...?
PLANS ...
I DO HAVE PLANS TONIGHT ...
ANYWAY, THE PLACE IS AL-READY...
CLOSED
IT'S OKAY.
I UNDER-STAND.
BEEP
OH HEY.
EVERY-THING OKAY?
YES...
UM... THOSE PLANS YOU HAD FOR TODAY...

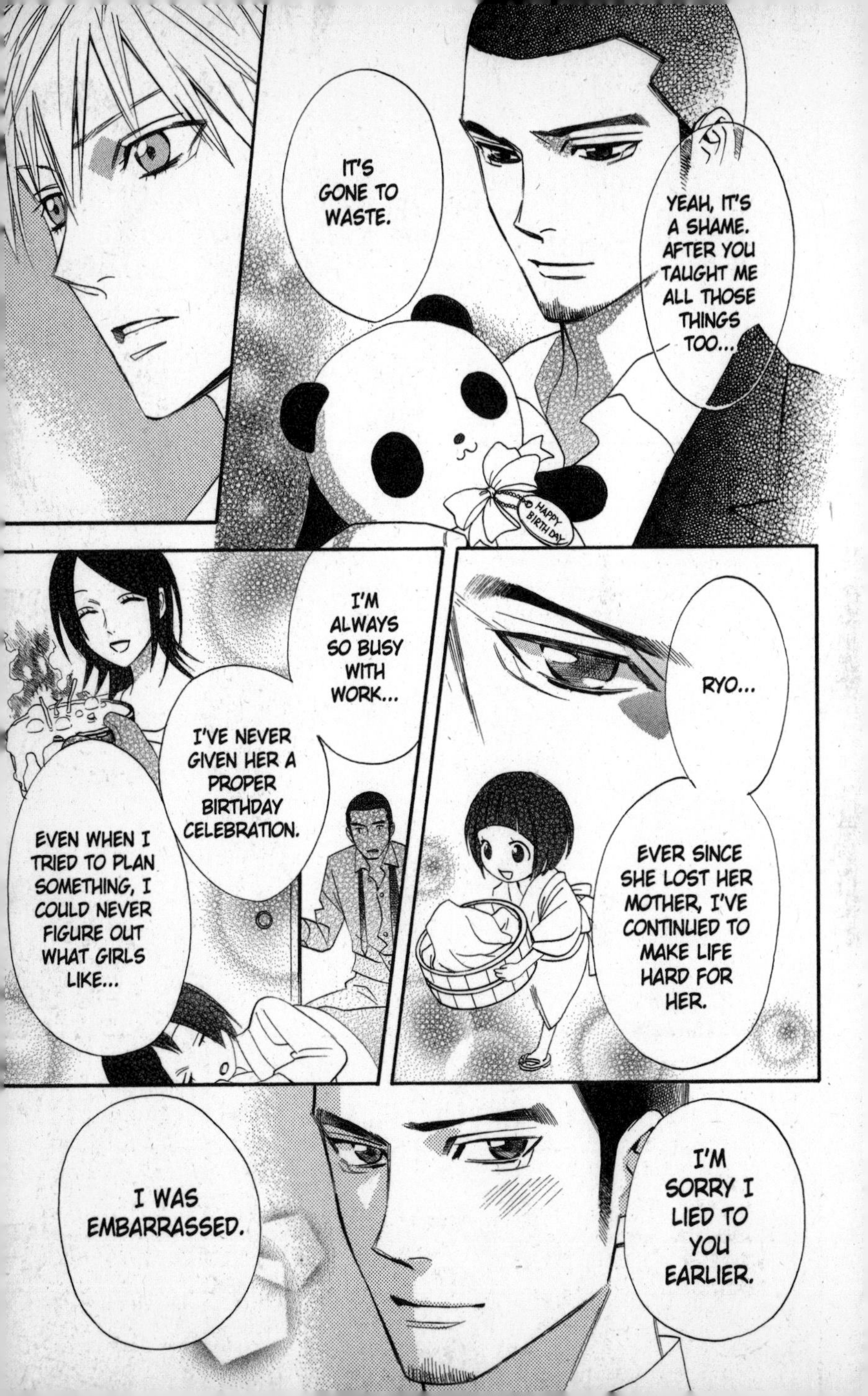
IT'S GONE TO WASTE.
YEAH, IT'S A SHAME. AFTER YOU TAUGHT ME ALL THOSE THINGS TOO...
HAPPY BIRTHDAY
RYO...
EVER SINCE SHE LOST HER MOTHER, I'VE CONTINUED TO MAKE LIFE HARD FOR HER.
I'M ALWAYS SO BUSY WITH WORK...
I'VE NEVER GIVEN HER A PROPER BIRTHDAY CELEBRATION.
EVEN WHEN I TRIED TO PLAN SOMETHING, I COULD NEVER FIGURE OUT WHAT GIRLS LIKE...
I'M SORRY I LIED TO YOU EARLIER.
I WAS EMBARRASSED.

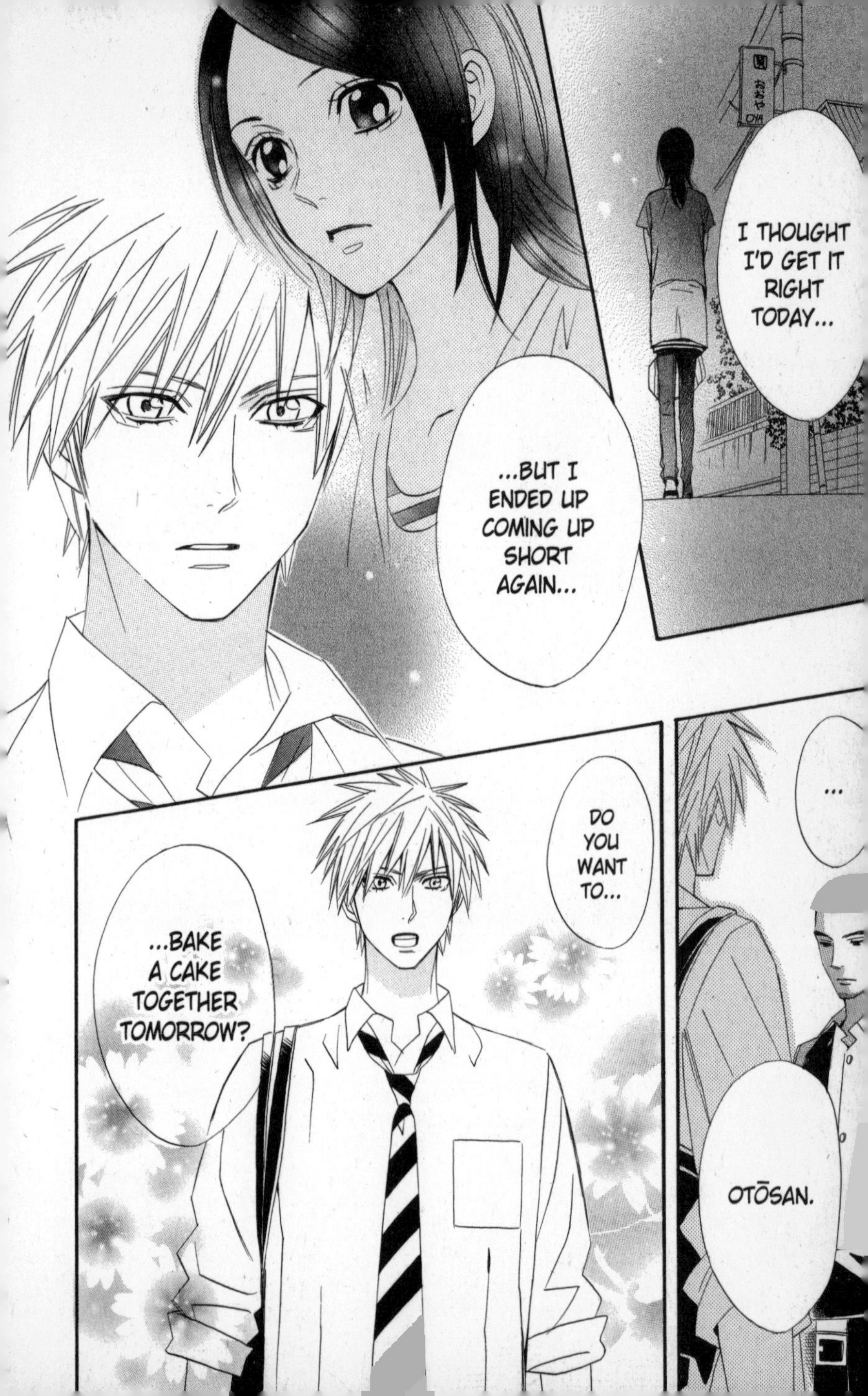
I THOUGHT I'D GET IT RIGHT TODAY...
...BUT I ENDED UP COMING UP SHORT AGAIN...
...
OTŌSAN.
DO YOU WANT TO...
...BAKE A CAKE TOGETHER TOMORROW?

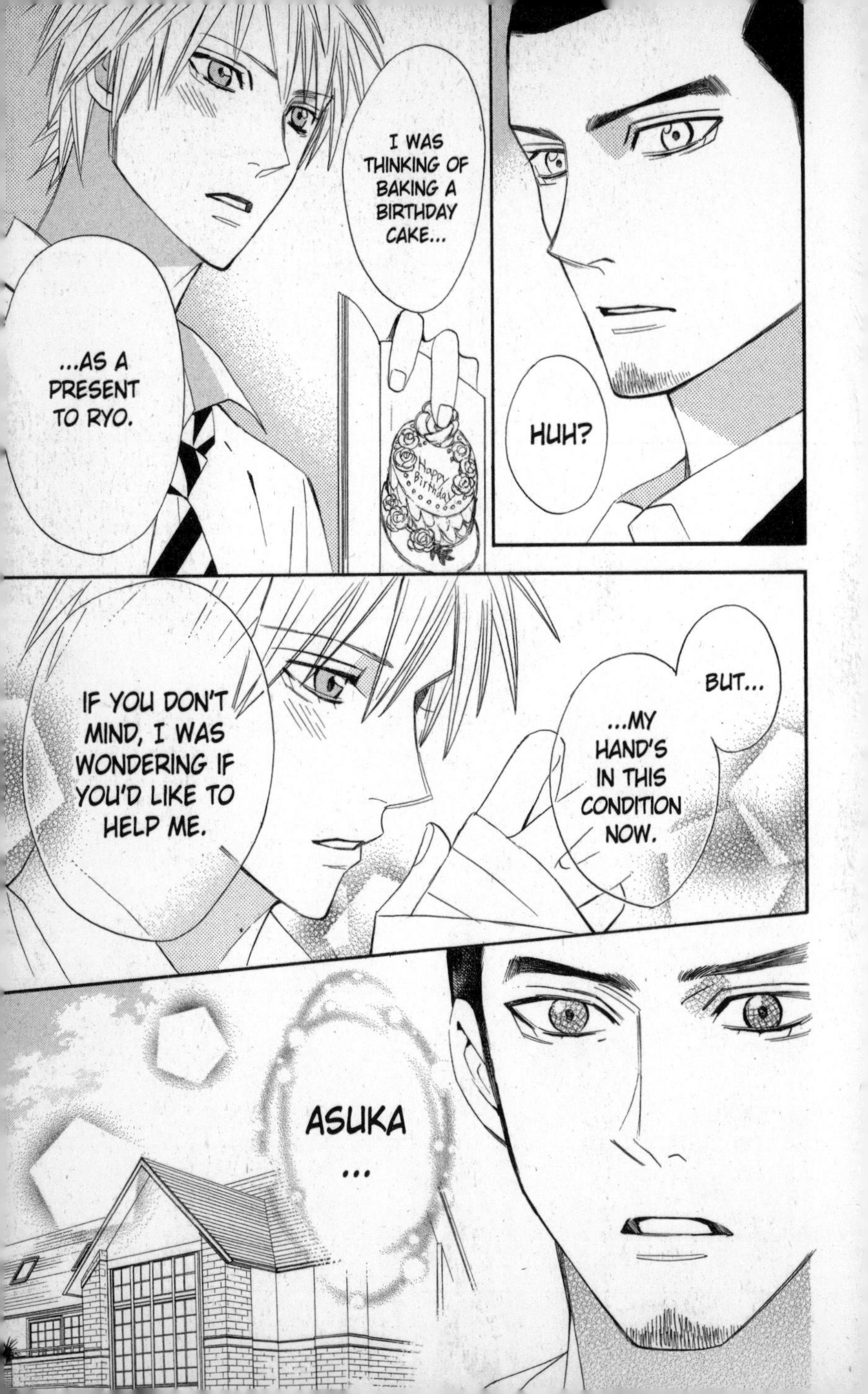
HUH?
I WAS THINKING OF BAKING A BIRTHDAY CAKE...
Happy Birthday
...AS A PRESENT TO RYO.
BUT...
...MY HAND'S IN THIS CONDITION NOW.
IF YOU DON'T MIND, I WAS WONDERING IF YOU'D LIKE TO HELP ME.
ASUKA
...

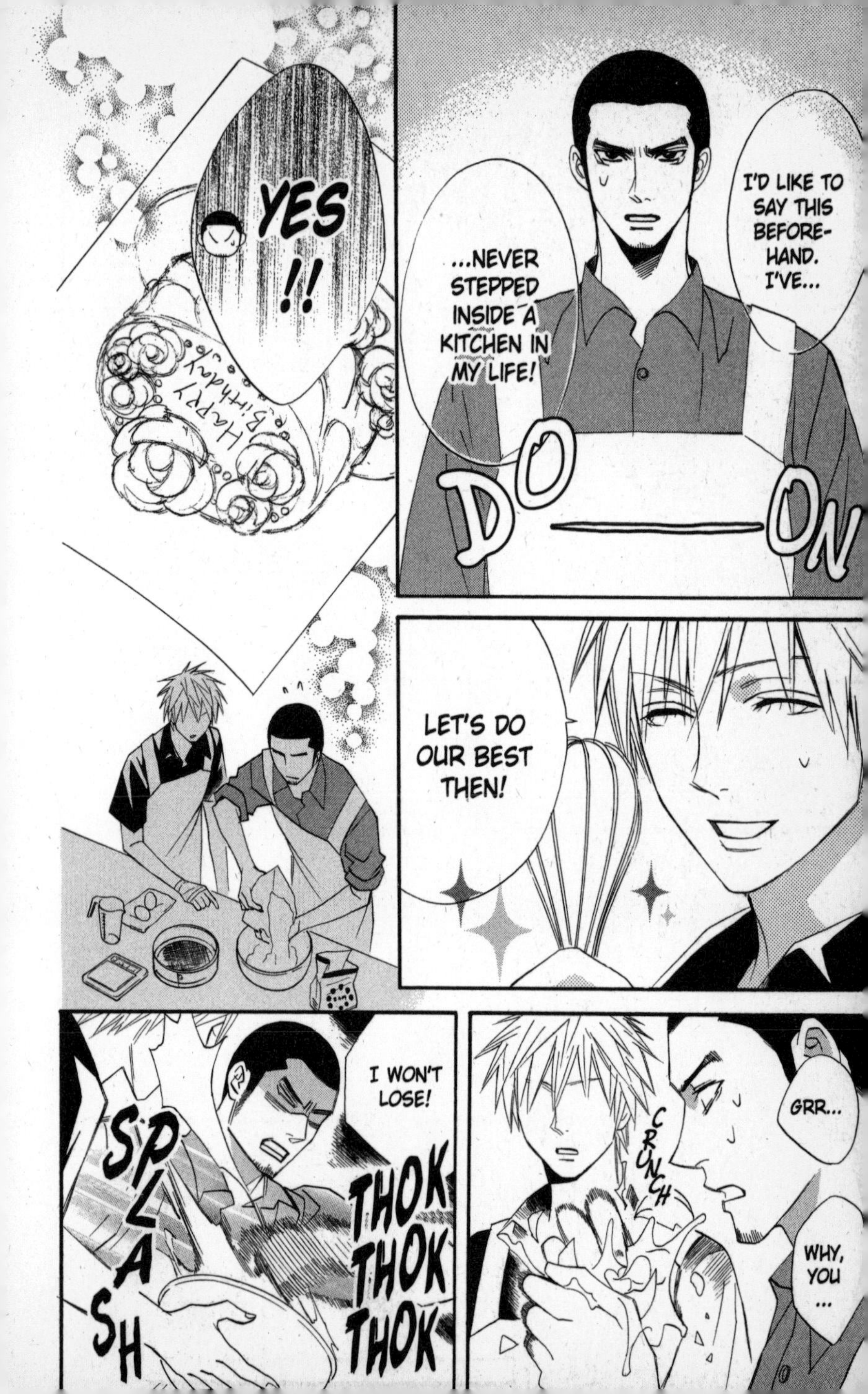
I'D LIKE TO SAY THIS BEFORE-HAND. I'VE...
...NEVER STEPPED INSIDE A KITCHEN IN MY LIFE!
DO—ON
LET'S DO OUR BEST THEN!
YES!!
Happy Birthday
GRR...
WHY, YOU...
CRUNCH
I WON'T LOSE!
SPLASH
THOK THOK THOK

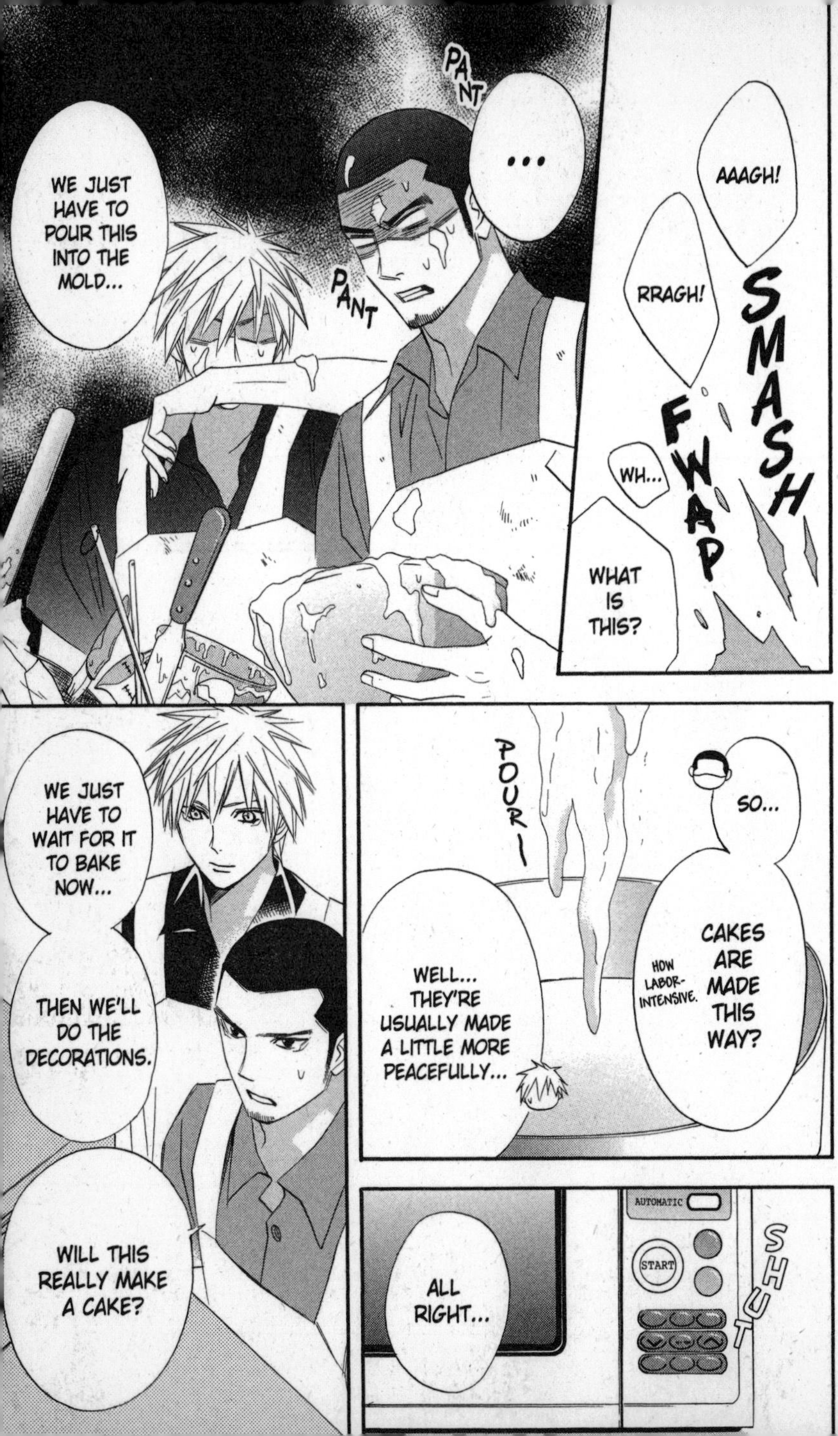
AAAGH!
RRAGH!
SMASH
FWAP
WH...
WHAT IS THIS?
PANT
...
PANT
WE JUST HAVE TO POUR THIS INTO THE MOLD...
POURI
SO...
CAKES ARE MADE THIS WAY?
HOW LABOR-INTENSIVE.
WELL... THEY'RE USUALLY MADE A LITTLE MORE PEACEFULLY...
SHUT
AUTOMATIC
START
ALL RIGHT...
WE JUST HAVE TO WAIT FOR IT TO BAKE NOW...
THEN WE'LL DO THE DECORATIONS.
WILL THIS REALLY MAKE A CAKE?

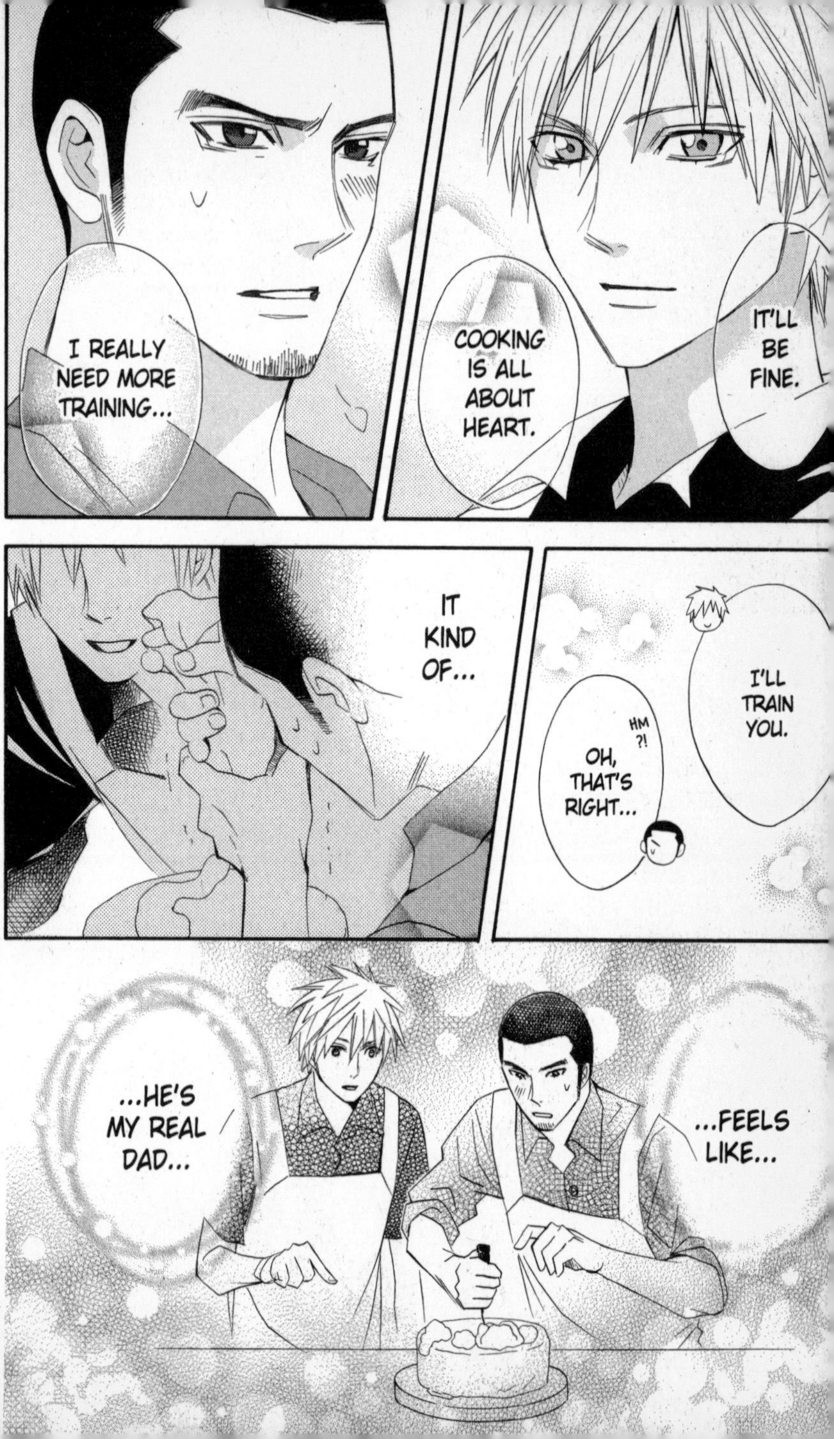
IT'LL BE FINE.
COOKING IS ALL ABOUT HEART.
I REALLY NEED MORE TRAINING...
I'LL TRAIN YOU.
HM ?!
OH, THAT'S RIGHT...
IT KIND OF...
...FEELS LIKE...
...HE'S MY REAL DAD...

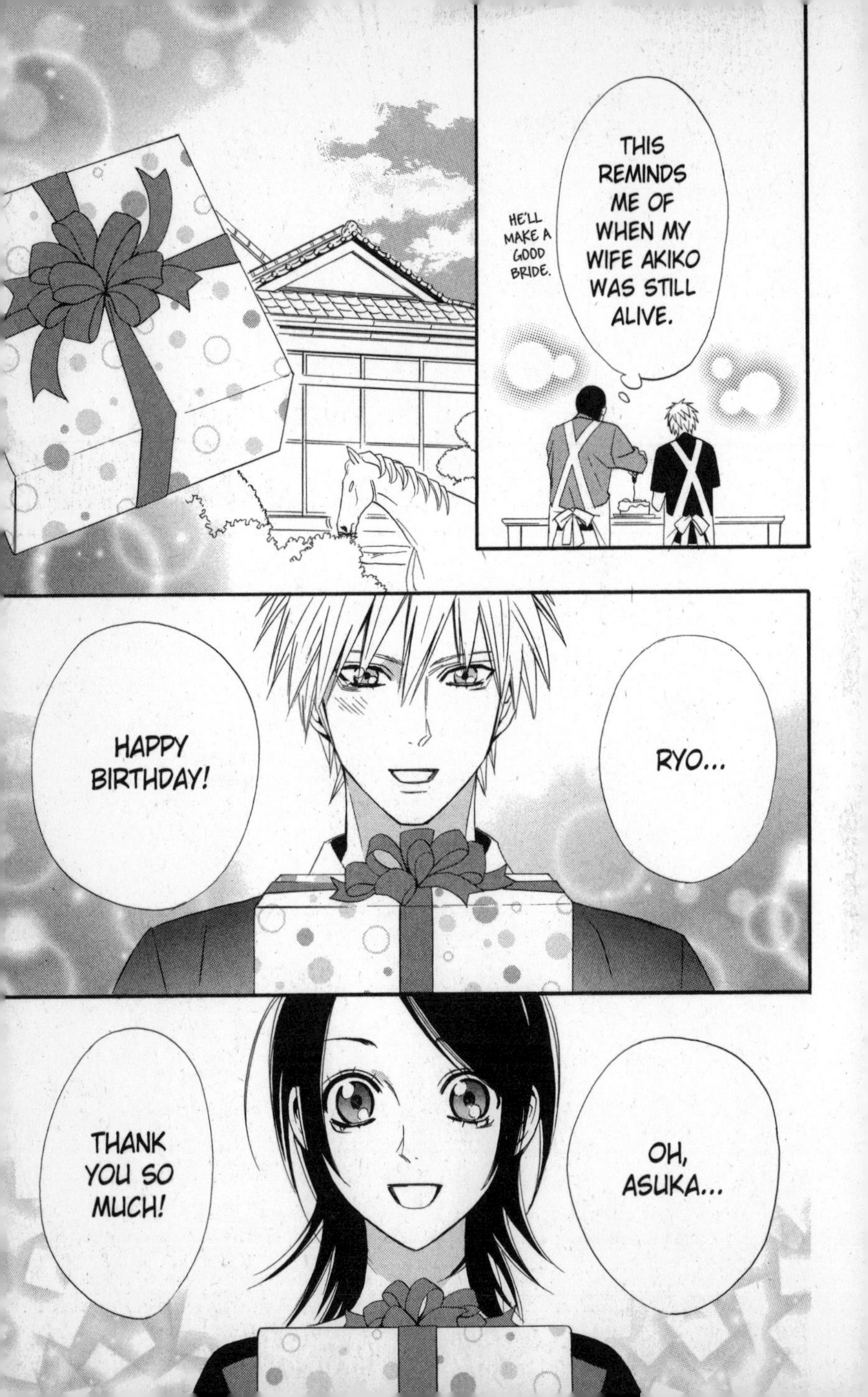
THIS REMINDS ME OF WHEN MY WIFE AKIKO WAS STILL ALIVE.
HE'LL MAKE A GOOD BRIDE.
RYO...
HAPPY BIRTHDAY!
OH, ASUKA...
THANK YOU SO MUCH!

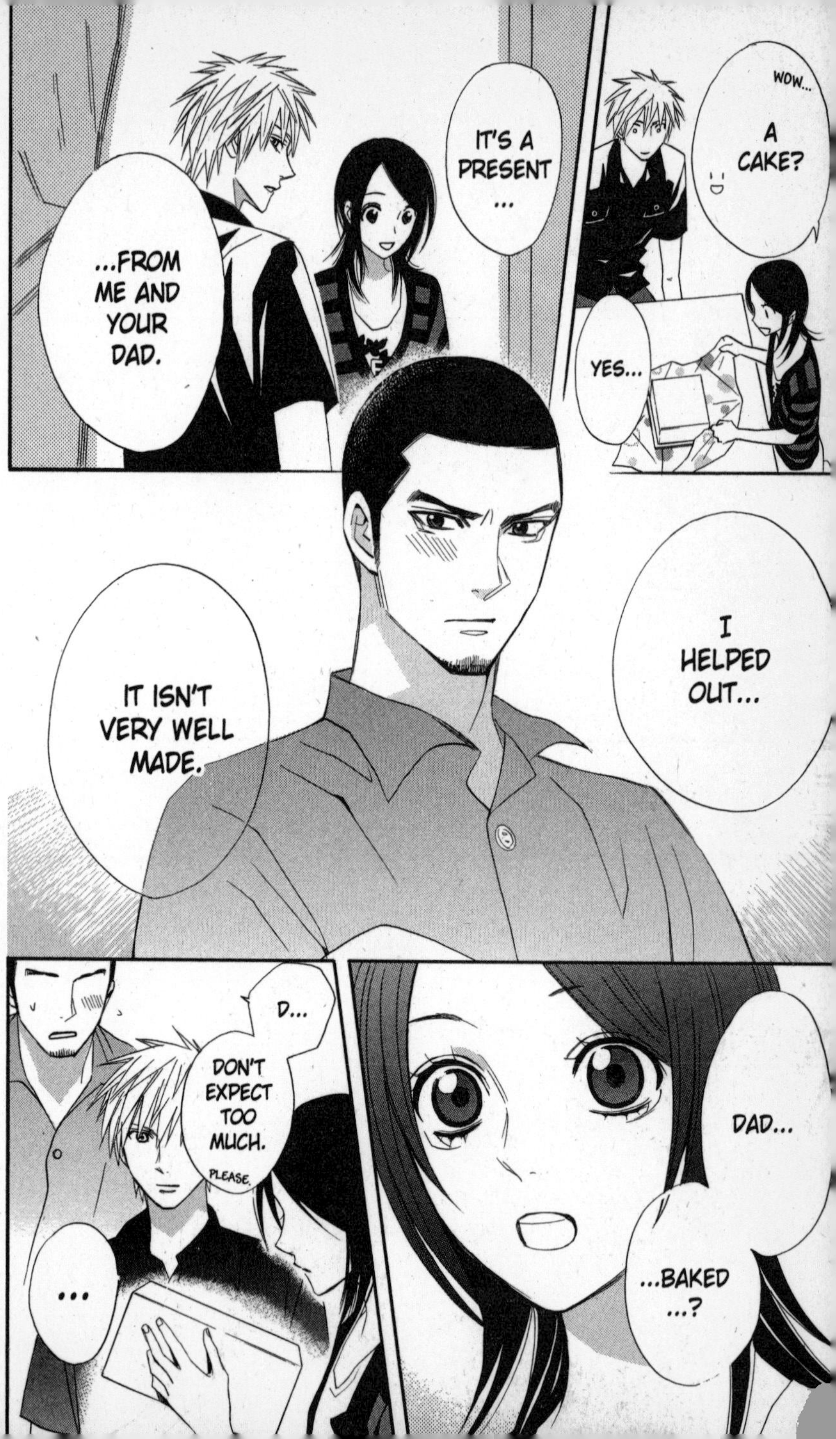
WOW... A CAKE?
YES...
IT'S A PRESENT...
...FROM ME AND YOUR DAD.
I HELPED OUT...
IT ISN'T VERY WELL MADE.
DAD...
...BAKED...?
D...
DON'T EXPECT TOO MUCH.
PLEASE.
...

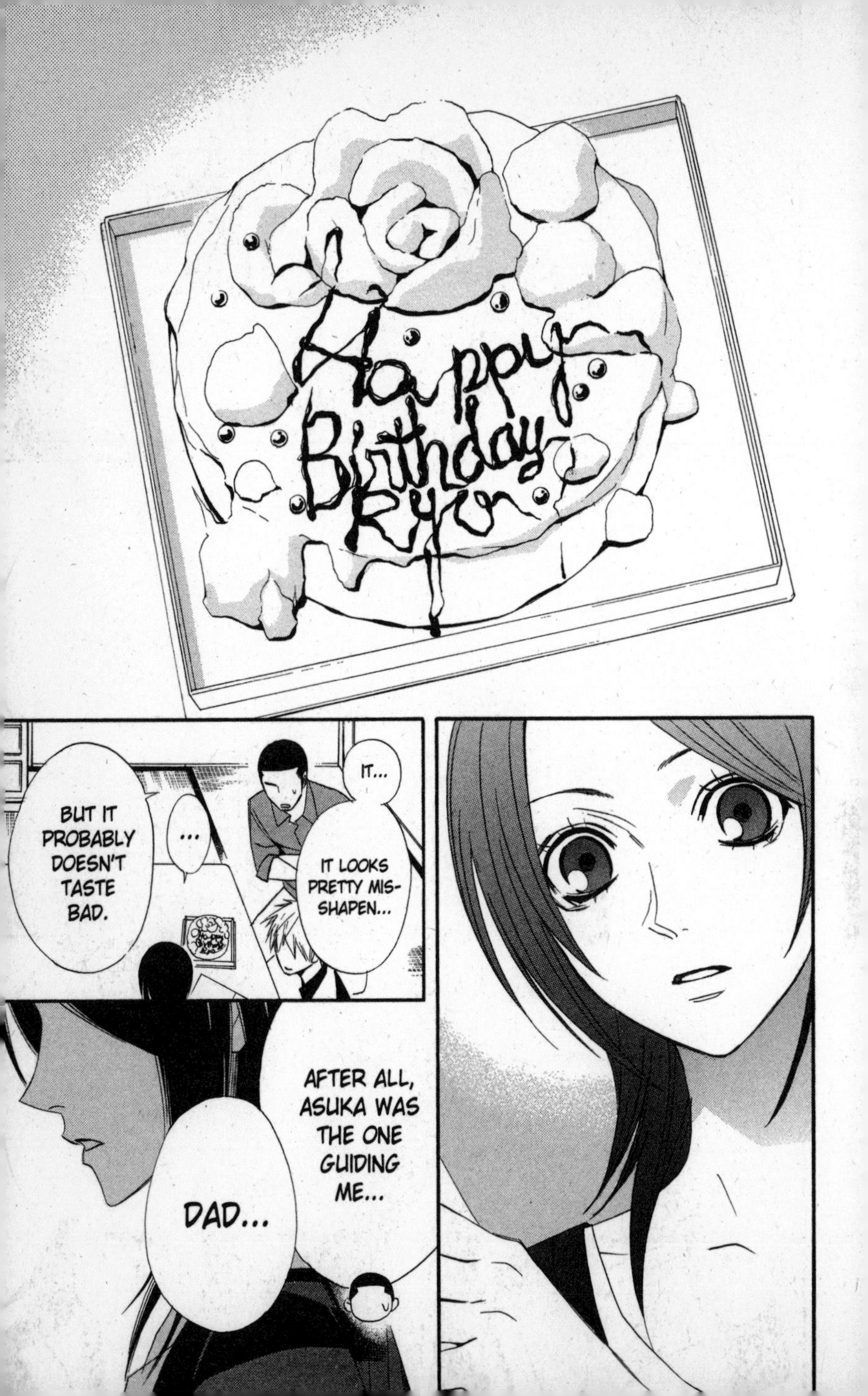
Happy Birthday Ryo
IT...
IT LOOKS PRETTY MIS-SHAPEN...
...
BUT IT PROBABLY DOESN'T TASTE BAD.
AFTER ALL, ASUKA WAS THE ONE GUIDING ME...
DAD...

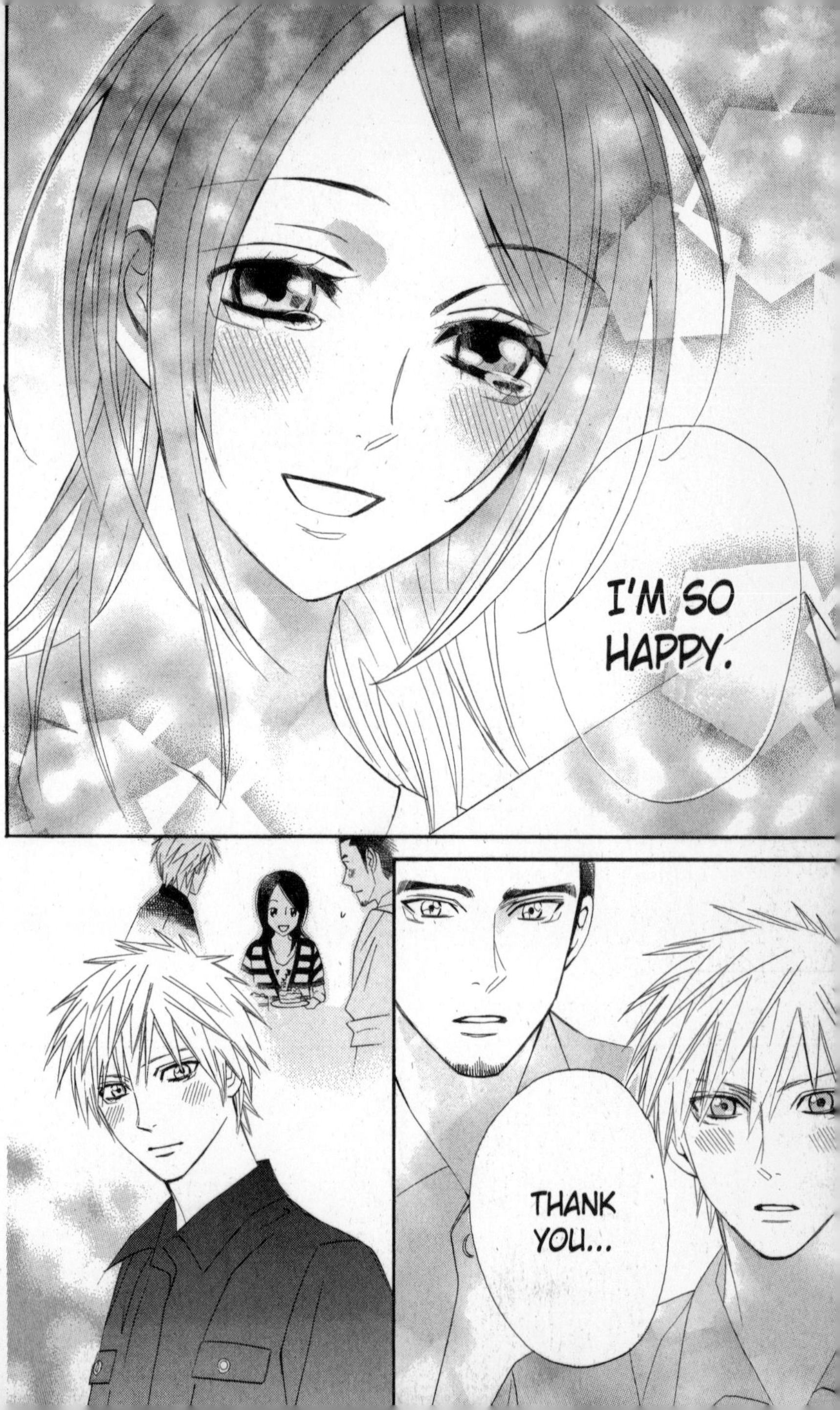
I'M SO HAPPY.
THANK YOU...

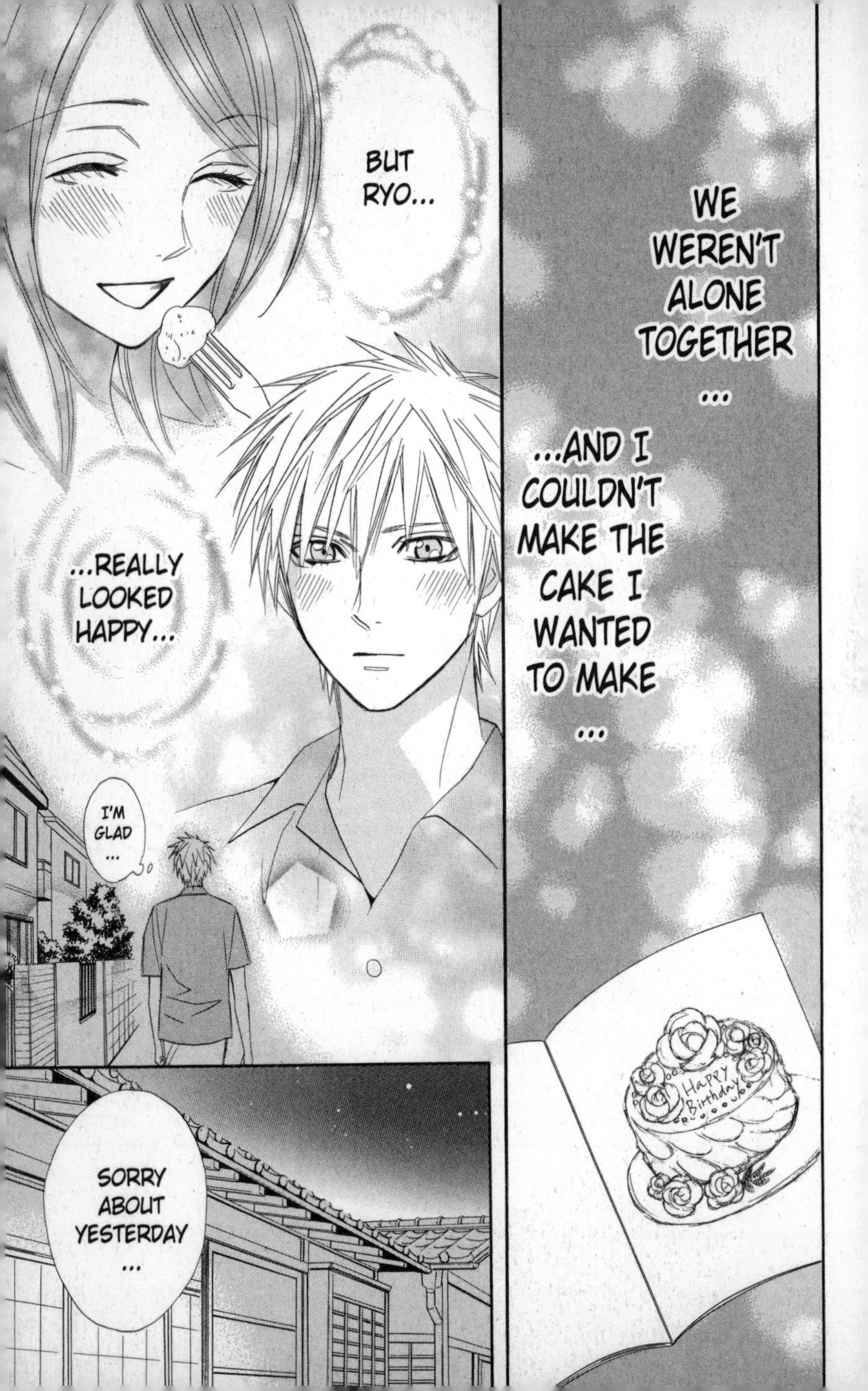
WE WEREN'T ALONE TOGETHER...
...AND I COULDN'T MAKE THE CAKE I WANTED TO MAKE...
Happy Birthday
BUT RYO...
...REALLY LOOKED HAPPY...
I'M GLAD...
SORRY ABOUT YESTERDAY...

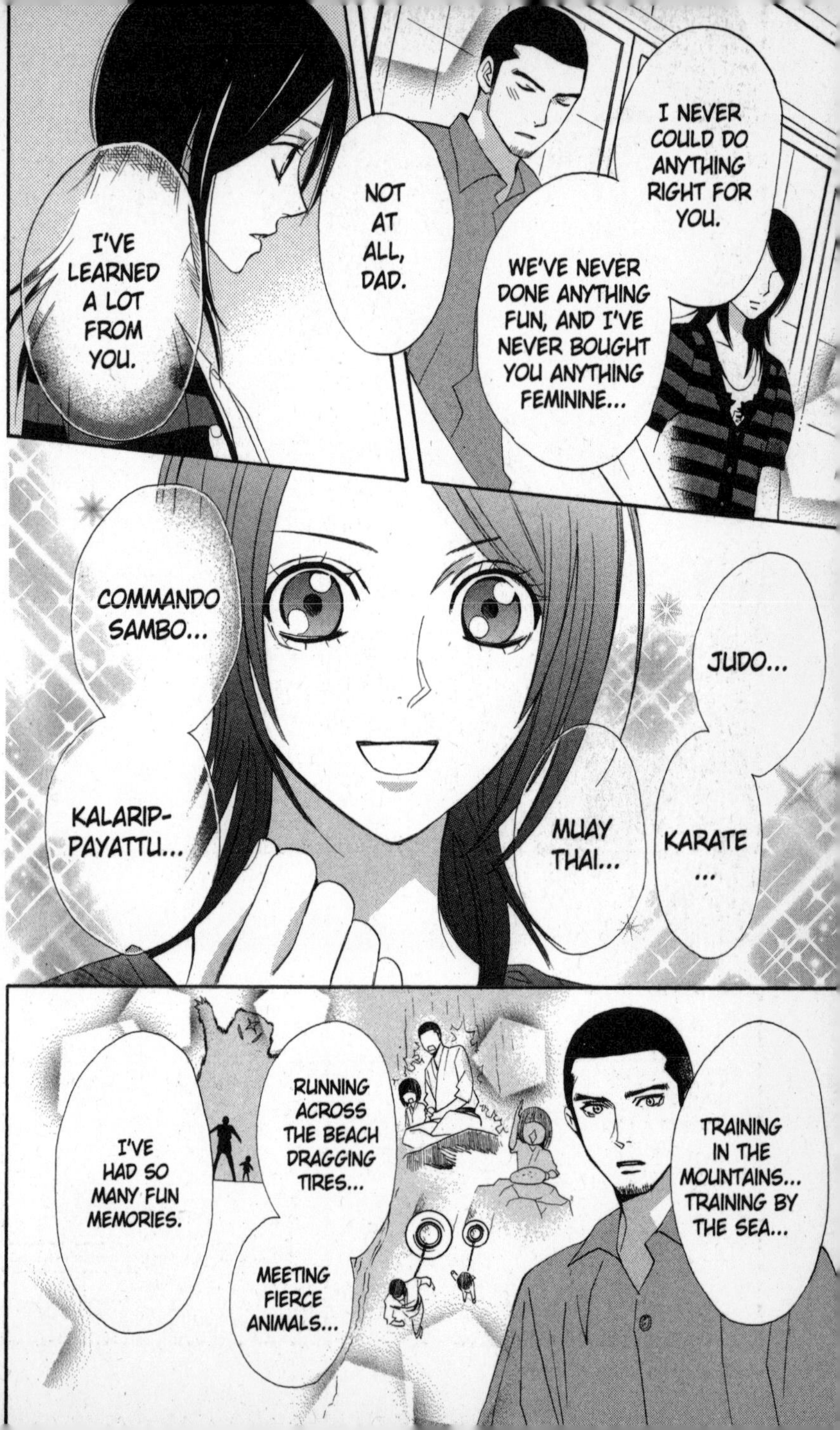
I NEVER COULD DO ANYTHING RIGHT FOR YOU.
WE'VE NEVER DONE ANYTHING FUN, AND I'VE NEVER BOUGHT YOU ANYTHING FEMININE...
NOT AT ALL, DAD.
I'VE LEARNED A LOT FROM YOU.
JUDO...
KARATE...
MUAY THAI...
COMMANDO SAMBO...
KALARIP-PAYATTU...
TRAINING IN THE MOUNTAINS... TRAINING BY THE SEA...
RUNNING ACROSS THE BEACH DRAGGING TIRES...
MEETING FIERCE ANIMALS...
I'VE HAD SO MANY FUN MEMORIES.

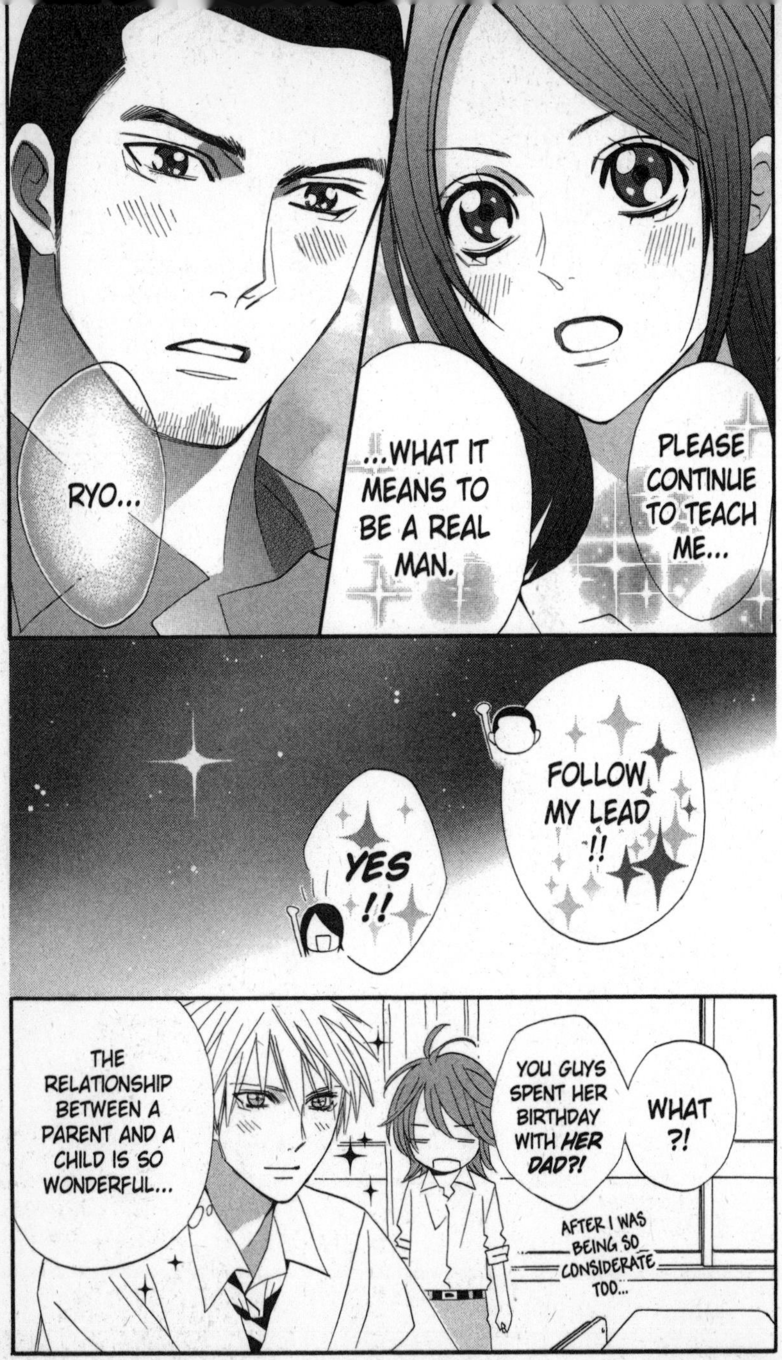
PLEASE CONTINUE TO TEACH ME...
...WHAT IT MEANS TO BE A REAL MAN.
RYO...
FOLLOW MY LEAD!!
YES!!
WHAT?!
YOU GUYS SPENT HER BIRTHDAY WITH HER DAD?!
AFTER I WAS BEING SO CONSIDERATE TOO...
THE RELATIONSHIP BETWEEN A PARENT AND A CHILD IS SO WONDERFUL...

OTOMEN

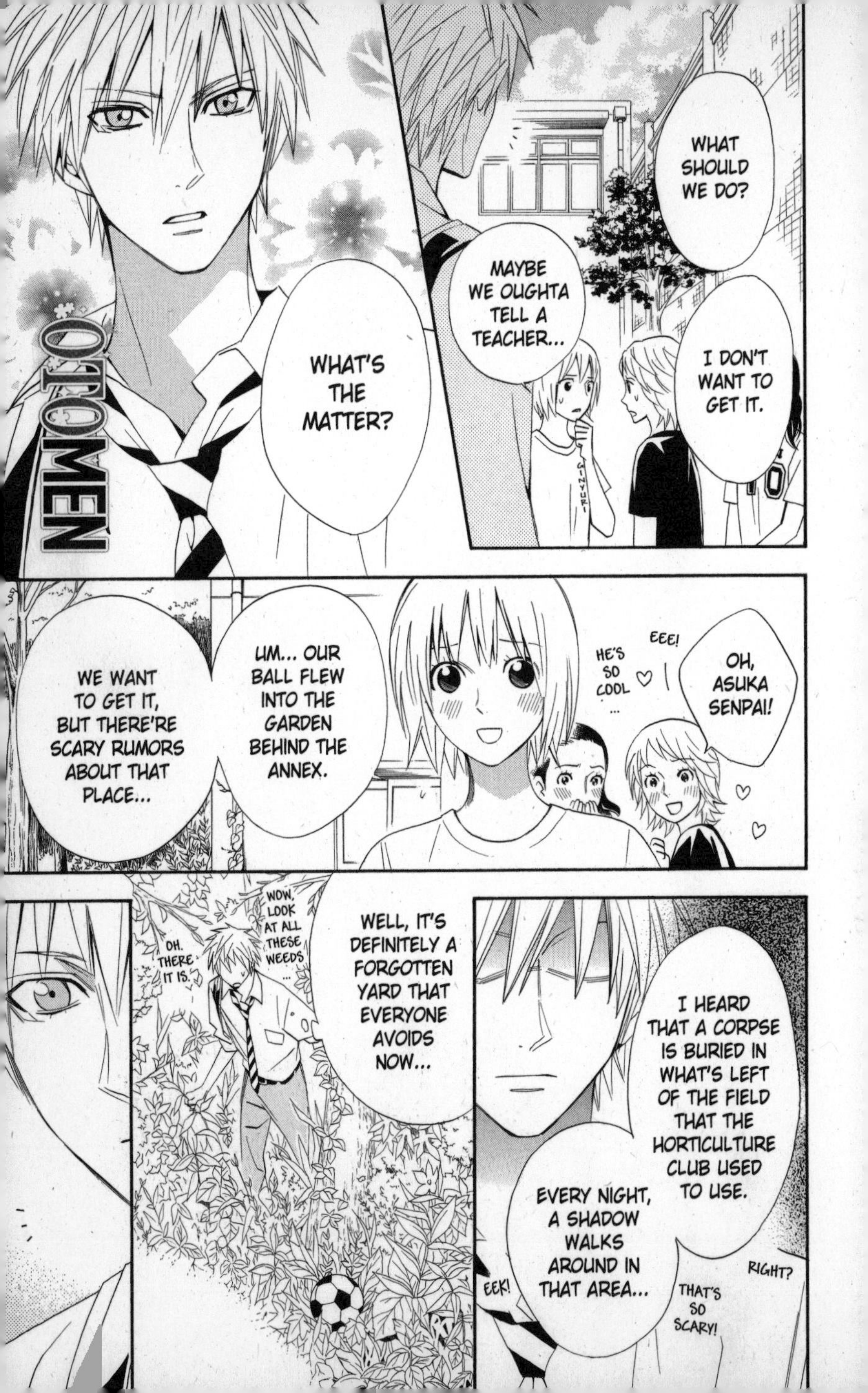
WHAT SHOULD WE DO?
MAYBE WE OUGHTA TELL A TEACHER...
I DON'T WANT TO GET IT.
WHAT'S THE MATTER?
OTOMEN
OH, ASUKA SENPAI!
EEE!
HE'S SO COOL...
UM... OUR BALL FLEW INTO THE GARDEN BEHIND THE ANNEX.
WE WANT TO GET IT, BUT THERE'RE SCARY RUMORS ABOUT THAT PLACE...
I HEARD THAT A CORPSE IS BURIED IN WHAT'S LEFT OF THE FIELD THAT THE HORTICULTURE CLUB USED TO USE.
EVERY NIGHT, A SHADOW WALKS AROUND IN THAT AREA...
RIGHT?
THAT'S SO SCARY!
EEK!
WELL, IT'S DEFINITELY A FORGOTTEN YARD THAT EVERYONE AVOIDS NOW...
WOW, LOOK AT ALL THESE WEEDS...
OH. THERE IT IS.

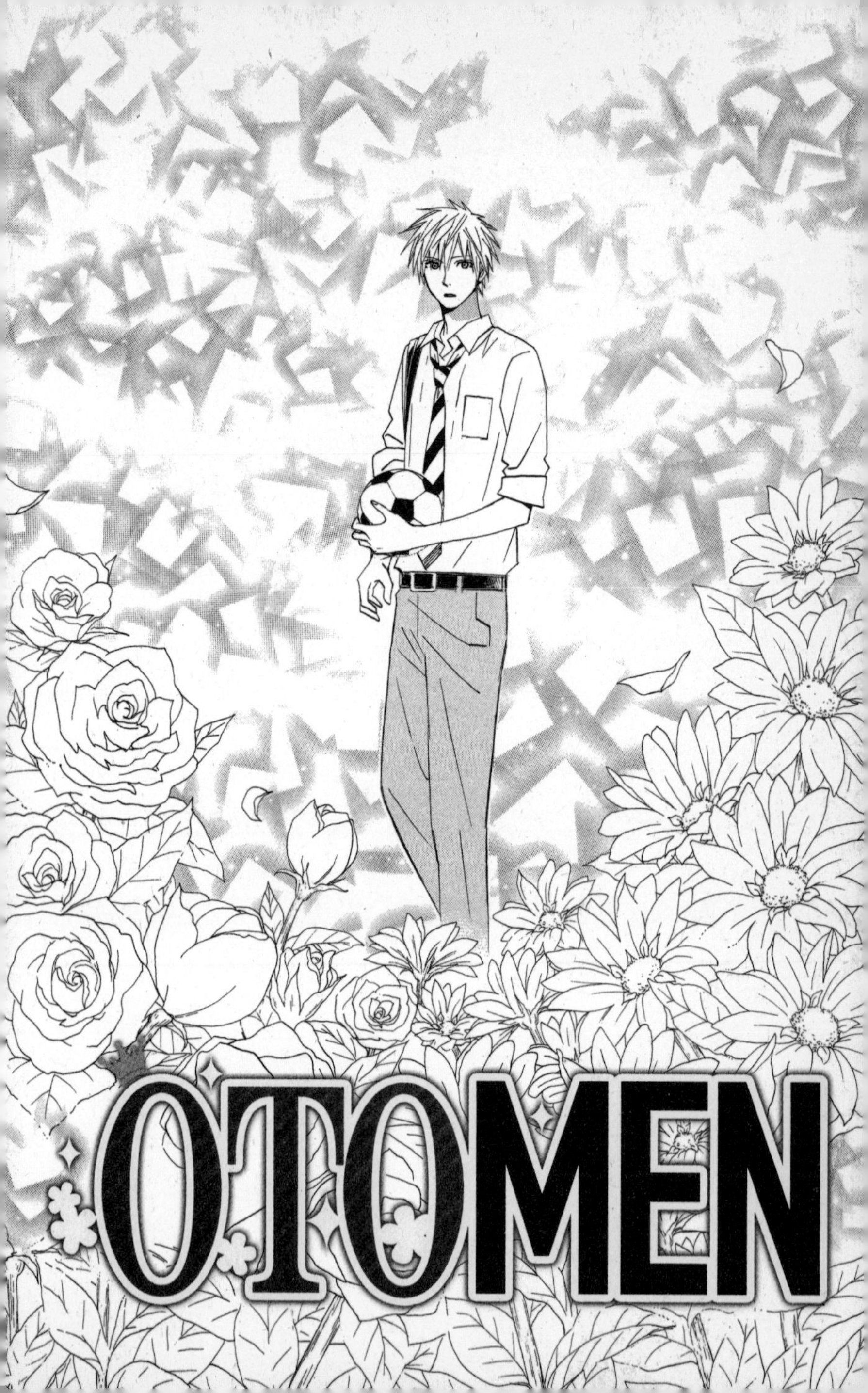
OTOMEN

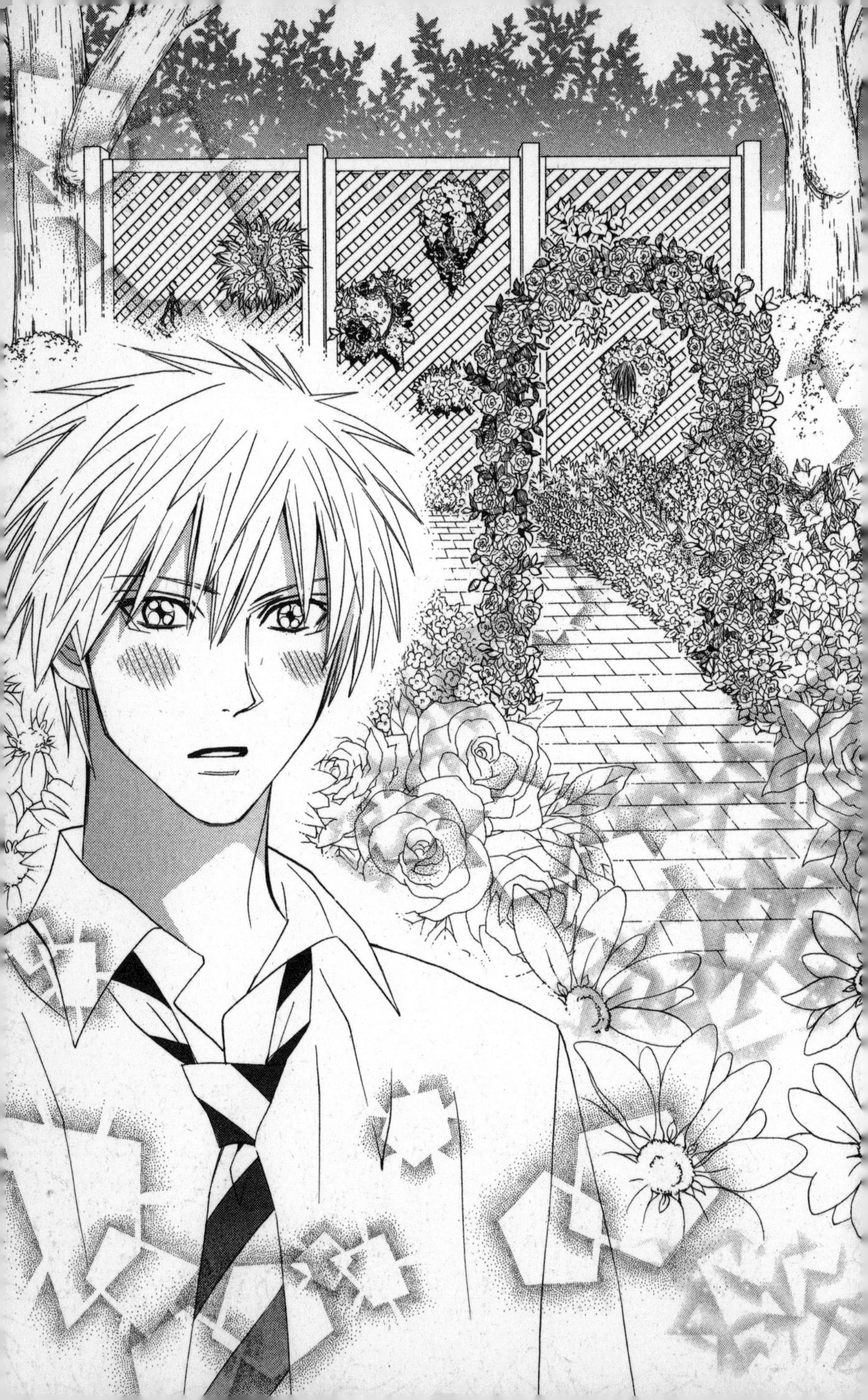

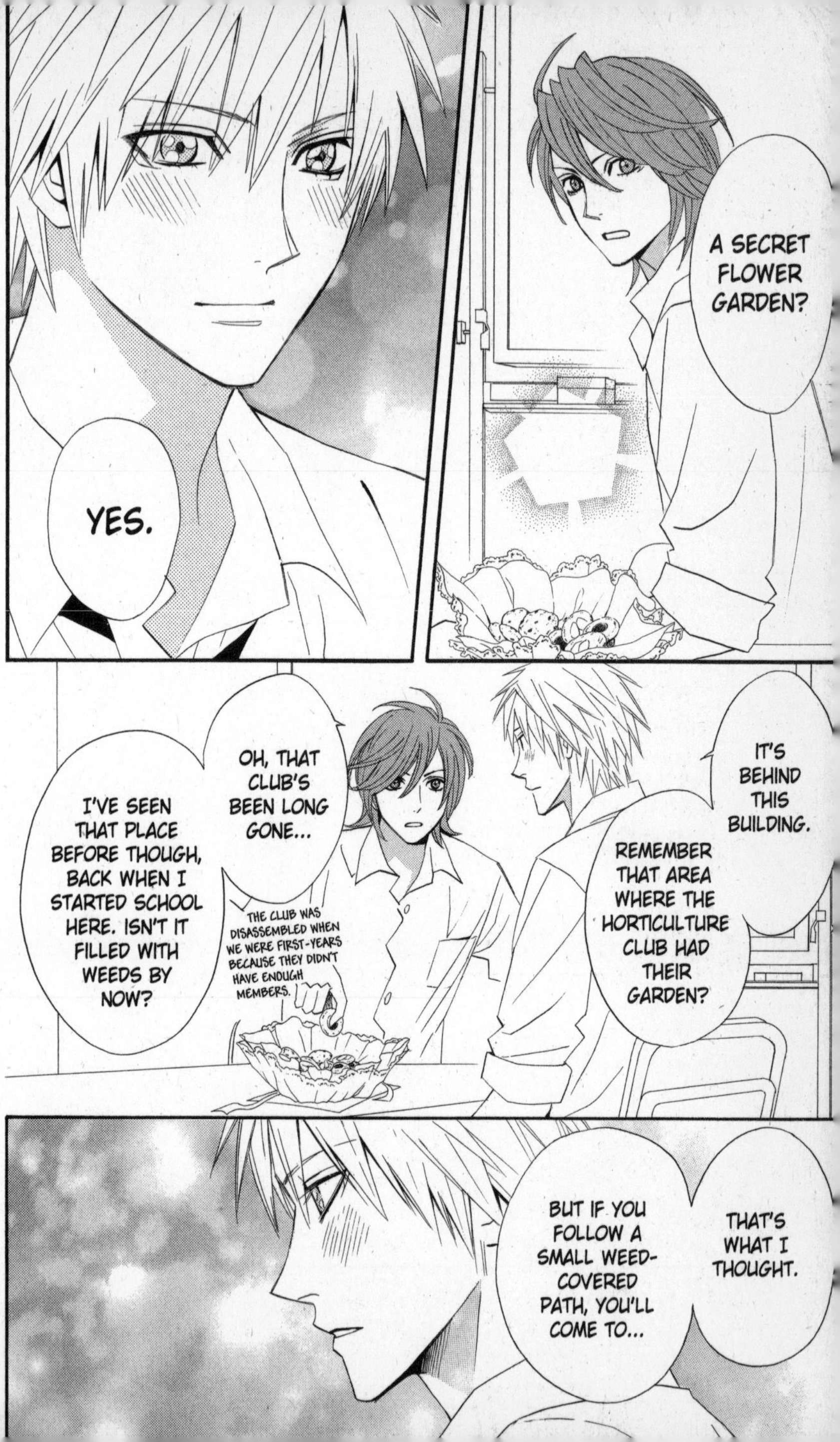
A SECRET FLOWER GARDEN?
YES.
IT'S BEHIND THIS BUILDING.
REMEMBER THAT AREA WHERE THE HORTICULTURE CLUB HAD THEIR GARDEN?
OH, THAT CLUB'S BEEN LONG GONE...
THE CLUB WAS DISASSEMBLED WHEN WE WERE FIRST-YEARS BECAUSE THEY DIDN'T HAVE ENOUGH MEMBERS.
I'VE SEEN THAT PLACE BEFORE THOUGH, BACK WHEN I STARTED SCHOOL HERE. ISN'T IT FILLED WITH WEEDS BY NOW?
THAT'S WHAT I THOUGHT.
BUT IF YOU FOLLOW A SMALL WEED-COVERED PATH, YOU'LL COME TO...

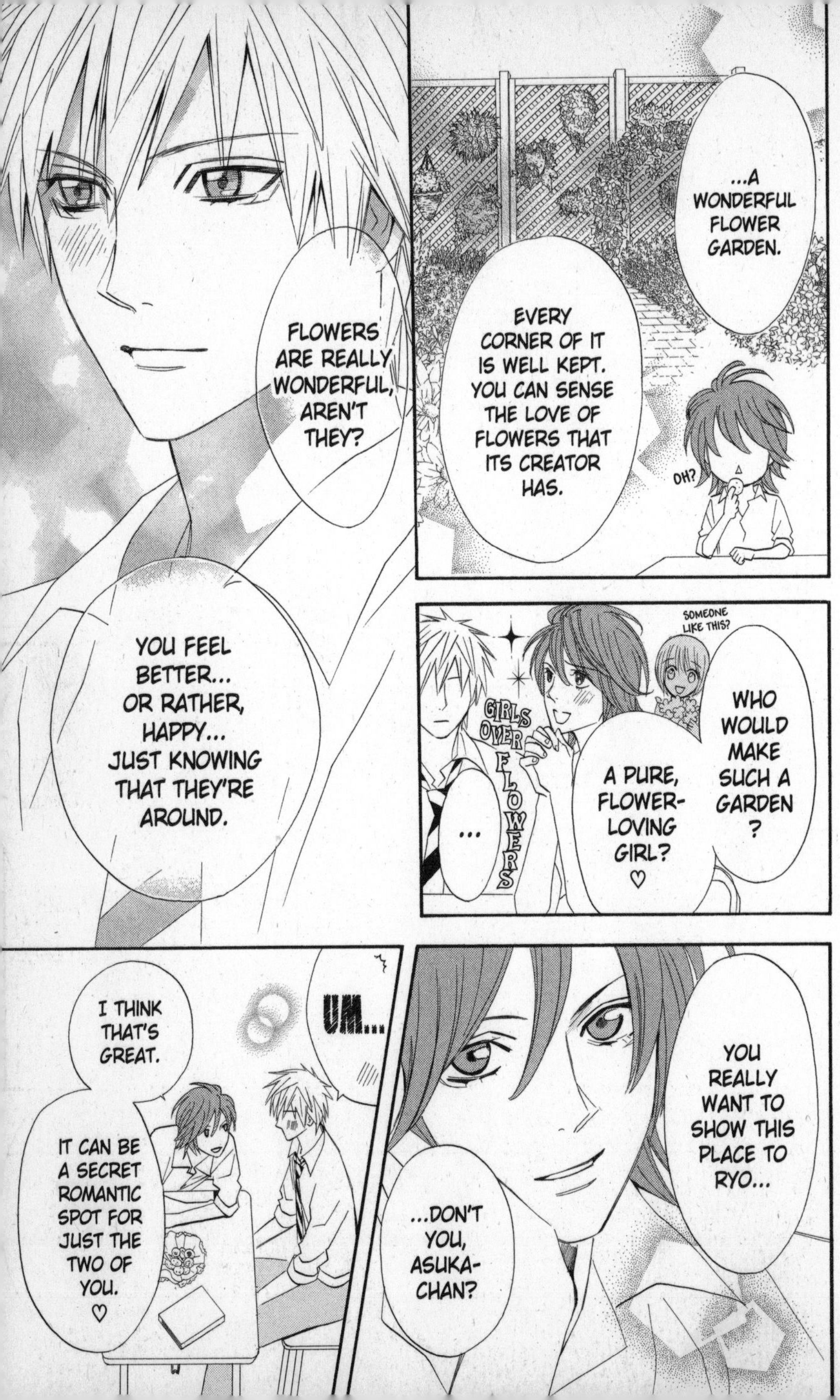
...A WONDERFUL FLOWER GARDEN.
EVERY CORNER OF IT IS WELL KEPT. YOU CAN SENSE THE LOVE OF FLOWERS THAT ITS CREATOR HAS.
OH?
WHO WOULD MAKE SUCH A GARDEN?
SOMEONE LIKE THIS?
A PURE, FLOWER-LOVING GIRL? ♡
GIRLS OVER FLOWERS
...
FLOWERS ARE REALLY WONDERFUL, AREN'T THEY?
YOU FEEL BETTER... OR RATHER, HAPPY... JUST KNOWING THAT THEY'RE AROUND.
YOU REALLY WANT TO SHOW THIS PLACE TO RYO...
...DON'T YOU, ASUKA-CHAN?
UM...
I THINK THAT'S GREAT.
IT CAN BE A SECRET ROMANTIC SPOT FOR JUST THE TWO OF YOU. ♡

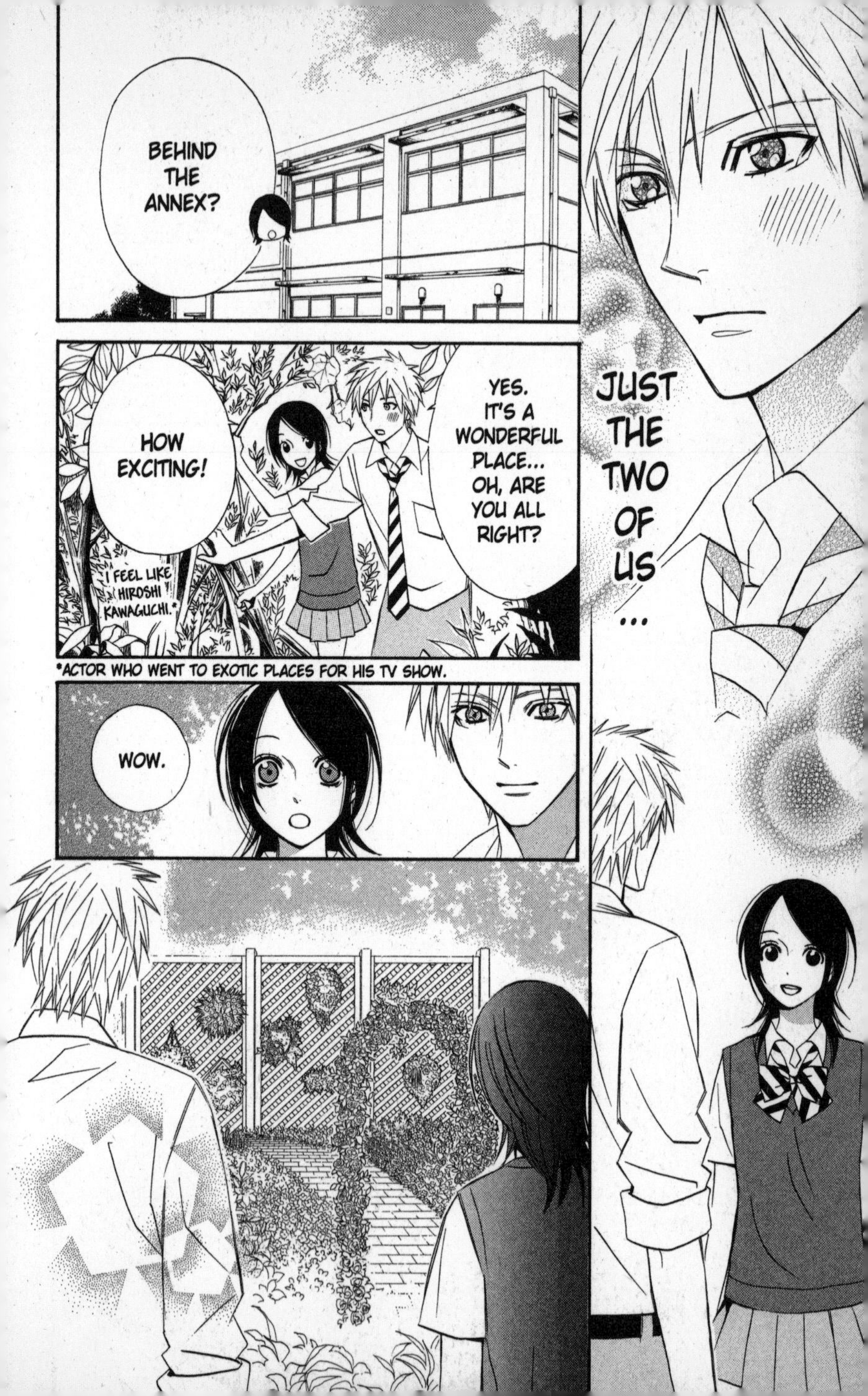
JUST THE TWO OF US ...
BEHIND THE ANNEX?
YES. IT'S A WONDERFUL PLACE... OH, ARE YOU ALL RIGHT?
HOW EXCITING!
I FEEL LIKE HIROSHI KAWAGUCHI.*
*ACTOR WHO WENT TO EXOTIC PLACES FOR HIS TV SHOW.
WOW.

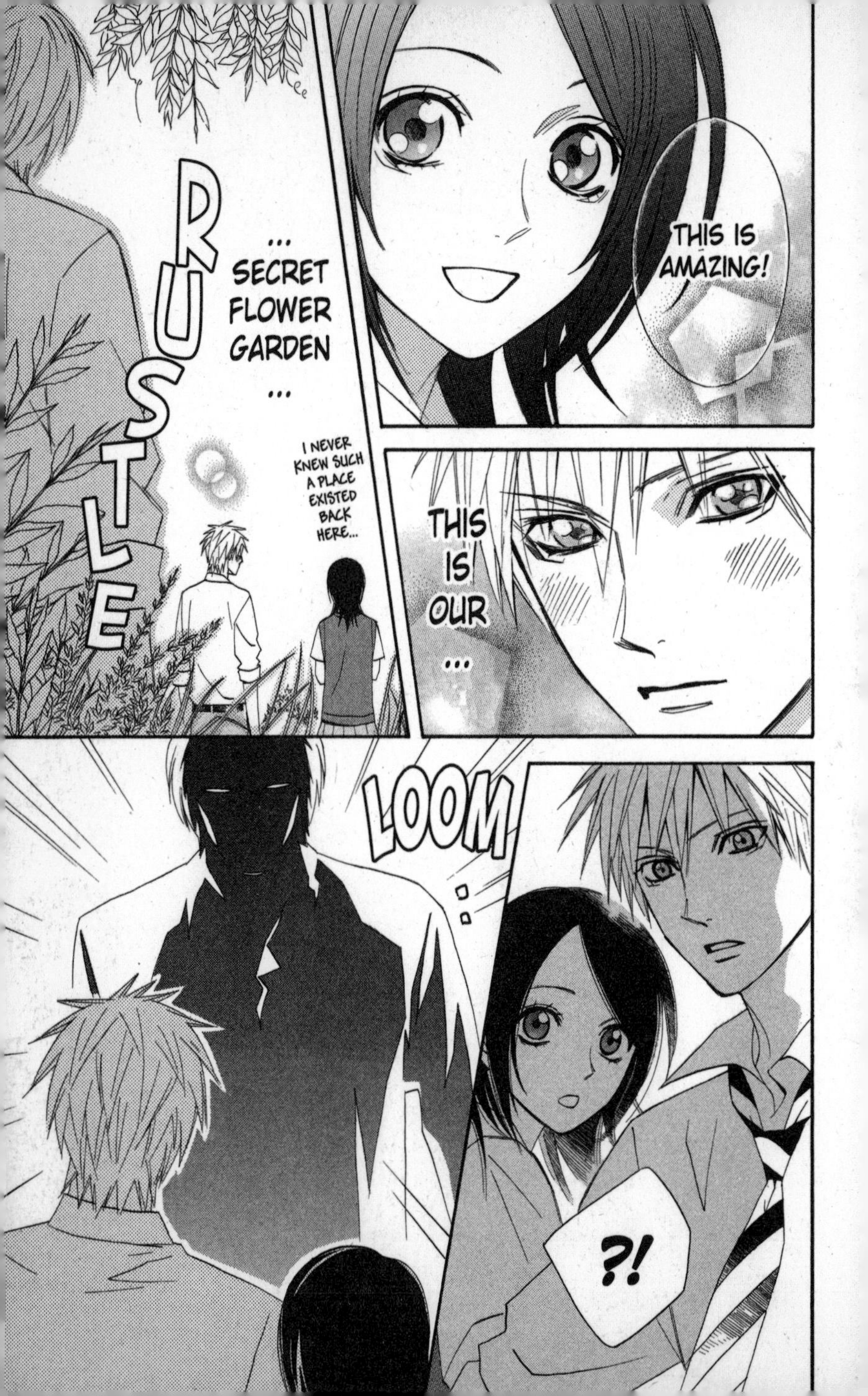
THIS IS AMAZING!
THIS IS OUR ...
RUSTLE
... SECRET FLOWER GARDEN ...
I NEVER KNEW SUCH A PLACE EXISTED BACK HERE...
LOOM
?!

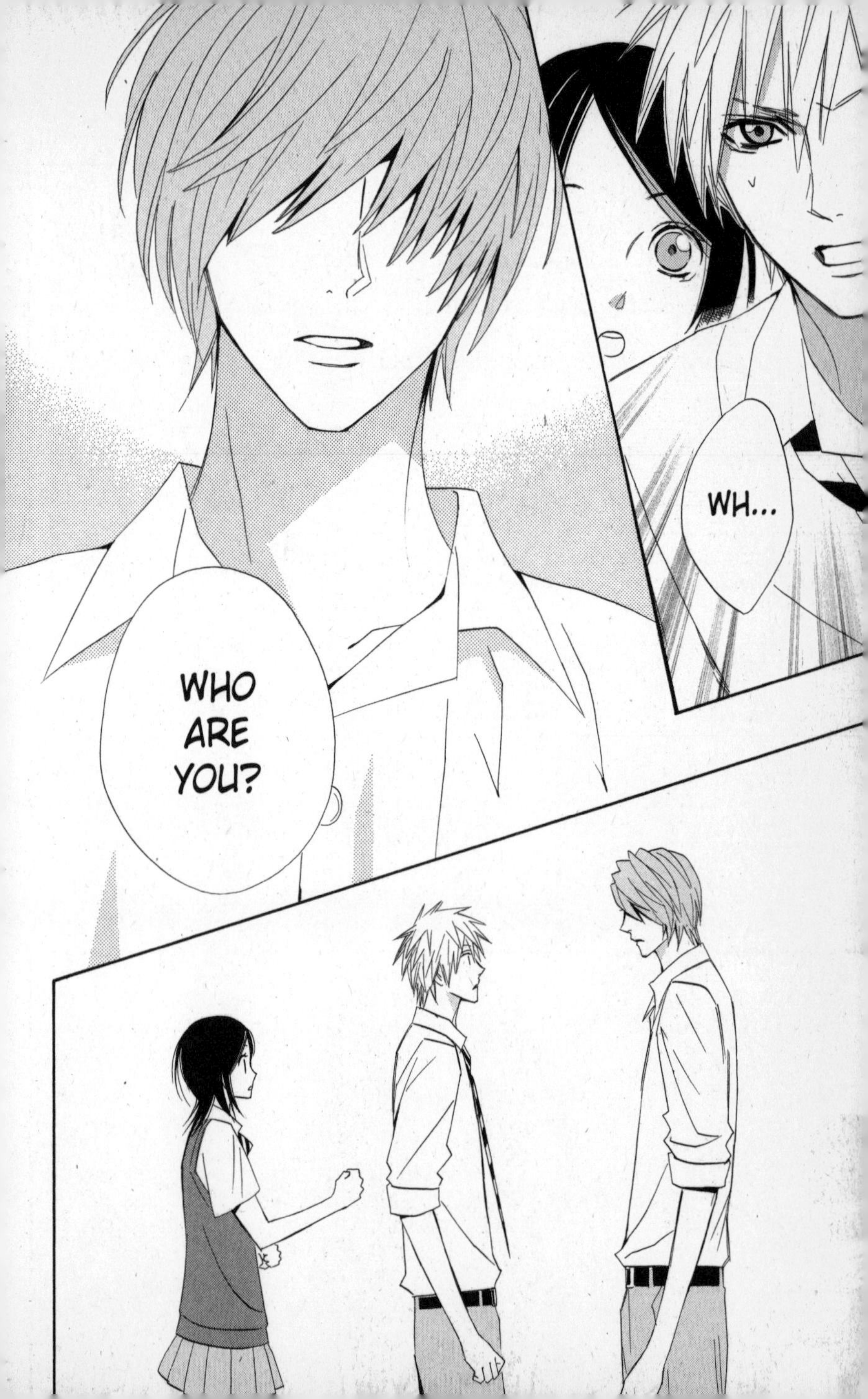
WH...
WHO ARE YOU?

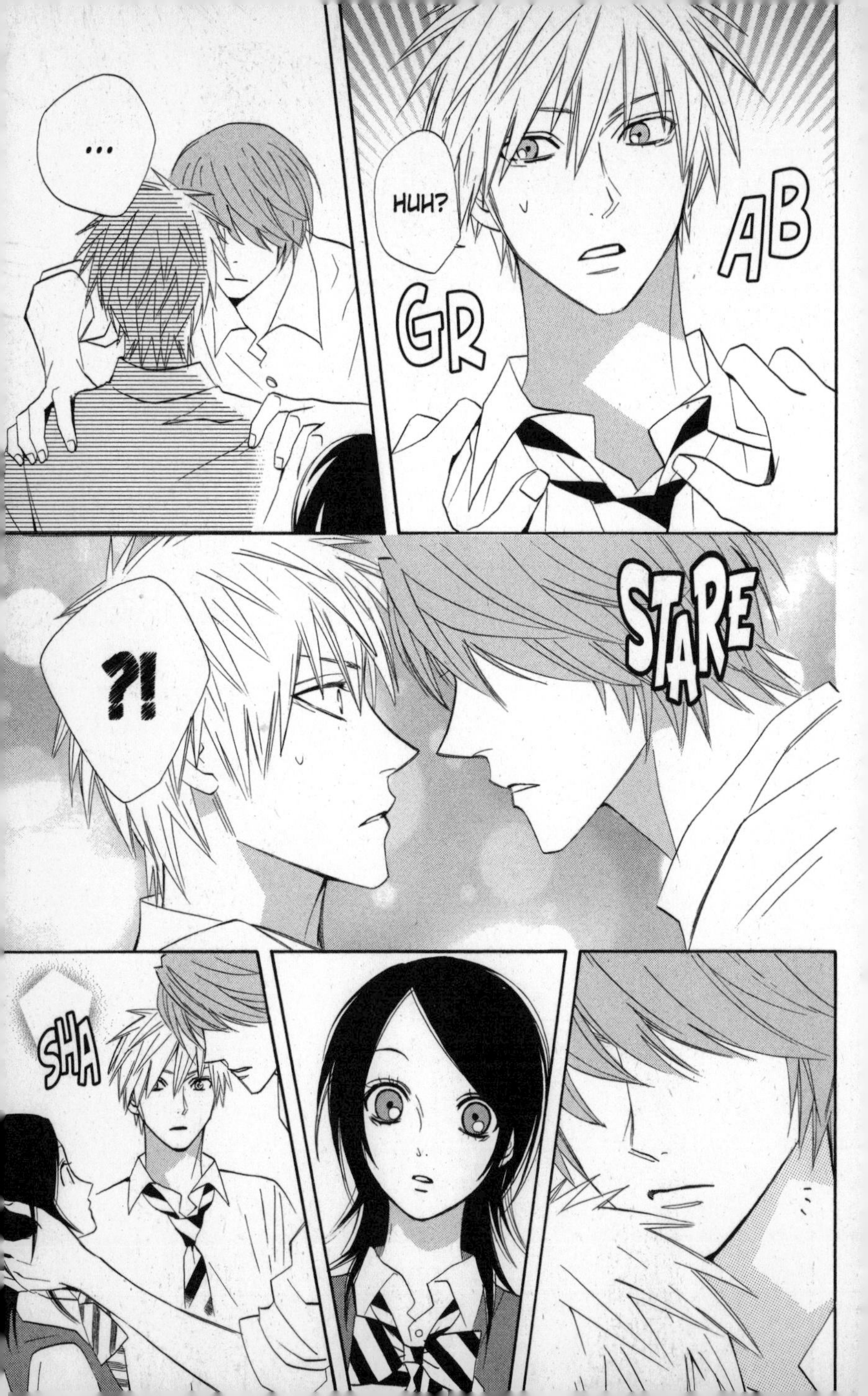

HUH?
GR
AB
...
STARE
?!
SHA

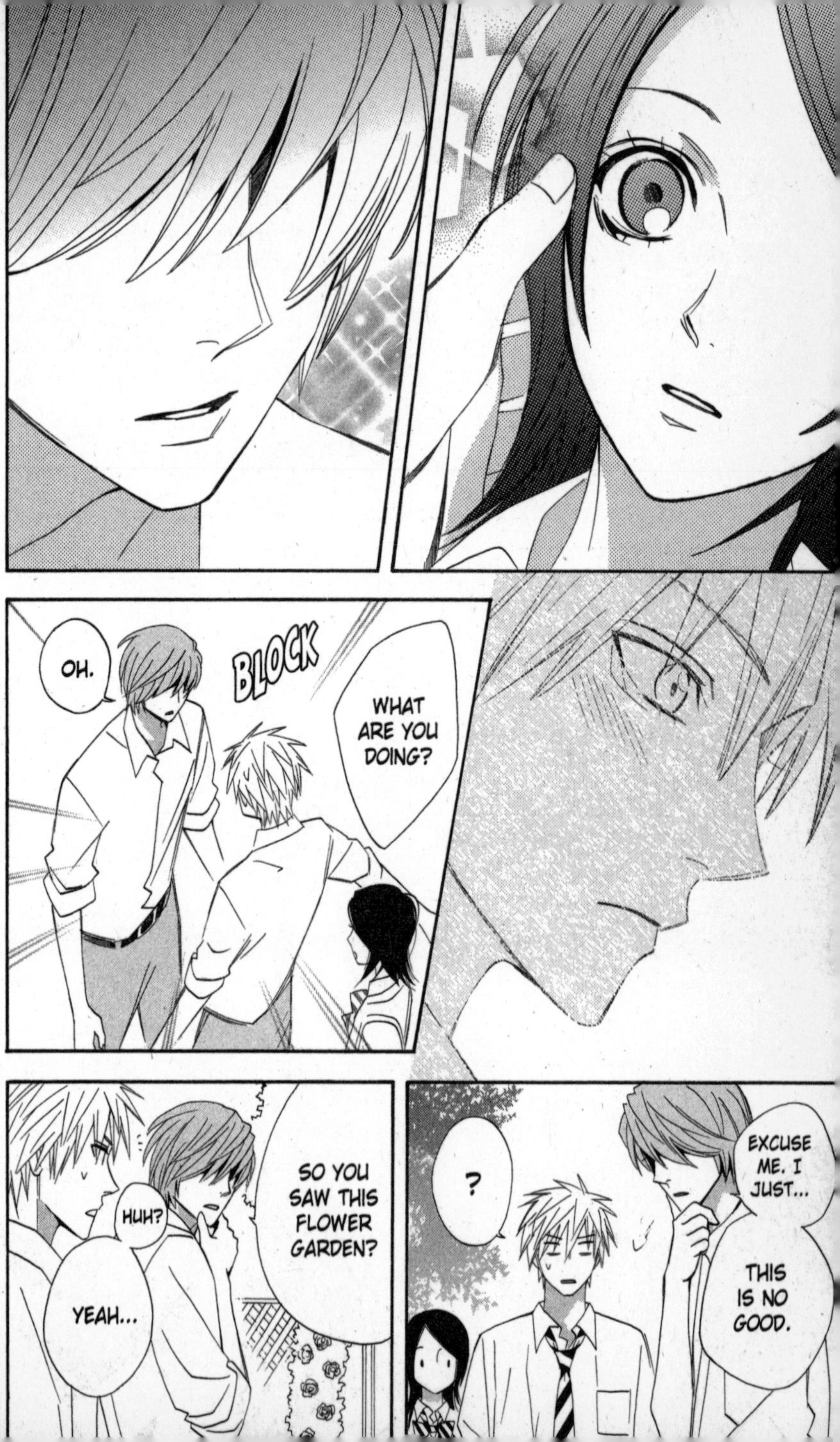
WHAT ARE YOU DOING?
BLOCK
OH.
EXCUSE ME. I JUST...
THIS IS NO GOOD.
?
SO YOU SAW THIS FLOWER GARDEN?
HUH?
YEAH...

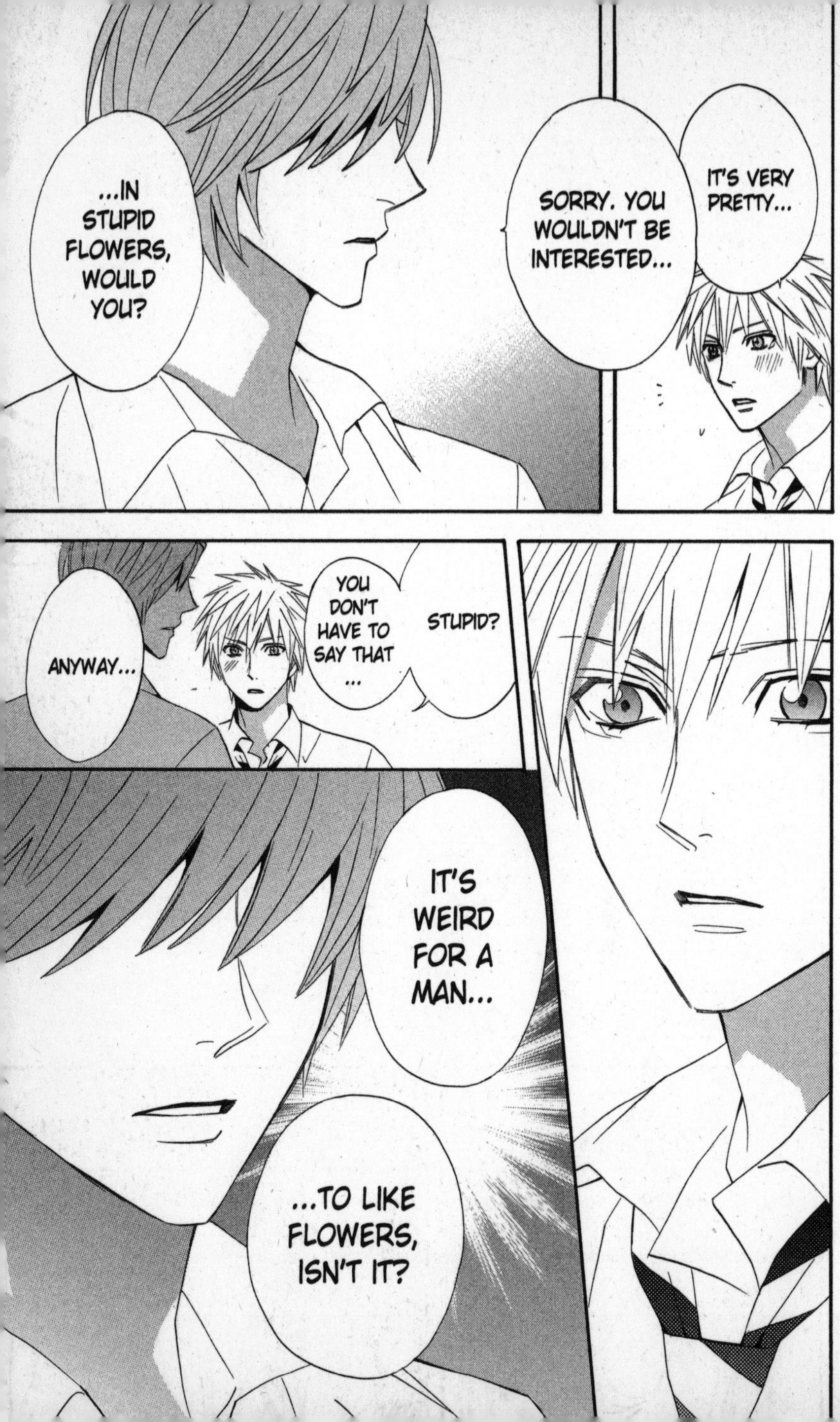
IT'S VERY PRETTY...
SORRY. YOU WOULDN'T BE INTERESTED...
...IN STUPID FLOWERS, WOULD YOU?
STUPID?
YOU DON'T HAVE TO SAY THAT ...
ANYWAY...
IT'S WEIRD FOR A MAN...
...TO LIKE FLOWERS, ISN'T IT?

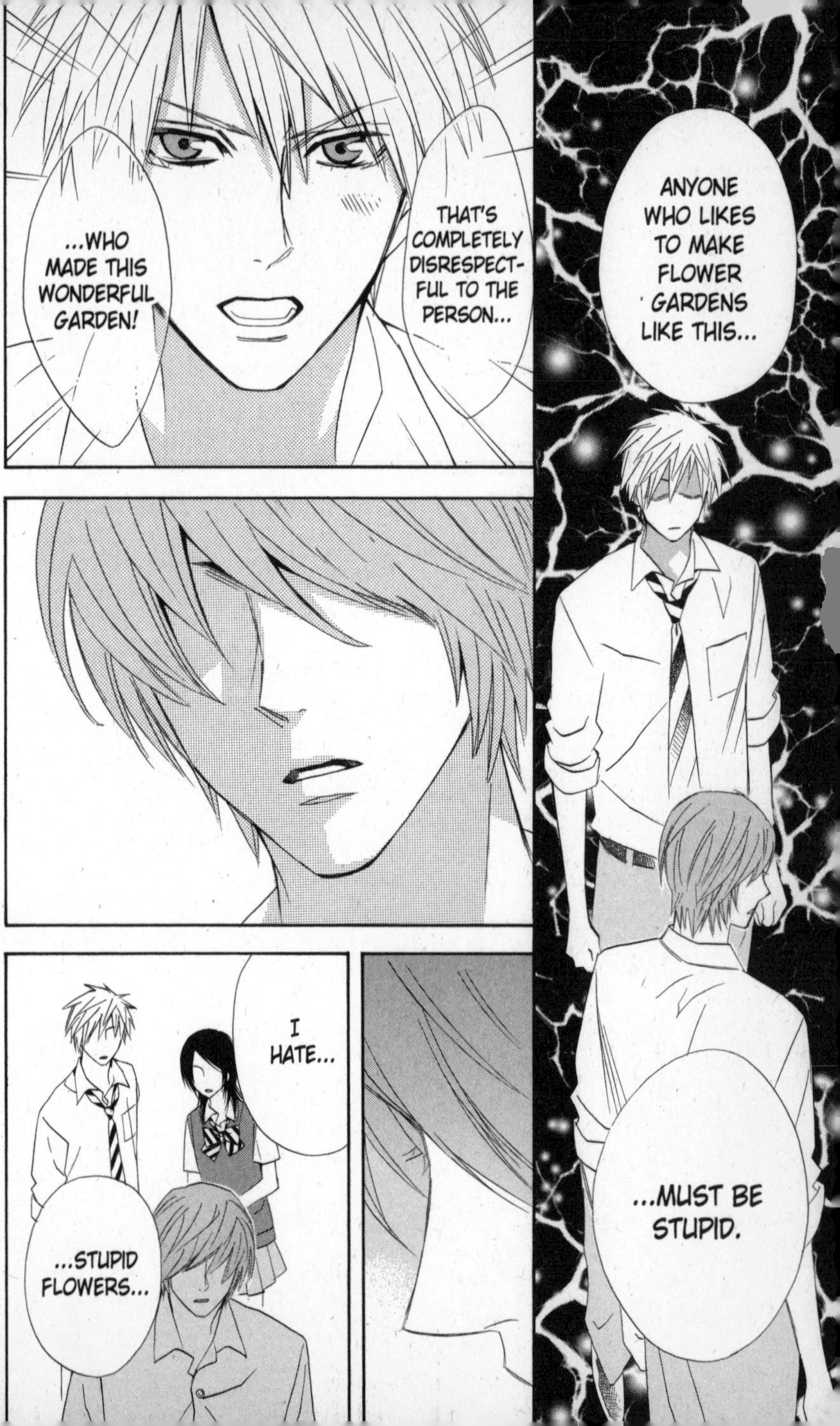
ANYONE WHO LIKES TO MAKE FLOWER GARDENS LIKE THIS...
...MUST BE STUPID.
THAT'S COMPLETELY DISRESPECT-FUL TO THE PERSON...
...WHO MADE THIS WONDERFUL GARDEN!
I HATE...
...STUPID FLOWERS...

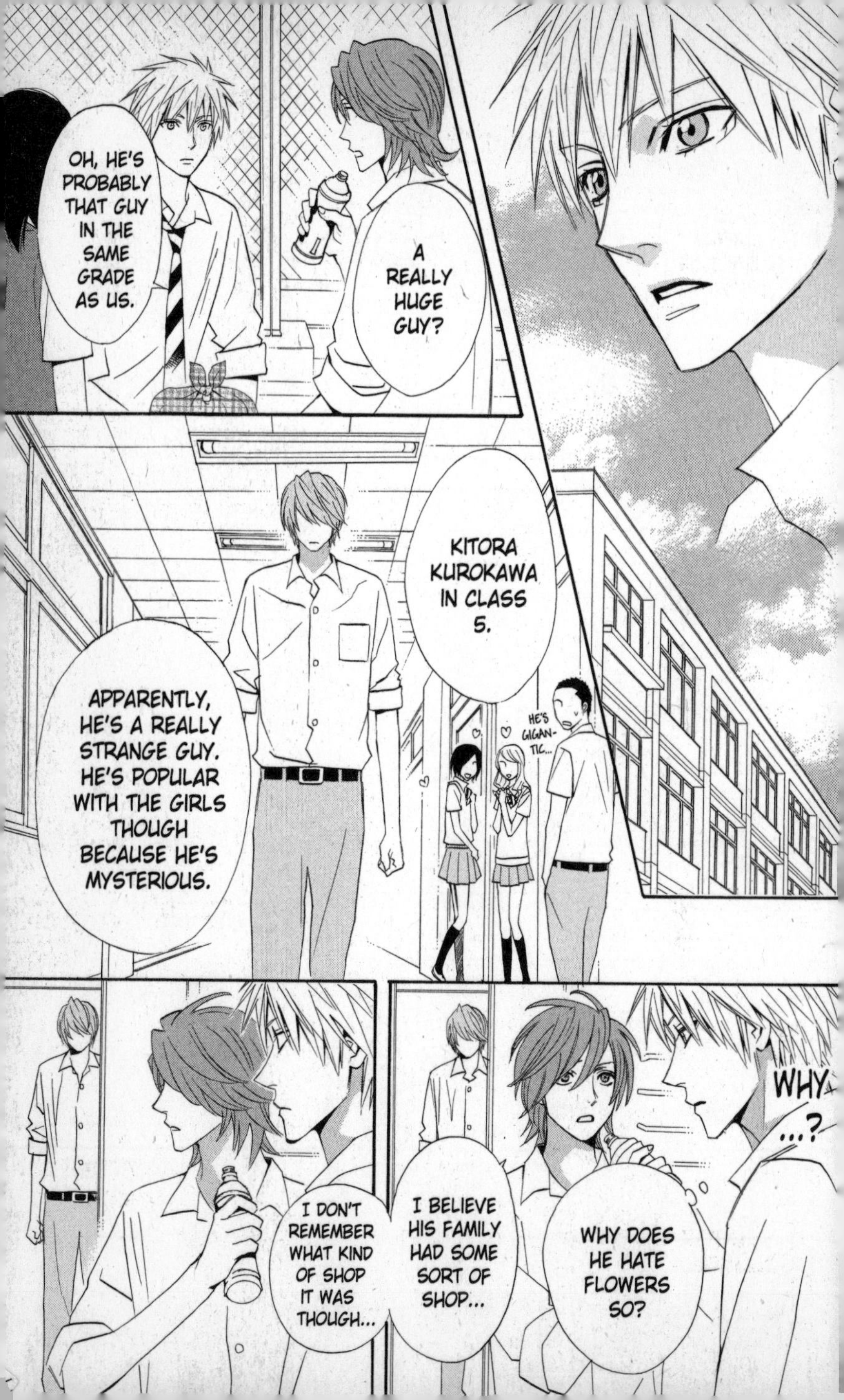
A REALLY HUGE GUY?
OH, HE'S PROBABLY THAT GUY IN THE SAME GRADE AS US.
KITORA KUROKAWA IN CLASS 5.
HE'S GIGAN-TIC...
APPARENTLY, HE'S A REALLY STRANGE GUY. HE'S POPULAR WITH THE GIRLS THOUGH BECAUSE HE'S MYSTERIOUS.
WHY ...?
WHY DOES HE HATE FLOWERS SO?
I BELIEVE HIS FAMILY HAD SOME SORT OF SHOP...
I DON'T REMEMBER WHAT KIND OF SHOP IT WAS THOUGH...

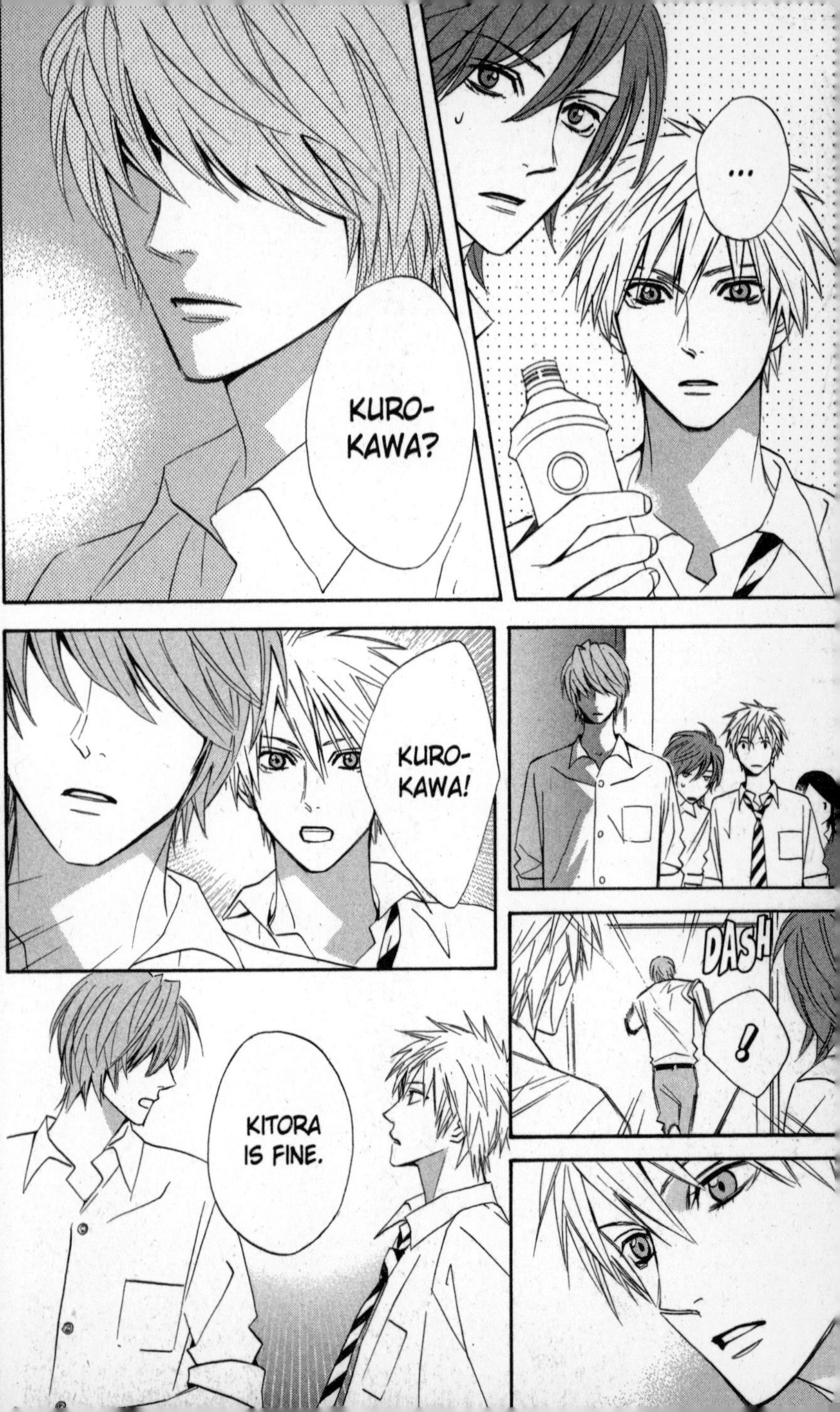
...
KURO-KAWA?
KURO-KAWA!
DASH
!
KITORA IS FINE.

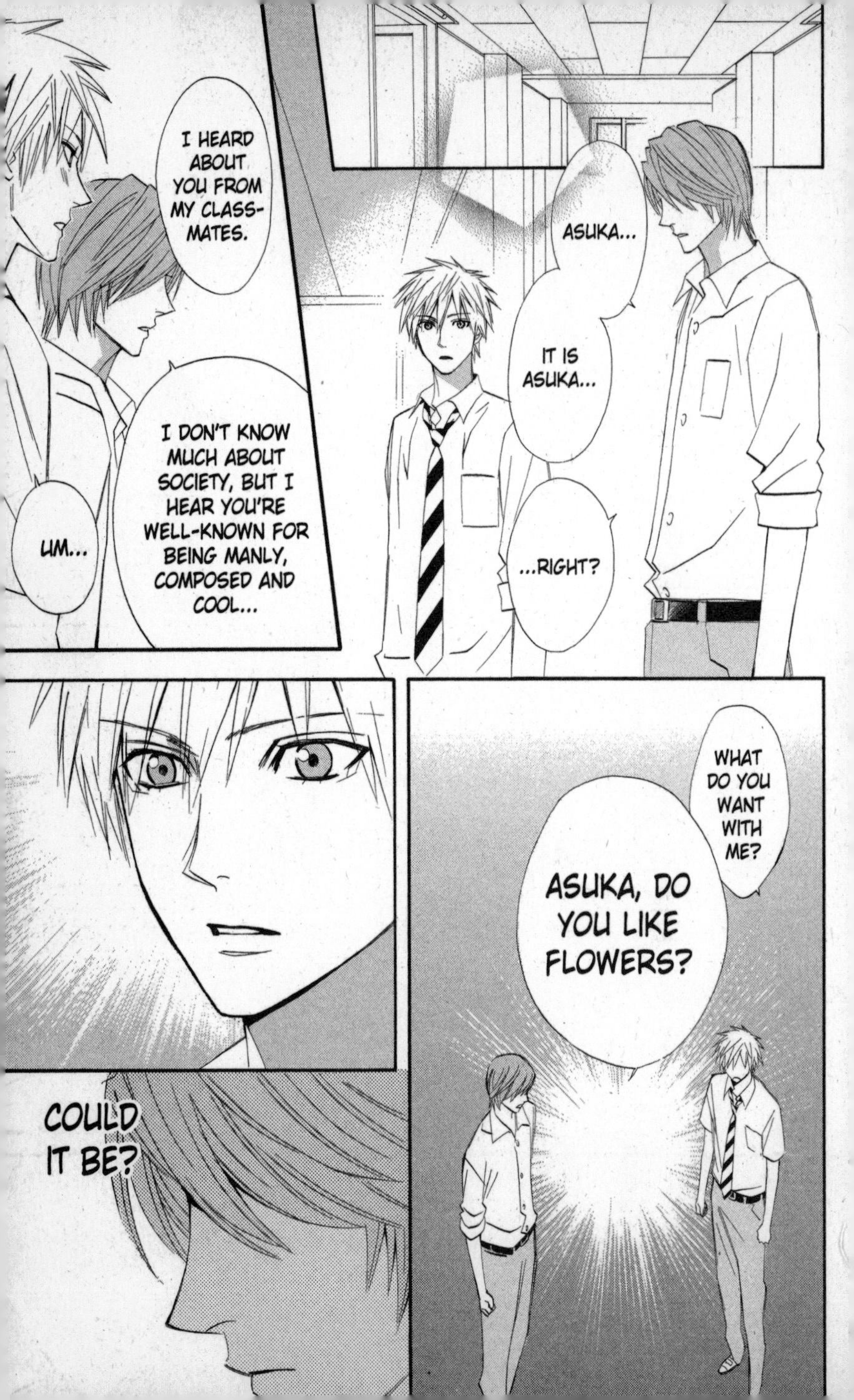
ASUKA...
IT IS ASUKA...
...RIGHT?
I HEARD ABOUT YOU FROM MY CLASS-MATES.
I DON'T KNOW MUCH ABOUT SOCIETY, BUT I HEAR YOU'RE WELL-KNOWN FOR BEING MANLY, COMPOSED AND COOL...
UM...
WHAT DO YOU WANT WITH ME?
ASUKA, DO YOU LIKE FLOWERS?
COULD IT BE?

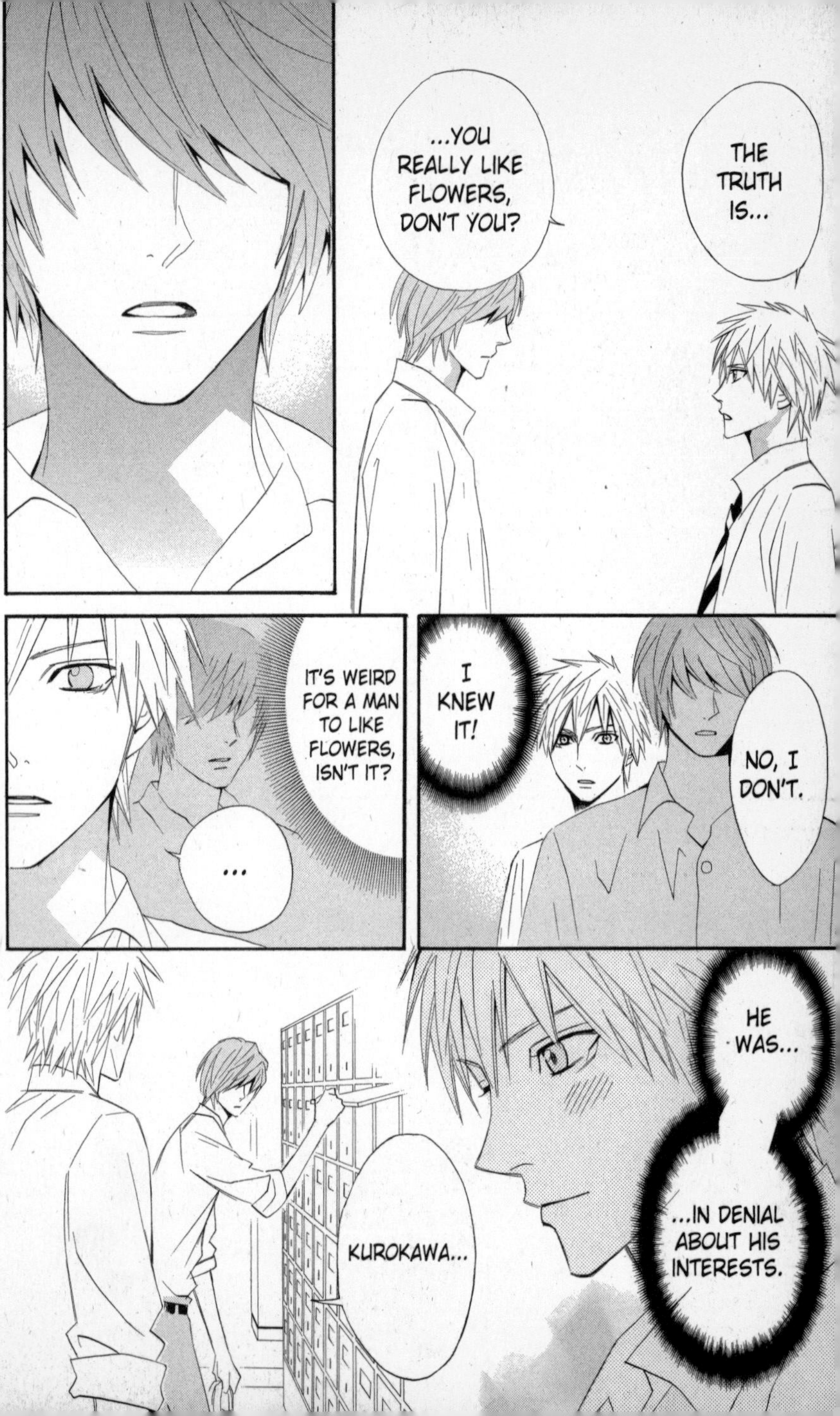
THE TRUTH IS...
...YOU REALLY LIKE FLOWERS, DON'T YOU?
NO, I DON'T.
I KNEW IT!
IT'S WEIRD FOR A MAN TO LIKE FLOWERS, ISN'T IT?
...
HE WAS...
...IN DENIAL ABOUT HIS INTERESTS.
KUROKAWA...

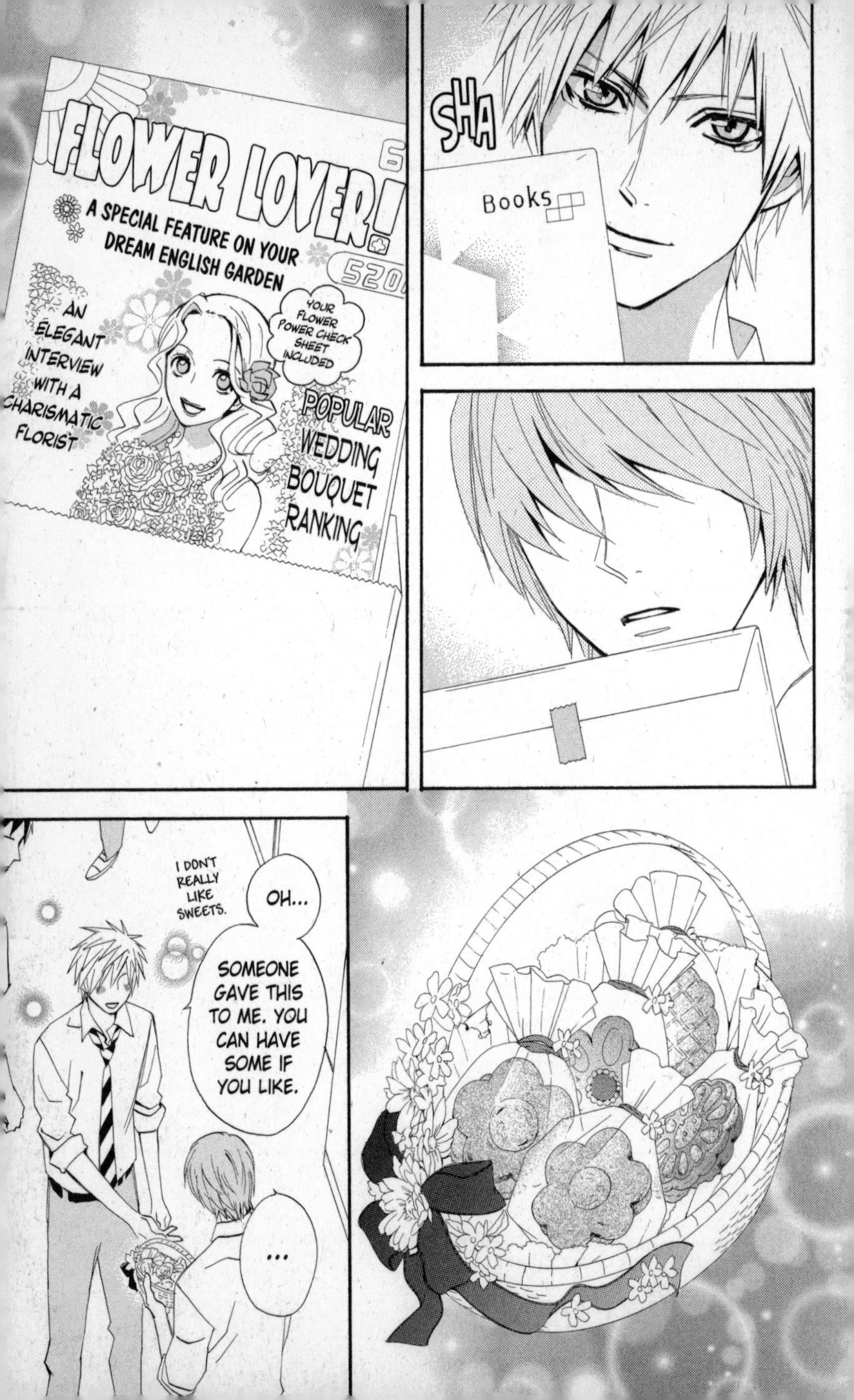
SHA
Books
FLOWER LOVER!
A SPECIAL FEATURE ON YOUR DREAM ENGLISH GARDEN
YOUR FLOWER POWER CHECK SHEET INCLUDED
AN ELEGANT INTERVIEW WITH A CHARISMATIC FLORIST
POPULAR WEDDING BOUQUET RANKING
OH...
I DON'T REALLY LIKE SWEETS.
SOMEONE GAVE THIS TO ME. YOU CAN HAVE SOME IF YOU LIKE.
...

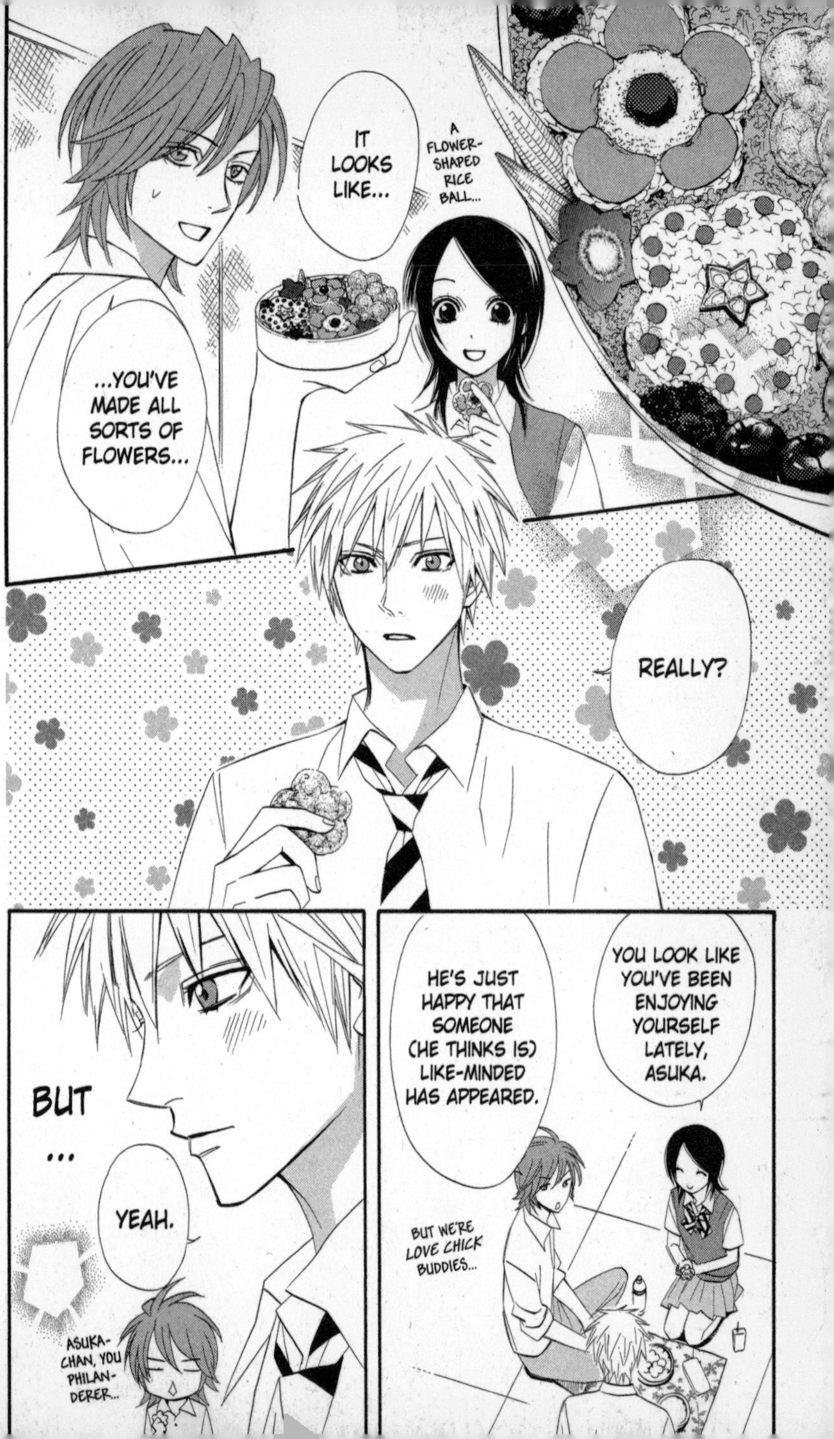
A FLOWER-SHAPED RICE BALL...
IT LOOKS LIKE...
...YOU'VE MADE ALL SORTS OF FLOWERS...
REALLY?
YOU LOOK LIKE YOU'VE BEEN ENJOYING YOURSELF LATELY, ASUKA.
HE'S JUST HAPPY THAT SOMEONE (HE THINKS IS) LIKE-MINDED HAS APPEARED.
BUT WE'RE LOVE CHICK BUDDIES...
BUT...
YEAH.
ASUKA-CHAN, YOU PHILANDERER...

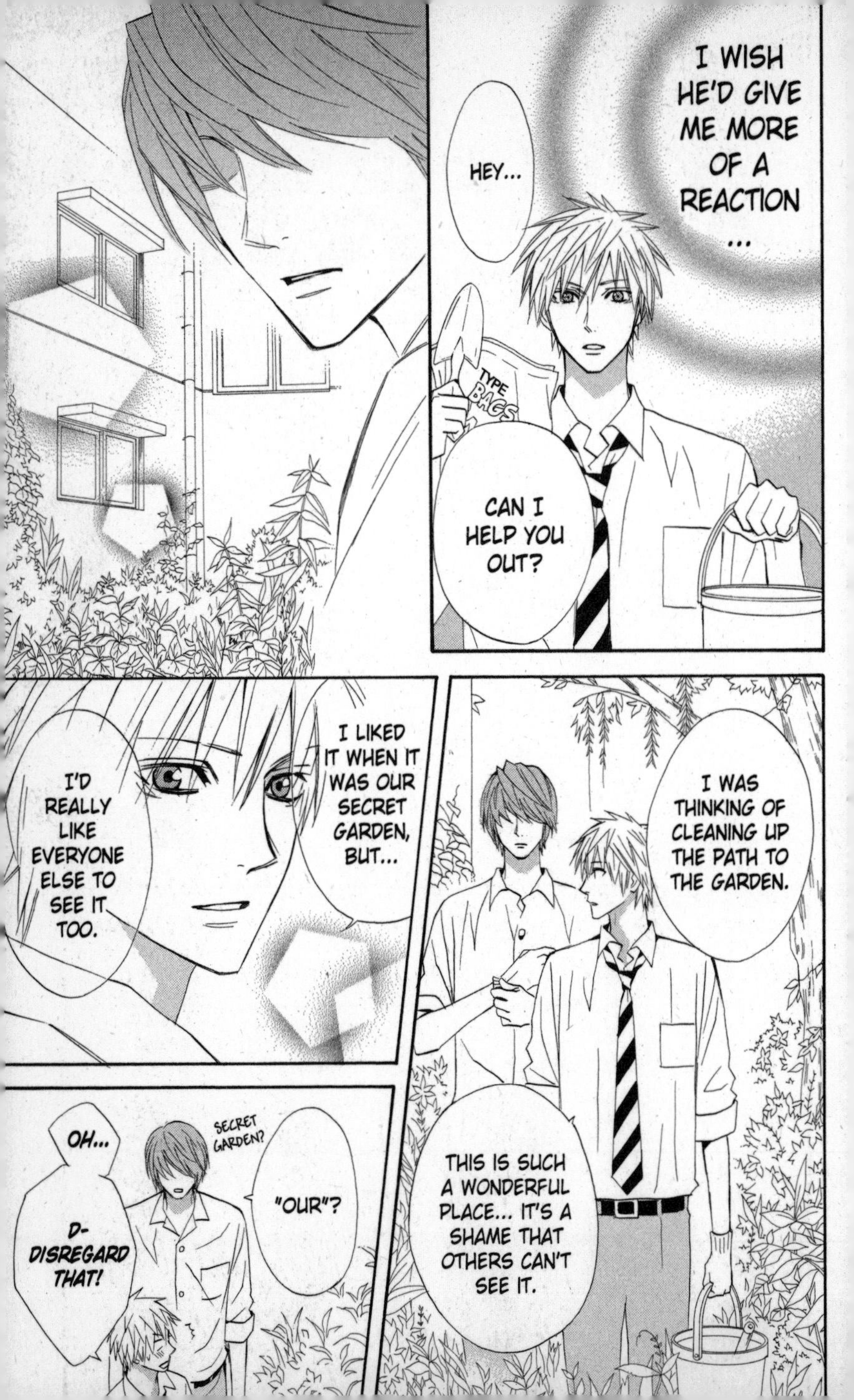
I WISH HE'D GIVE ME MORE OF A REACTION ...
HEY...
TYPE BAGS
CAN I HELP YOU OUT?
I WAS THINKING OF CLEANING UP THE PATH TO THE GARDEN.
THIS IS SUCH A WONDERFUL PLACE... IT'S A SHAME THAT OTHERS CAN'T SEE IT.
I LIKED IT WHEN IT WAS OUR SECRET GARDEN, BUT...
I'D REALLY LIKE EVERYONE ELSE TO SEE IT TOO.
SECRET GARDEN?
"OUR"?
OH...
D-DISREGARD THAT!

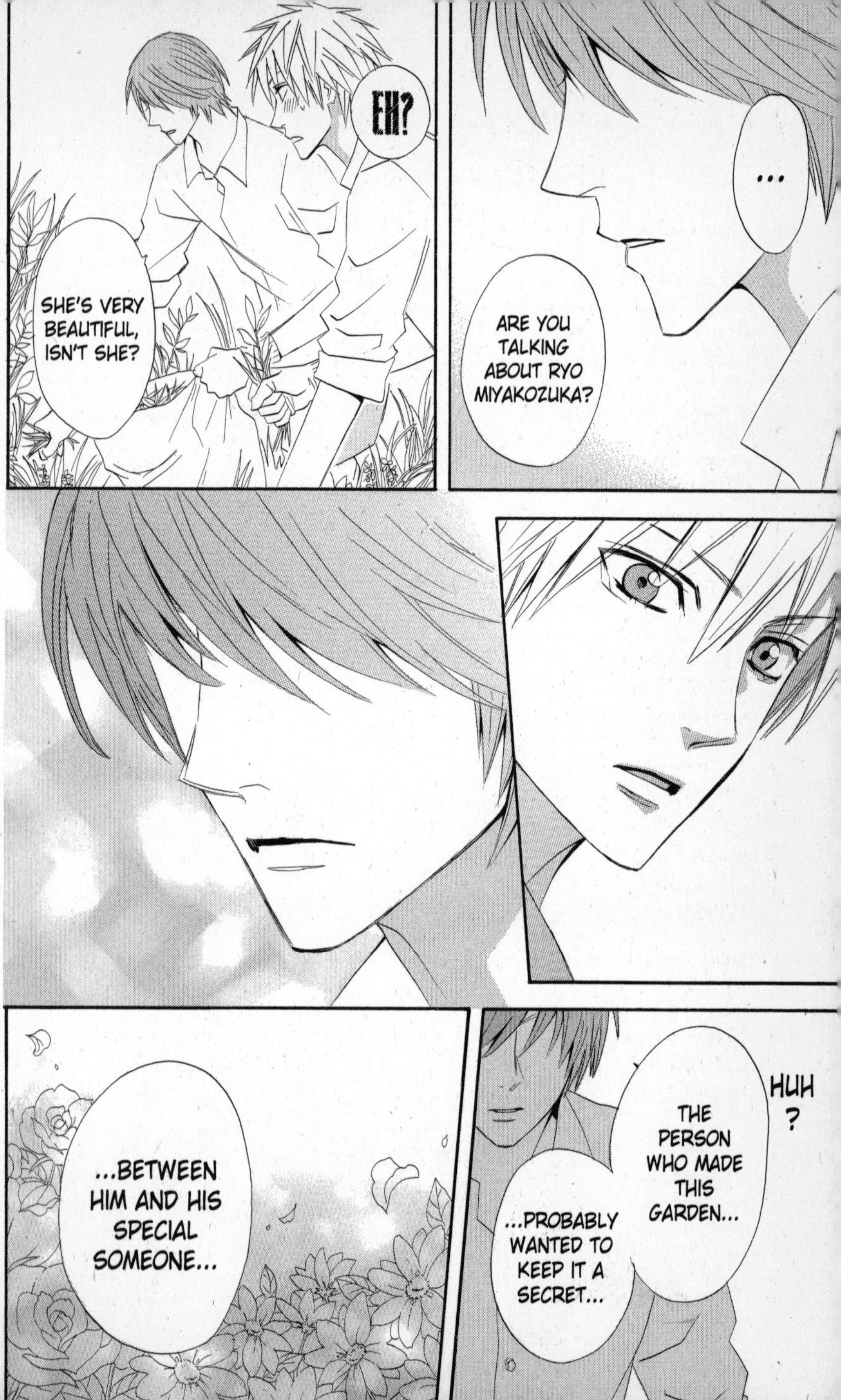
...
ARE YOU TALKING ABOUT RYO MIYAKOZUKA?
EH?
SHE'S VERY BEAUTIFUL, ISN'T SHE?
HUH?
THE PERSON WHO MADE THIS GARDEN...
...PROBABLY WANTED TO KEEP IT A SECRET...
...BETWEEN HIM AND HIS SPECIAL SOMEONE...

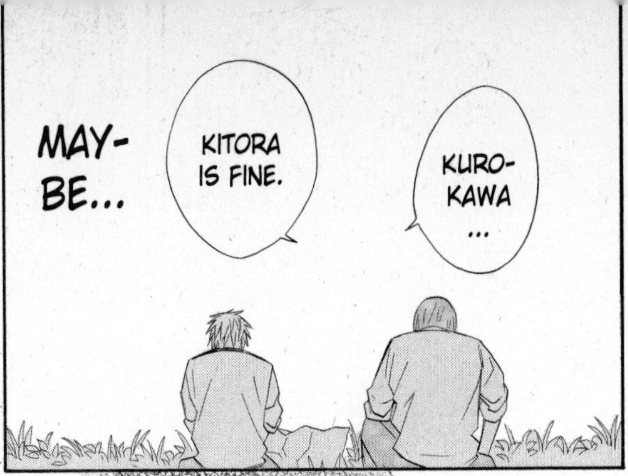
KURO-KAWA ...
KITORA IS FINE.
MAY-BE...

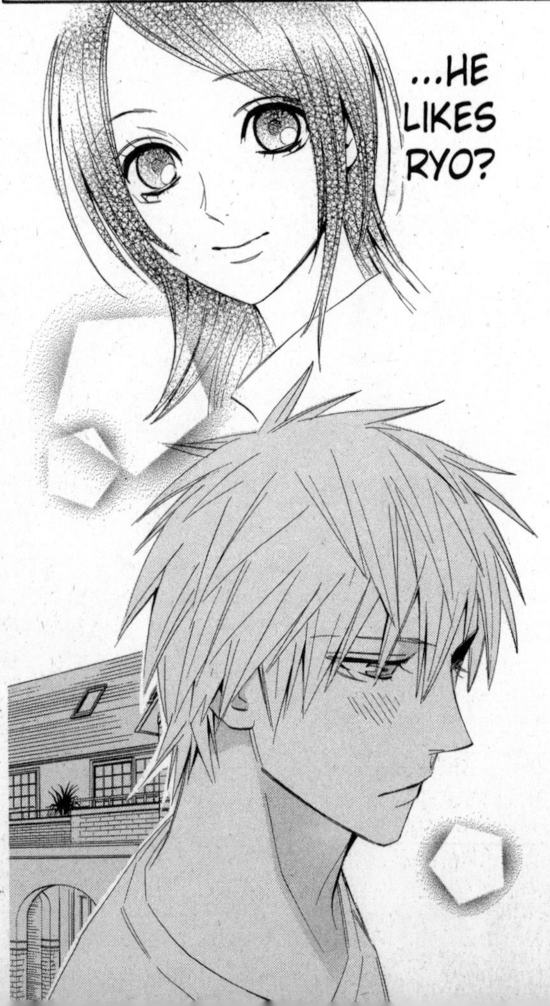
...HE LIKES RYO?

A new character.

I wanted to draw a character whose bangs cover his face... I come from a generation that immediately thinks of Yo Nihiruda when you mention a character who has bangs covering his eyes. I'm glad I don't have to draw his eyes, but he's too tall. It's very difficult to place him in the same frame as the other characters... I'd like to explore his character more in the future.

The florist in the series *Flowers for the Heart!!* that I wrote before was very fictitious, and I ended up doing it again... I've worked at a flower shop before, but I can't arrange flowers at all.

I love flowers.

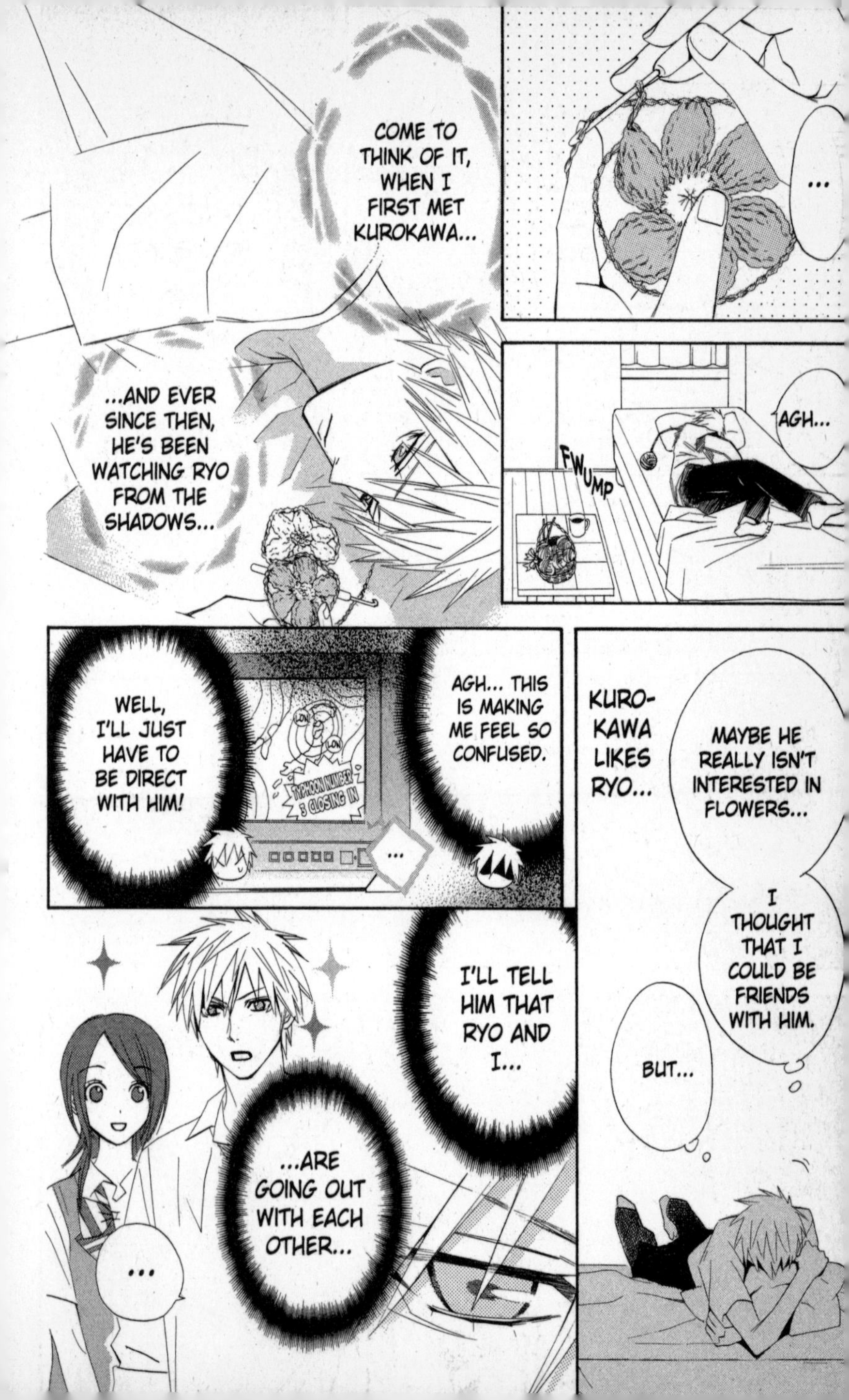
...
FWUMP
AGH...
COME TO THINK OF IT, WHEN I FIRST MET KUROKAWA...
...AND EVER SINCE THEN, HE'S BEEN WATCHING RYO FROM THE SHADOWS...
KURO-KAWA LIKES RYO...
MAYBE HE REALLY ISN'T INTERESTED IN FLOWERS...
I THOUGHT THAT I COULD BE FRIENDS WITH HIM.
BUT...
AGH... THIS IS MAKING ME FEEL SO CONFUSED.
WELL, I'LL JUST HAVE TO BE DIRECT WITH HIM!
TYPHOON NUMBER 3 CLOSING IN
...
I'LL TELL HIM THAT RYO AND I...
...ARE GOING OUT WITH EACH OTHER...
...

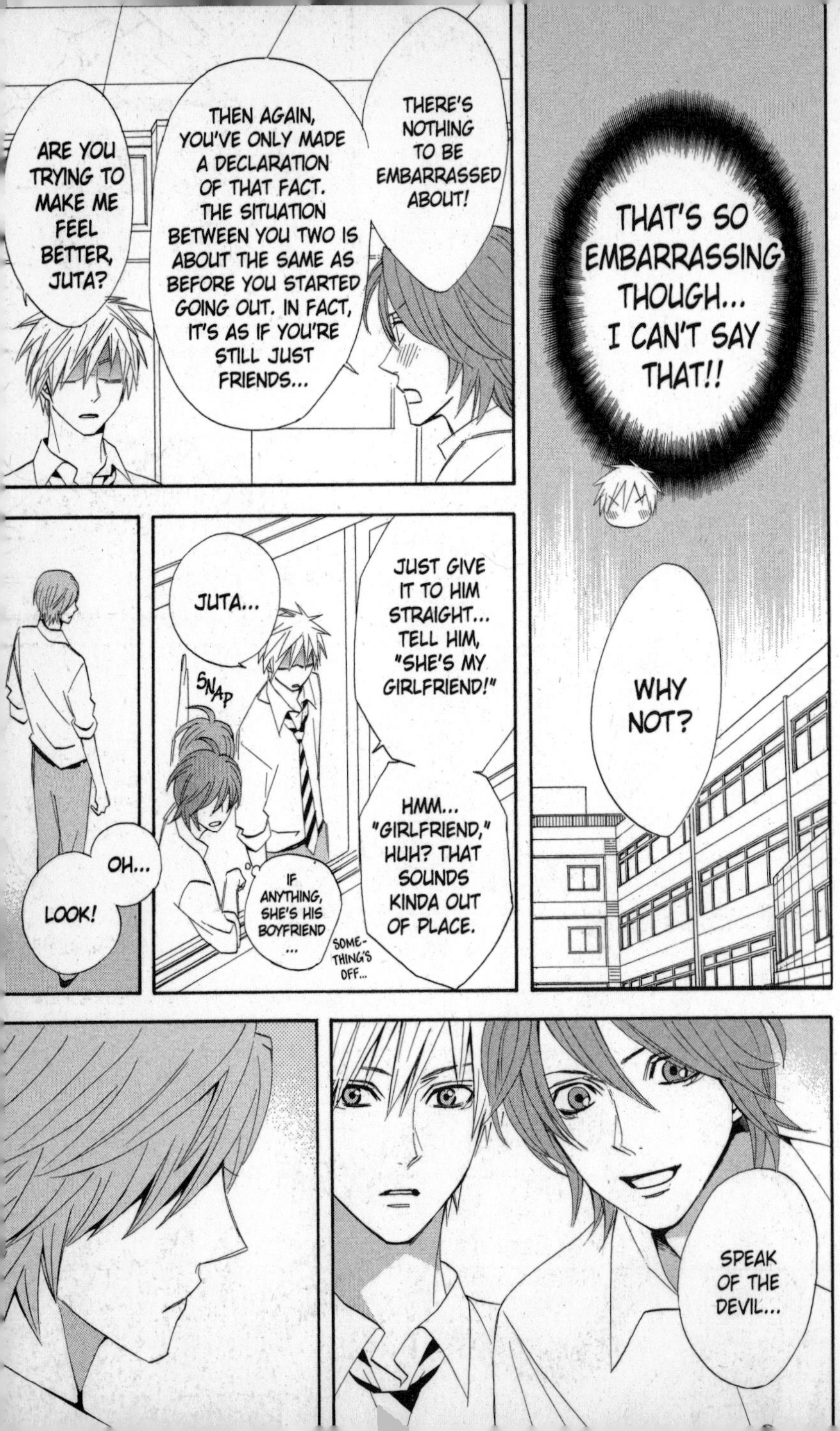
THERE'S NOTHING TO BE EMBARRASSED ABOUT!
THEN AGAIN, YOU'VE ONLY MADE A DECLARATION OF THAT FACT. THE SITUATION BETWEEN YOU TWO IS ABOUT THE SAME AS BEFORE YOU STARTED GOING OUT. IN FACT, IT'S AS IF YOU'RE STILL JUST FRIENDS...
ARE YOU TRYING TO MAKE ME FEEL BETTER, JUTA?
THAT'S SO EMBARRASSING THOUGH... I CAN'T SAY THAT!!
WHY NOT?
JUST GIVE IT TO HIM STRAIGHT... TELL HIM, "SHE'S MY GIRLFRIEND!"
HMM... "GIRLFRIEND," HUH? THAT SOUNDS KINDA OUT OF PLACE.
JUTA...
SNAP
IF ANYTHING, SHE'S HIS BOYFRIEND...
SOME-THING'S OFF...
OH...
LOOK!
SPEAK OF THE DEVIL...

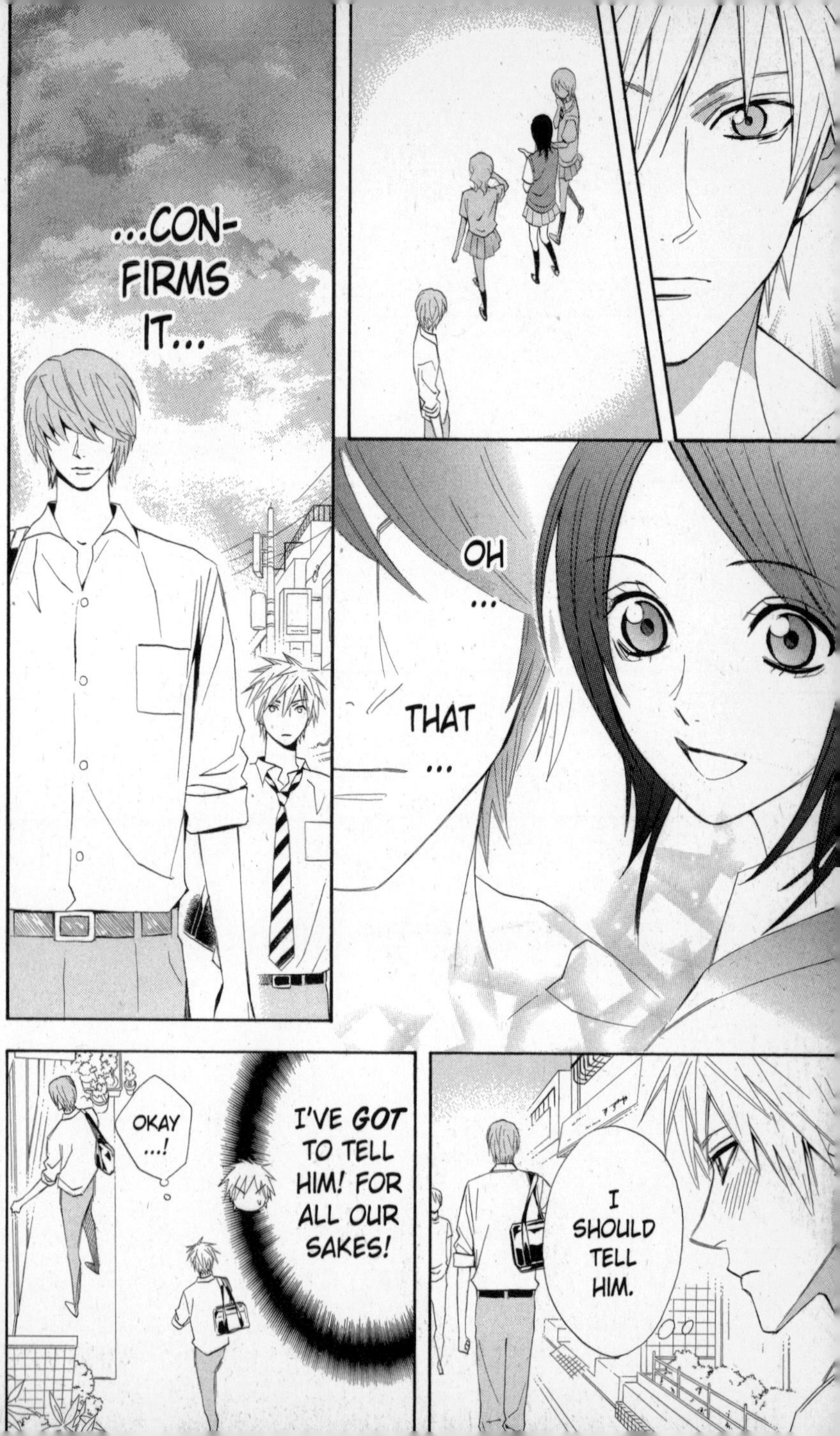
OH ... THAT ...
...CON-FIRMS IT...
I SHOULD TELL HIM.
I'VE GOT TO TELL HIM! FOR ALL OUR SAKES!
OKAY ...!

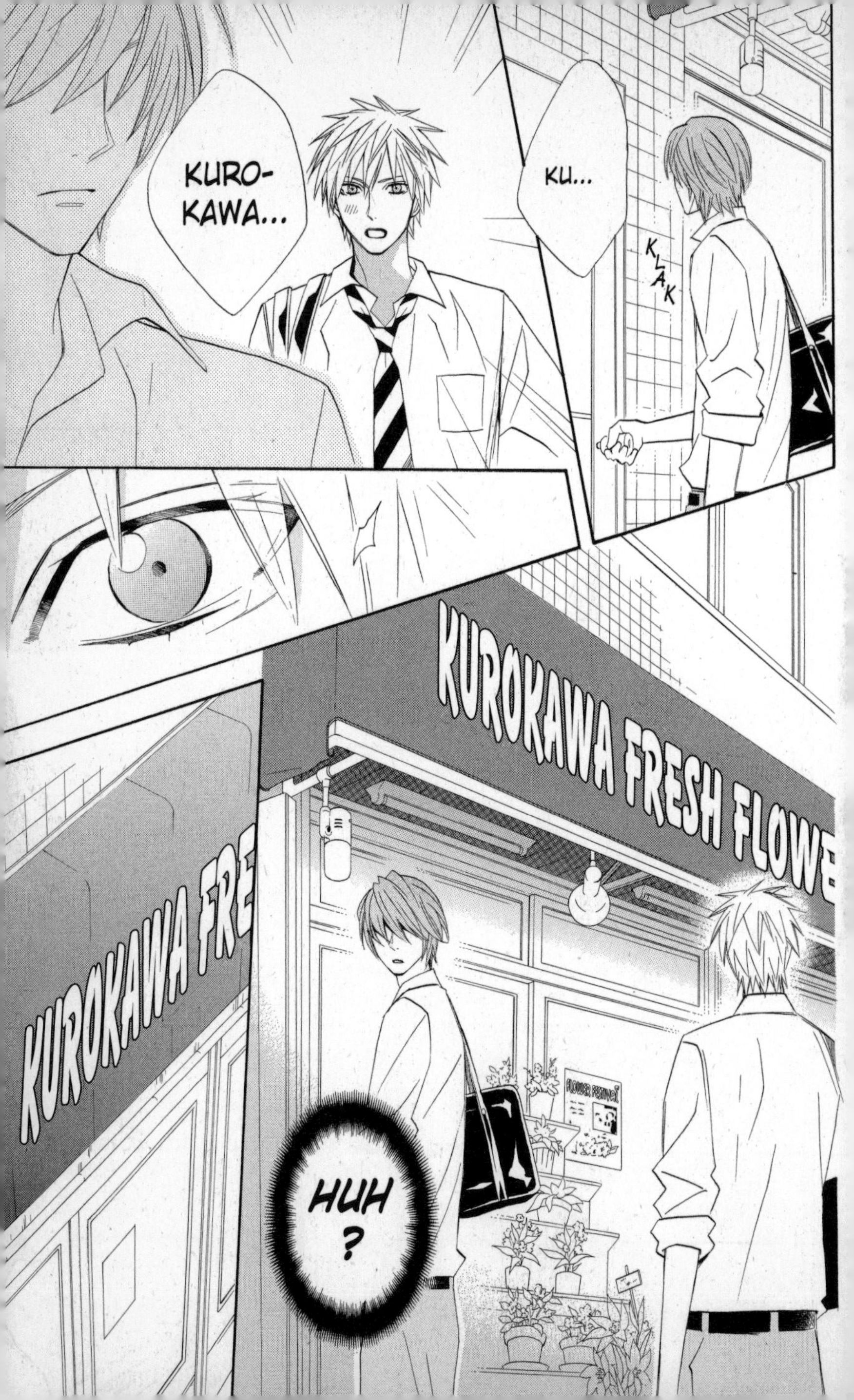
KU...
KLAK
KURO-KAWA...
KUROKAWA FRESH FLOWE
HUH?
KUROKAWA FRE

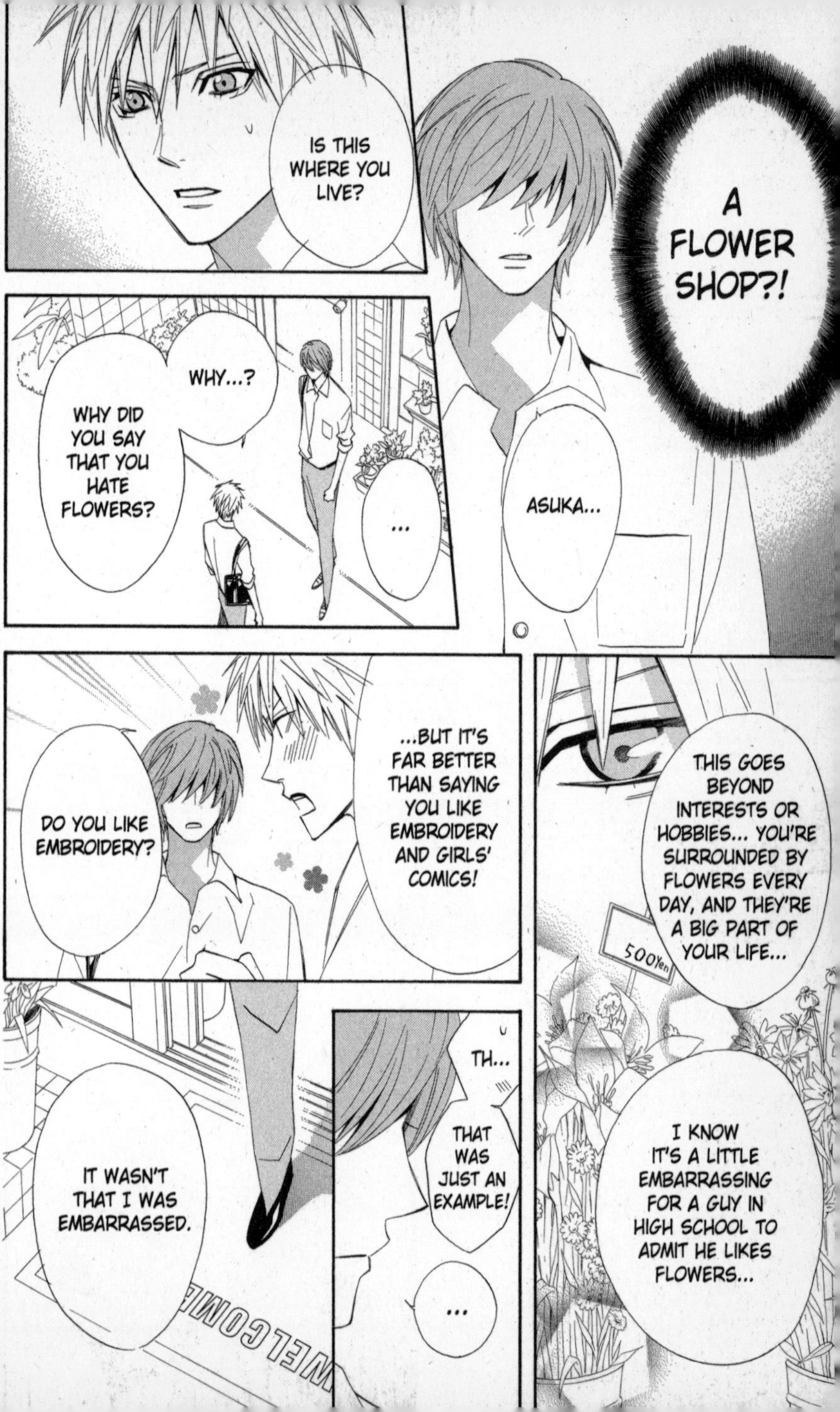
A FLOWER SHOP?!
ASUKA...
IS THIS WHERE YOU LIVE?
WHY...?
...
WHY DID YOU SAY THAT YOU HATE FLOWERS?
THIS GOES BEYOND INTERESTS OR HOBBIES... YOU'RE SURROUNDED BY FLOWERS EVERY DAY, AND THEY'RE A BIG PART OF YOUR LIFE...
500Yen
I KNOW IT'S A LITTLE EMBARRASSING FOR A GUY IN HIGH SCHOOL TO ADMIT HE LIKES FLOWERS...
...BUT IT'S FAR BETTER THAN SAYING YOU LIKE EMBROIDERY AND GIRLS' COMICS!
DO YOU LIKE EMBROIDERY?
TH...
THAT WAS JUST AN EXAMPLE!
...
IT WASN'T THAT I WAS EMBARRASSED.

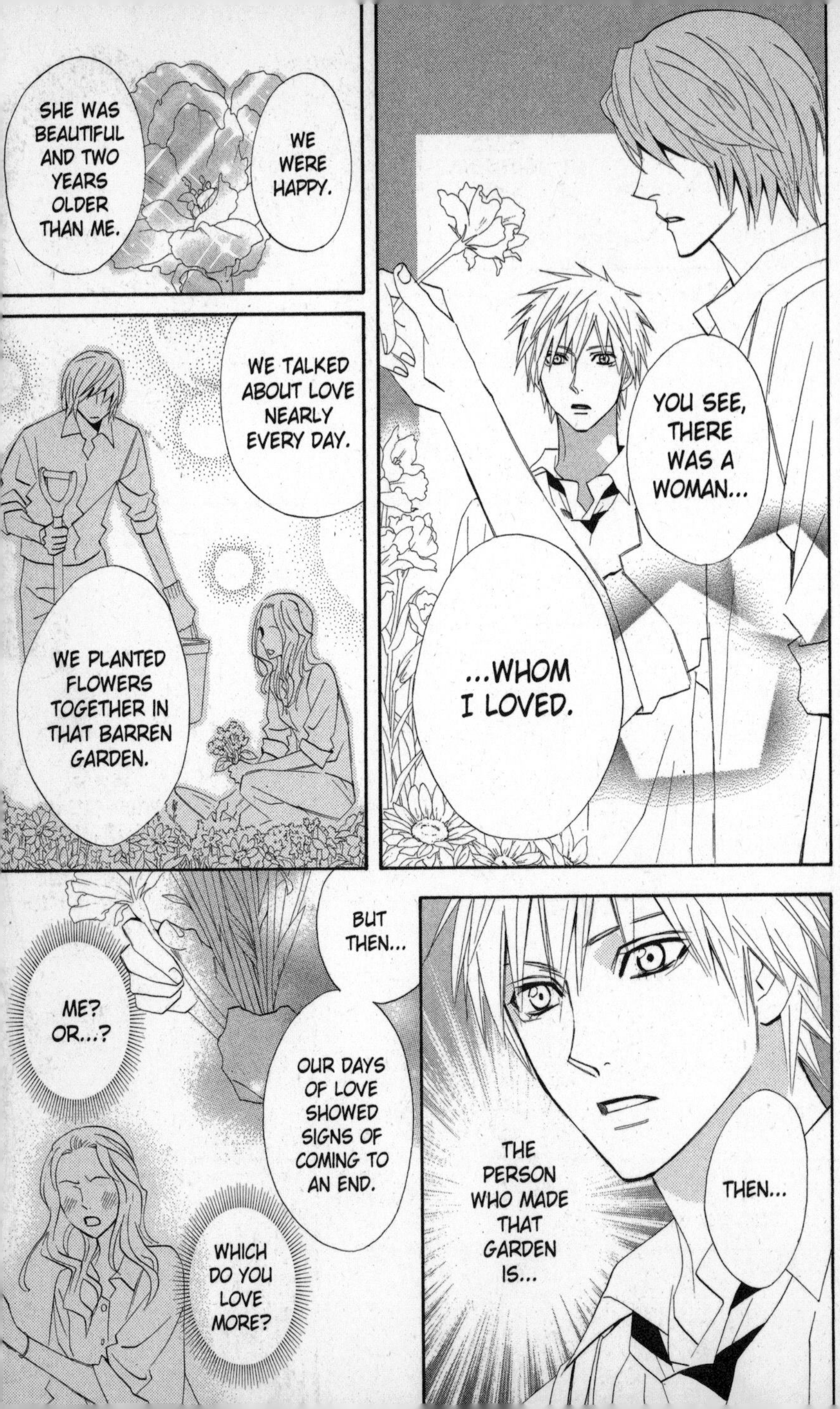
YOU SEE, THERE WAS A WOMAN...
...WHOM I LOVED.
WE WERE HAPPY.
SHE WAS BEAUTIFUL AND TWO YEARS OLDER THAN ME.
WE TALKED ABOUT LOVE NEARLY EVERY DAY.
WE PLANTED FLOWERS TOGETHER IN THAT BARREN GARDEN.
THEN...
THE PERSON WHO MADE THAT GARDEN IS...
BUT THEN...
OUR DAYS OF LOVE SHOWED SIGNS OF COMING TO AN END.
ME? OR...?
WHICH DO YOU LOVE MORE?

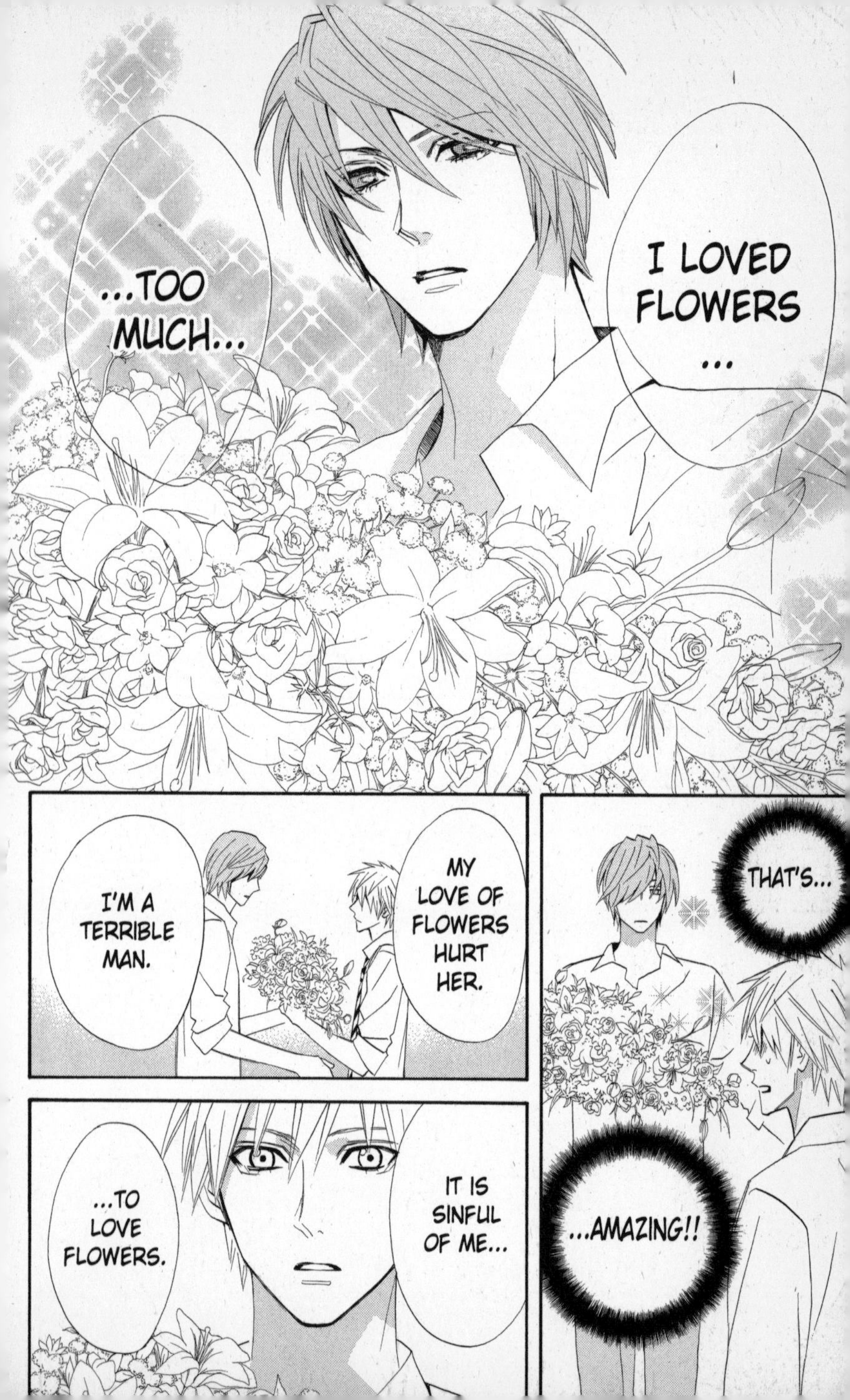
I LOVED FLOWERS ...
...TOO MUCH...
THAT'S...
...AMAZING!!
MY LOVE OF FLOWERS HURT HER.
I'M A TERRIBLE MAN.
IT IS SINFUL OF ME...
...TO LOVE FLOWERS.

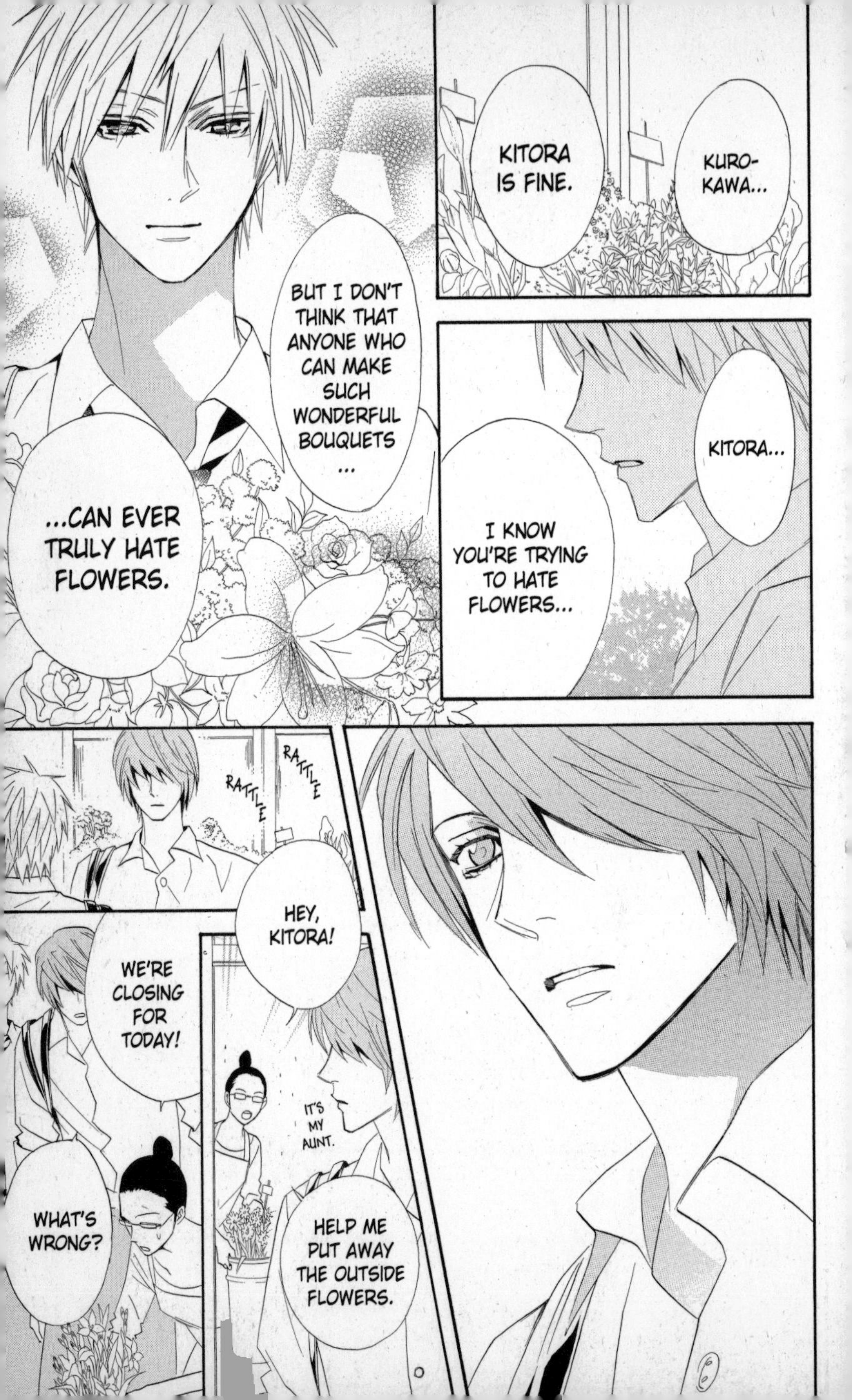
KURO-KAWA...
KITORA IS FINE.
KITORA...
I KNOW YOU'RE TRYING TO HATE FLOWERS...
BUT I DON'T THINK THAT ANYONE WHO CAN MAKE SUCH WONDERFUL BOUQUETS ...
...CAN EVER TRULY HATE FLOWERS.
RATTLE
RATTLE
HEY, KITORA!
WE'RE CLOSING FOR TODAY!
HELP ME PUT AWAY THE OUTSIDE FLOWERS.
WHAT'S WRONG?
IT'S MY AUNT.

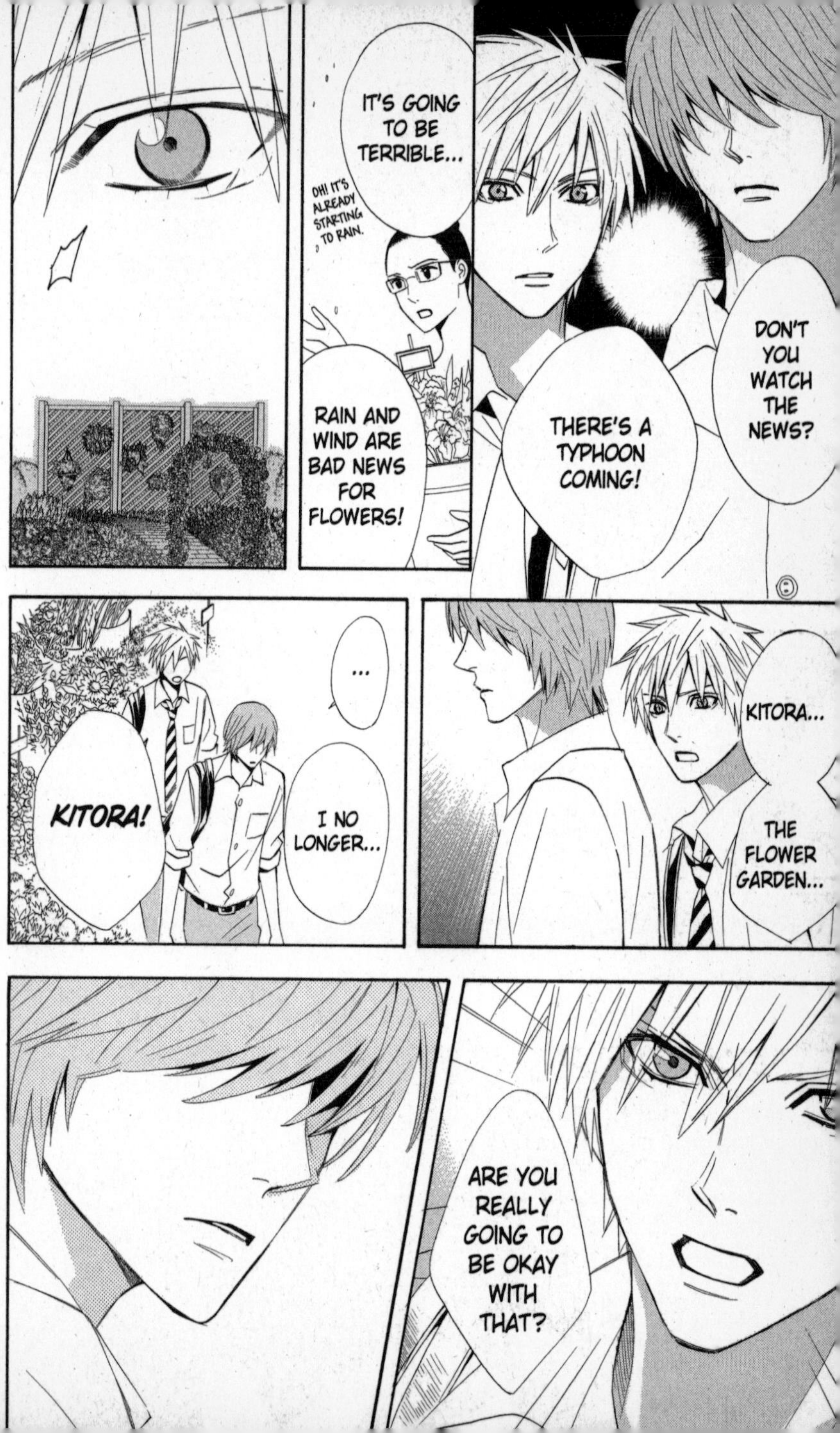
DON'T YOU WATCH THE NEWS?
THERE'S A TYPHOON COMING!
IT'S GOING TO BE TERRIBLE...
OH! IT'S ALREADY STARTING TO RAIN.
RAIN AND WIND ARE BAD NEWS FOR FLOWERS!
KITORA...
THE FLOWER GARDEN...
...
I NO LONGER...
KITORA!
ARE YOU REALLY GOING TO BE OKAY WITH THAT?

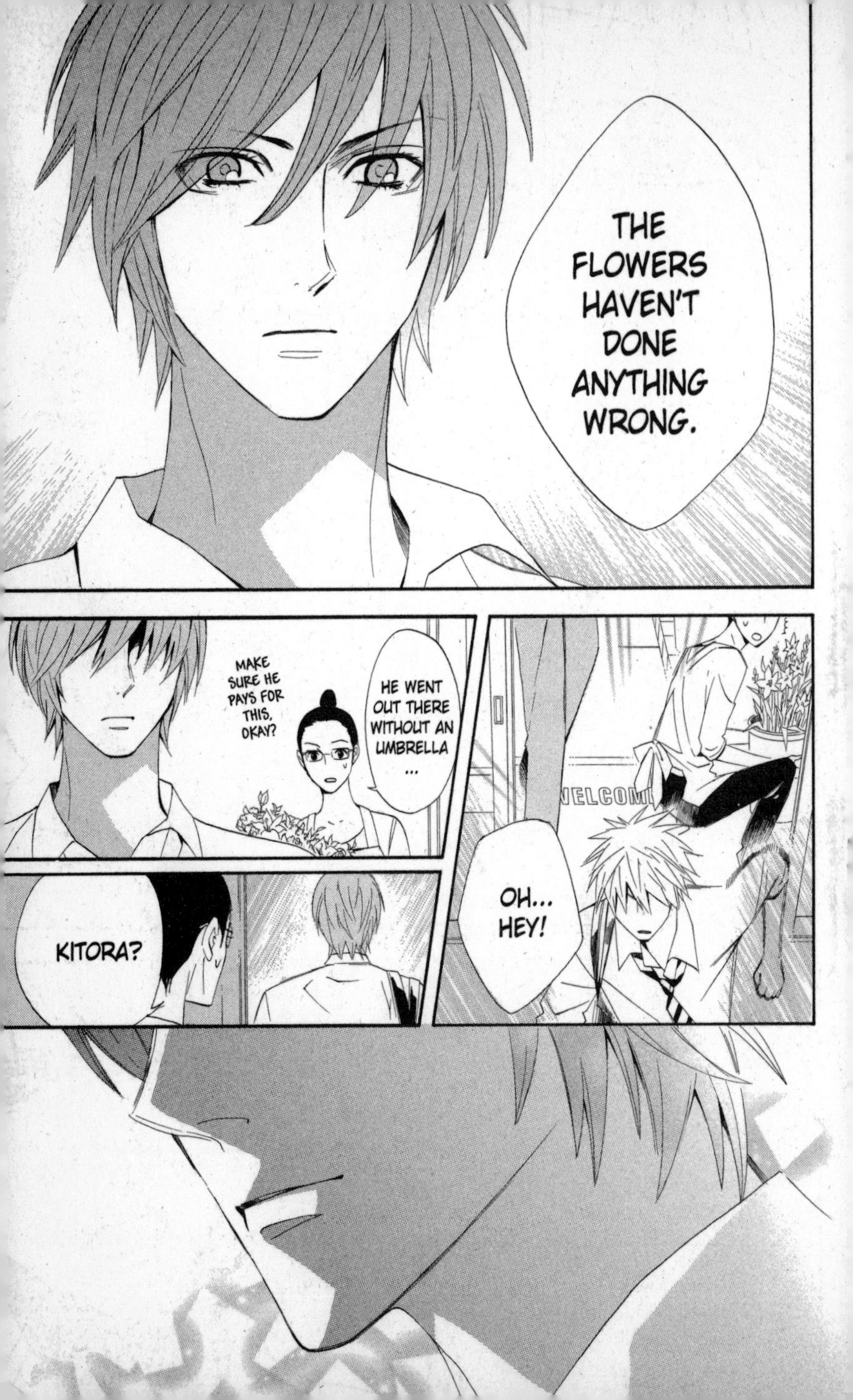
THE FLOWERS HAVEN'T DONE ANYTHING WRONG.
OH... HEY!
HE WENT OUT THERE WITHOUT AN UMBRELLA ...
MAKE SURE HE PAYS FOR THIS, OKAY?
KITORA?

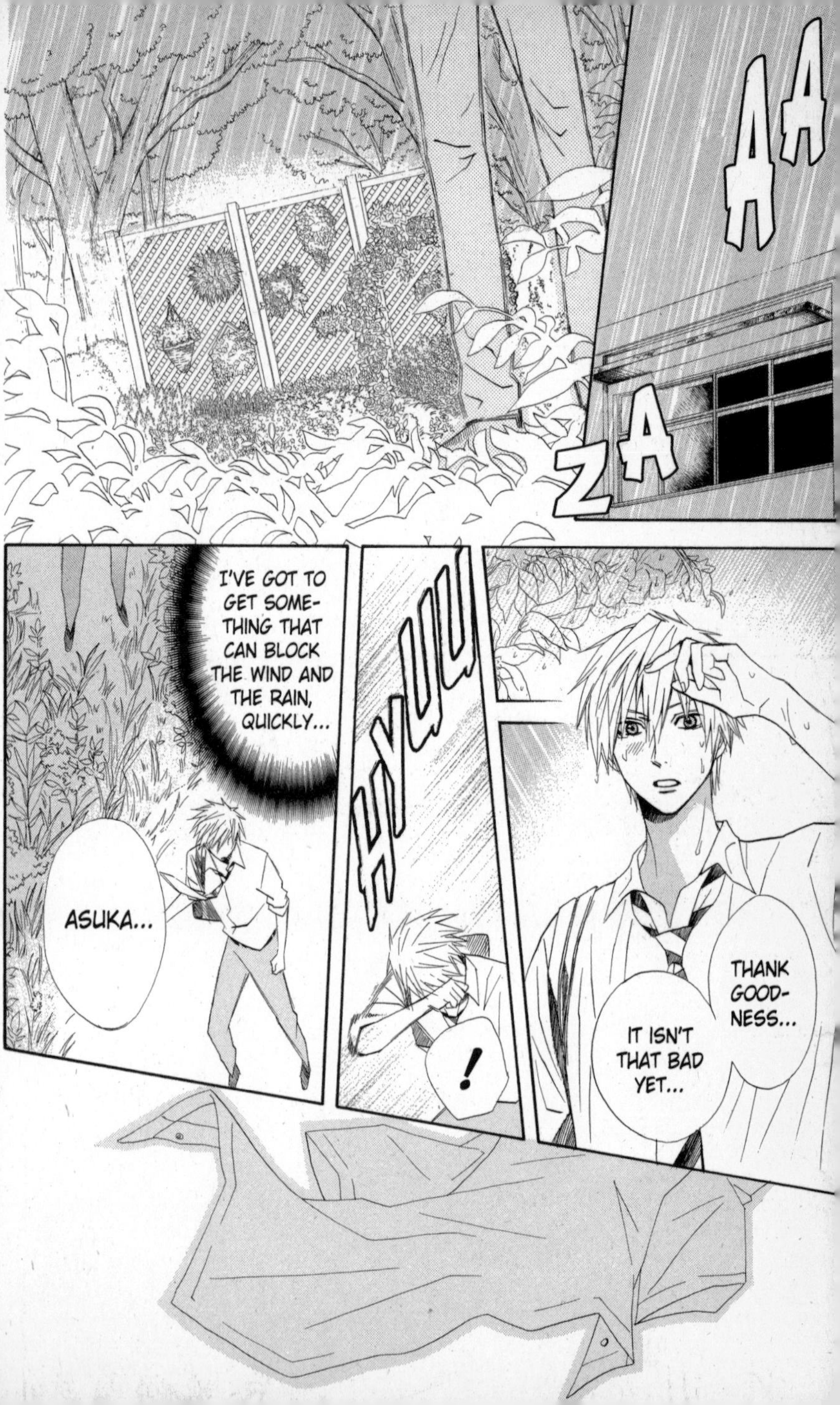
ZAAAA
THANK GOODNESS...
IT ISN'T THAT BAD YET...
HYUUU
!
I'VE GOT TO GET SOMETHING THAT CAN BLOCK THE WIND AND THE RAIN, QUICKLY...
ASUKA...

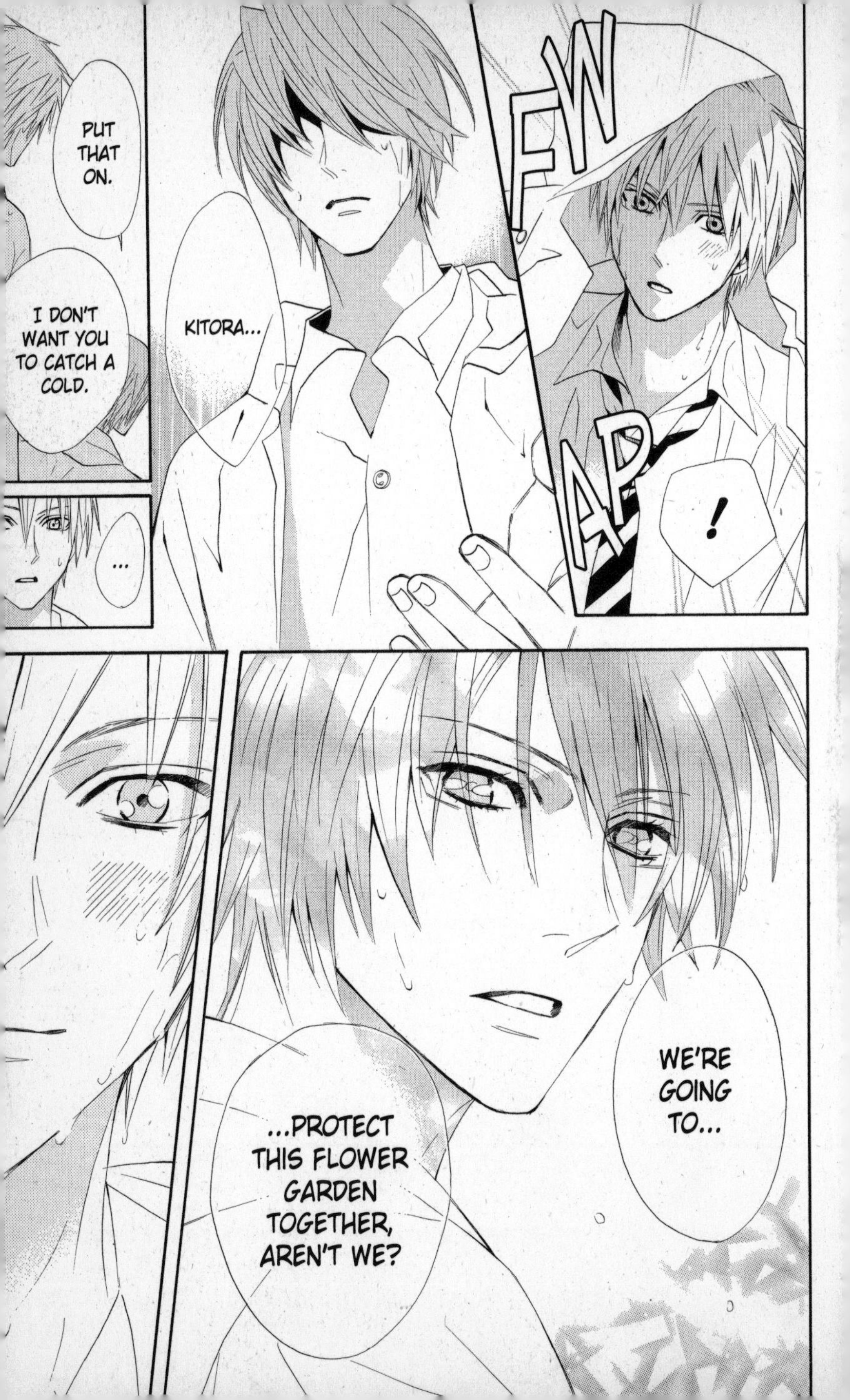
FWAP
!
KITORA...
PUT THAT ON.
I DON'T WANT YOU TO CATCH A COLD.
...
WE'RE GOING TO...
...PROTECT THIS FLOWER GARDEN TOGETHER, AREN'T WE?

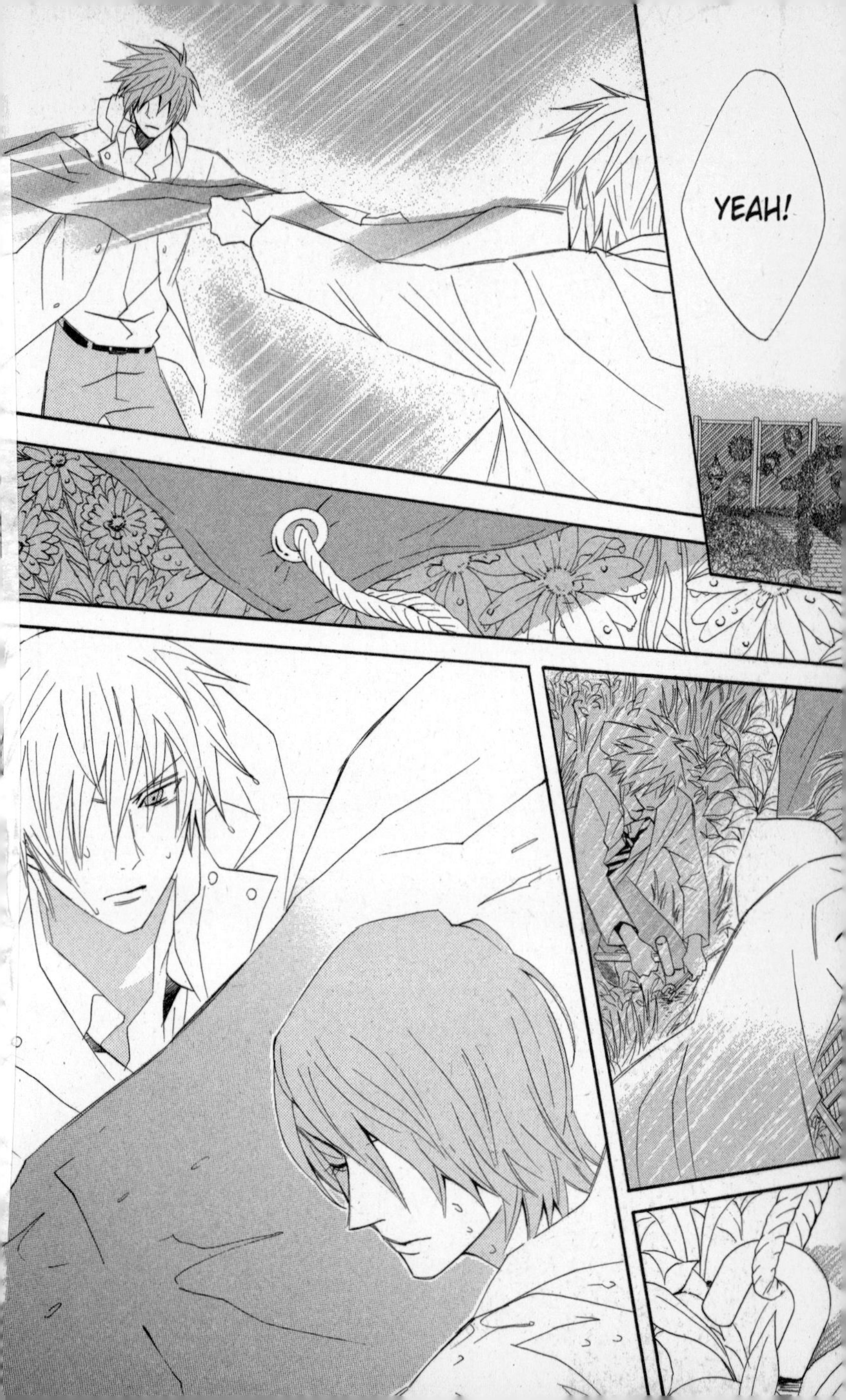
YEAH!

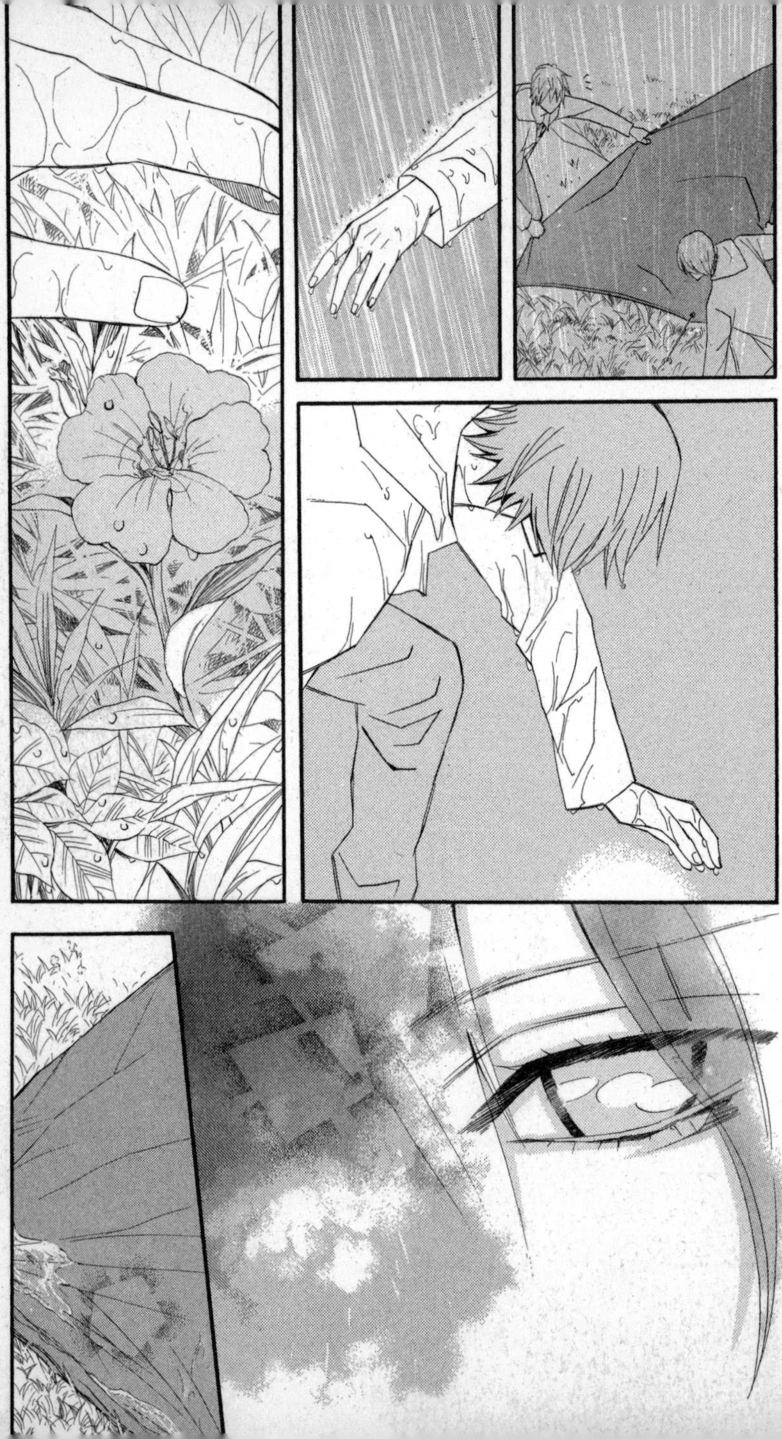

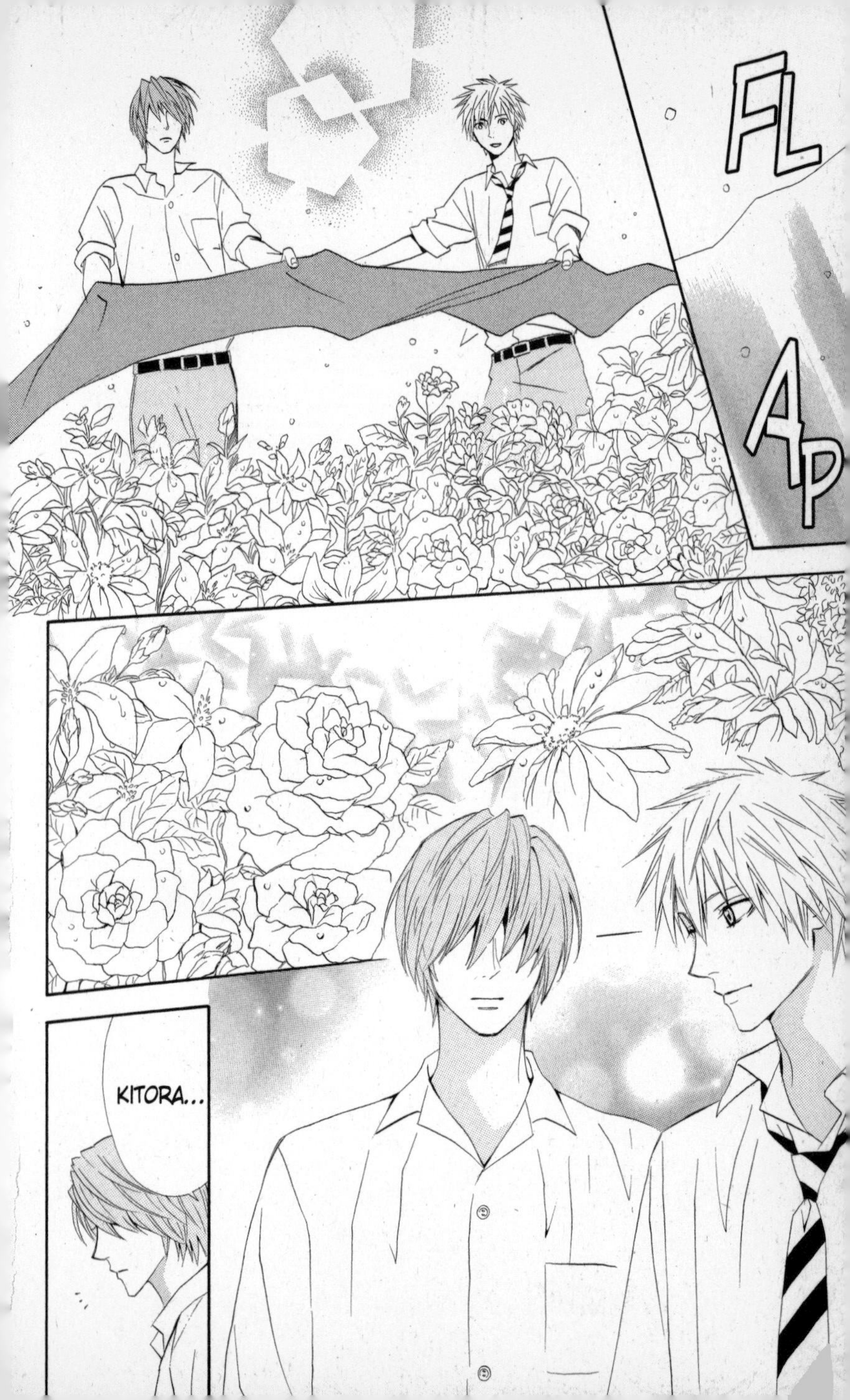
FLAP
KITORA...

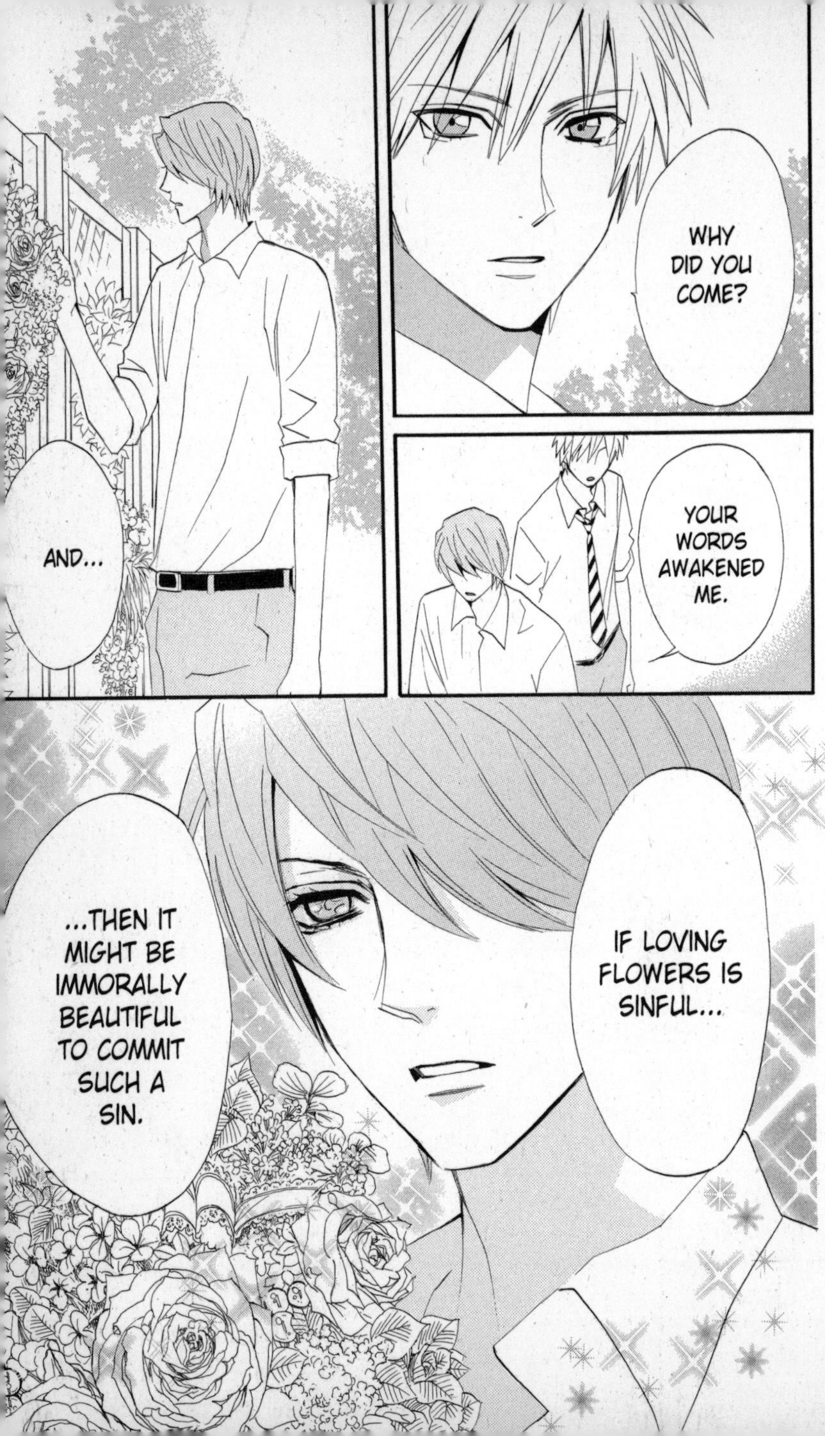
WHY DID YOU COME?
YOUR WORDS AWAKENED ME.
AND...
IF LOVING FLOWERS IS SINFUL...
...THEN IT MIGHT BE IMMORALLY BEAUTIFUL TO COMMIT SUCH A SIN.

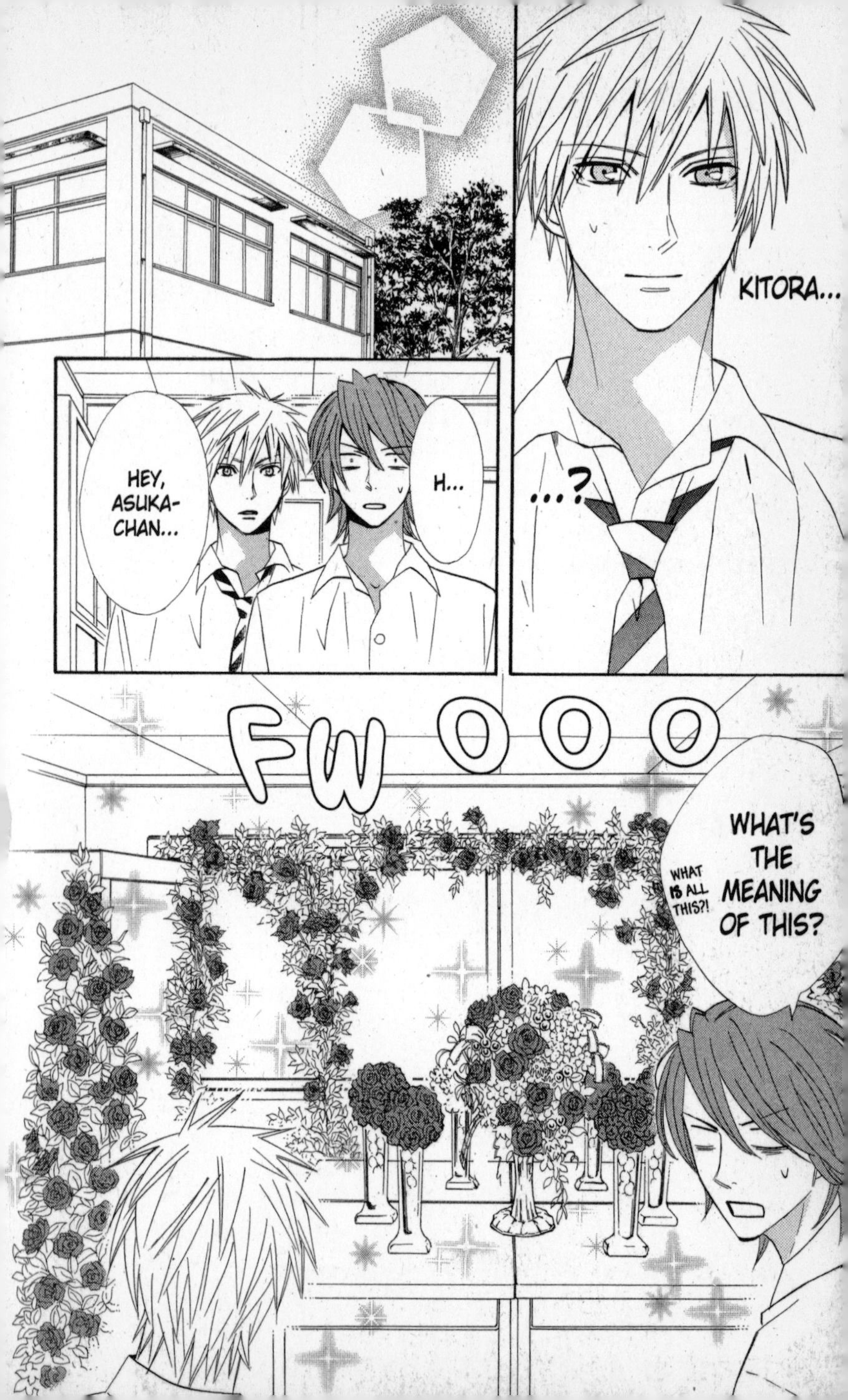
KITORA...
...?
H...
HEY, ASUKA-CHAN...
FWOOO
WHAT'S THE MEANING OF THIS?
WHAT IS ALL THIS?!

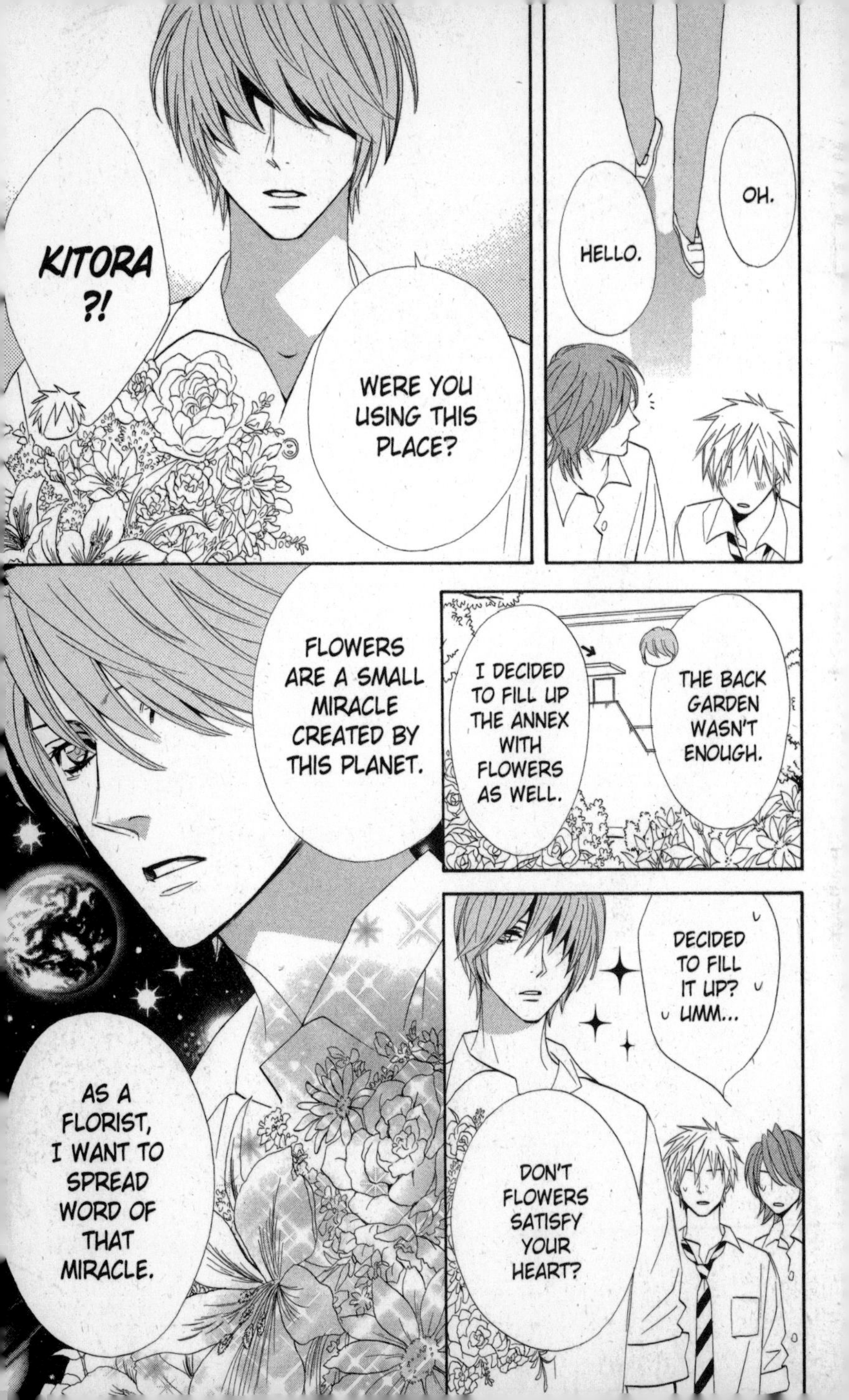
OH.
HELLO.
KITORA ?!
WERE YOU USING THIS PLACE?
THE BACK GARDEN WASN'T ENOUGH.
I DECIDED TO FILL UP THE ANNEX WITH FLOWERS AS WELL.
DECIDED TO FILL IT UP? UMM...
DON'T FLOWERS SATISFY YOUR HEART?
FLOWERS ARE A SMALL MIRACLE CREATED BY THIS PLANET.
AS A FLORIST, I WANT TO SPREAD WORD OF THAT MIRACLE.

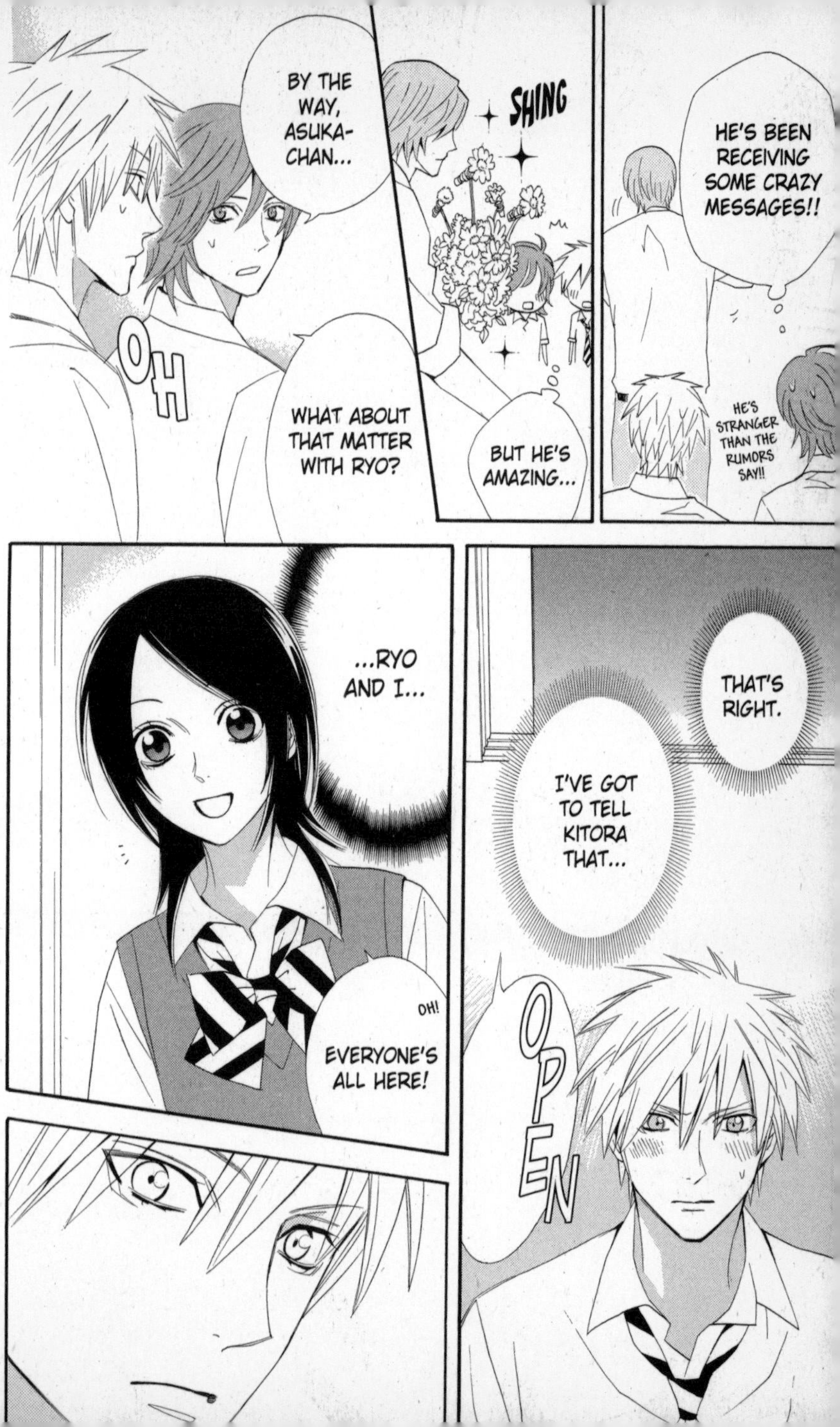
HE'S BEEN RECEIVING SOME CRAZY MESSAGES!!
HE'S STRANGER THAN THE RUMORS SAY!!
SHING
BUT HE'S AMAZING...
BY THE WAY, ASUKA-CHAN...
OH
WHAT ABOUT THAT MATTER WITH RYO?
THAT'S RIGHT.
I'VE GOT TO TELL KITORA THAT...
OPEN
...RYO AND I...
OH!
EVERYONE'S ALL HERE!

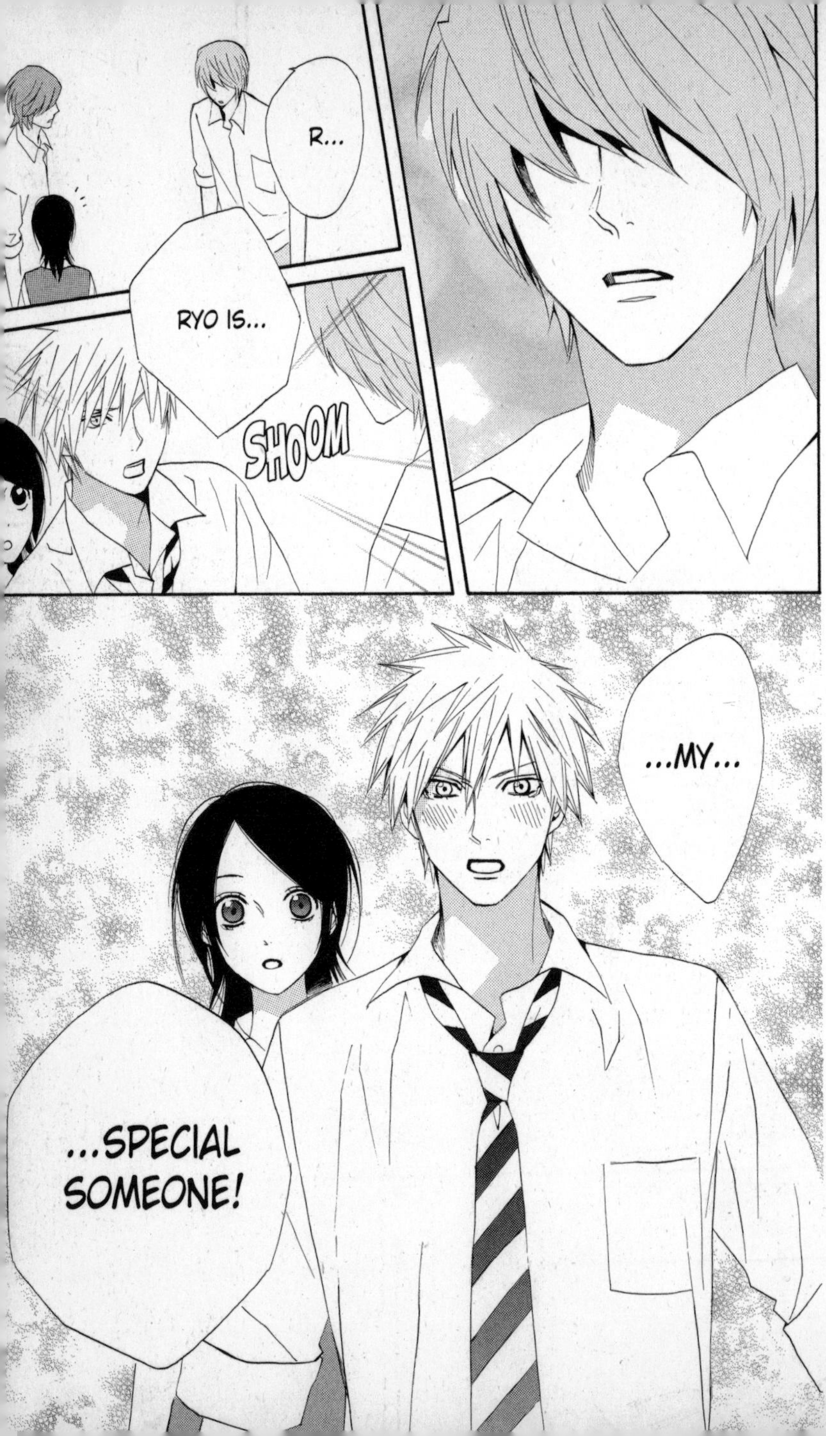
R...
RYO IS...
SHOOM
...MY...
...SPECIAL SOMEONE!

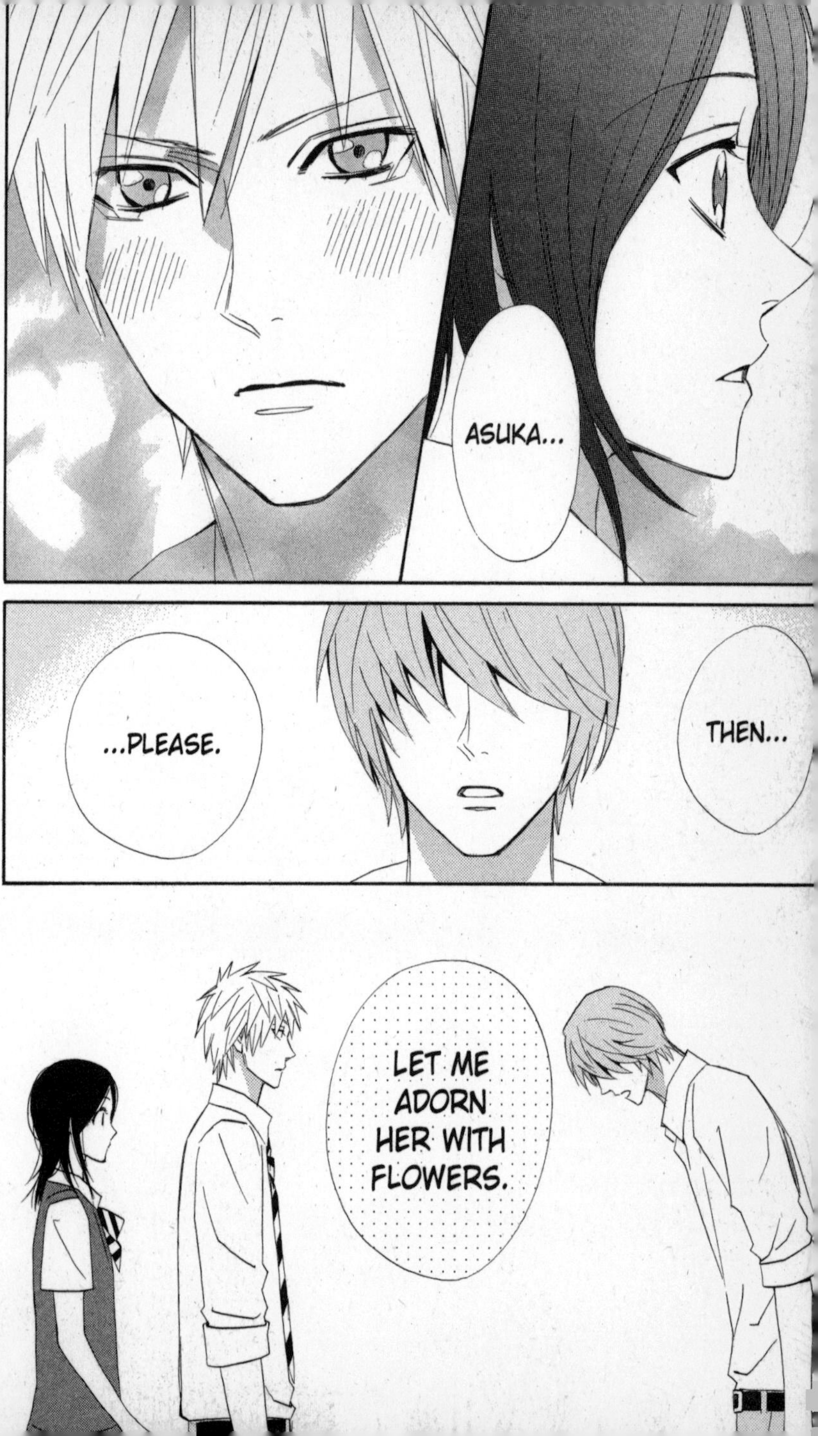
ASUKA...
THEN...
...PLEASE.
LET ME ADORN HER WITH FLOWERS.

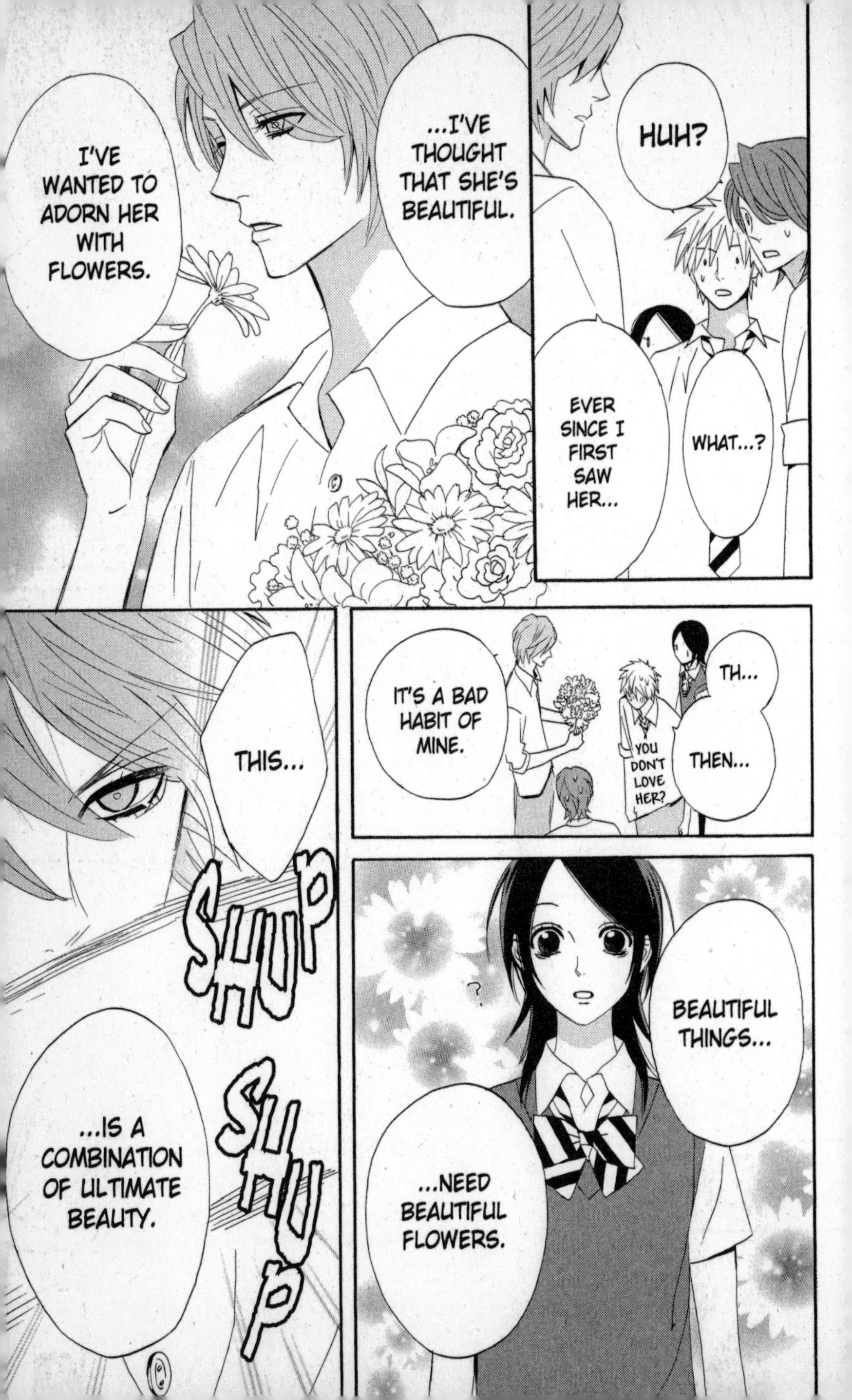
HUH?
WHAT...?
EVER SINCE I FIRST SAW HER...
...I'VE THOUGHT THAT SHE'S BEAUTIFUL.
I'VE WANTED TO ADORN HER WITH FLOWERS.
TH...
THEN...
YOU DON'T LOVE HER?
IT'S A BAD HABIT OF MINE.
BEAUTIFUL THINGS...
...NEED BEAUTIFUL FLOWERS.
THIS...
SHUP
SHUP
...IS A COMBINATION OF ULTIMATE BEAUTY.

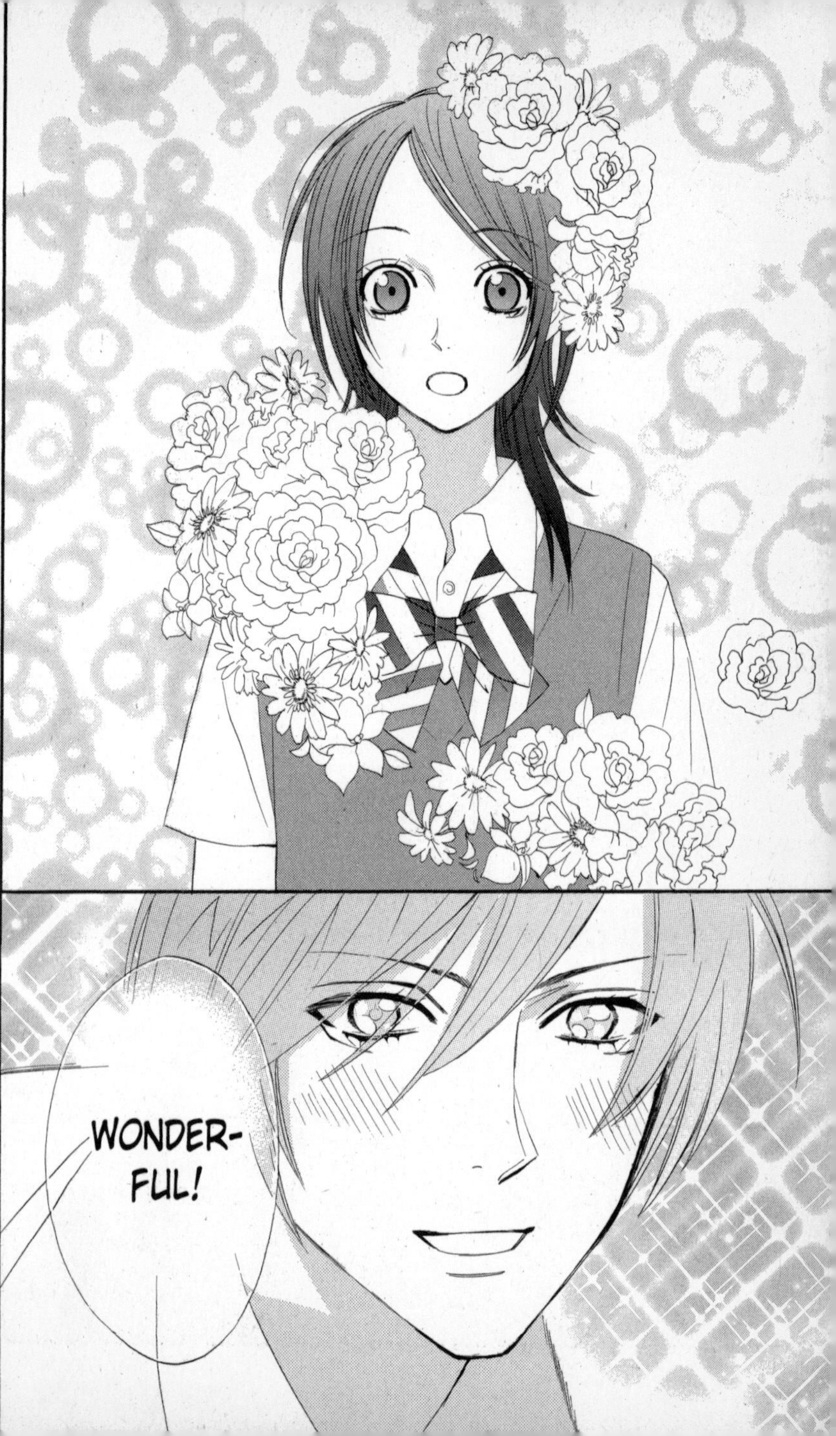
WONDER-
FUL!

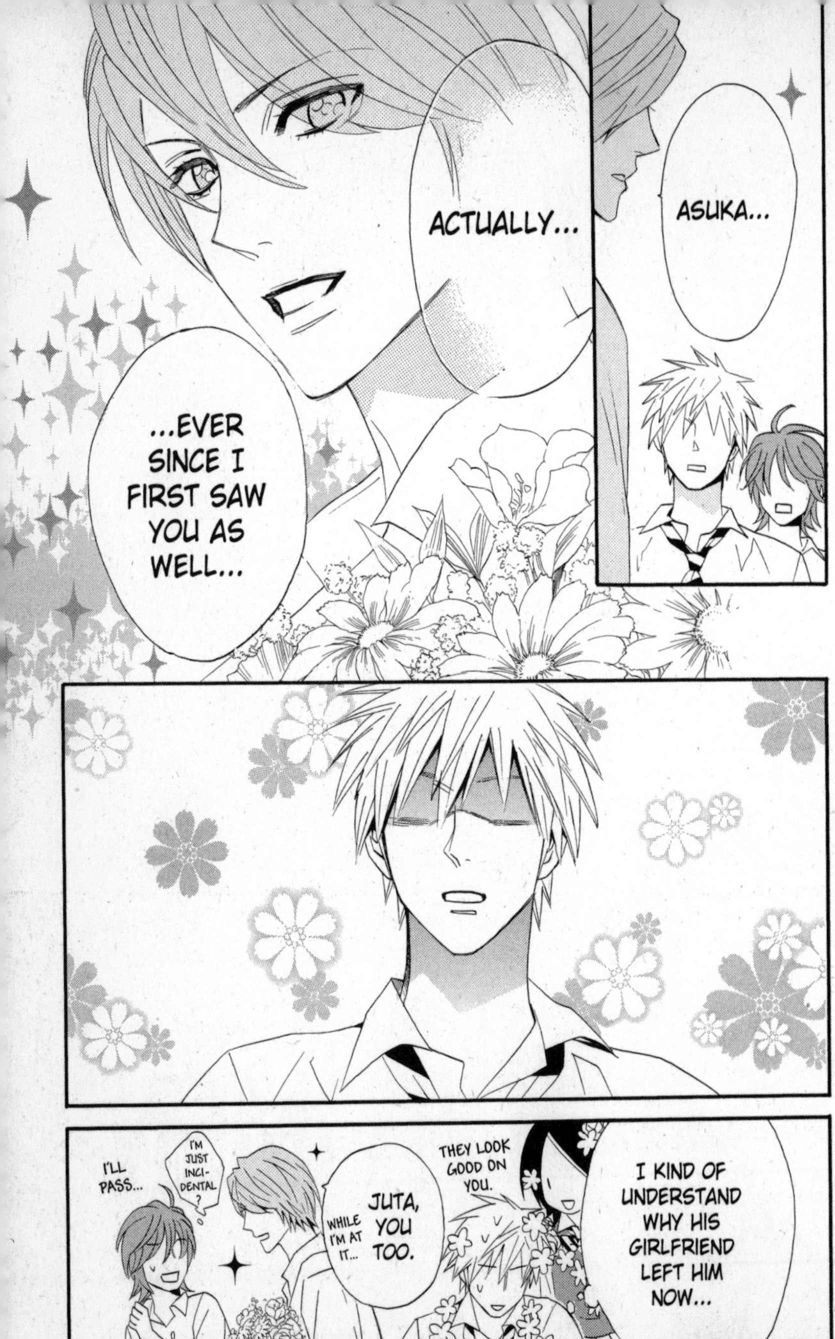
ASUKA...
ACTUALLY...
...EVER SINCE I FIRST SAW YOU AS WELL...
I KIND OF UNDERSTAND WHY HIS GIRLFRIEND LEFT HIM NOW...
THEY LOOK GOOD ON YOU.
JUTA, YOU TOO.
WHILE I'M AT IT...
I'M JUST INCI-DENTAL?
I'LL PASS...

OTOMEN

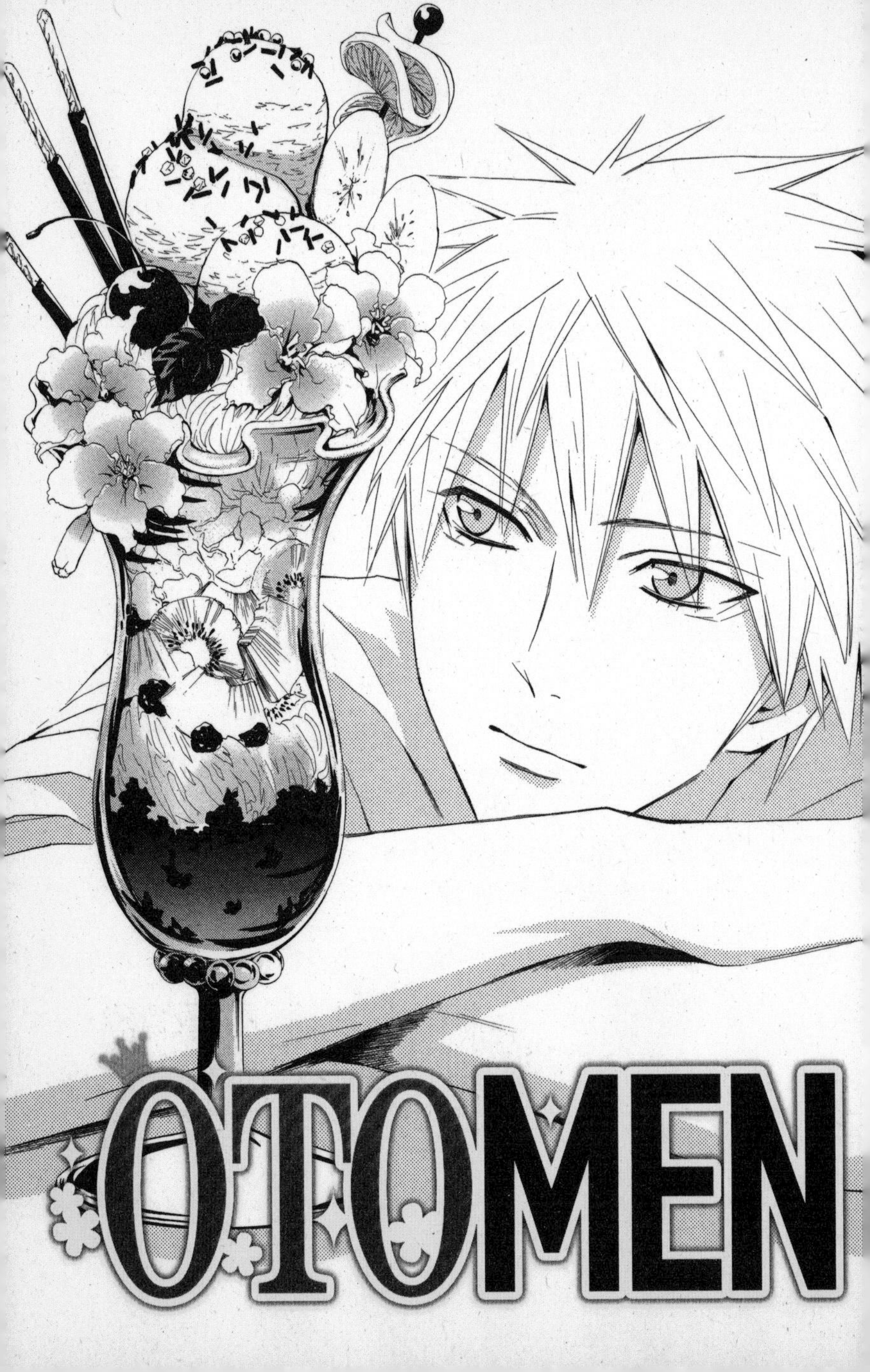
OTOMEN

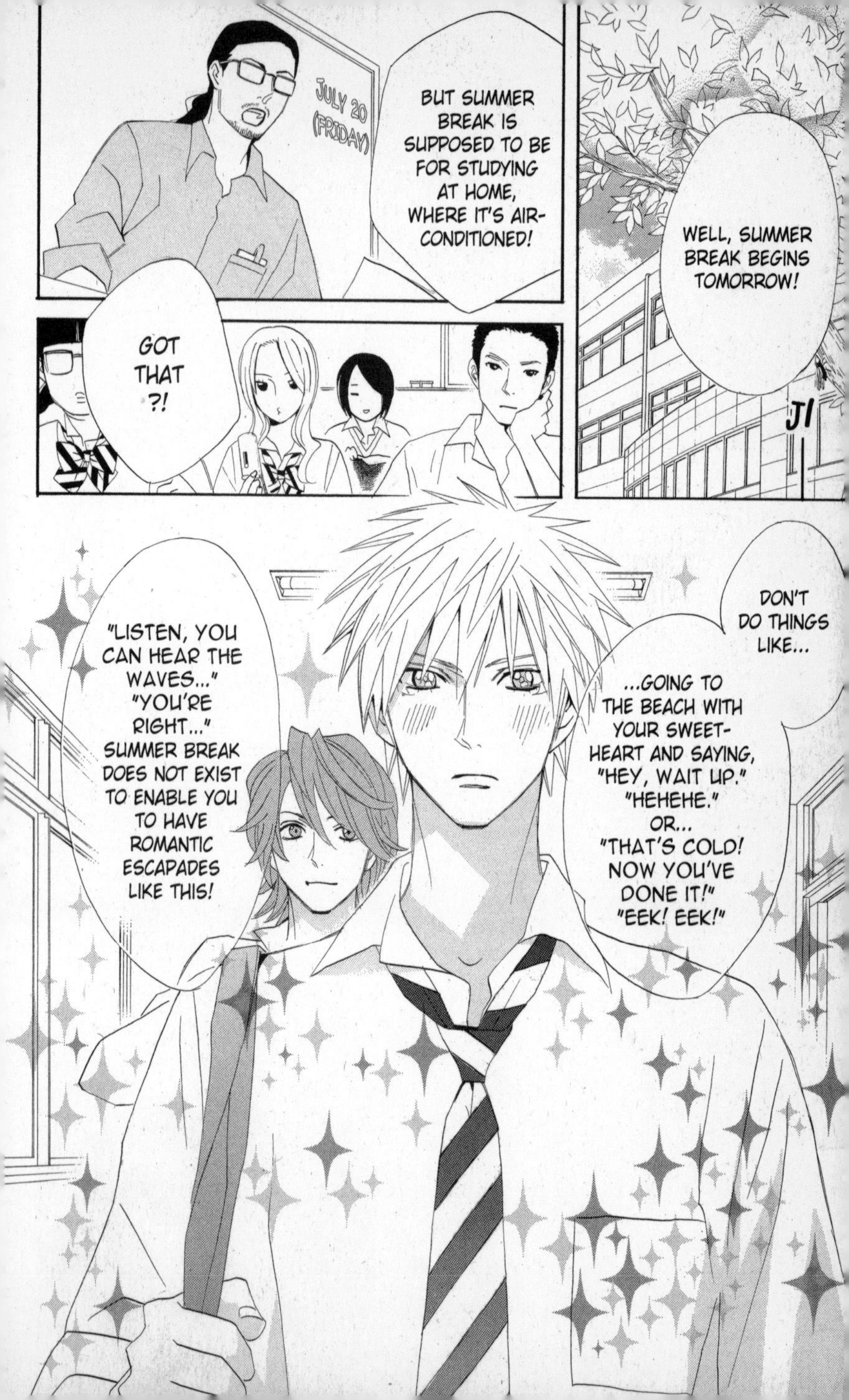
WELL, SUMMER BREAK BEGINS TOMORROW!
JI
JULY 20 (FRIDAY)
BUT SUMMER BREAK IS SUPPOSED TO BE FOR STUDYING AT HOME, WHERE IT'S AIR-CONDITIONED!
GOT THAT ?!
DON'T DO THINGS LIKE...
...GOING TO THE BEACH WITH YOUR SWEET-HEART AND SAYING, "HEY, WAIT UP." "HEHEHE." OR... "THAT'S COLD! NOW YOU'VE DONE IT!" "EEK! EEK!"
"LISTEN, YOU CAN HEAR THE WAVES..." "YOU'RE RIGHT..." SUMMER BREAK DOES NOT EXIST TO ENABLE YOU TO HAVE ROMANTIC ESCAPADES LIKE THIS!

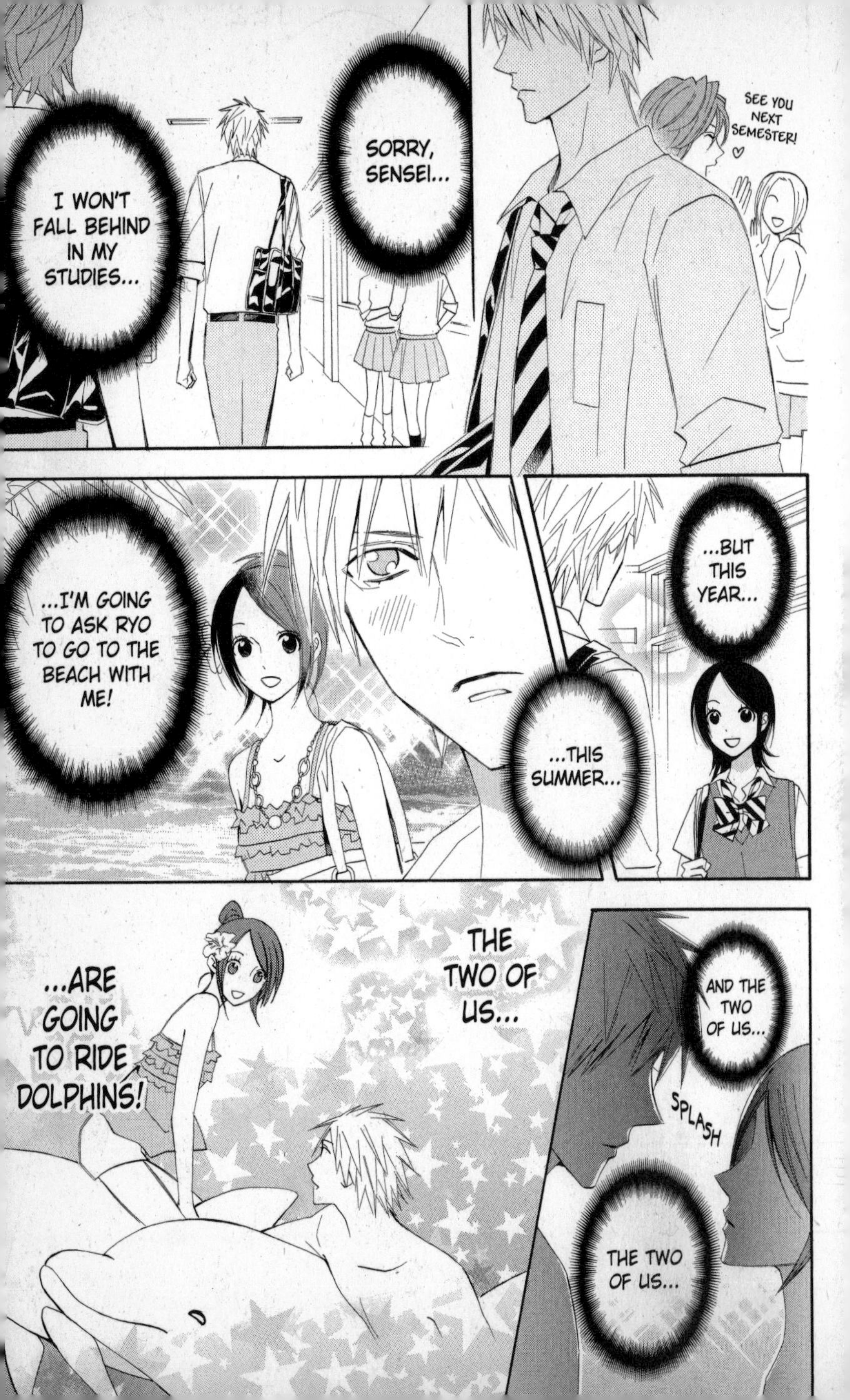
SEE YOU NEXT SEMESTER! ♡
SORRY, SENSEI...
I WON'T FALL BEHIND IN MY STUDIES...
...BUT THIS YEAR...
...THIS SUMMER...
...I'M GOING TO ASK RYO TO GO TO THE BEACH WITH ME!
AND THE TWO OF US...
SPLASH
THE TWO OF US...
THE TWO OF US...
...ARE GOING TO RIDE DOLPHINS!

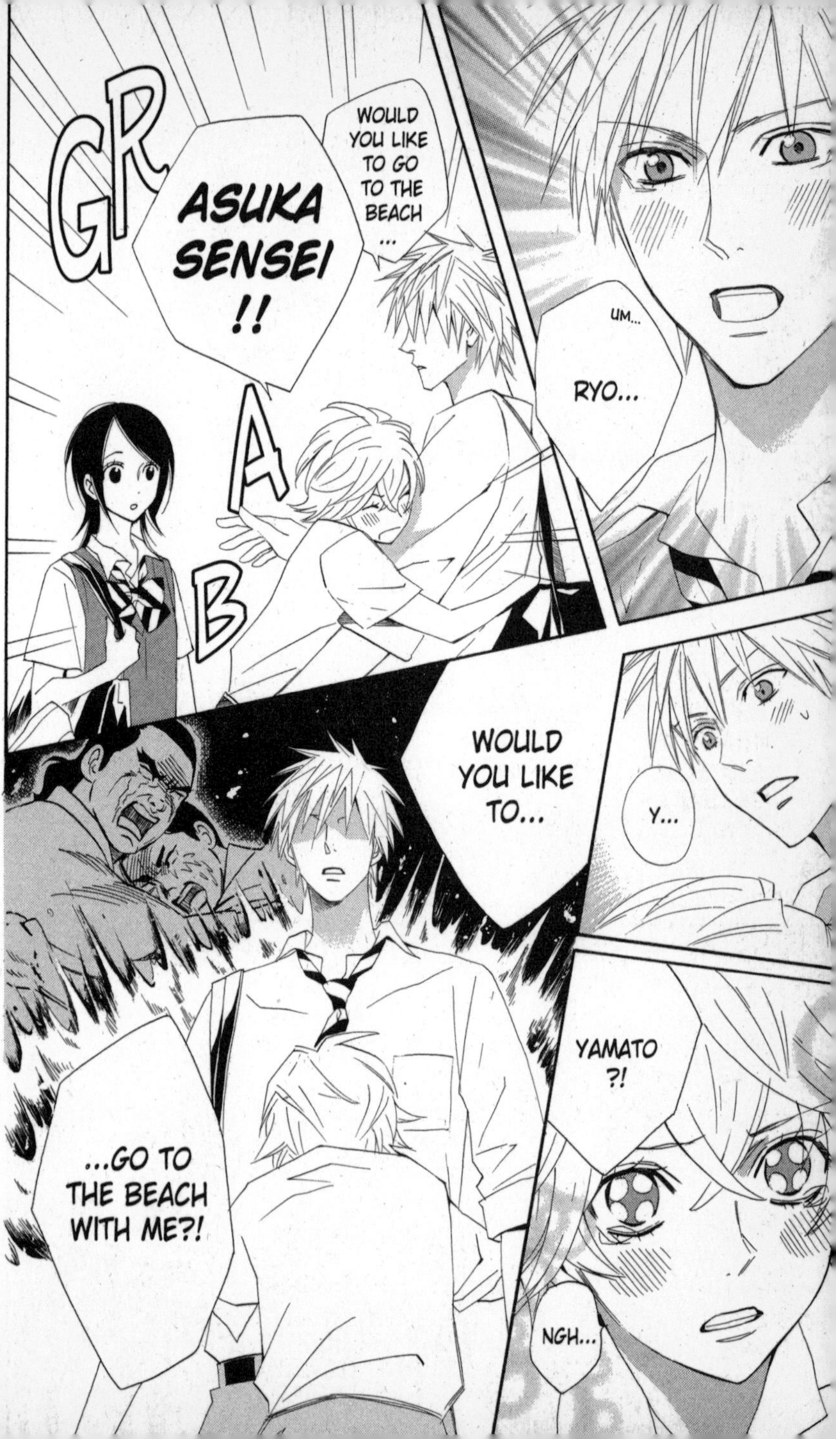
UM...
RYO...
WOULD YOU LIKE TO GO TO THE BEACH ...
ASUKA SENSEI !!
GRAB
Y...
YAMATO ?!
NGH...
WOULD YOU LIKE TO...
...GO TO THE BEACH WITH ME?!

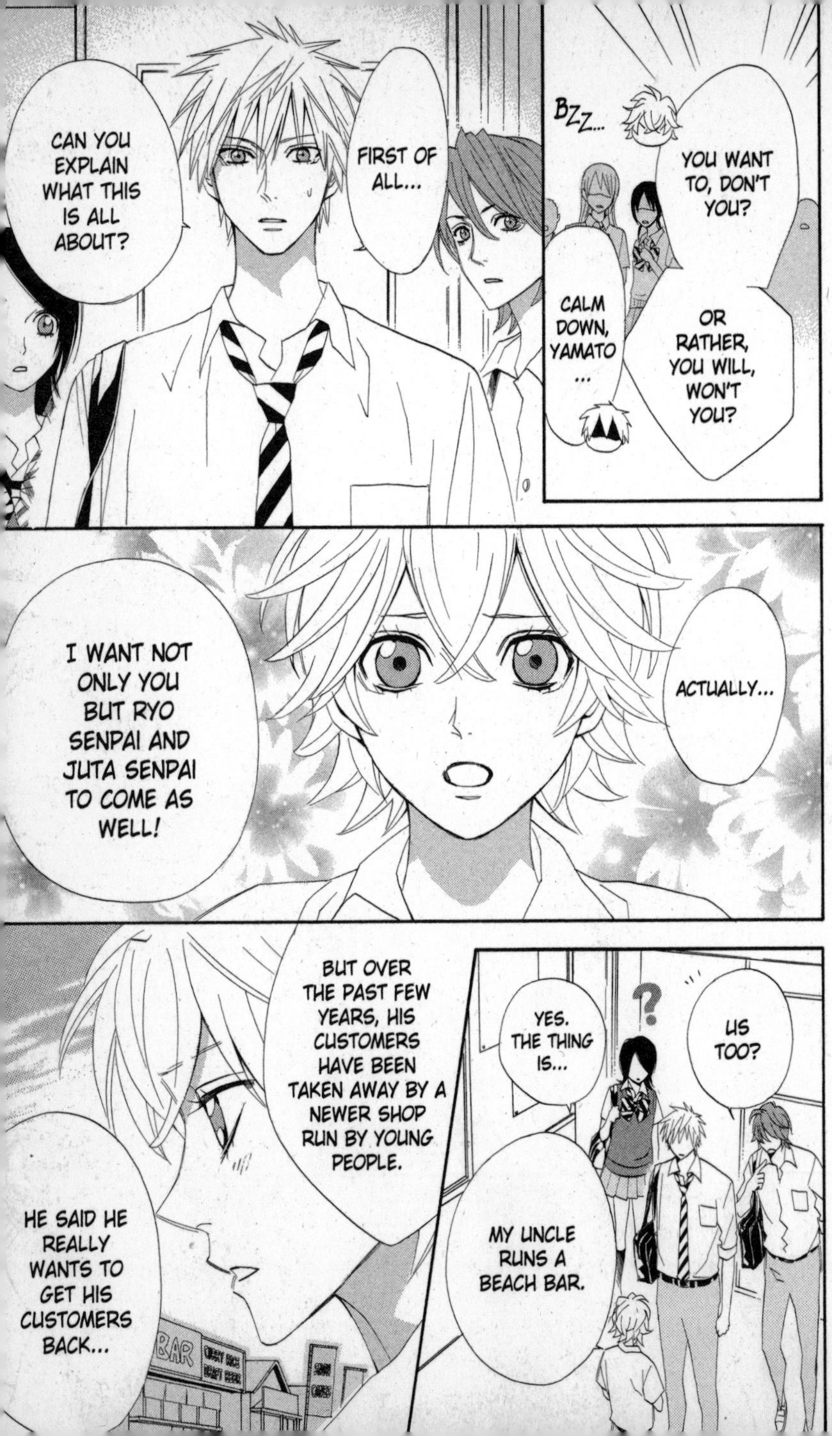
BZZ...
YOU WANT TO, DON'T YOU?
OR RATHER, YOU WILL, WON'T YOU?
CALM DOWN, YAMATO...
FIRST OF ALL...
CAN YOU EXPLAIN WHAT THIS IS ALL ABOUT?
ACTUALLY...
I WANT NOT ONLY YOU BUT RYO SENPAI AND JUTA SENPAI TO COME AS WELL!
US TOO?
YES. THE THING IS...
MY UNCLE RUNS A BEACH BAR.
BUT OVER THE PAST FEW YEARS, HIS CUSTOMERS HAVE BEEN TAKEN AWAY BY A NEWER SHOP RUN BY YOUNG PEOPLE.
HE SAID HE REALLY WANTS TO GET HIS CUSTOMERS BACK...
BAR

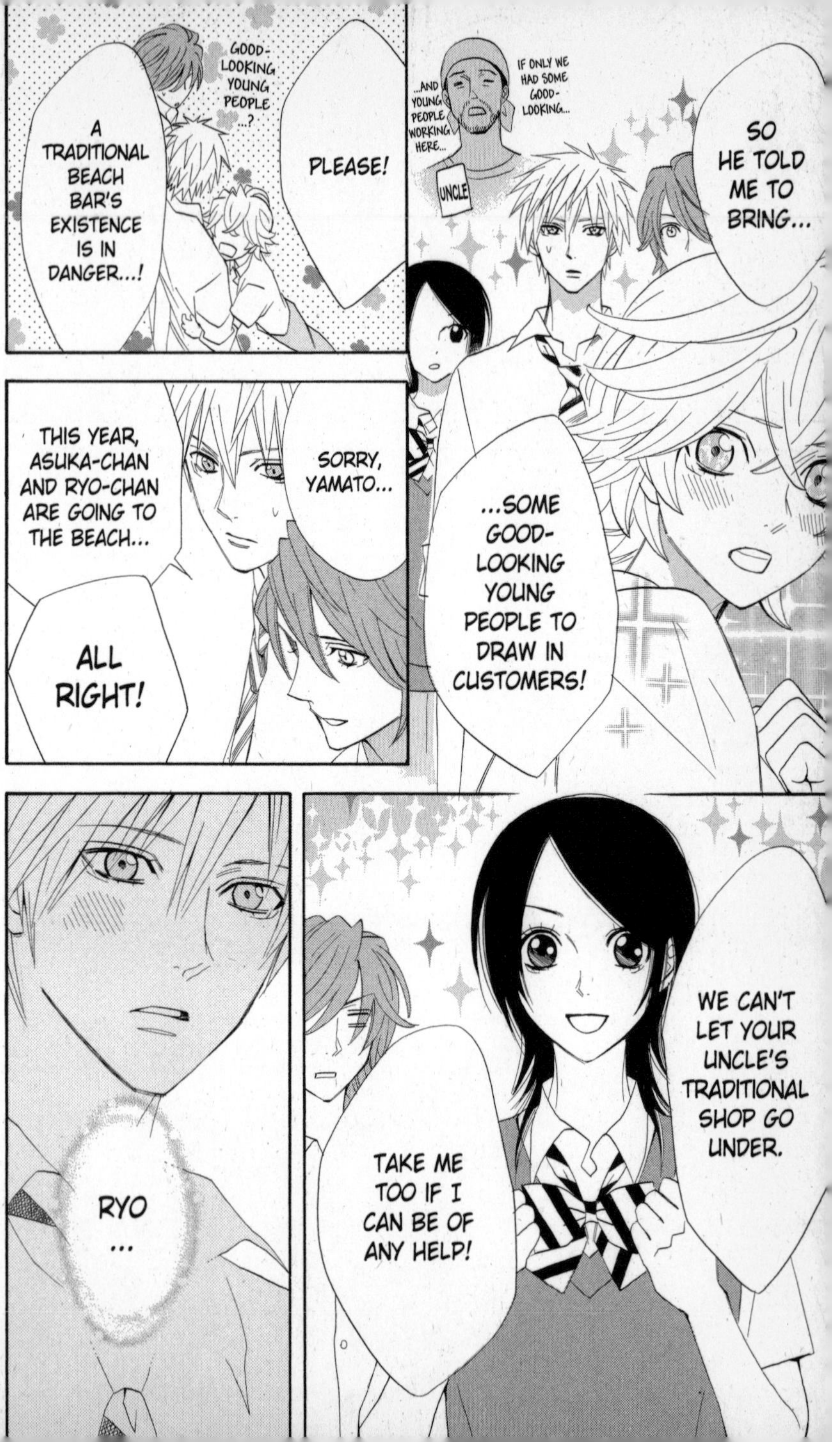
SO HE TOLD ME TO BRING...
IF ONLY WE HAD SOME GOOD-LOOKING...
...AND YOUNG PEOPLE WORKING HERE...
UNCLE
...SOME GOOD-LOOKING YOUNG PEOPLE TO DRAW IN CUSTOMERS!
PLEASE!
GOOD-LOOKING YOUNG PEOPLE ...?
A TRADITIONAL BEACH BAR'S EXISTENCE IS IN DANGER...!
SORRY, YAMATO...
THIS YEAR, ASUKA-CHAN AND RYO-CHAN ARE GOING TO THE BEACH...
ALL RIGHT!
WE CAN'T LET YOUR UNCLE'S TRADITIONAL SHOP GO UNDER.
TAKE ME TOO IF I CAN BE OF ANY HELP!
RYO ...

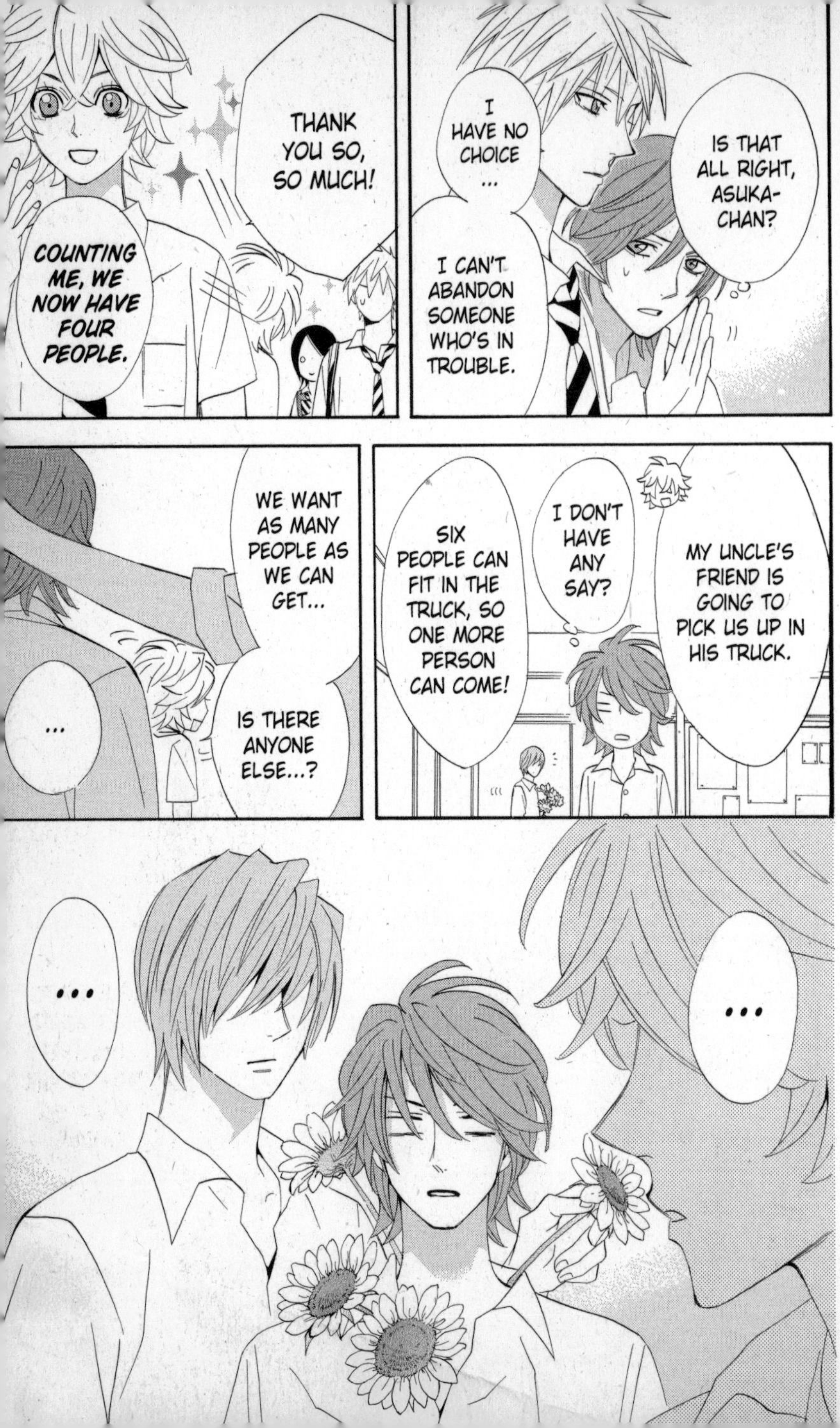
IS THAT ALL RIGHT, ASUKA-CHAN?
I HAVE NO CHOICE ...
I CAN'T ABANDON SOMEONE WHO'S IN TROUBLE.
THANK YOU SO, SO MUCH!
COUNTING ME, WE NOW HAVE FOUR PEOPLE.
MY UNCLE'S FRIEND IS GOING TO PICK US UP IN HIS TRUCK.
I DON'T HAVE ANY SAY?
SIX PEOPLE CAN FIT IN THE TRUCK, SO ONE MORE PERSON CAN COME!
WE WANT AS MANY PEOPLE AS WE CAN GET...
IS THERE ANYONE ELSE...?
...
...
...

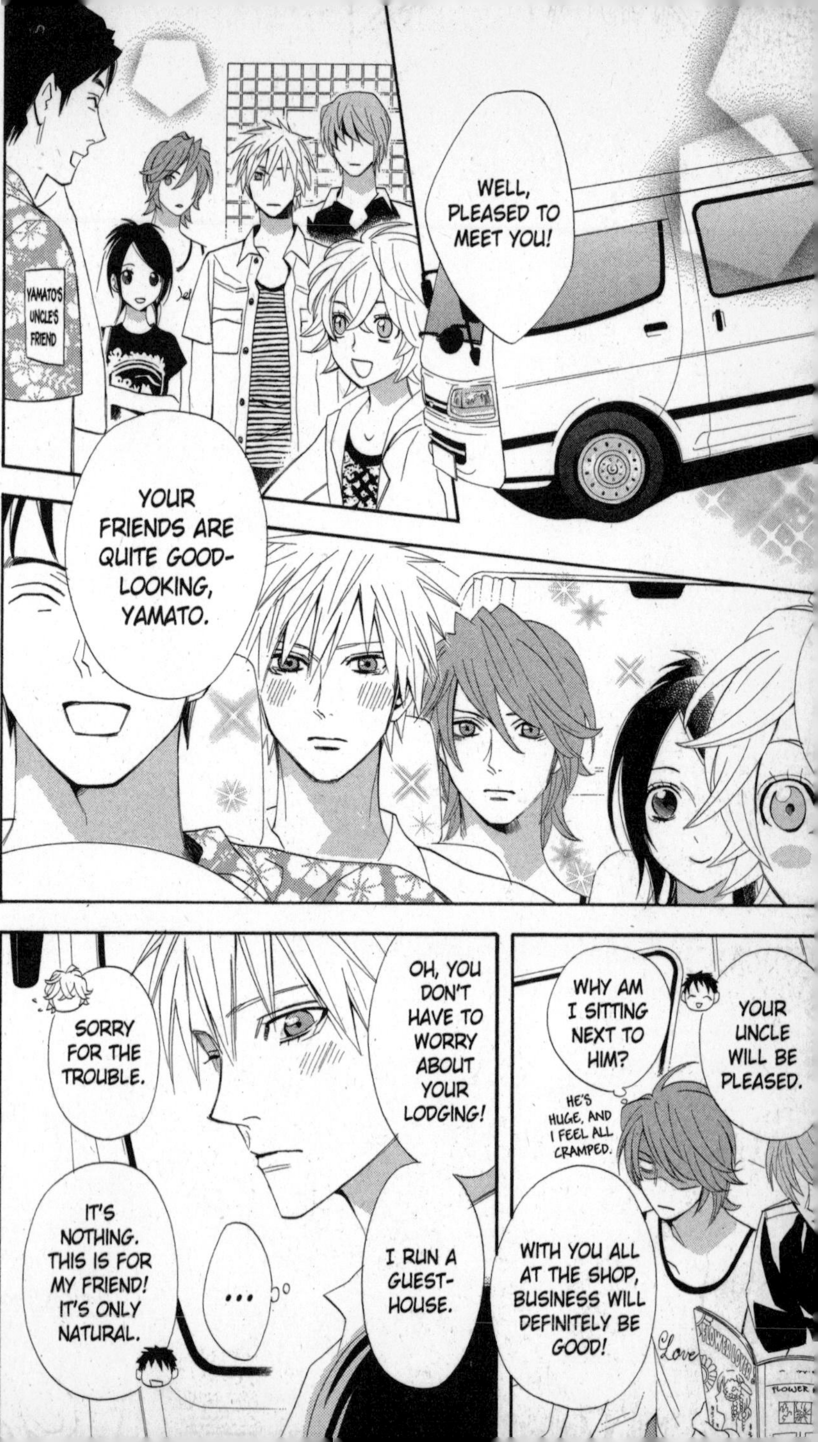
WELL, PLEASED TO MEET YOU!
YAMATO'S UNCLE'S FRIEND
YOUR FRIENDS ARE QUITE GOOD-LOOKING, YAMATO.
YOUR UNCLE WILL BE PLEASED.
WHY AM I SITTING NEXT TO HIM?
HE'S HUGE, AND I FEEL ALL CRAMPED.
WITH YOU ALL AT THE SHOP, BUSINESS WILL DEFINITELY BE GOOD!
OH, YOU DON'T HAVE TO WORRY ABOUT YOUR LODGING!
SORRY FOR THE TROUBLE.
I RUN A GUEST-HOUSE.
...
IT'S NOTHING. THIS IS FOR MY FRIEND! IT'S ONLY NATURAL.

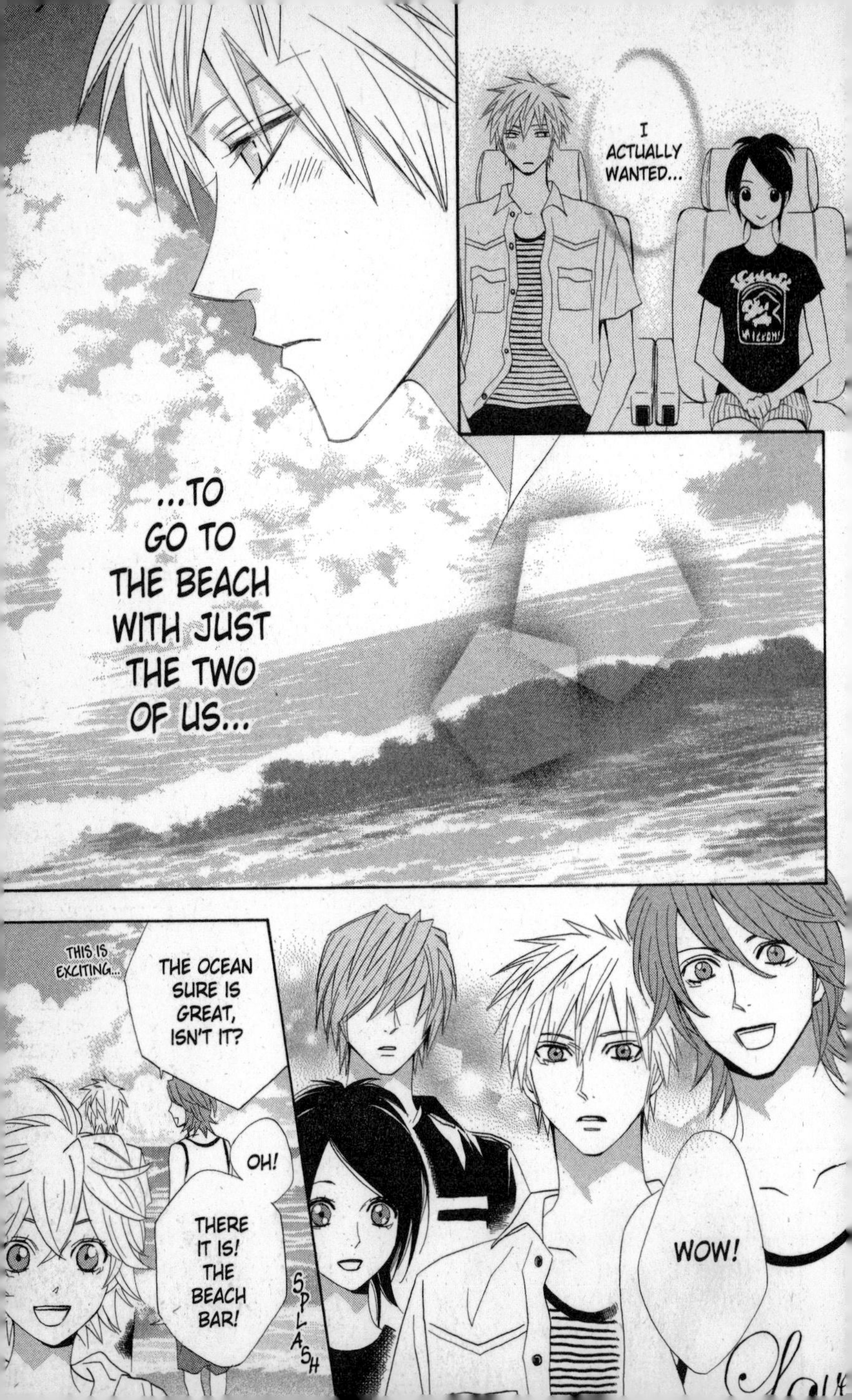
I ACTUALLY WANTED...
...TO GO TO THE BEACH WITH JUST THE TWO OF US...
WOW!
THERE IT IS! THE BEACH BAR!
OH!
SPLASH
THE OCEAN SURE IS GREAT, ISN'T IT?
THIS IS EXCITING...

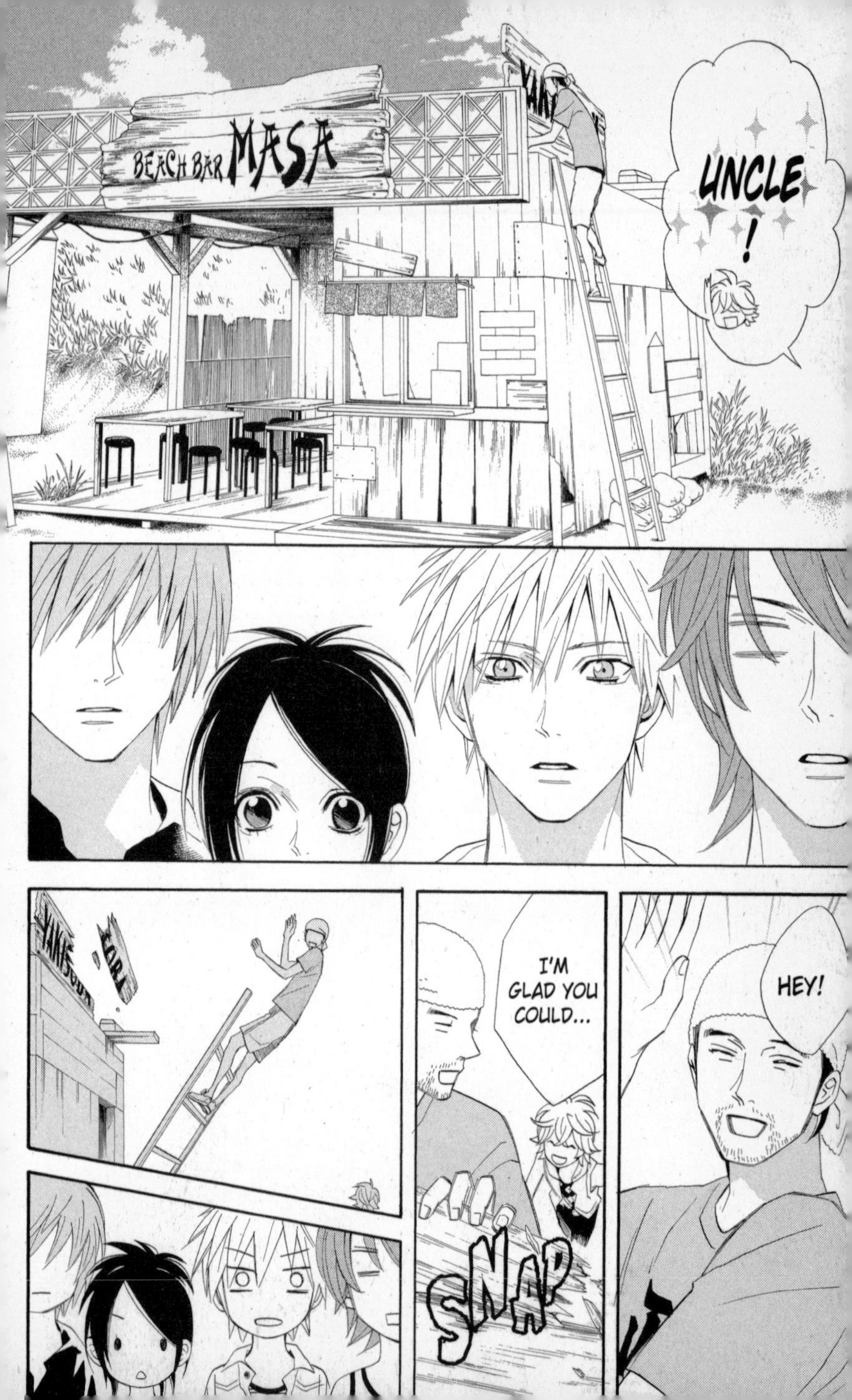
BEACH BAR MASA
UNCLE!
HEY!
I'M GLAD YOU COULD...
SNAP

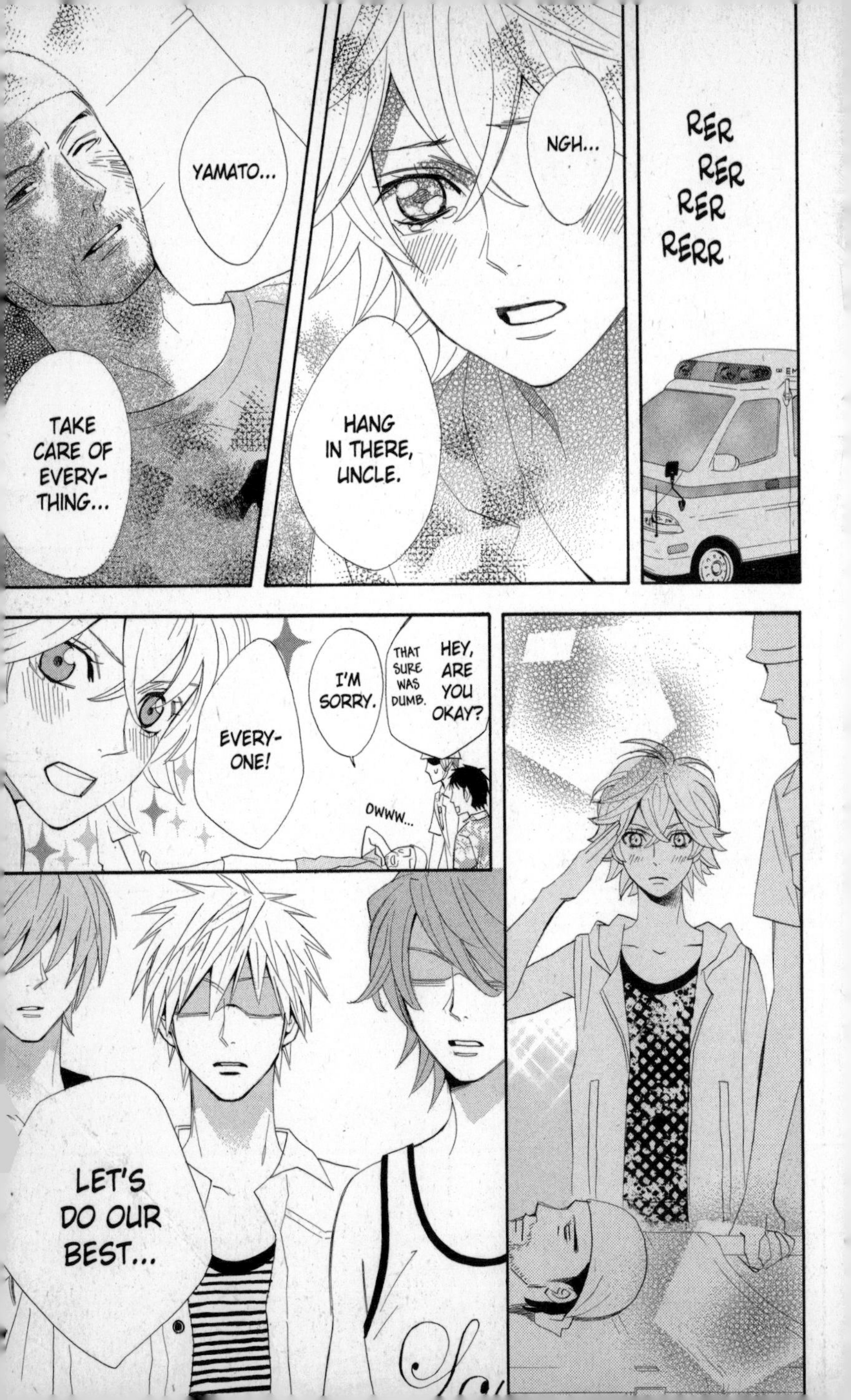
RER RER RER RERR
NGH...
HANG IN THERE, UNCLE.
YAMATO...
TAKE CARE OF EVERY-THING...
HEY, ARE YOU OKAY?
THAT SURE WAS DUMB.
I'M SORRY.
OWWW...
EVERY-ONE!
LET'S DO OUR BEST...

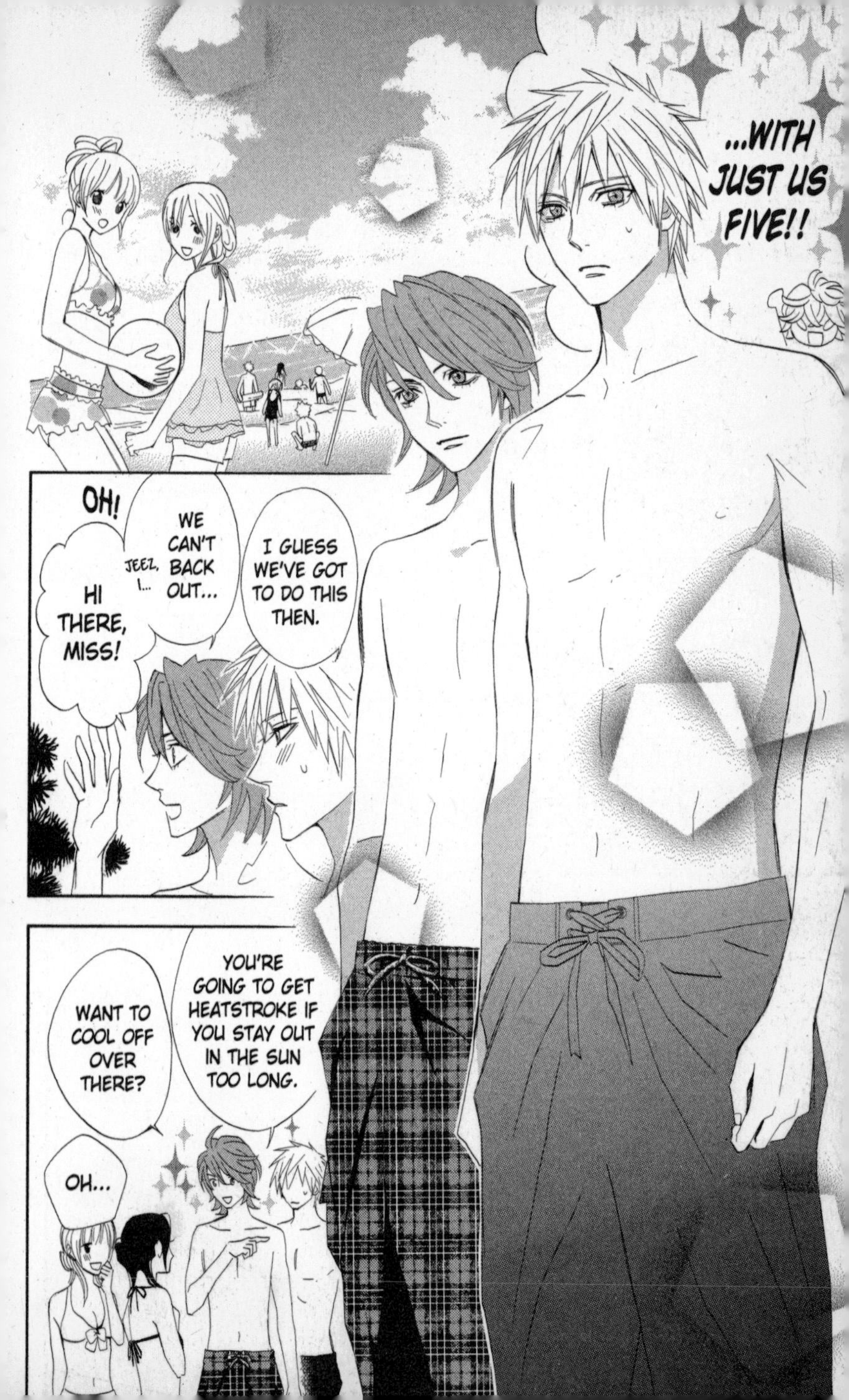
...WITH JUST US FIVE!!
I GUESS WE'VE GOT TO DO THIS THEN.
WE CAN'T BACK OUT...
JEEZ, I...
OH!
HI THERE, MISS!
YOU'RE GOING TO GET HEATSTROKE IF YOU STAY OUT IN THE SUN TOO LONG.
WANT TO COOL OFF OVER THERE?
OH...

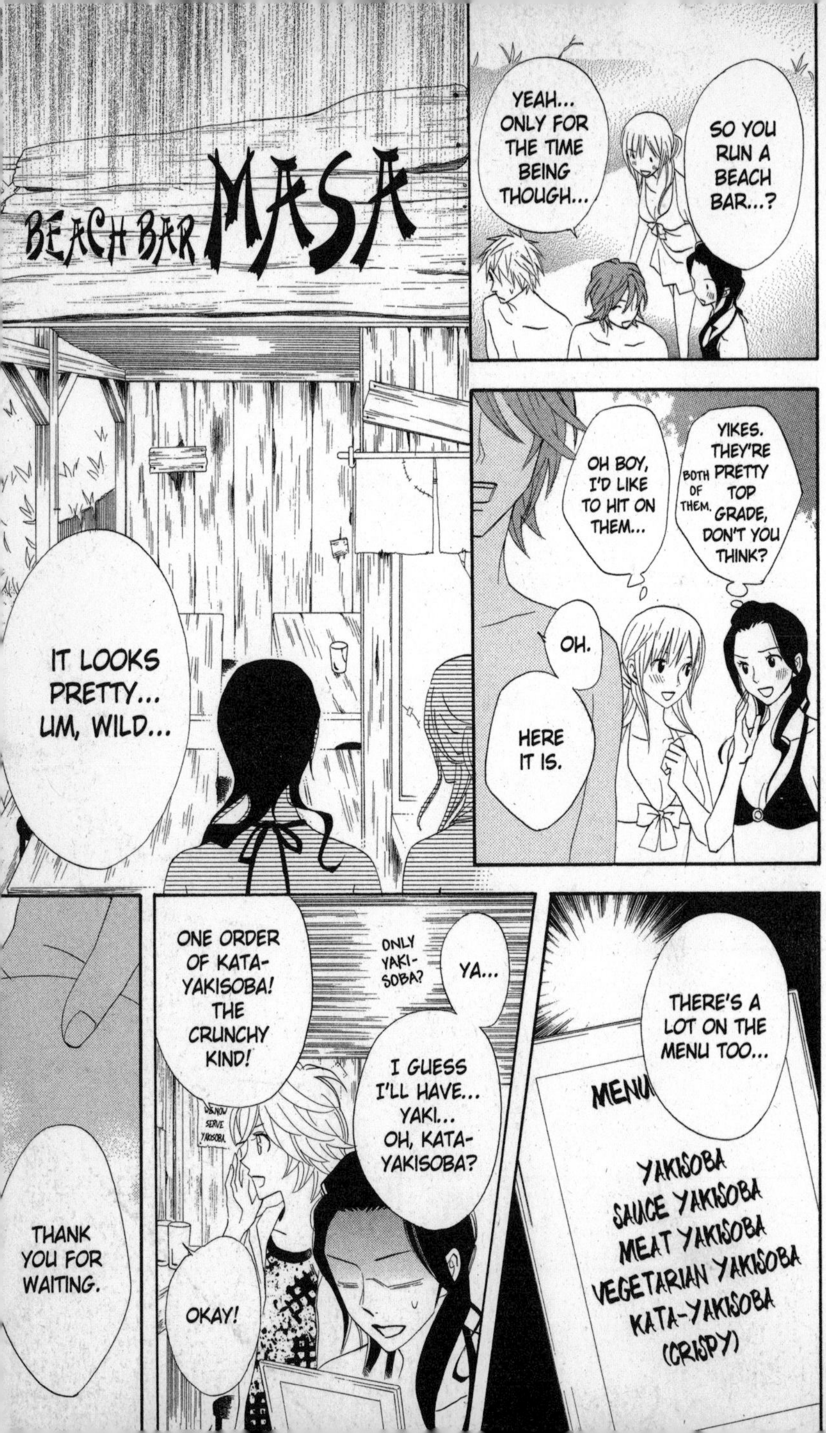
SO YOU RUN A BEACH BAR...?
YEAH... ONLY FOR THE TIME BEING THOUGH...
YIKES. THEY'RE PRETTY TOP GRADE, DON'T YOU THINK?
BOTH OF THEM.
OH BOY, I'D LIKE TO HIT ON THEM...
OH.
HERE IT IS.
BEACH BAR MASA
IT LOOKS PRETTY... UM, WILD...
THERE'S A LOT ON THE MENU TOO...
MENU
YAKISOBA
SAUCE YAKISOBA
MEAT YAKISOBA
VEGETARIAN YAKISOBA
KATA-YAKISOBA (CRISPY)
YA...
ONLY YAKI-SOBA?
ONE ORDER OF KATA-YAKISOBA! THE CRUNCHY KIND!
I GUESS I'LL HAVE... YAKI... OH, KATA-YAKISOBA?
WE NOW SERVE YAKISOBA.
OKAY!
THANK YOU FOR WAITING.

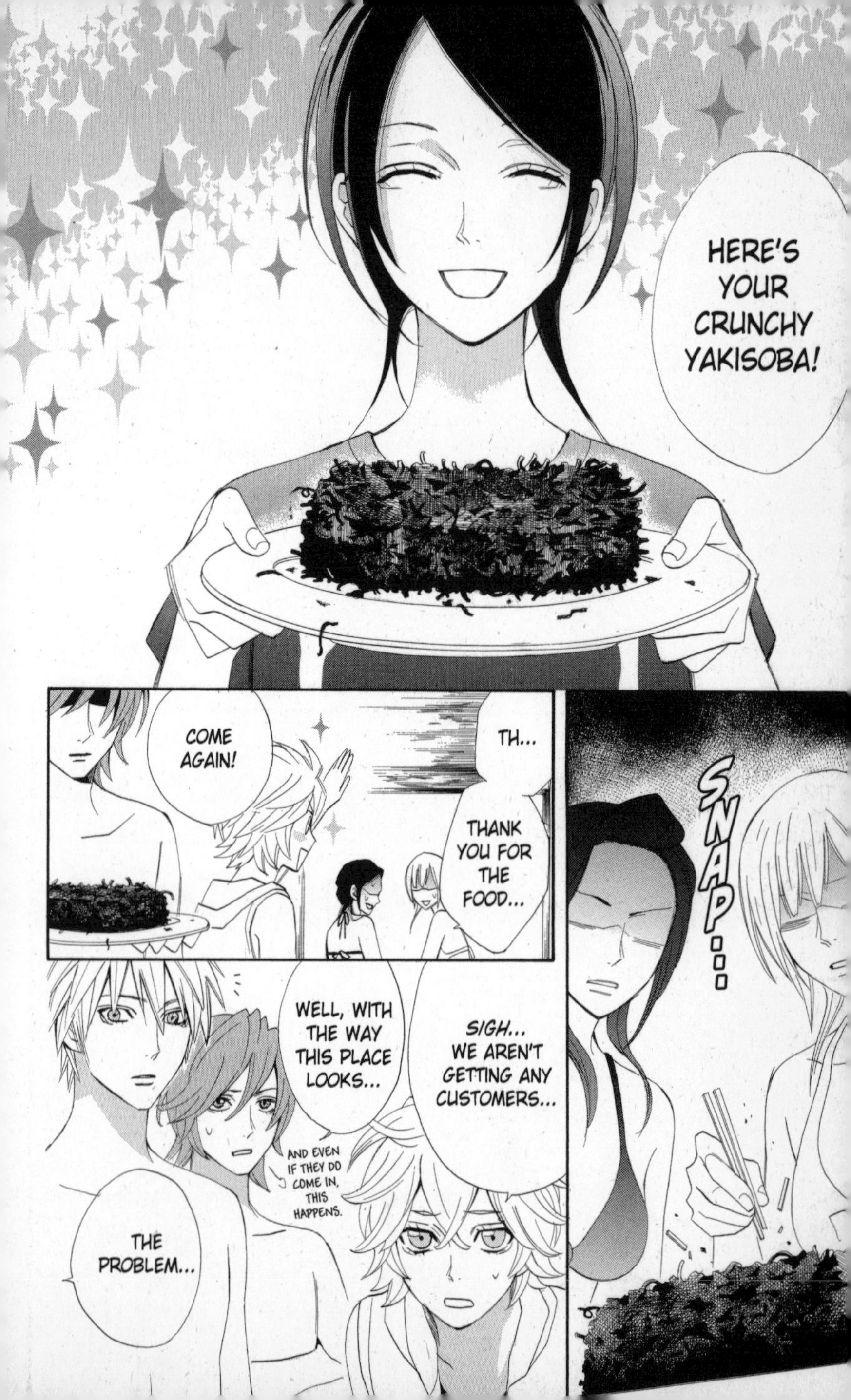
HERE'S YOUR CRUNCHY YAKISOBA!
SNAP...
TH...
THANK YOU FOR THE FOOD...
COME AGAIN!
SIGH... WE AREN'T GETTING ANY CUSTOMERS...
WELL, WITH THE WAY THIS PLACE LOOKS...
AND EVEN IF THEY DO COME IN, THIS HAPPENS.
THE PROBLEM...

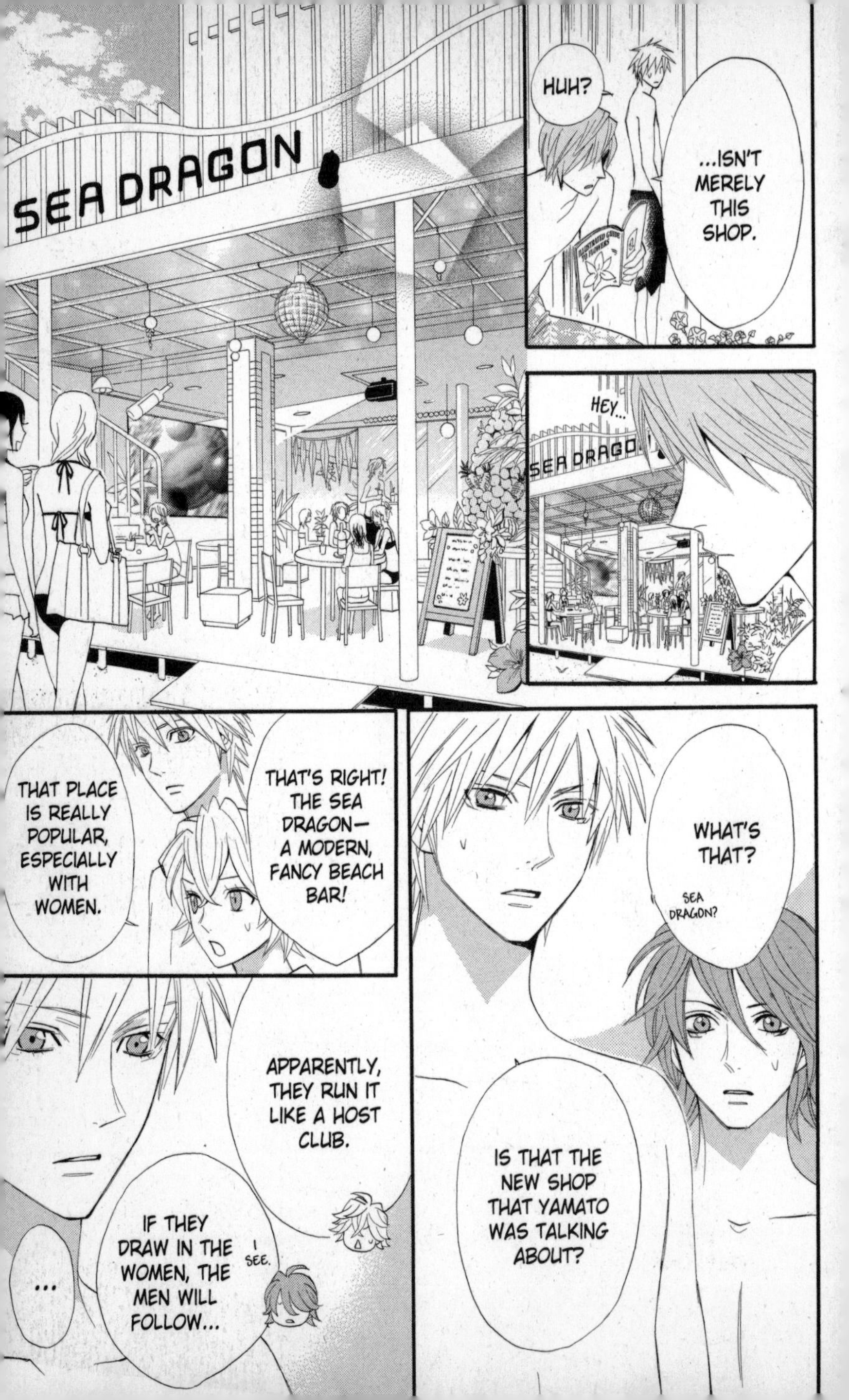
...ISN'T MERELY THIS SHOP.
HUH?
ILLUSTRATED GUIDE TO FLOWERS
HEY...
SEA DRAGON
SEA DRAGON
WHAT'S THAT?
SEA DRAGON?
IS THAT THE NEW SHOP THAT YAMATO WAS TALKING ABOUT?
THAT'S RIGHT! THE SEA DRAGON— A MODERN, FANCY BEACH BAR!
THAT PLACE IS REALLY POPULAR, ESPECIALLY WITH WOMEN.
APPARENTLY, THEY RUN IT LIKE A HOST CLUB.
I SEE.
IF THEY DRAW IN THE WOMEN, THE MEN WILL FOLLOW...
...

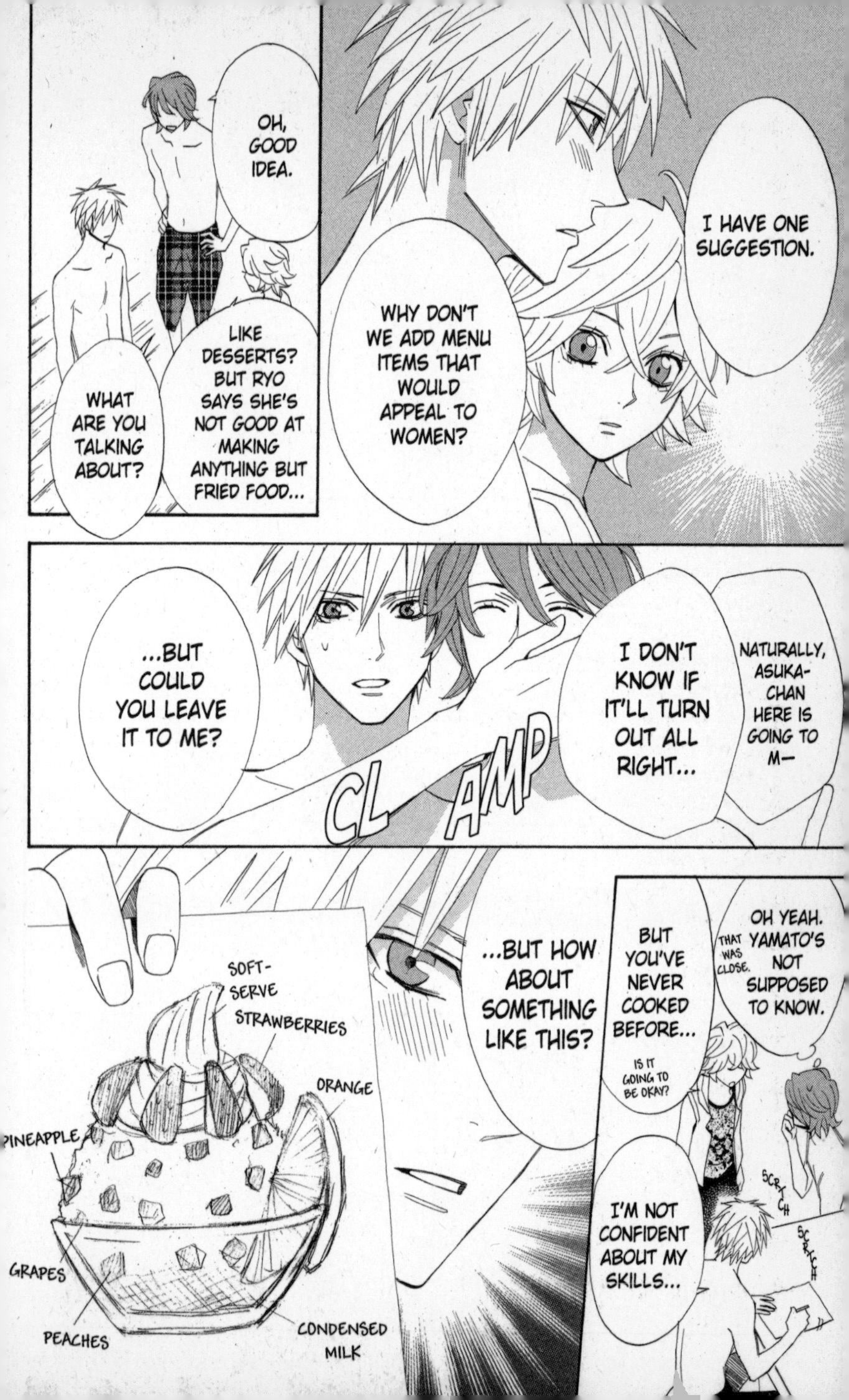
I HAVE ONE SUGGESTION.
WHY DON'T WE ADD MENU ITEMS THAT WOULD APPEAL TO WOMEN?
OH, GOOD IDEA.
LIKE DESSERTS? BUT RYO SAYS SHE'S NOT GOOD AT MAKING ANYTHING BUT FRIED FOOD...
WHAT ARE YOU TALKING ABOUT?
NATURALLY, ASUKA-CHAN HERE IS GOING TO M—
CLAMP
I DON'T KNOW IF IT'LL TURN OUT ALL RIGHT...
...BUT COULD YOU LEAVE IT TO ME?
OH YEAH. YAMATO'S NOT SUPPOSED TO KNOW.
THAT WAS CLOSE.
BUT YOU'VE NEVER COOKED BEFORE...
IS IT GOING TO BE OKAY?
I'M NOT CONFIDENT ABOUT MY SKILLS...
SCRATCH
SCRATCH
...BUT HOW ABOUT SOMETHING LIKE THIS?
SOFT-SERVE
STRAWBERRIES
ORANGE
PINEAPPLE
GRAPES
PEACHES
CONDENSED MILK

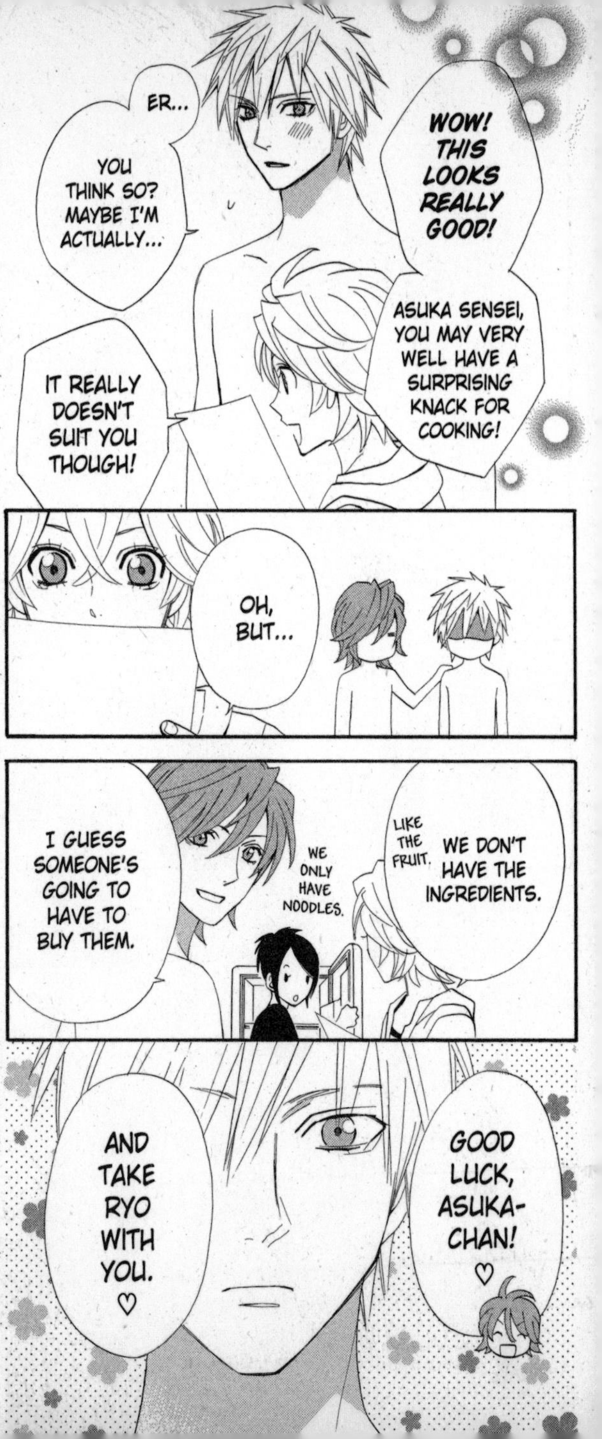
WOW! THIS LOOKS REALLY GOOD!
ASUKA SENSEI, YOU MAY VERY WELL HAVE A SURPRISING KNACK FOR COOKING!
ER...
YOU THINK SO? MAYBE I'M ACTUALLY...
IT REALLY DOESN'T SUIT YOU THOUGH!
OH, BUT...
WE DON'T HAVE THE INGREDIENTS.
LIKE THE FRUIT.
WE ONLY HAVE NOODLES.
I GUESS SOMEONE'S GOING TO HAVE TO BUY THEM.
GOOD LUCK, ASUKA-CHAN! ♡
AND TAKE RYO WITH YOU. ♡

The beach! Swimsuits!

I wanted to do all of the cliché stories. I've covered every cliché once I've made everyone go to the beach during summer break. In this chapter, Asuka and his friends spend the entire time nearly naked, so my assistants kept asking me how much muscle we should draw, whether we could draw abs and what we should do about nipples. This is what we settled on. I think that this is about right for a girls' comic.

There are a lot of recurring characters. I'm glad that I can finally draw Yamato again.

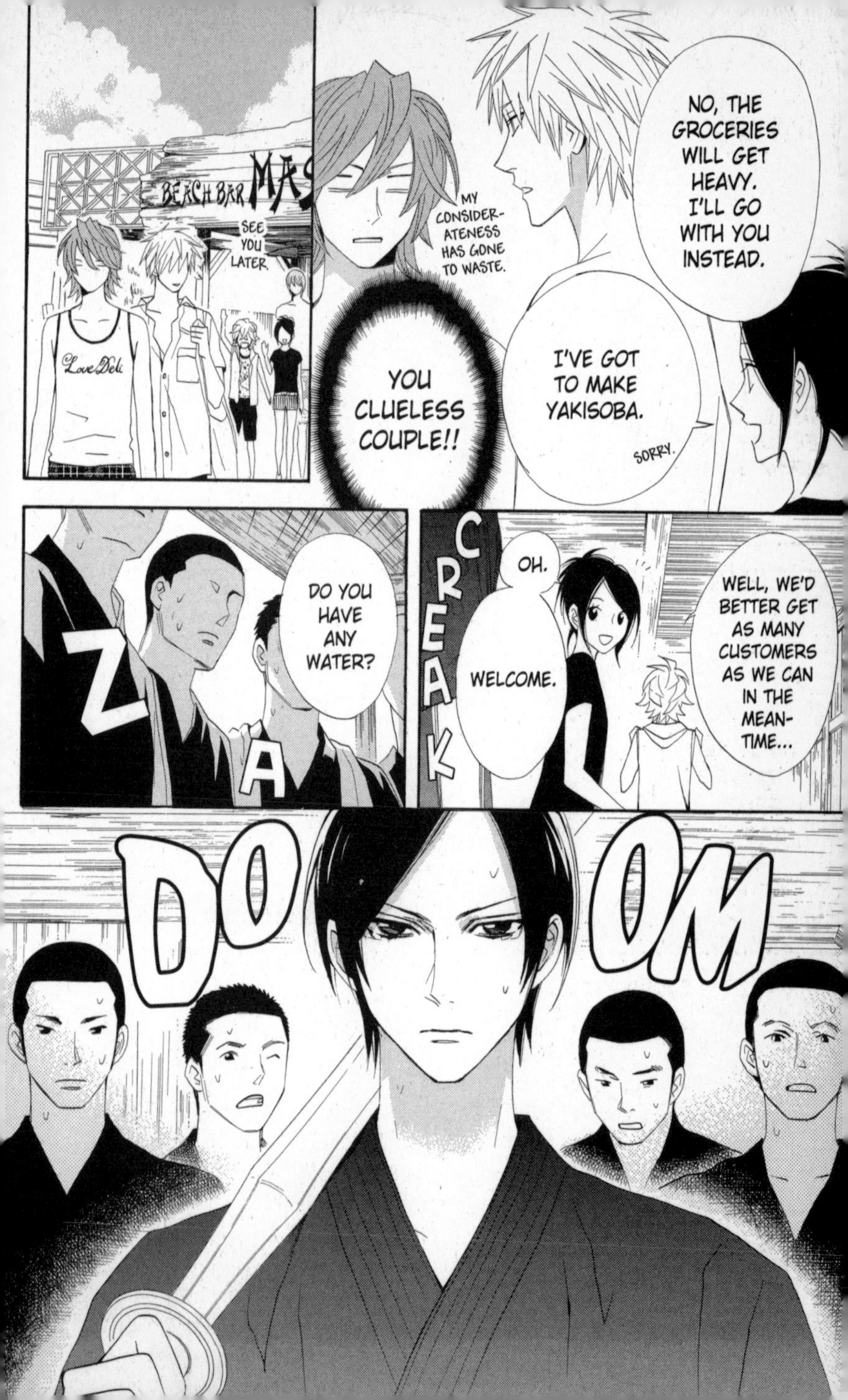
NO, THE GROCERIES WILL GET HEAVY. I'LL GO WITH YOU INSTEAD.
I'VE GOT TO MAKE YAKISOBA.
SORRY.
MY CONSIDER-ATENESS HAS GONE TO WASTE.
YOU CLUELESS COUPLE!!
BEACH BAR MAS
SEE YOU LATER.
Love Deli
WELL, WE'D BETTER GET AS MANY CUSTOMERS AS WE CAN IN THE MEAN-TIME...
OH.
WELCOME.
CREAK
DO YOU HAVE ANY WATER?
ZA
DOOM

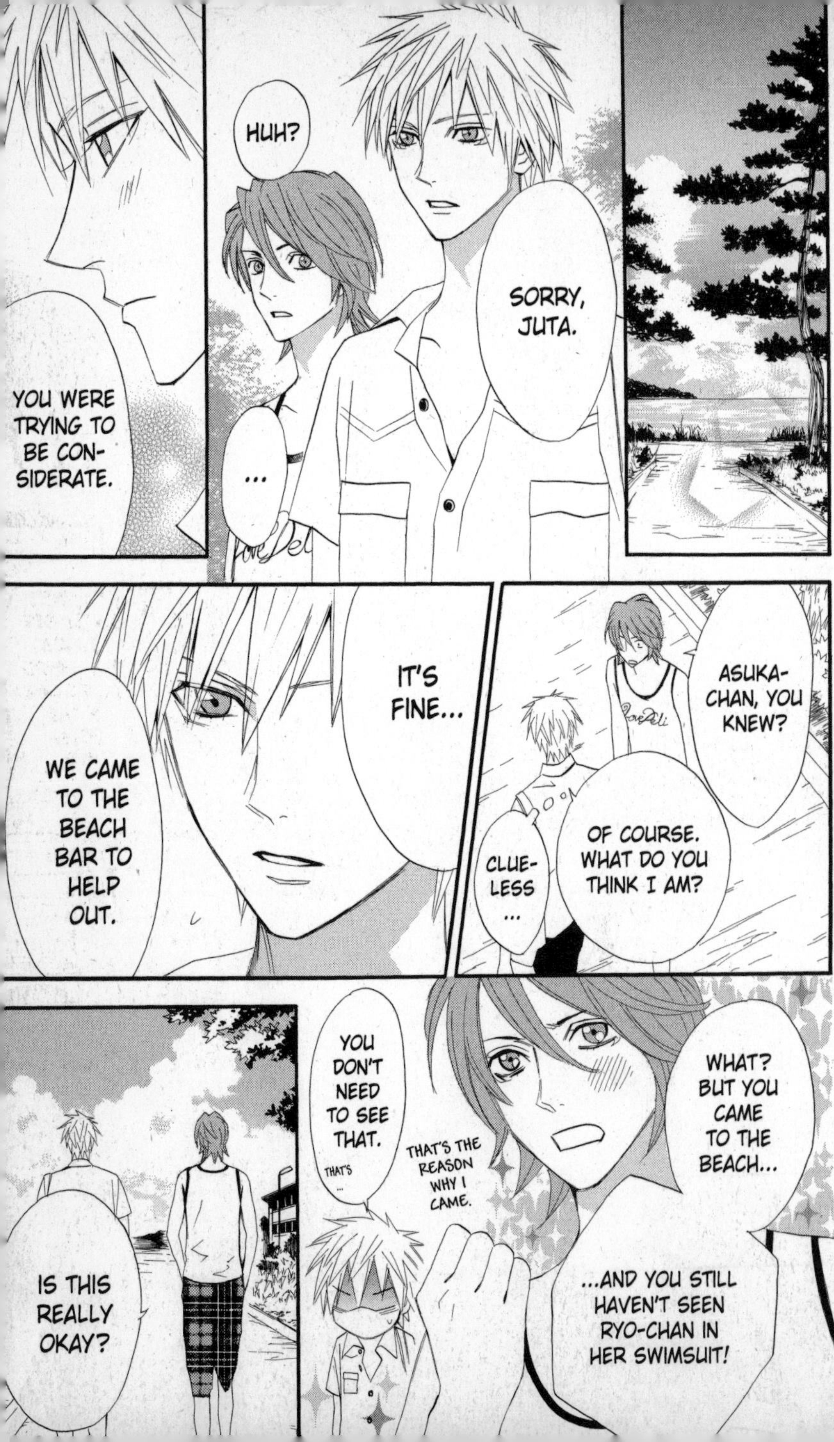
HUH?
SORRY, JUTA.
...
YOU WERE TRYING TO BE CON-SIDERATE.
ASUKA-CHAN, YOU KNEW?
OF COURSE. WHAT DO YOU THINK I AM?
CLUE-LESS ...
IT'S FINE...
WE CAME TO THE BEACH BAR TO HELP OUT.
WHAT? BUT YOU CAME TO THE BEACH...
...AND YOU STILL HAVEN'T SEEN RYO-CHAN IN HER SWIMSUIT!
THAT'S THE REASON WHY I CAME.
YOU DON'T NEED TO SEE THAT.
THAT'S ...
IS THIS REALLY OKAY?

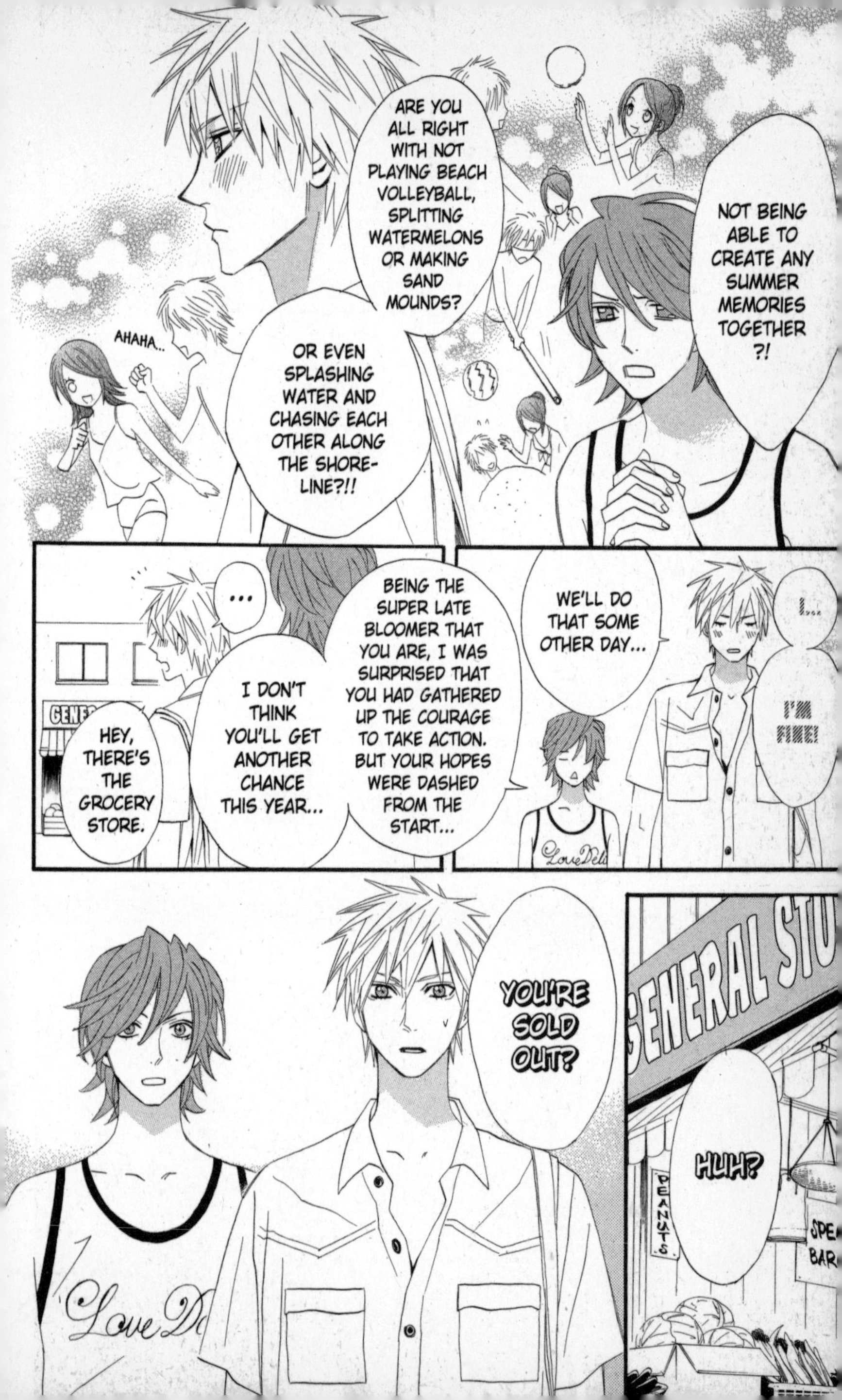
ARE YOU ALL RIGHT WITH NOT PLAYING BEACH VOLLEYBALL, SPLITTING WATERMELONS OR MAKING SAND MOUNDS?
OR EVEN SPLASHING WATER AND CHASING EACH OTHER ALONG THE SHORE-LINE?!!
NOT BEING ABLE TO CREATE ANY SUMMER MEMORIES TOGETHER?!
AHAHA...
I...
I'M FINE!
WE'LL DO THAT SOME OTHER DAY...
BEING THE SUPER LATE BLOOMER THAT YOU ARE, I WAS SURPRISED THAT YOU HAD GATHERED UP THE COURAGE TO TAKE ACTION. BUT YOUR HOPES WERE DASHED FROM THE START...
...
I DON'T THINK YOU'LL GET ANOTHER CHANCE THIS YEAR...
HEY, THERE'S THE GROCERY STORE.
GENERAL STO
HUH?
PEANUTS
SPE
BAR
YOU'RE SOLD OUT?

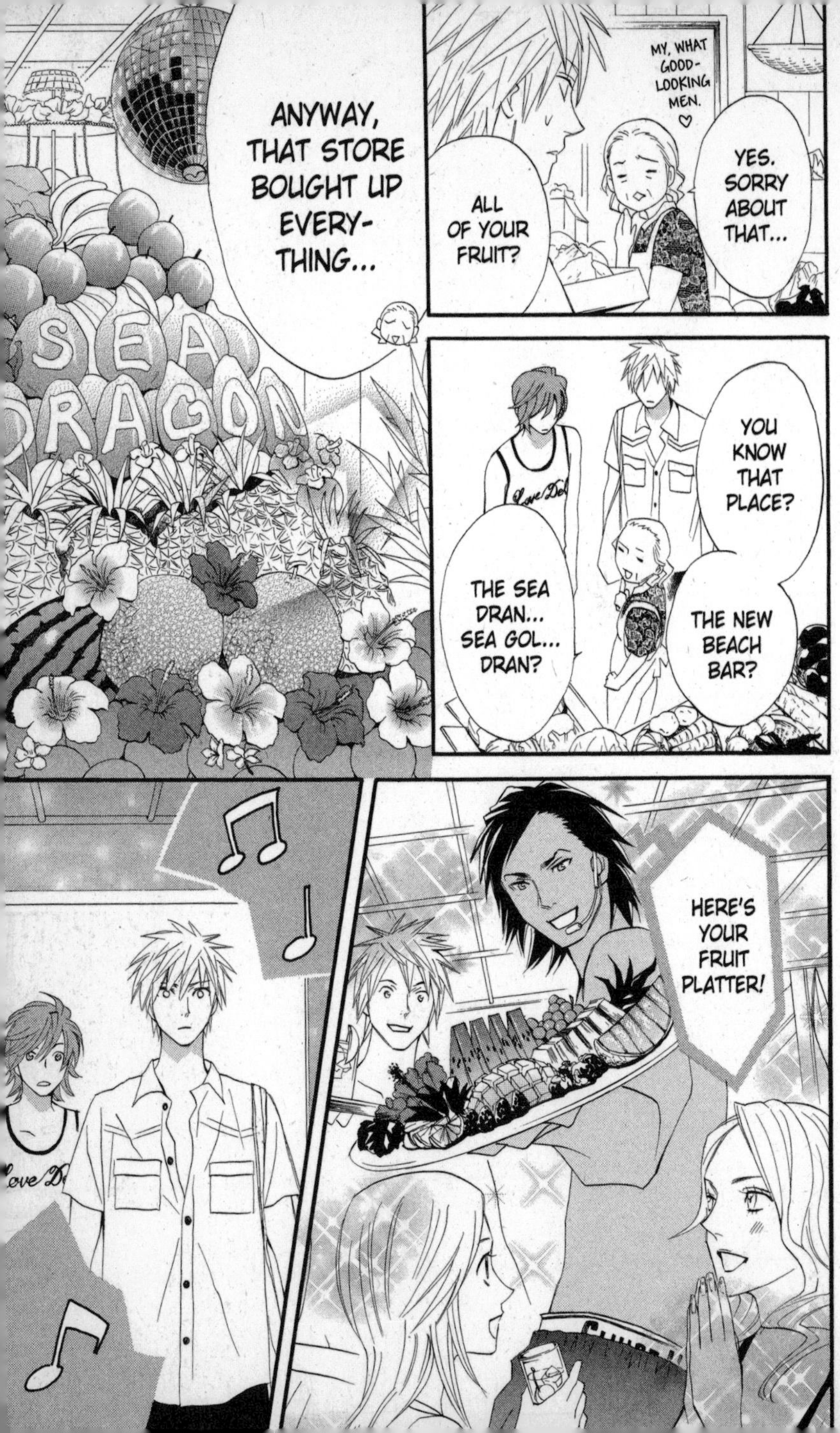
MY, WHAT GOOD-LOOKING MEN. ♡
YES. SORRY ABOUT THAT...
ALL OF YOUR FRUIT?
YOU KNOW THAT PLACE?
THE NEW BEACH BAR?
THE SEA DRAN... SEA GOL... DRAN?
ANYWAY, THAT STORE BOUGHT UP EVERY-THING...
SEA DRAGON
HERE'S YOUR FRUIT PLATTER!

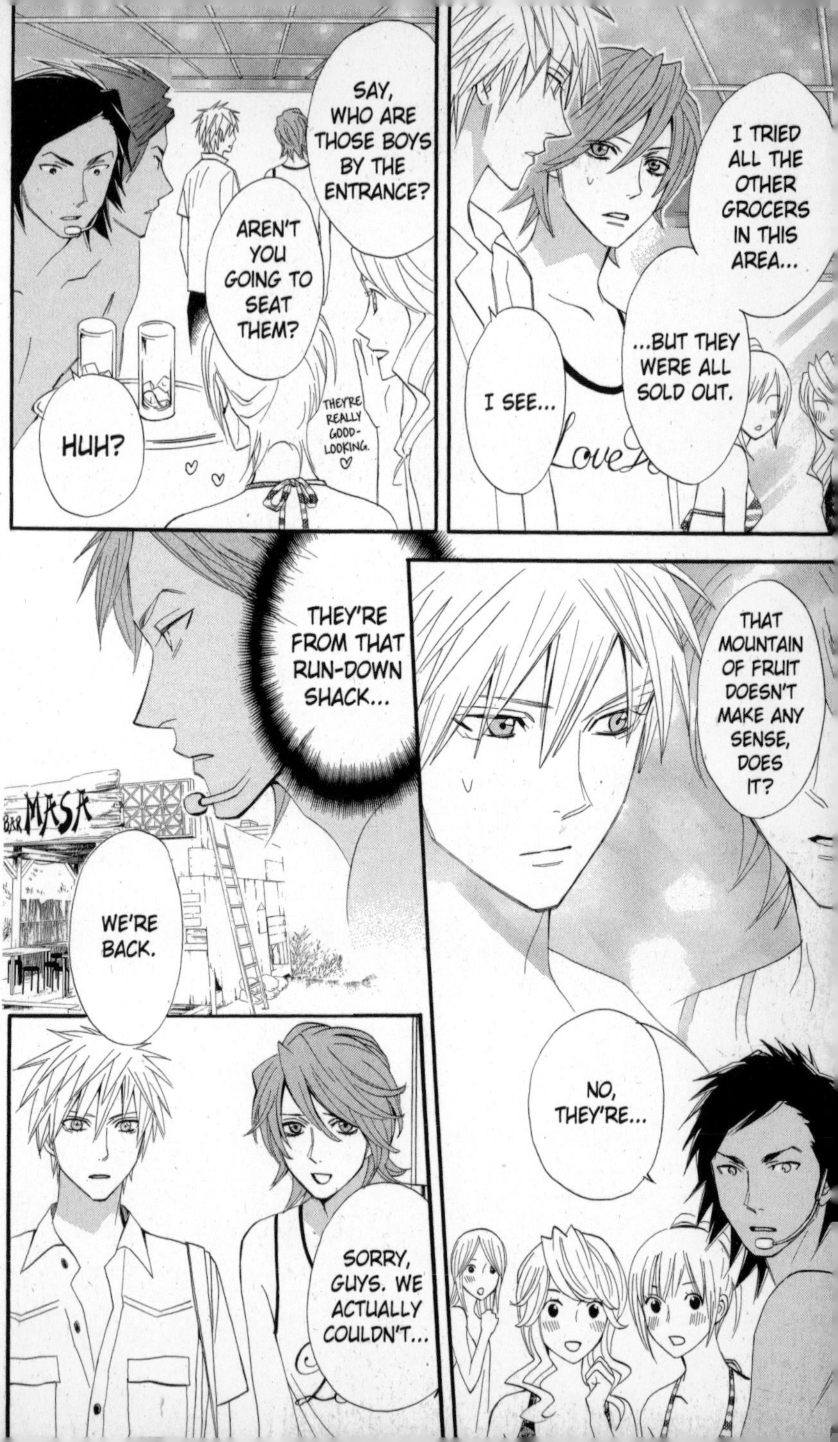
I TRIED ALL THE OTHER GROCERS IN THIS AREA...
...BUT THEY WERE ALL SOLD OUT.
I SEE...
SAY, WHO ARE THOSE BOYS BY THE ENTRANCE?
AREN'T YOU GOING TO SEAT THEM?
THEY'RE REALLY GOOD-LOOKING.
HUH?
THAT MOUNTAIN OF FRUIT DOESN'T MAKE ANY SENSE, DOES IT?
THEY'RE FROM THAT RUN-DOWN SHACK...
BAR MASA
WE'RE BACK.
NO, THEY'RE...
SORRY, GUYS. WE ACTUALLY COULDN'T...

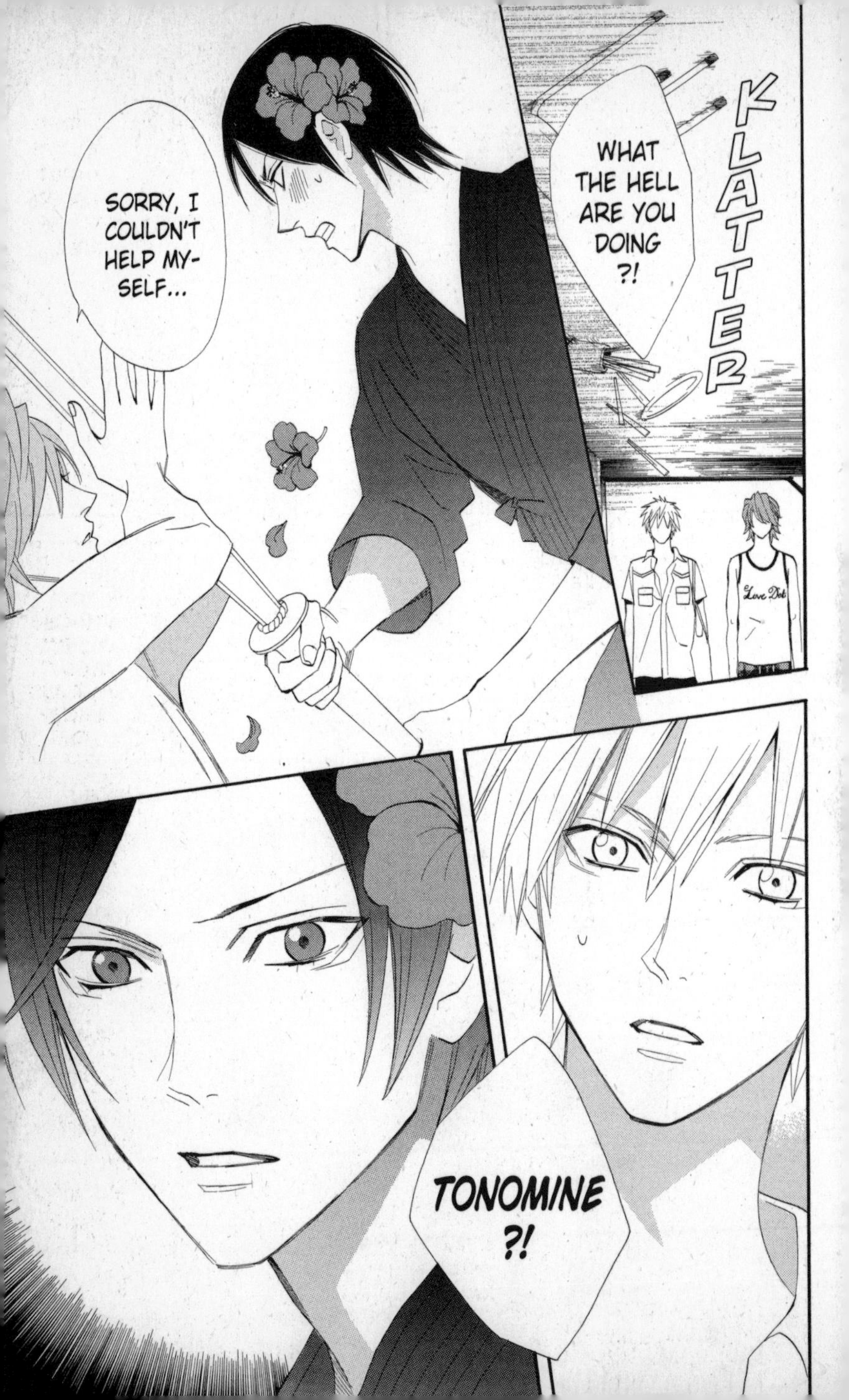
KLATTER
WHAT THE HELL ARE YOU DOING ?!
SORRY, I COULDN'T HELP MY-SELF...
TONOMINE ?!

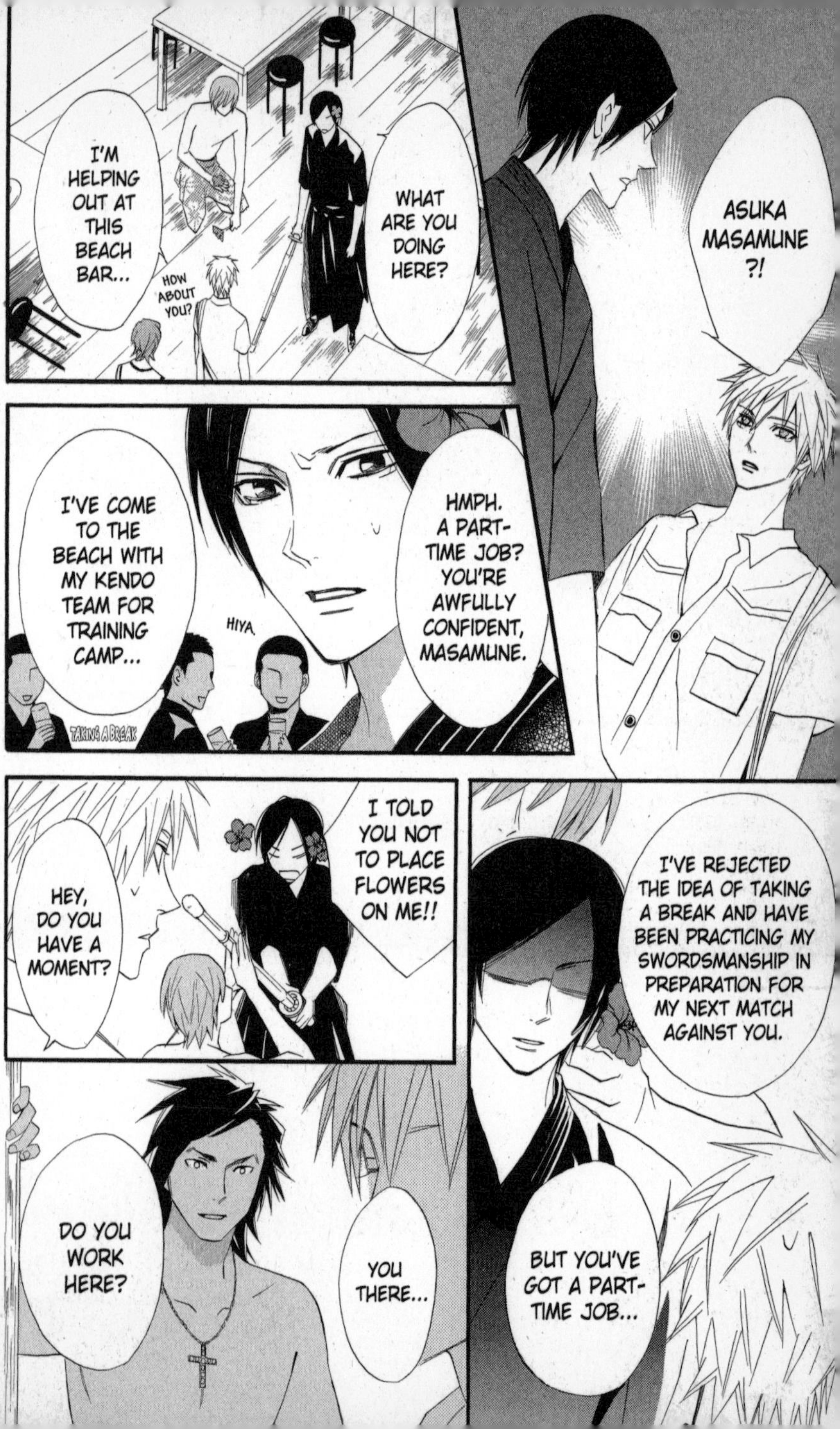
ASUKA MASAMUNE ?!
WHAT ARE YOU DOING HERE?
I'M HELPING OUT AT THIS BEACH BAR...
HOW ABOUT YOU?
HMPH. A PART-TIME JOB? YOU'RE AWFULLY CONFIDENT, MASAMUNE.
I'VE COME TO THE BEACH WITH MY KENDO TEAM FOR TRAINING CAMP...
HIYA.
TAKING A BREAK
I'VE REJECTED THE IDEA OF TAKING A BREAK AND HAVE BEEN PRACTICING MY SWORDSMANSHIP IN PREPARATION FOR MY NEXT MATCH AGAINST YOU.
BUT YOU'VE GOT A PART-TIME JOB...
I TOLD YOU NOT TO PLACE FLOWERS ON ME!!
HEY, DO YOU HAVE A MOMENT?
YOU THERE...
DO YOU WORK HERE?

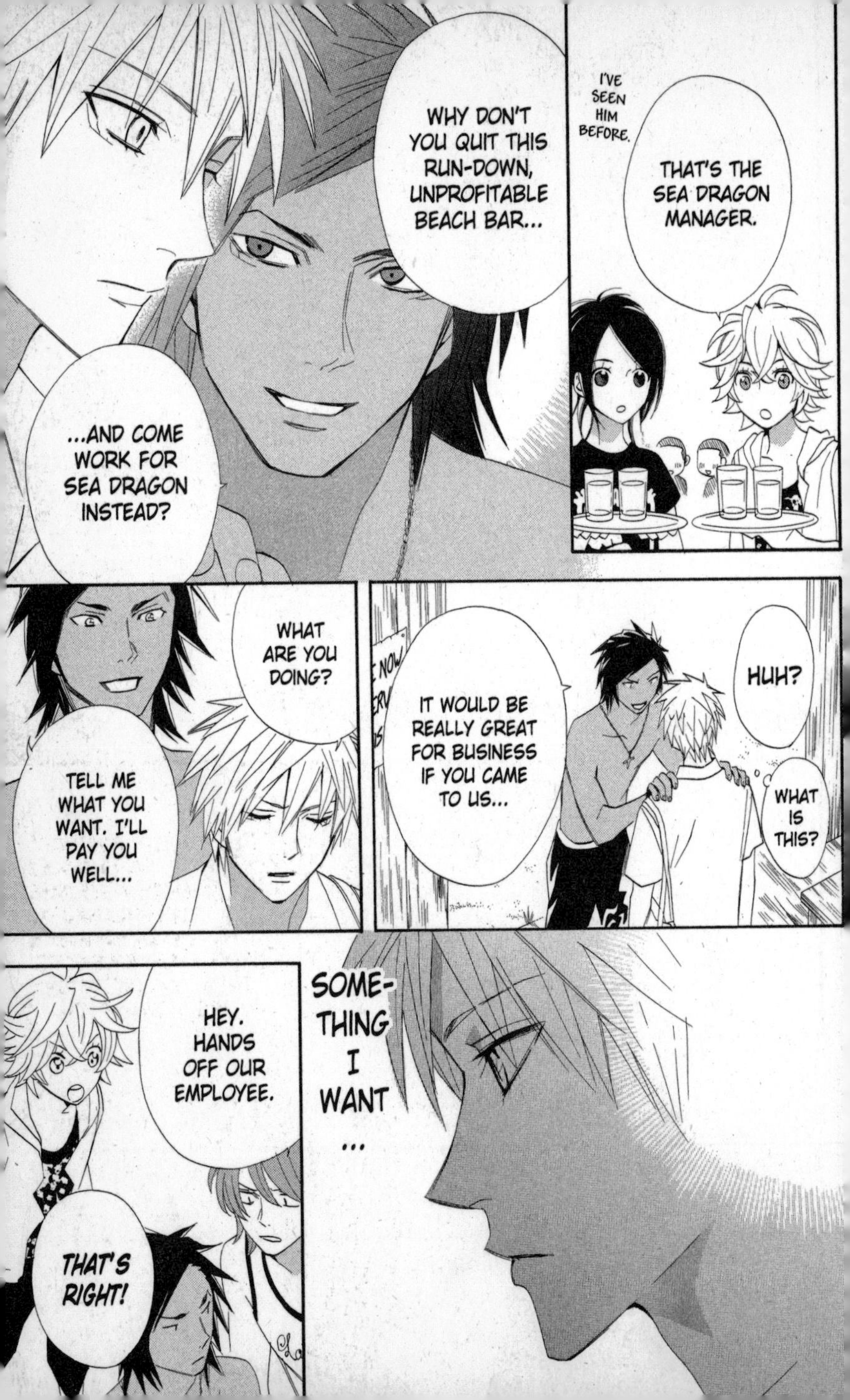
THAT'S THE SEA DRAGON MANAGER.
I'VE SEEN HIM BEFORE.
WHY DON'T YOU QUIT THIS RUN-DOWN, UNPROFITABLE BEACH BAR...
...AND COME WORK FOR SEA DRAGON INSTEAD?
HUH?
WHAT IS THIS?
IT WOULD BE REALLY GREAT FOR BUSINESS IF YOU CAME TO US...
WHAT ARE YOU DOING?
TELL ME WHAT YOU WANT. I'LL PAY YOU WELL...
SOME-THING I WANT ...
HEY. HANDS OFF OUR EMPLOYEE.
THAT'S RIGHT!

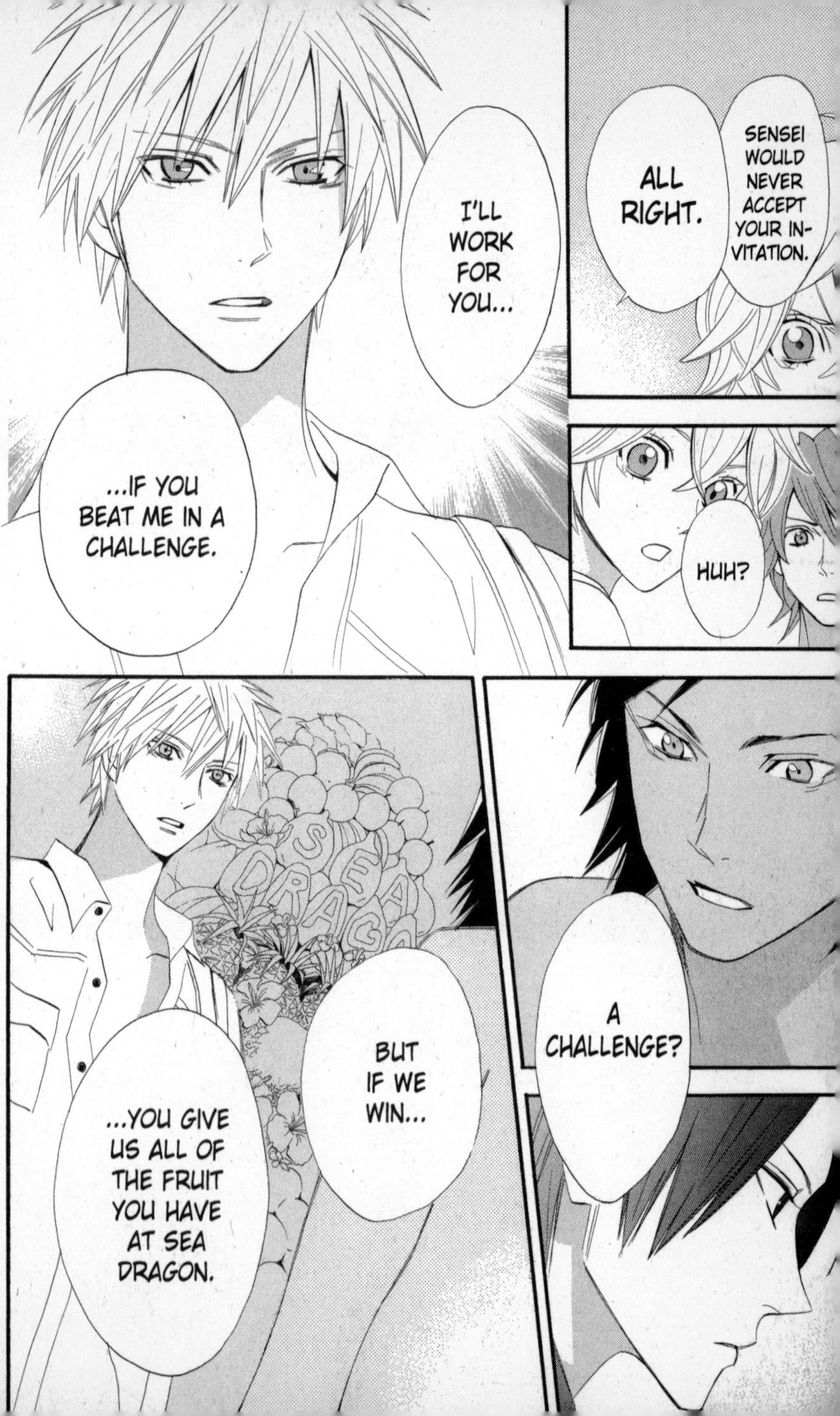
SENSEI WOULD NEVER ACCEPT YOUR IN-VITATION.
ALL RIGHT.
HUH?
I'LL WORK FOR YOU...
...IF YOU BEAT ME IN A CHALLENGE.
A CHALLENGE?
BUT IF WE WIN...
...YOU GIVE US ALL OF THE FRUIT YOU HAVE AT SEA DRAGON.

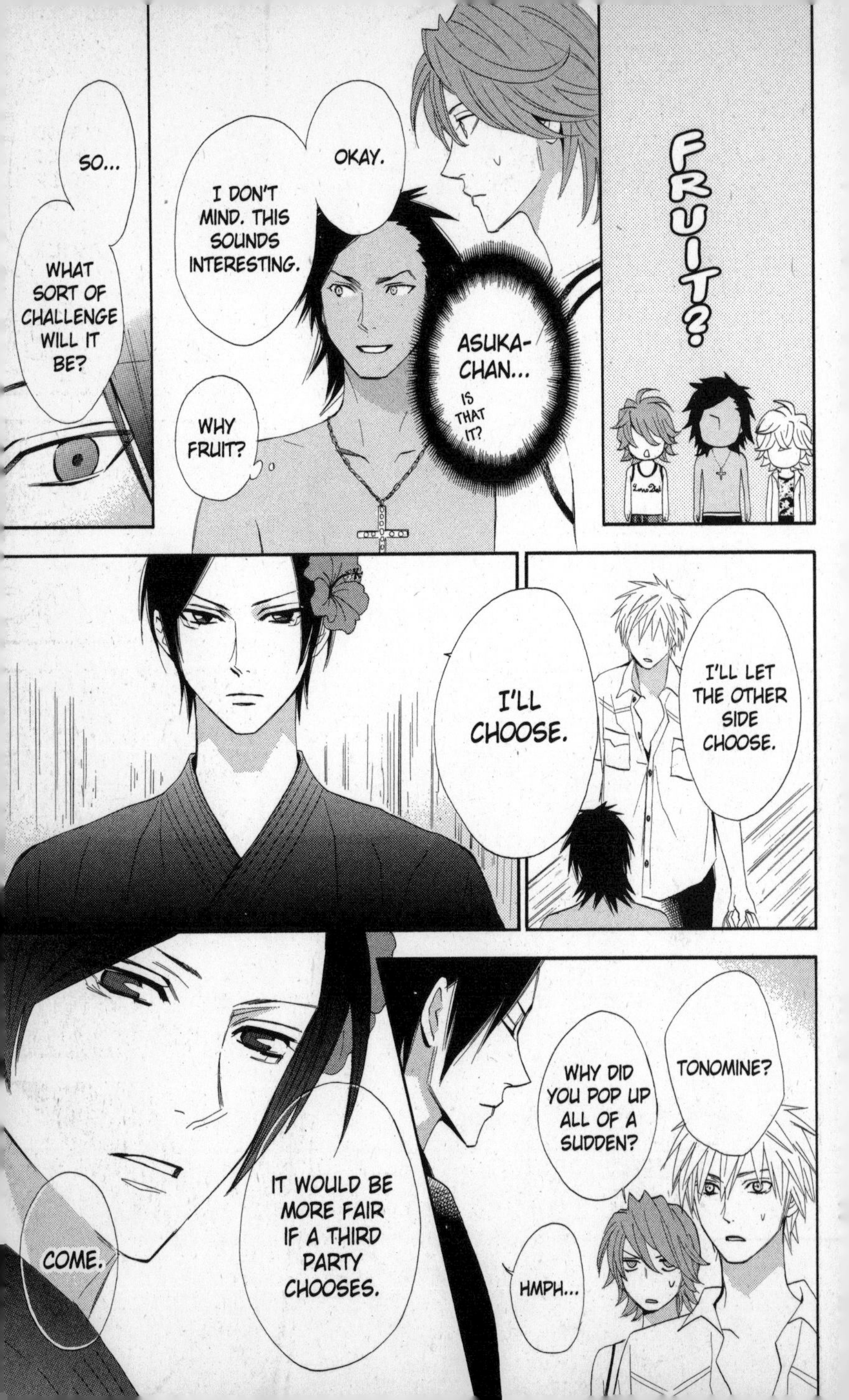
FRUIT?
ASUKA-CHAN... IS THAT IT?
OKAY.
I DON'T MIND. THIS SOUNDS INTERESTING.
WHY FRUIT?
SO...
WHAT SORT OF CHALLENGE WILL IT BE?
I'LL LET THE OTHER SIDE CHOOSE.
I'LL CHOOSE.
TONOMINE?
WHY DID YOU POP UP ALL OF A SUDDEN?
HMPH...
IT WOULD BE MORE FAIR IF A THIRD PARTY CHOOSES.
COME.

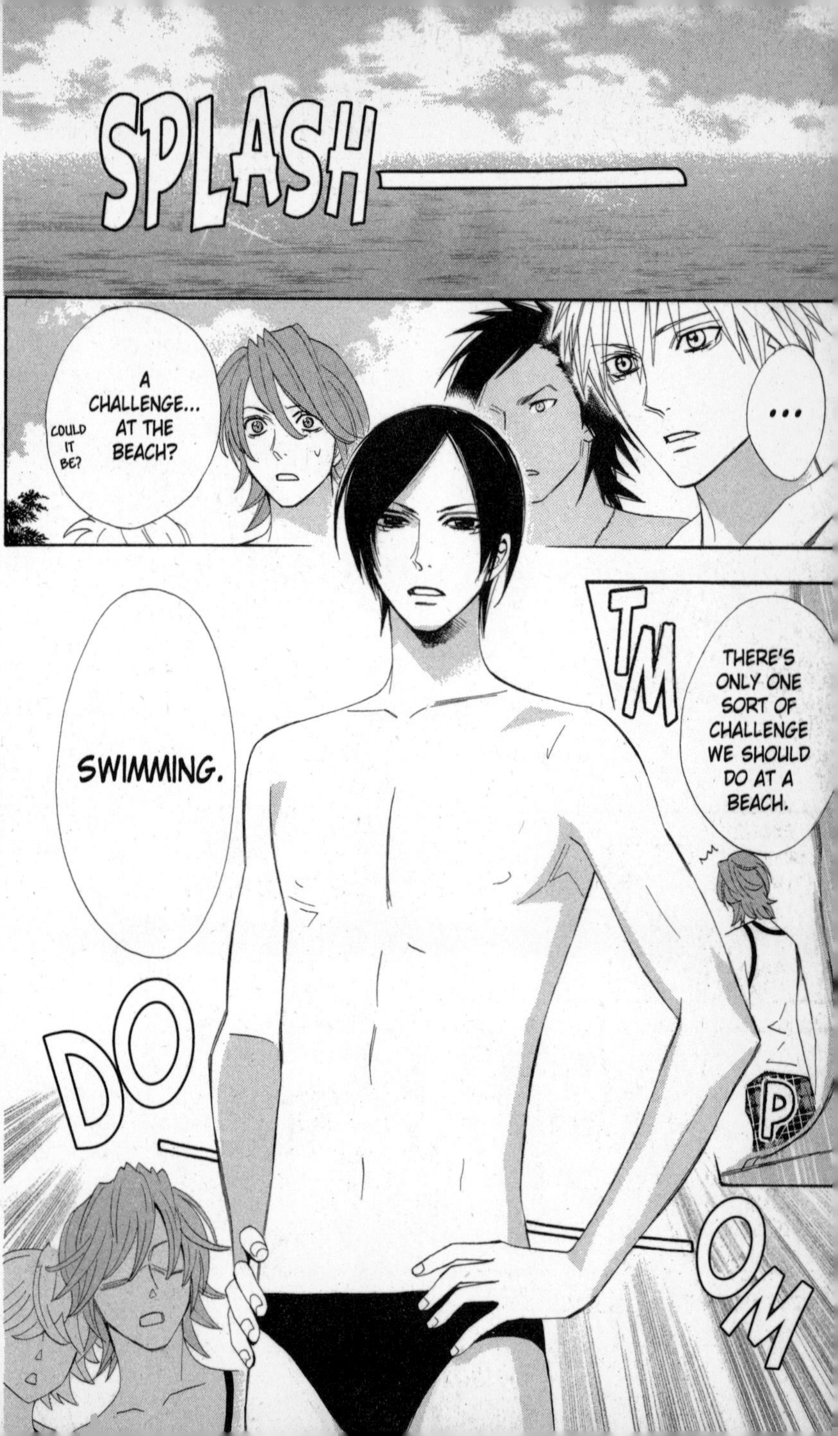
SPLASH——
...
A CHALLENGE... AT THE BEACH?
COULD IT BE?
TM
THERE'S ONLY ONE SORT OF CHALLENGE WE SHOULD DO AT A BEACH.
SWIMMING.
DO——OM

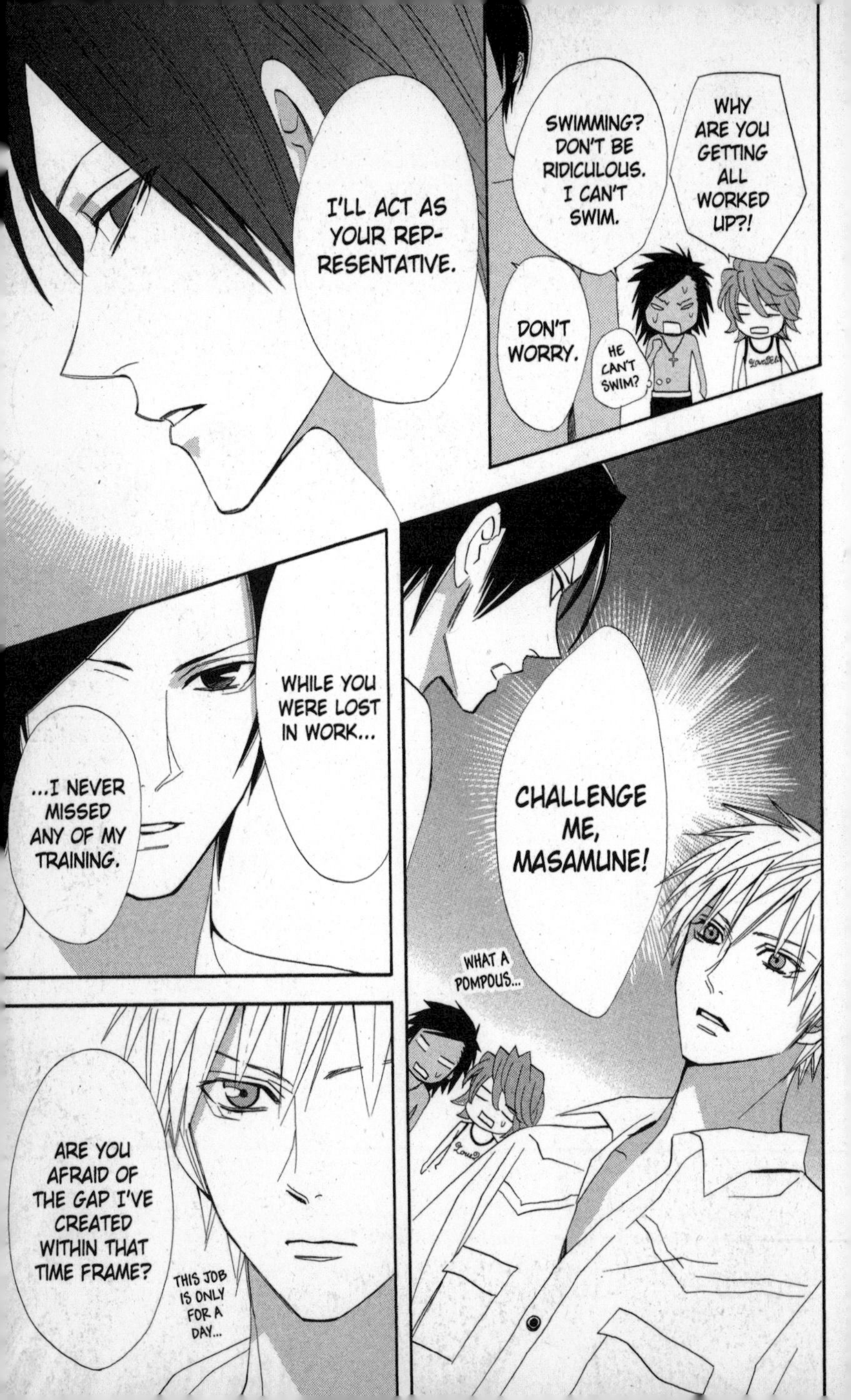
WHY ARE YOU GETTING ALL WORKED UP?!
SWIMMING? DON'T BE RIDICULOUS. I CAN'T SWIM.
DON'T WORRY.
HE CAN'T SWIM?
I'LL ACT AS YOUR REP-RESENTATIVE.
CHALLENGE ME, MASAMUNE!
WHAT A POMPOUS...
WHILE YOU WERE LOST IN WORK...
...I NEVER MISSED ANY OF MY TRAINING.
ARE YOU AFRAID OF THE GAP I'VE CREATED WITHIN THAT TIME FRAME?
THIS JOB IS ONLY FOR A DAY...

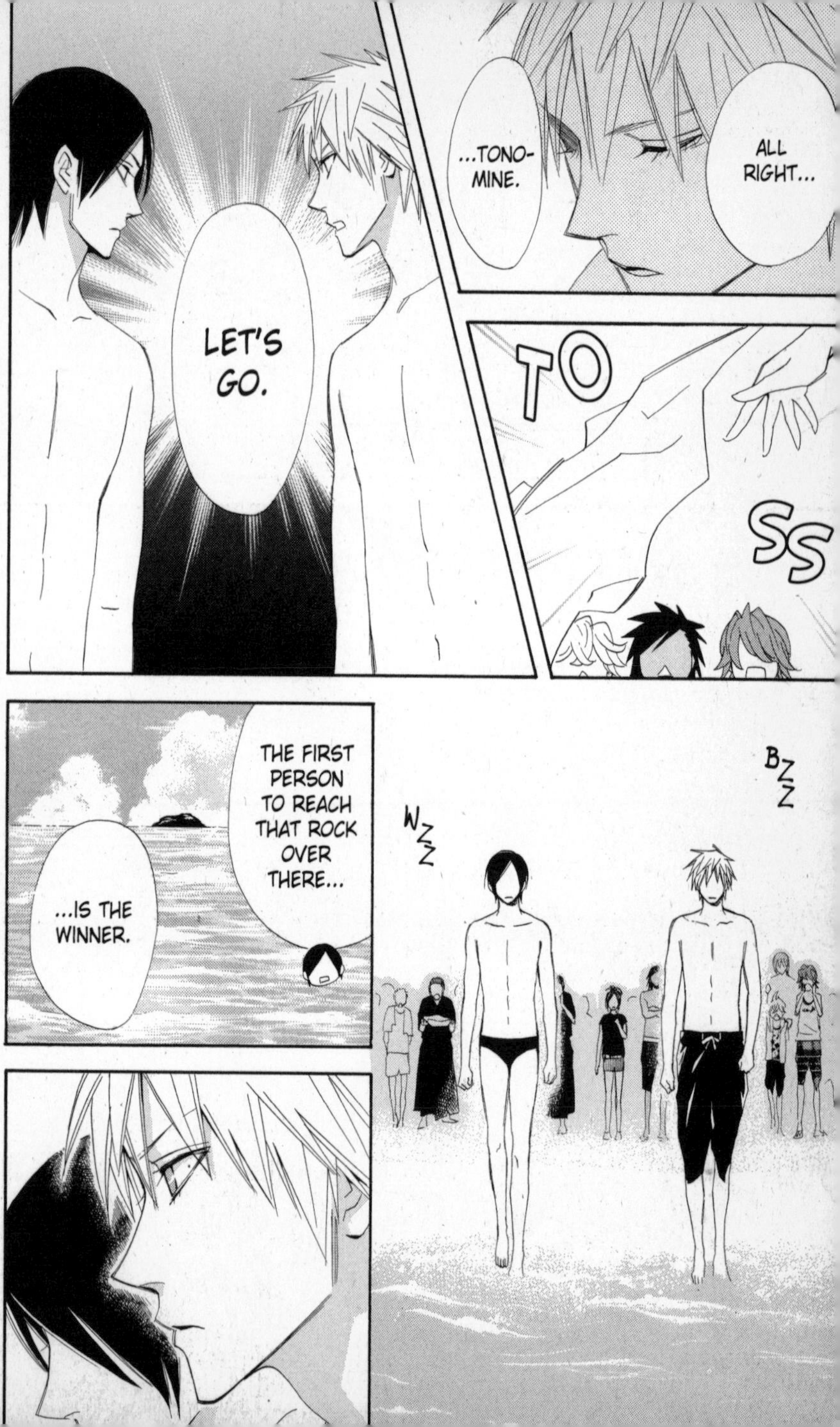
ALL RIGHT...
...TONO-MINE.
TO
SS
LET'S GO.
BZZ
WZZ
THE FIRST PERSON TO REACH THAT ROCK OVER THERE...
...IS THE WINNER.

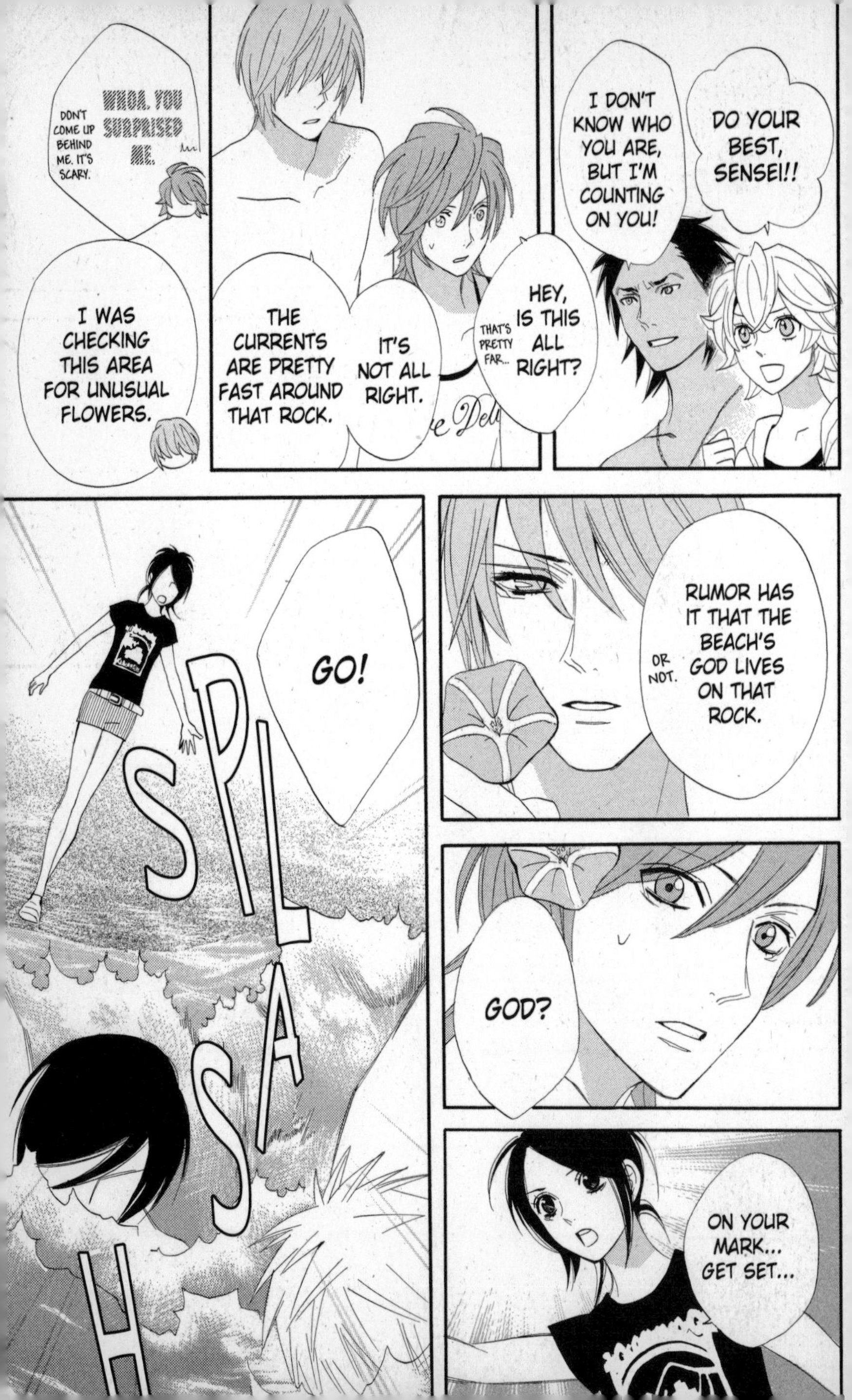
DO YOUR BEST, SENSEI!!
I DON'T KNOW WHO YOU ARE, BUT I'M COUNTING ON YOU!
HEY, IS THIS ALL RIGHT?
THAT'S PRETTY FAR...
IT'S NOT ALL RIGHT.
THE CURRENTS ARE PRETTY FAST AROUND THAT ROCK.
WHOA. YOU SURPRISED ME.
DON'T COME UP BEHIND ME. IT'S SCARY.
I WAS CHECKING THIS AREA FOR UNUSUAL FLOWERS.
RUMOR HAS IT THAT THE BEACH'S GOD LIVES ON THAT ROCK.
OR NOT.
GOD?
ON YOUR MARK... GET SET...
GO!
SPLASH

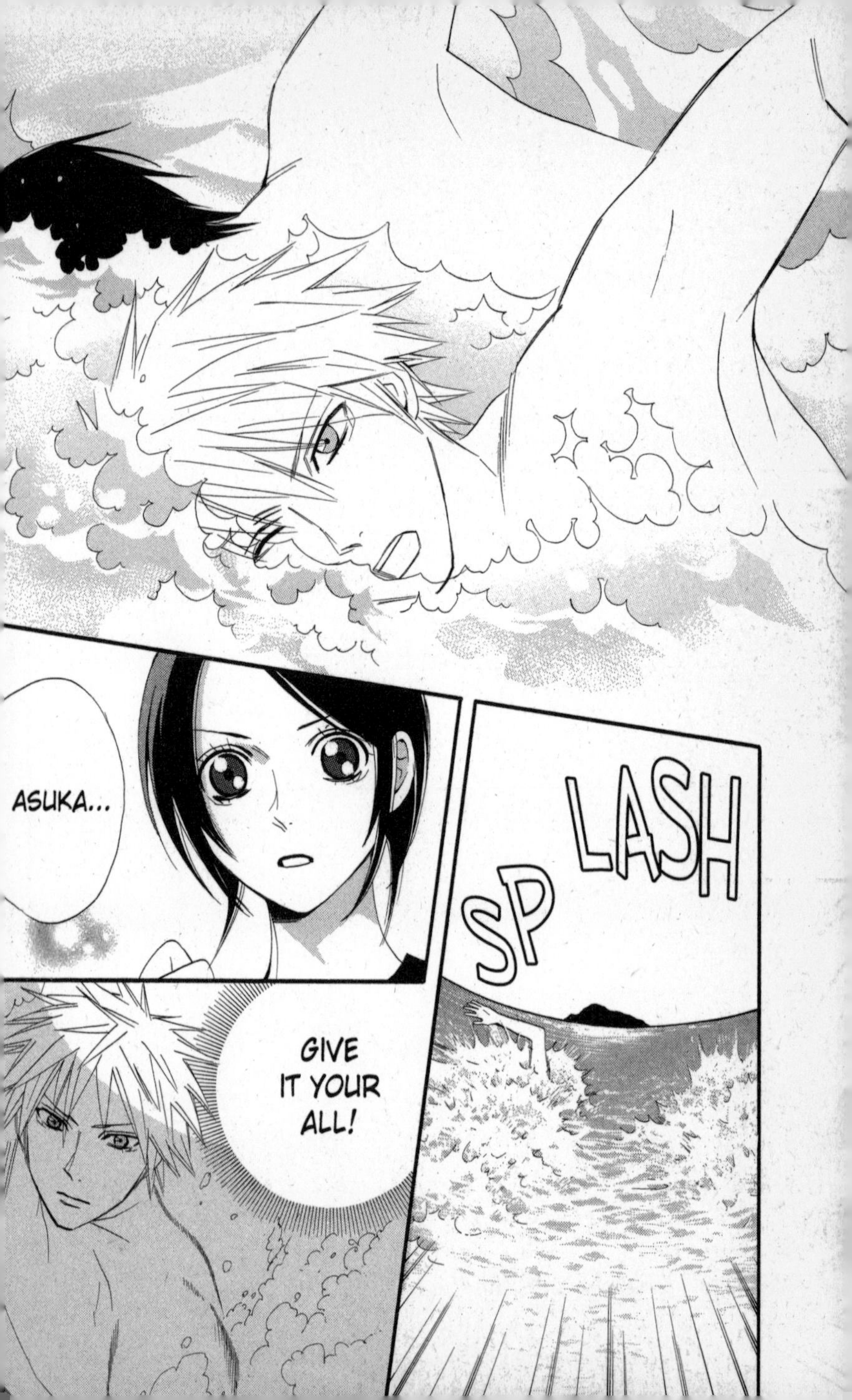
SPLASH
ASUKA...
GIVE IT YOUR ALL!

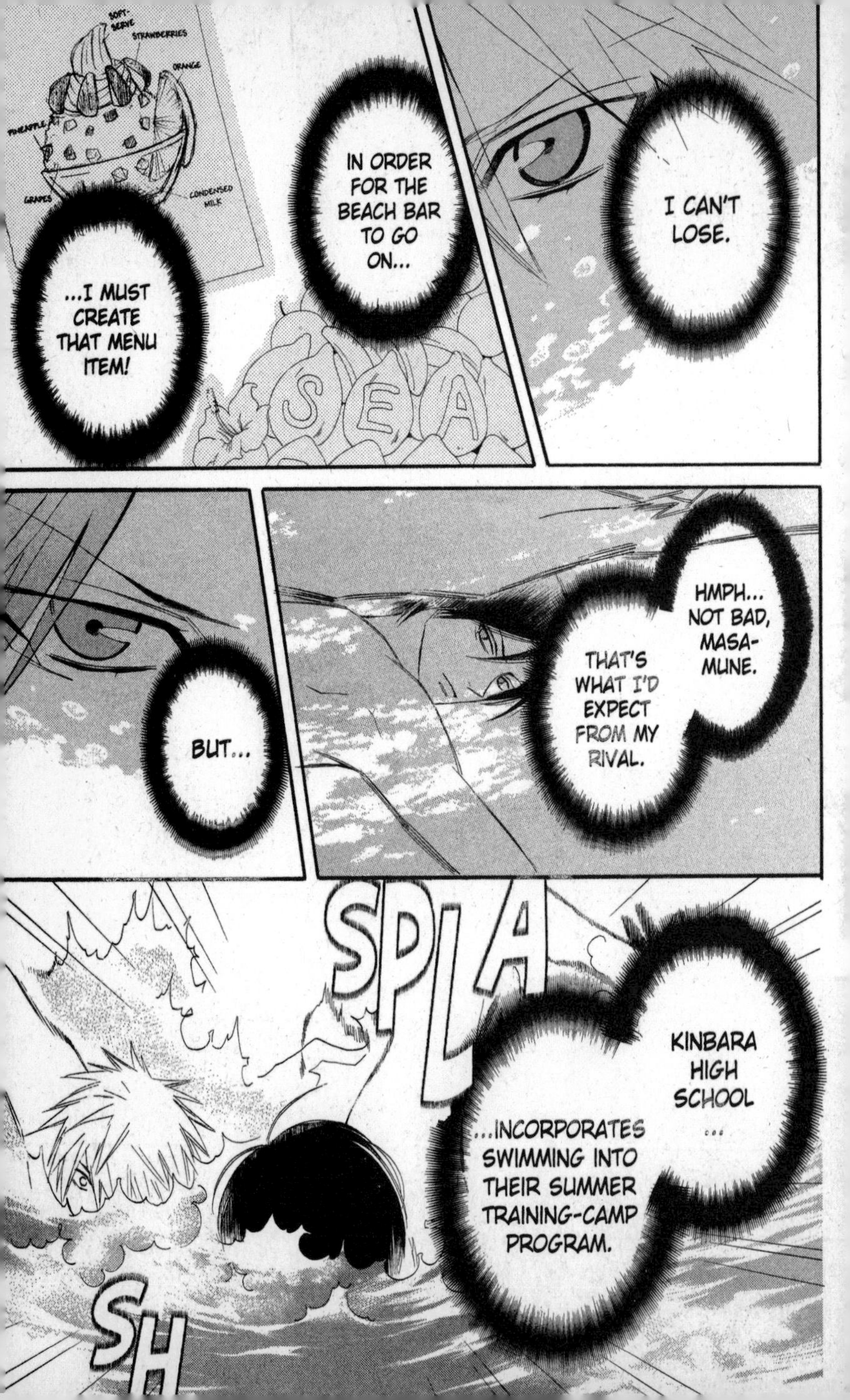
I CAN'T LOSE.
IN ORDER FOR THE BEACH BAR TO GO ON...
SOFT-SERVE
STRAWBERRIES
ORANGE
PINEAPPLE
GRAPES
CONDENSED MILK
SEA
...I MUST CREATE THAT MENU ITEM!
HMPH... NOT BAD, MASAMUNE.
THAT'S WHAT I'D EXPECT FROM MY RIVAL.
BUT...
SPLA
KINBARA HIGH SCHOOL...
...INCORPORATES SWIMMING INTO THEIR SUMMER TRAINING-CAMP PROGRAM.
SH

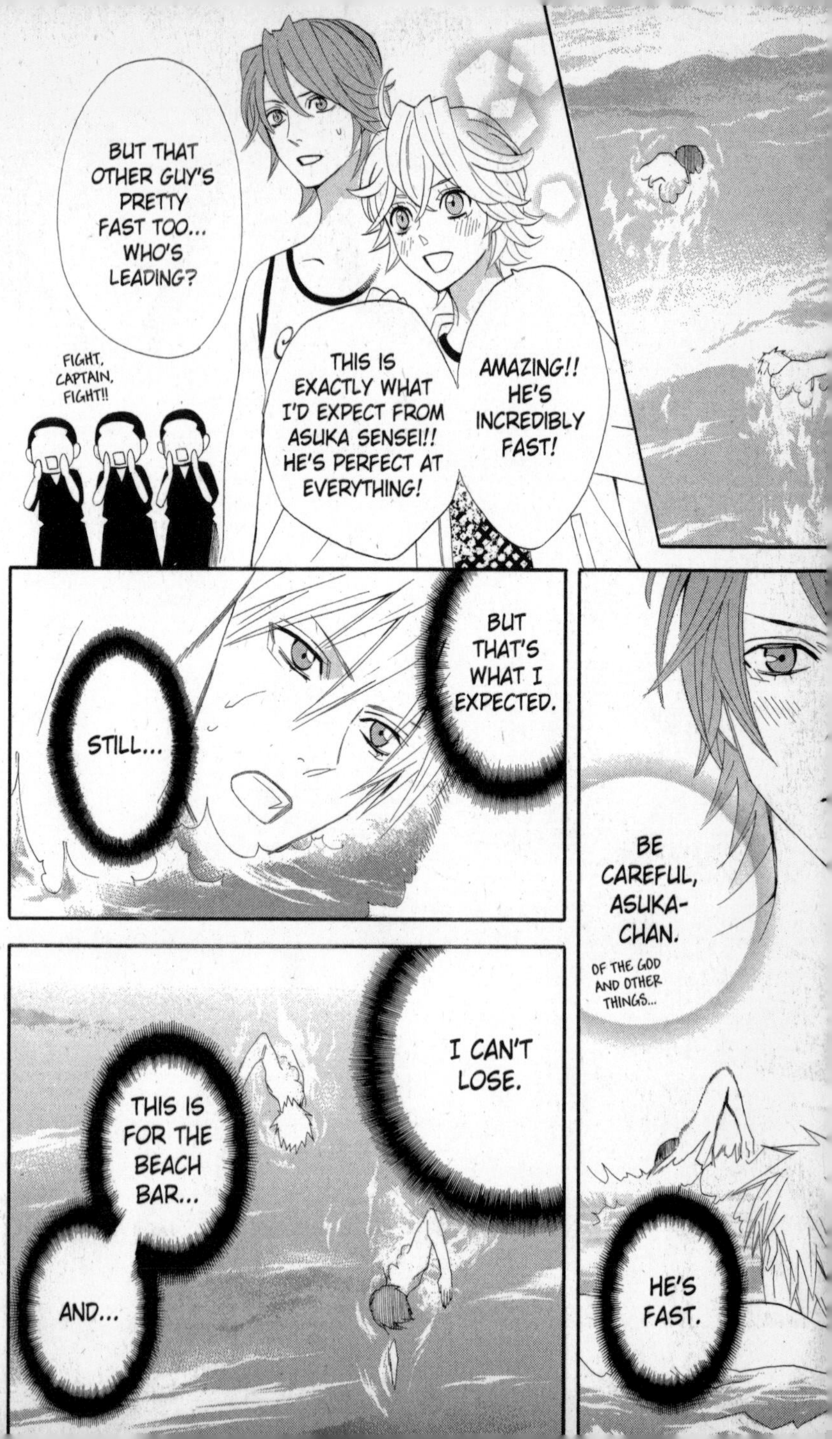
AMAZING!! HE'S INCREDIBLY FAST!
THIS IS EXACTLY WHAT I'D EXPECT FROM ASUKA SENSEI!! HE'S PERFECT AT EVERYTHING!
BUT THAT OTHER GUY'S PRETTY FAST TOO... WHO'S LEADING?
FIGHT, CAPTAIN, FIGHT!!
BE CAREFUL, ASUKA-CHAN.
OF THE GOD AND OTHER THINGS...
HE'S FAST.
BUT THAT'S WHAT I EXPECTED.
STILL...
I CAN'T LOSE.
THIS IS FOR THE BEACH BAR...
AND...

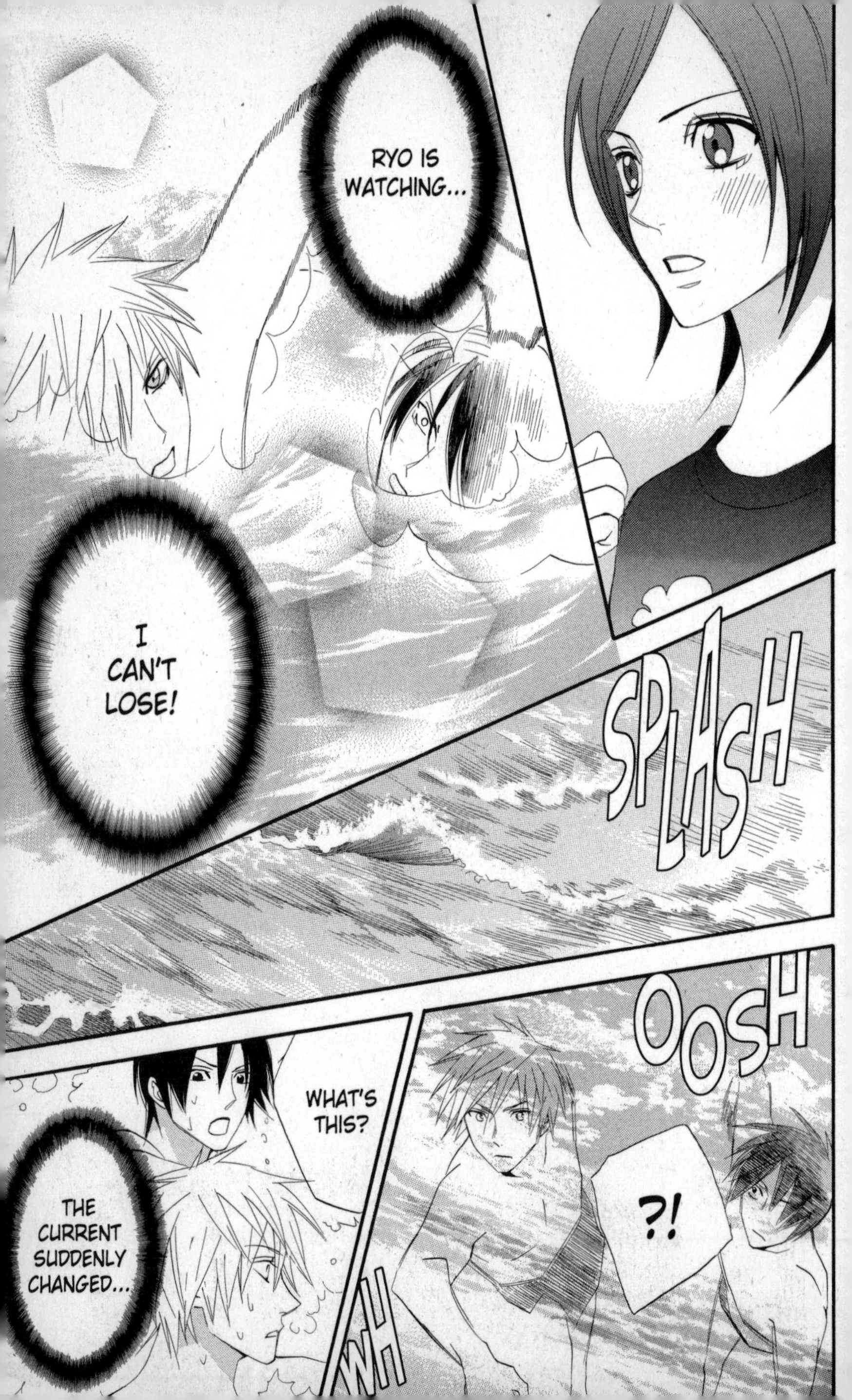
RYO IS WATCHING...
I CAN'T LOSE!
SPLASH
WH
OOSH
?!
WHAT'S THIS?
THE CURRENT SUDDENLY CHANGED...

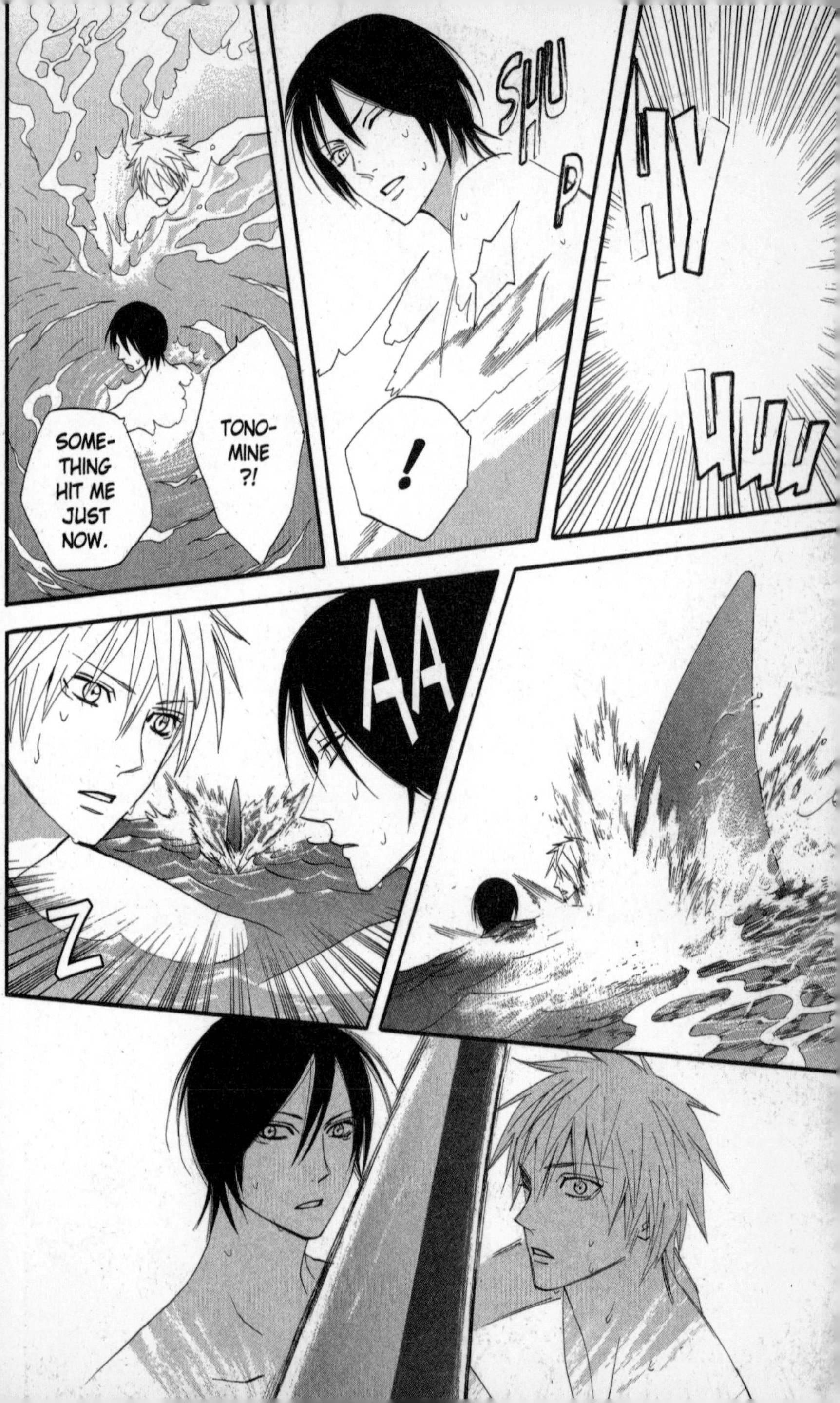

HYUUU
SHUP
!
TONO-MINE?!
SOME-THING HIT ME JUST NOW.
AA
Z

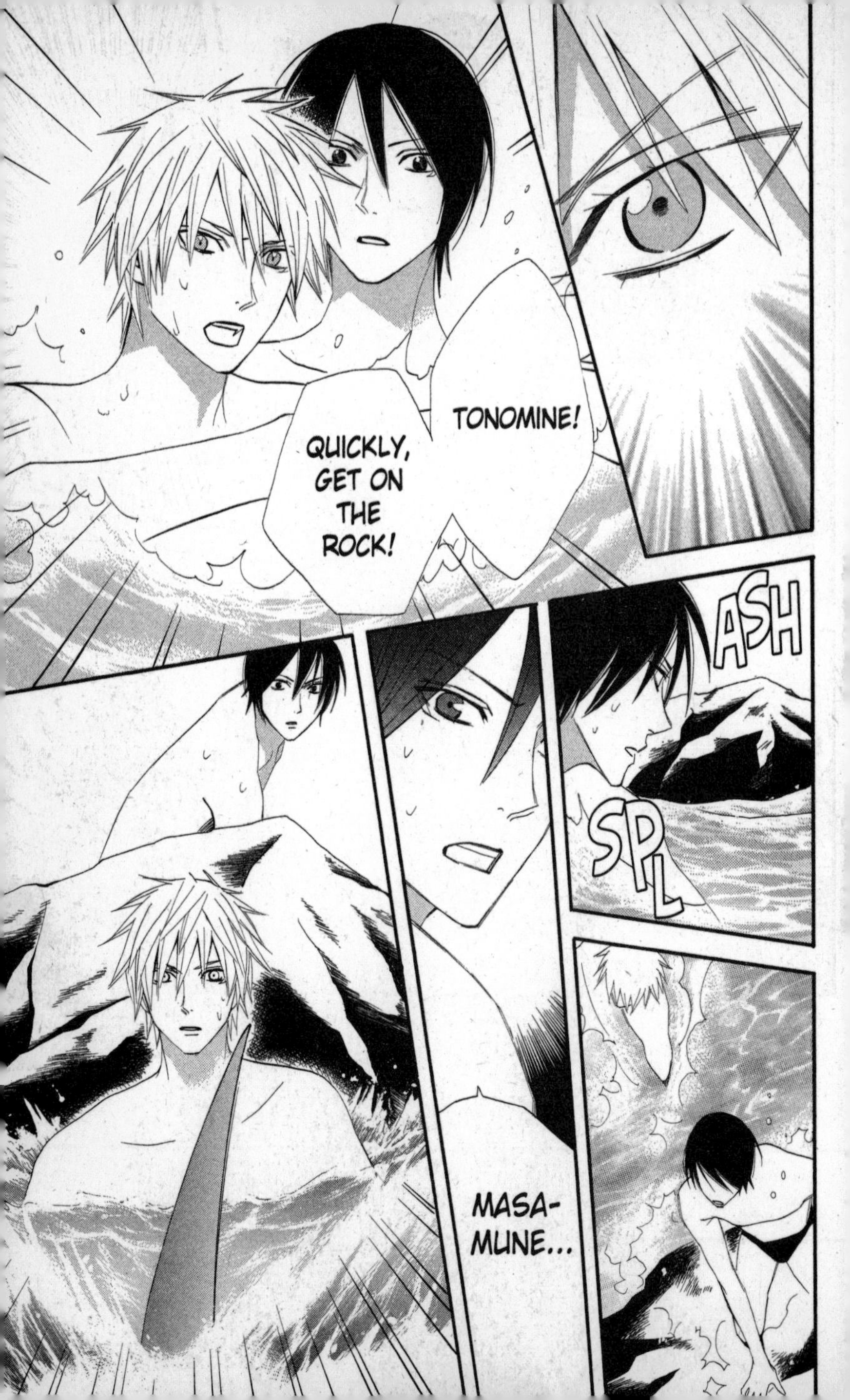

TONOMINE!
QUICKLY, GET ON THE ROCK!
SPLASH
MASA-MUNE...

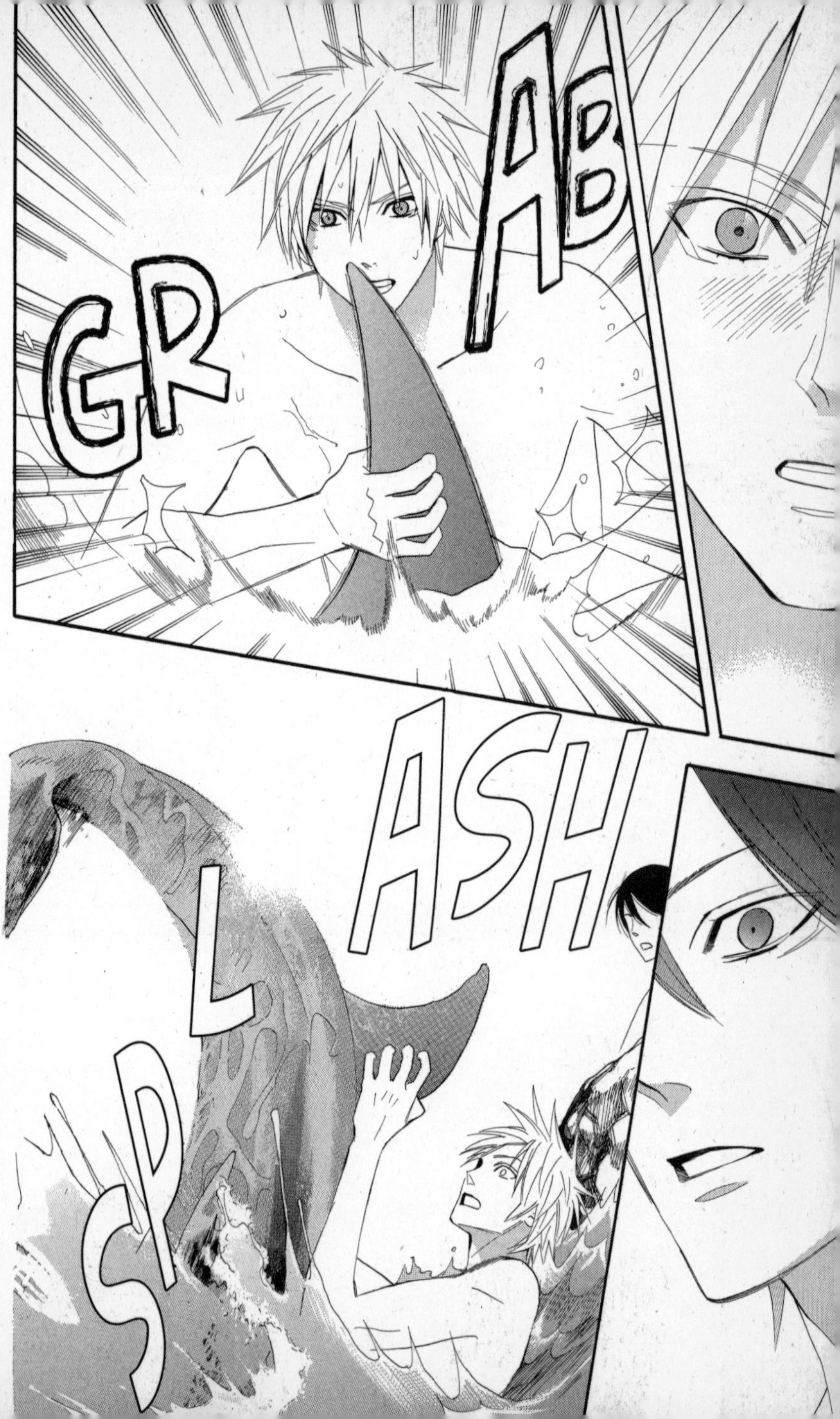
GRAB
SPLASH

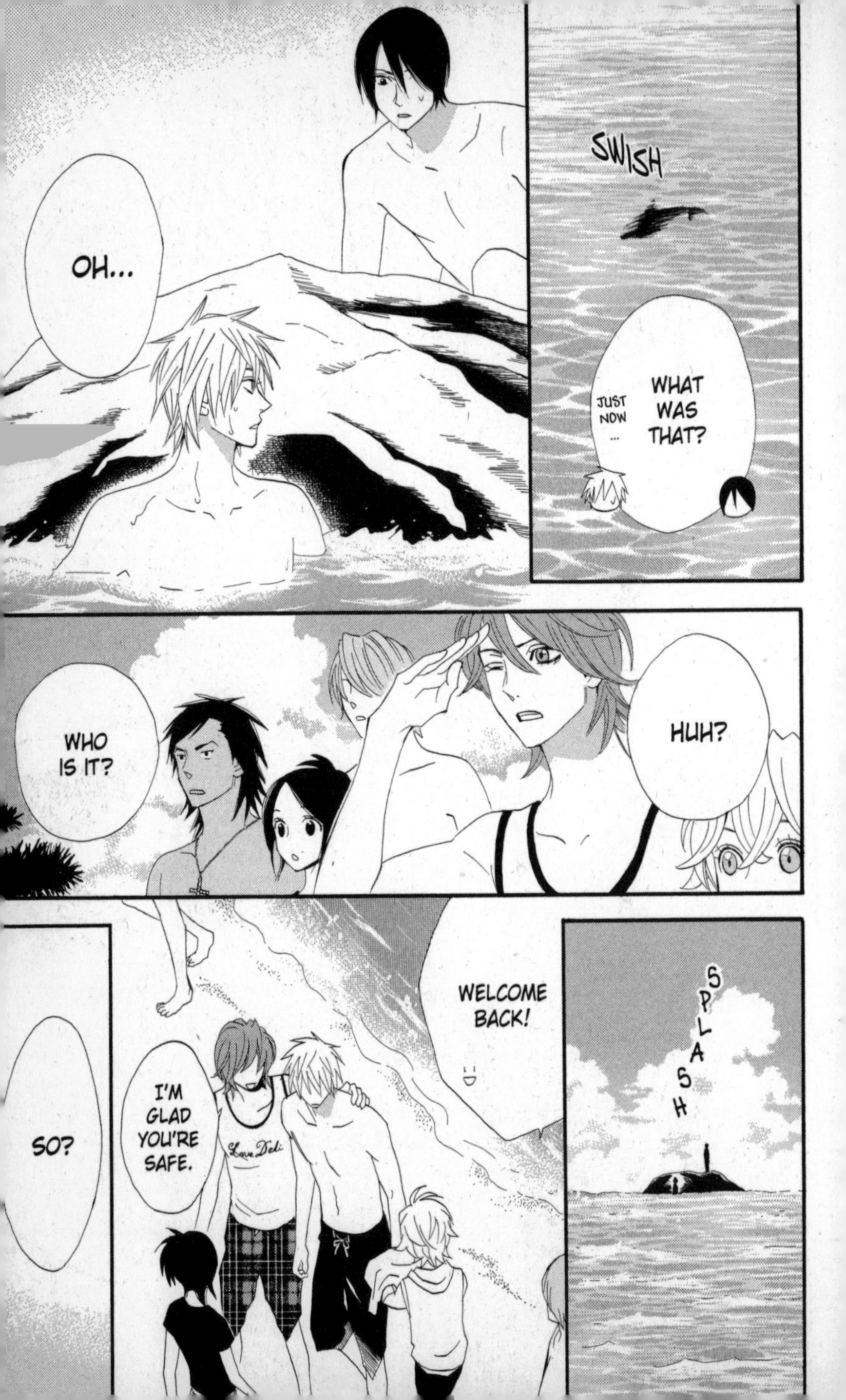
SWISH
WHAT WAS THAT?
JUST NOW...
OH...
HUH?
WHO IS IT?
SPLASH
WELCOME BACK!
I'M GLAD YOU'RE SAFE.
Love Deli
SO?

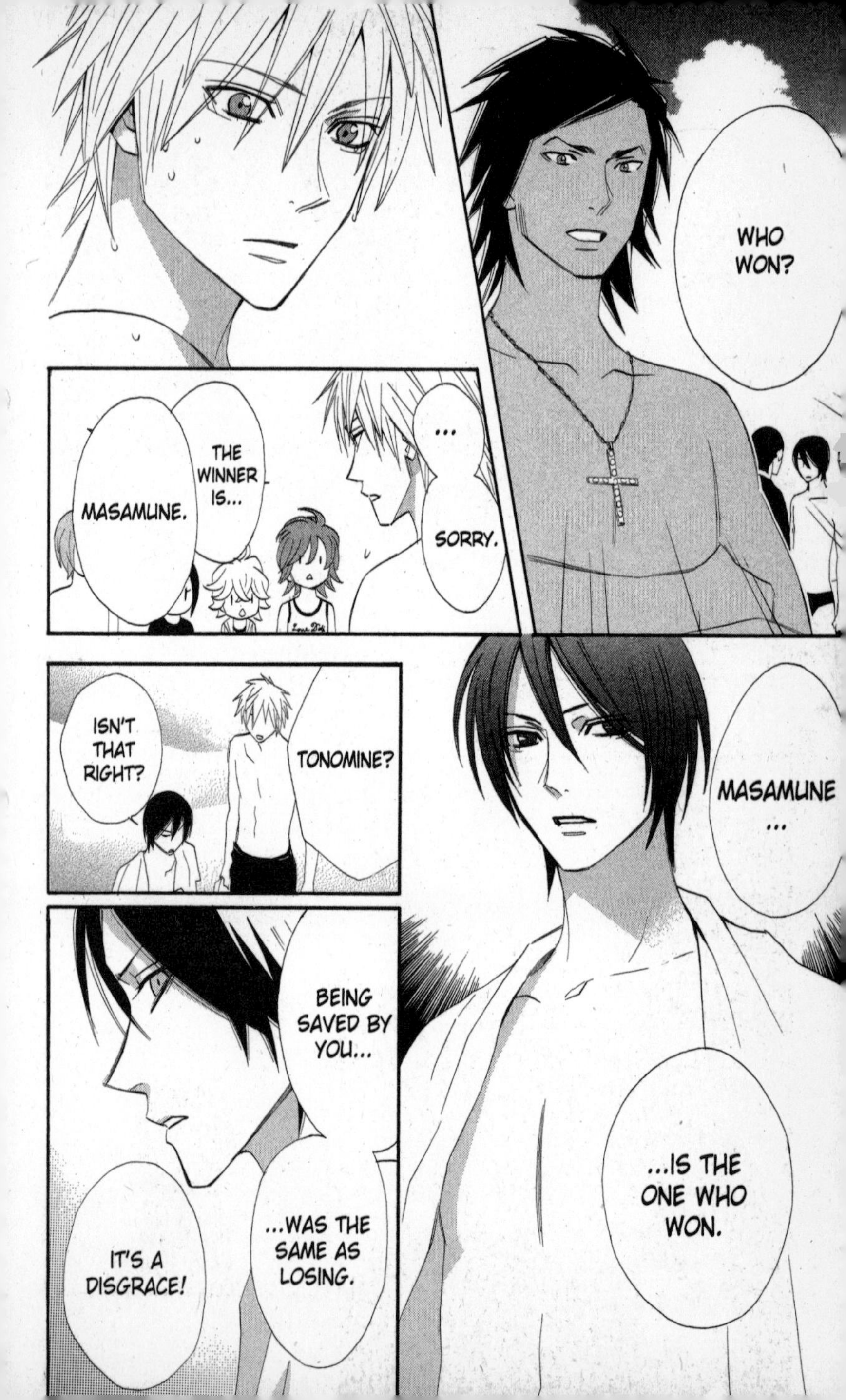
WHO WON?
...
SORRY.
THE WINNER IS...
MASAMUNE.
MASAMUNE ...
...IS THE ONE WHO WON.
TONOMINE?
ISN'T THAT RIGHT?
BEING SAVED BY YOU...
...WAS THE SAME AS LOSING.
IT'S A DISGRACE!

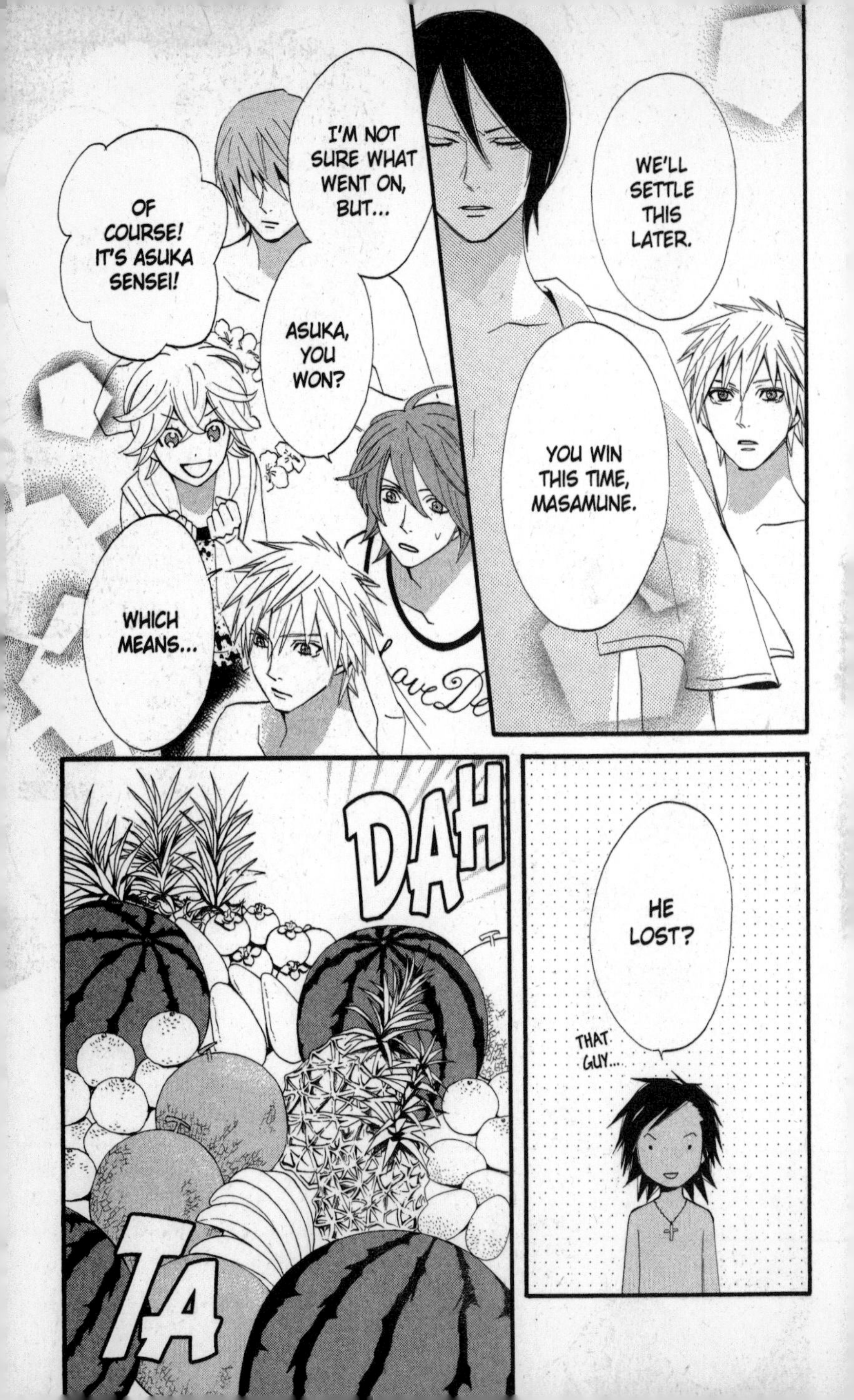
WE'LL SETTLE THIS LATER.
YOU WIN THIS TIME, MASAMUNE.
I'M NOT SURE WHAT WENT ON, BUT...
ASUKA, YOU WON?
OF COURSE! IT'S ASUKA SENSEI!
WHICH MEANS...
THAT GUY...
HE LOST?
DAH
TA

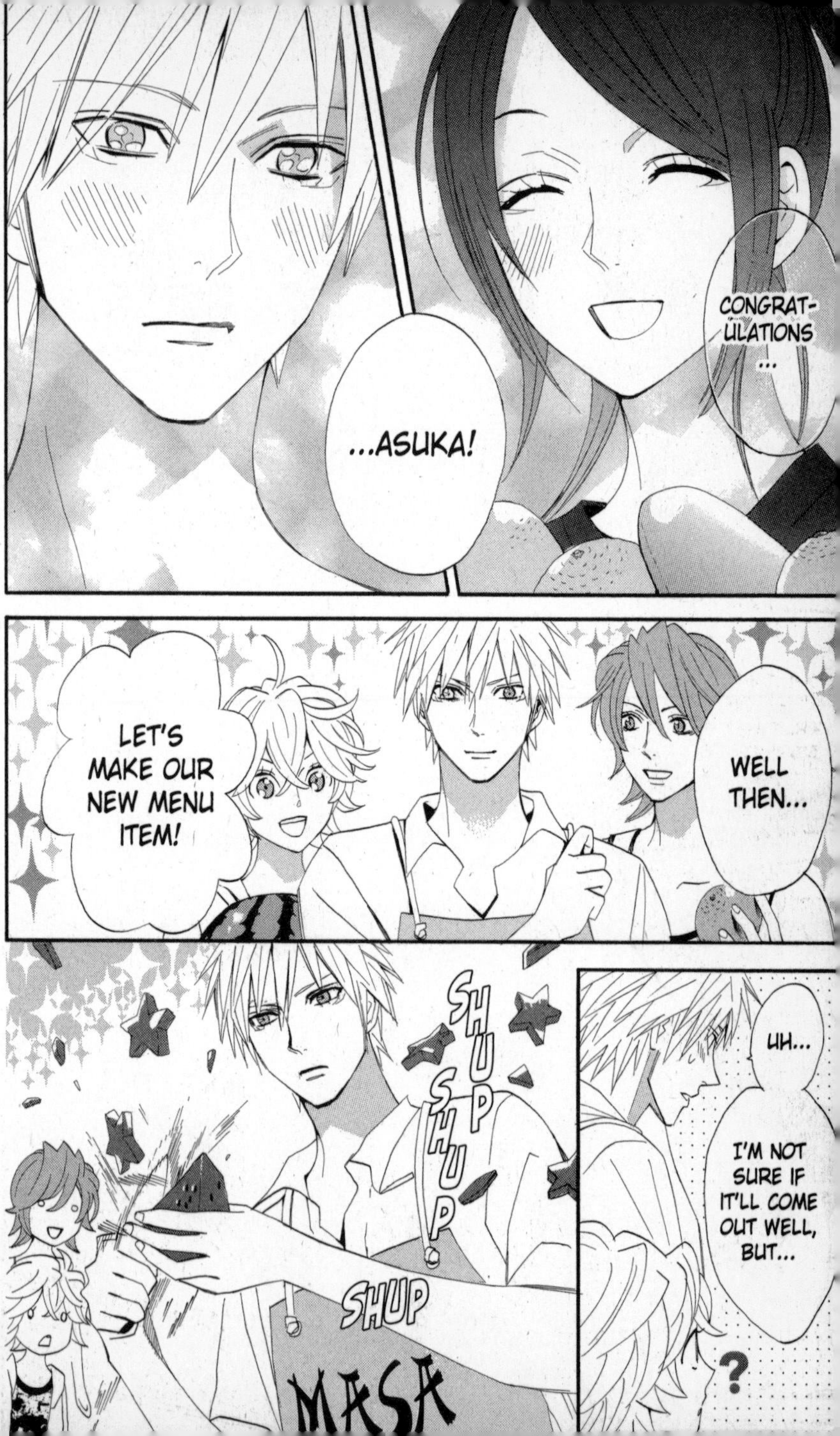
CONGRAT-ULATIONS...
...ASUKA!
WELL THEN...
LET'S MAKE OUR NEW MENU ITEM!
UH...
I'M NOT SURE IF IT'LL COME OUT WELL, BUT...
?
SHUP
SHUP
SHUP
MASA

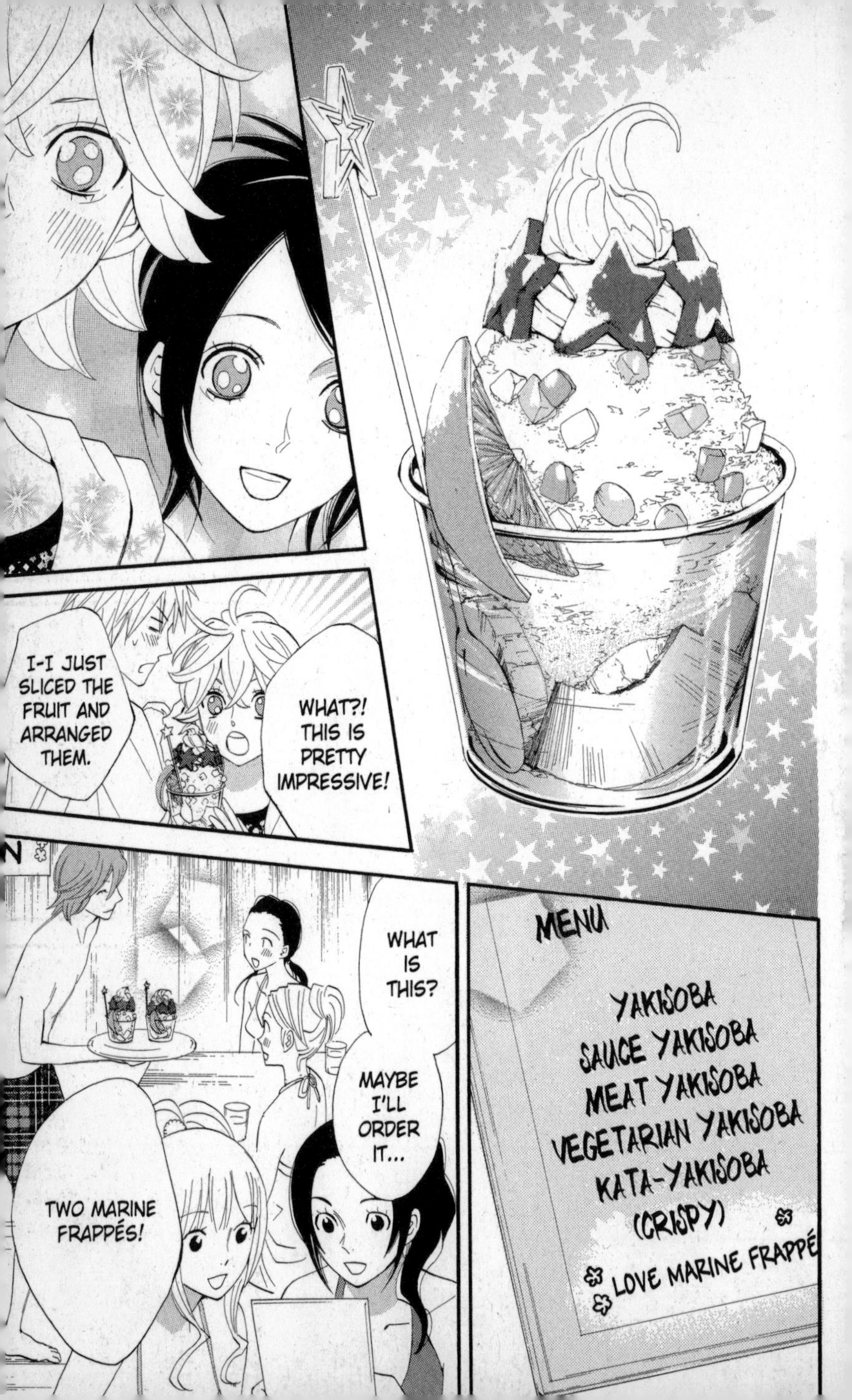
WHAT?! THIS IS PRETTY IMPRESSIVE!
I-I JUST SLICED THE FRUIT AND ARRANGED THEM.
MENU
YAKISOBA
SAUCE YAKISOBA
MEAT YAKISOBA
VEGETARIAN YAKISOBA
KATA-YAKISOBA (CRISPY)
LOVE MARINE FRAPPÉ
WHAT IS THIS?
MAYBE I'LL ORDER IT...
TWO MARINE FRAPPÉS!

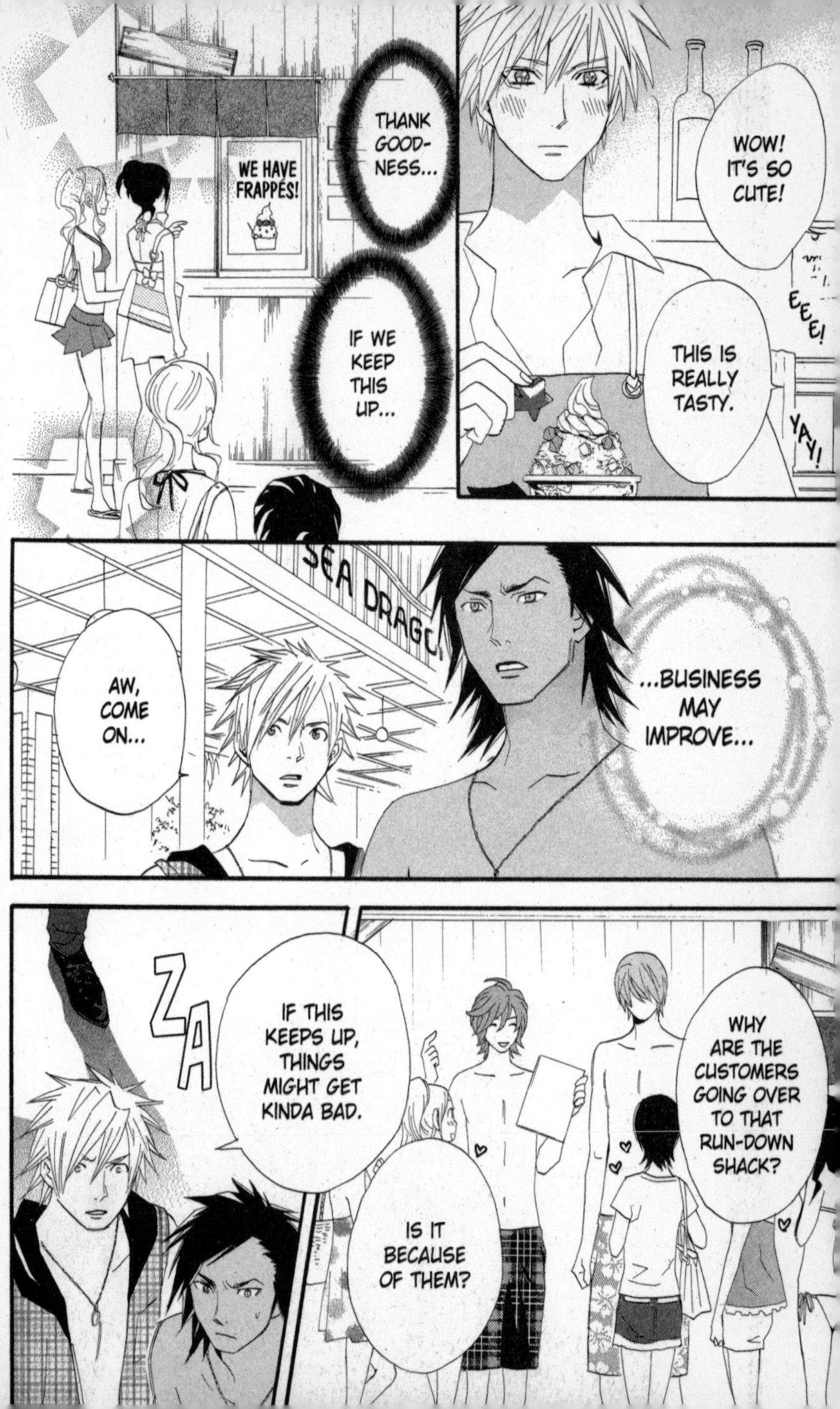
WOW! IT'S SO CUTE!
EEE!
THIS IS REALLY TASTY.
YAY!
WE HAVE FRAPPÉS!
THANK GOODNESS...
IF WE KEEP THIS UP...
...BUSINESS MAY IMPROVE...
SEA DRAGO
AW, COME ON...
WHY ARE THE CUSTOMERS GOING OVER TO THAT RUN-DOWN SHACK?
IS IT BECAUSE OF THEM?
IF THIS KEEPS UP, THINGS MIGHT GET KINDA BAD.
ZA

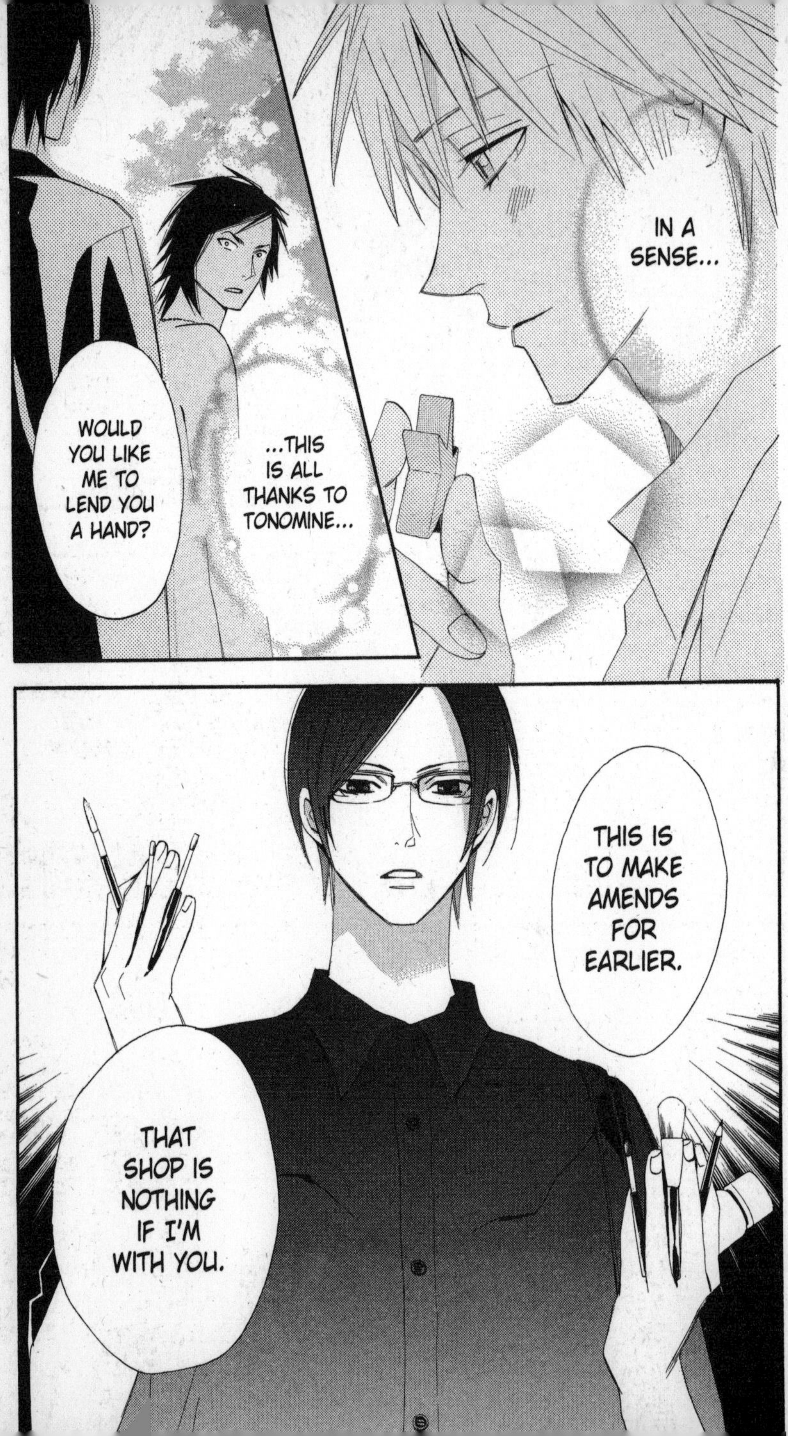
IN A SENSE...
...THIS IS ALL THANKS TO TONOMINE...
WOULD YOU LIKE ME TO LEND YOU A HAND?
THIS IS TO MAKE AMENDS FOR EARLIER.
THAT SHOP IS NOTHING IF I'M WITH YOU.

OTOMEN

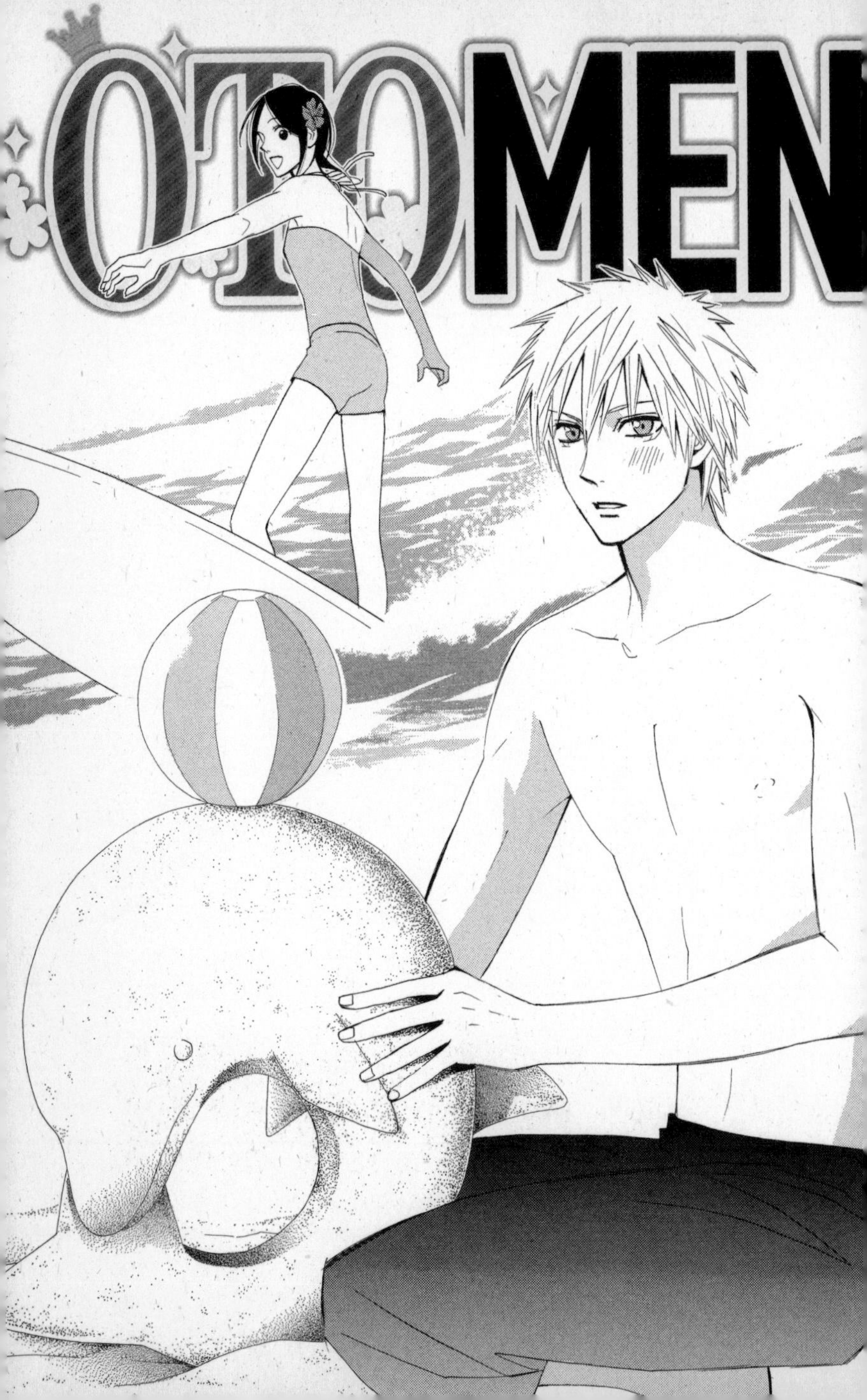
OTOMEN

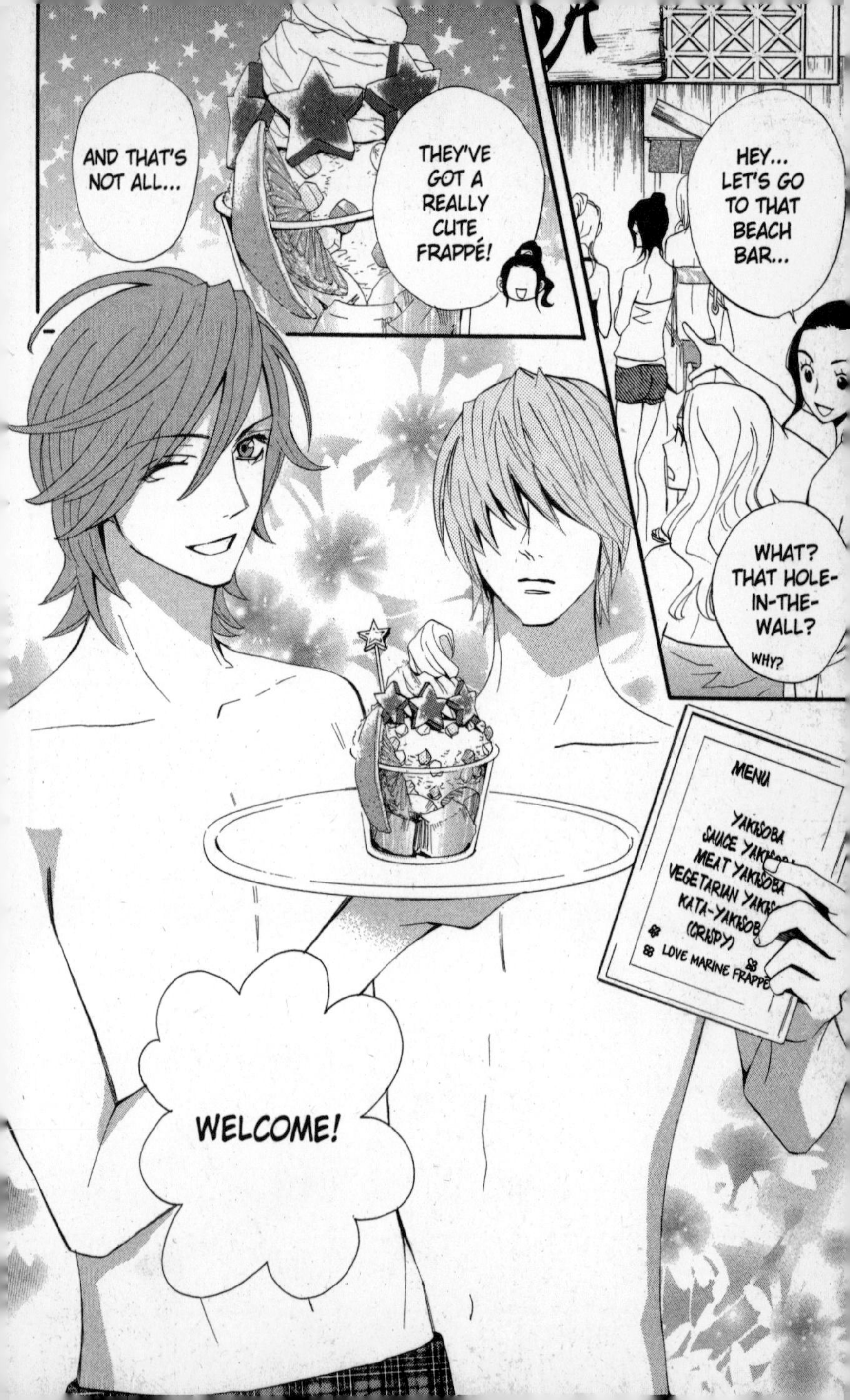
HEY... LET'S GO TO THAT BEACH BAR...
WHAT? THAT HOLE-IN-THE-WALL?
WHY?
THEY'VE GOT A REALLY CUTE FRAPPÉ!
AND THAT'S NOT ALL...
MENU
YAKISOBA
SAUCE YAKISOB
MEAT YAKISOBA
VEGETARIAN YAKIS
KATA-YAKISOBA
(CRISPY)
LOVE MARINE FRAPPÉ
WELCOME!

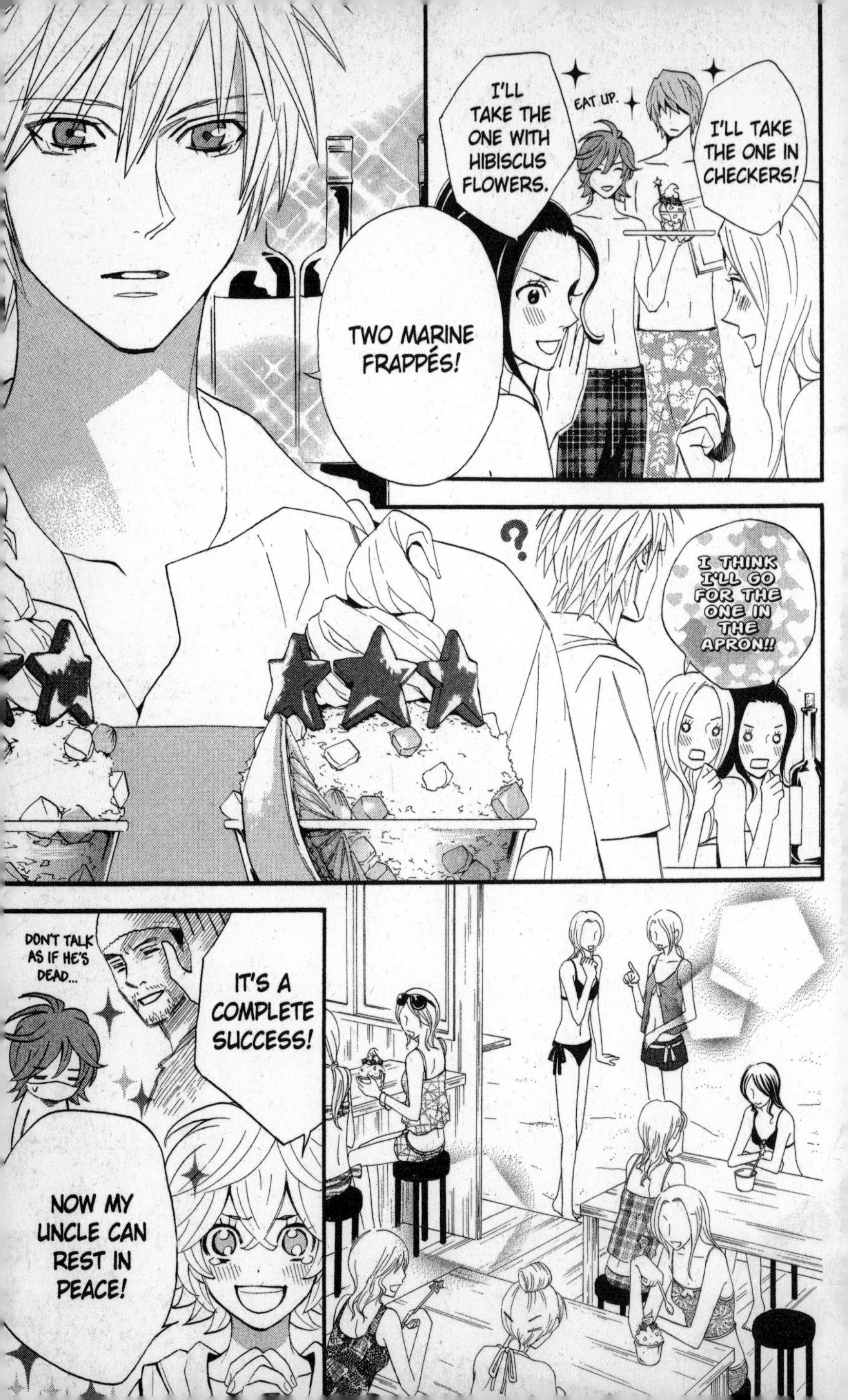
I'LL TAKE THE ONE IN CHECKERS!
EAT UP.
I'LL TAKE THE ONE WITH HIBISCUS FLOWERS.
TWO MARINE FRAPPÉS!
?
I THINK I'LL GO FOR THE ONE IN THE APRON!!
IT'S A COMPLETE SUCCESS!
DON'T TALK AS IF HE'S DEAD...
NOW MY UNCLE CAN REST IN PEACE!

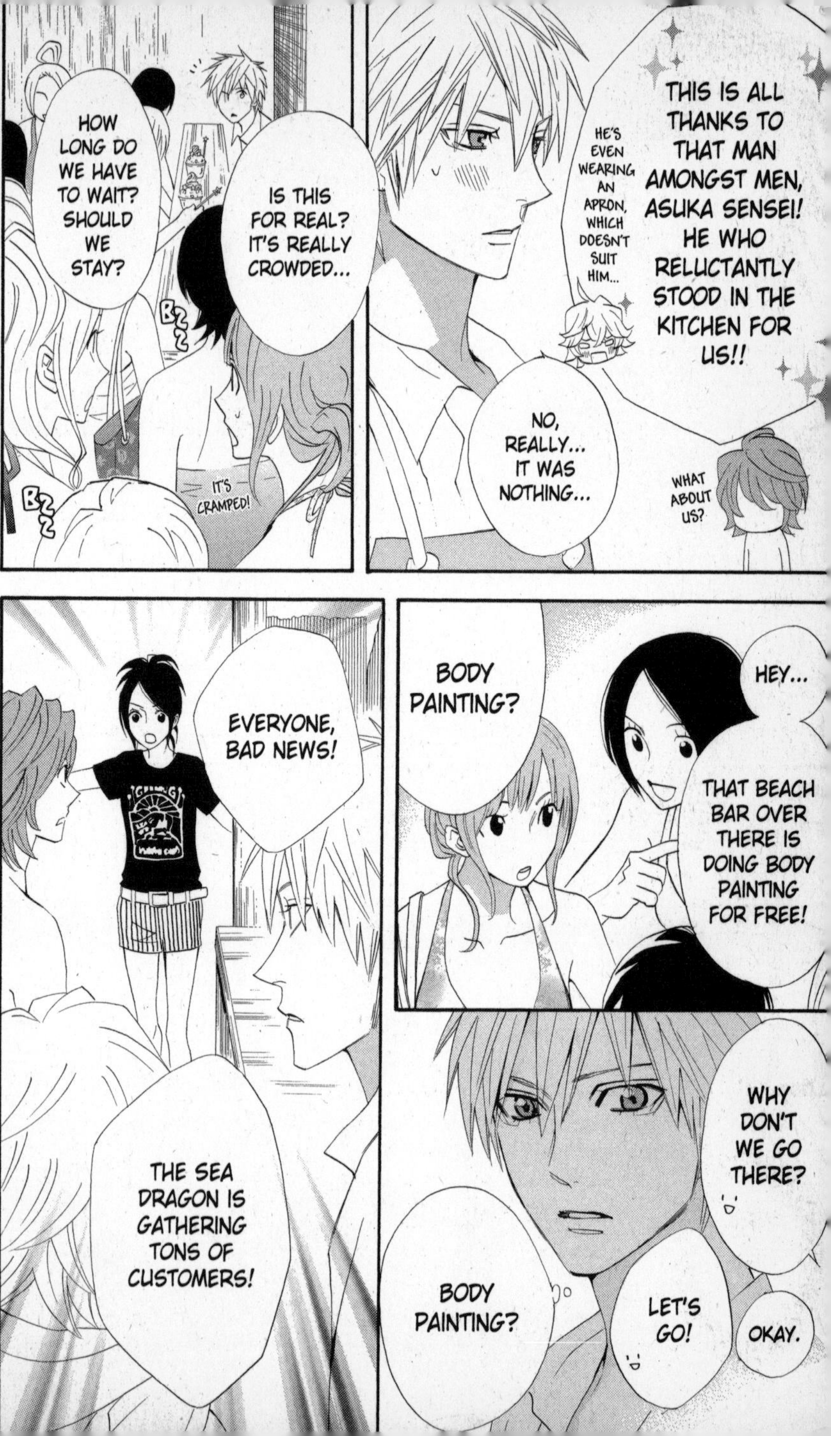
THIS IS ALL THANKS TO THAT MAN AMONGST MEN, ASUKA SENSEI! HE WHO RELUCTANTLY STOOD IN THE KITCHEN FOR US!!
HE'S EVEN WEARING AN APRON, WHICH DOESN'T SUIT HIM...
WHAT ABOUT US?
NO, REALLY... IT WAS NOTHING...
IS THIS FOR REAL? IT'S REALLY CROWDED...
HOW LONG DO WE HAVE TO WAIT? SHOULD WE STAY?
BZZ
IT'S CRAMPED!
BZZ
HEY...
THAT BEACH BAR OVER THERE IS DOING BODY PAINTING FOR FREE!
BODY PAINTING?
WHY DON'T WE GO THERE?
OKAY.
LET'S GO!
BODY PAINTING?
EVERYONE, BAD NEWS!
THE SEA DRAGON IS GATHERING TONS OF CUSTOMERS!

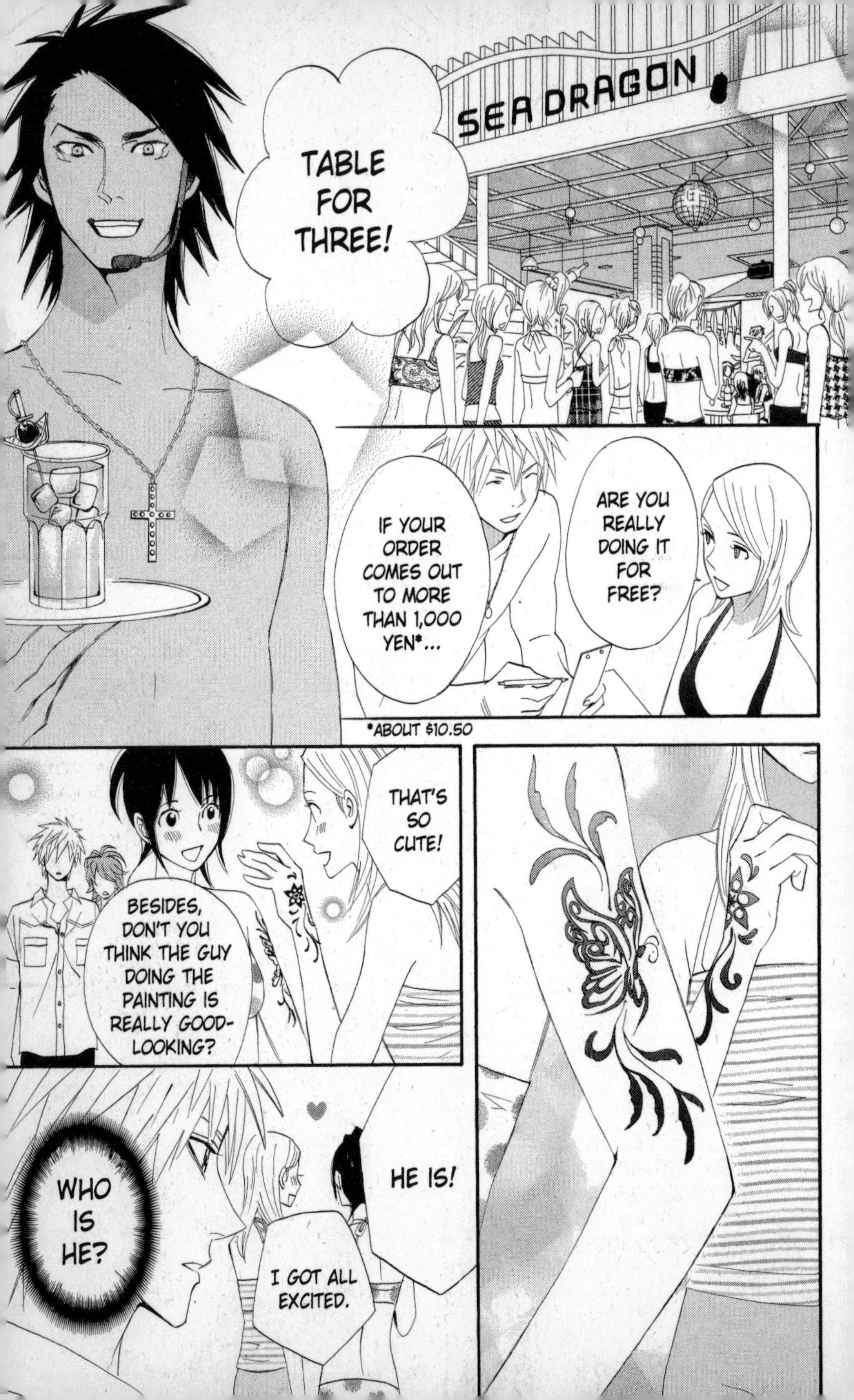
SEA DRAGON
ARE YOU REALLY DOING IT FOR FREE?
IF YOUR ORDER COMES OUT TO MORE THAN 1,000 YEN*...
*ABOUT $10.50
TABLE FOR THREE!
THAT'S SO CUTE!
BESIDES, DON'T YOU THINK THE GUY DOING THE PAINTING IS REALLY GOOD-LOOKING?
HE IS!
I GOT ALL EXCITED.
WHO IS HE?

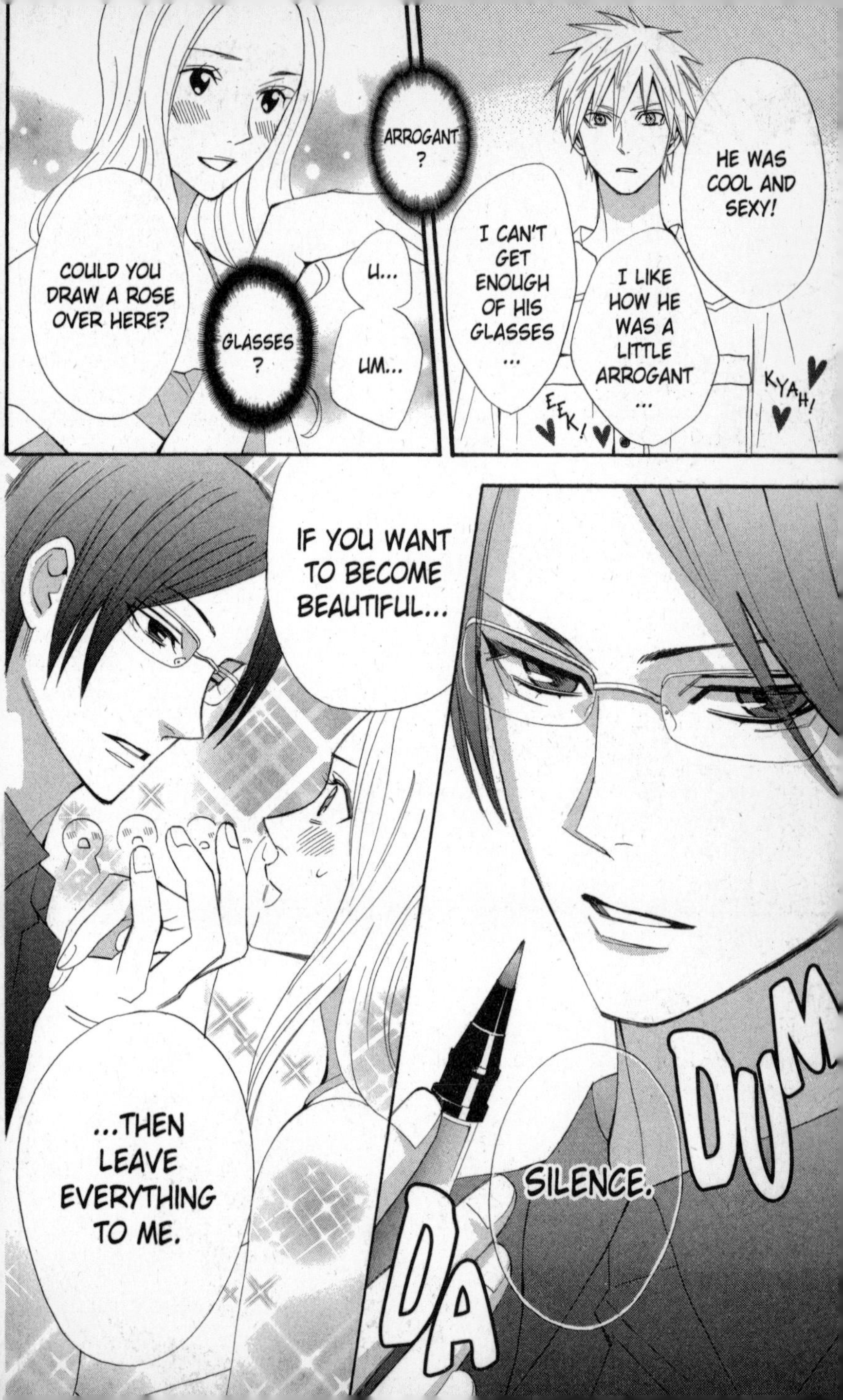
HE WAS COOL AND SEXY!
I LIKE HOW HE WAS A LITTLE ARROGANT...
I CAN'T GET ENOUGH OF HIS GLASSES...
KYAH!
EEEK!
ARROGANT?
U...
UM...
GLASSES?
COULD YOU DRAW A ROSE OVER HERE?
DA
DUM
SILENCE.
IF YOU WANT TO BECOME BEAUTIFUL...
...THEN LEAVE EVERYTHING TO ME.

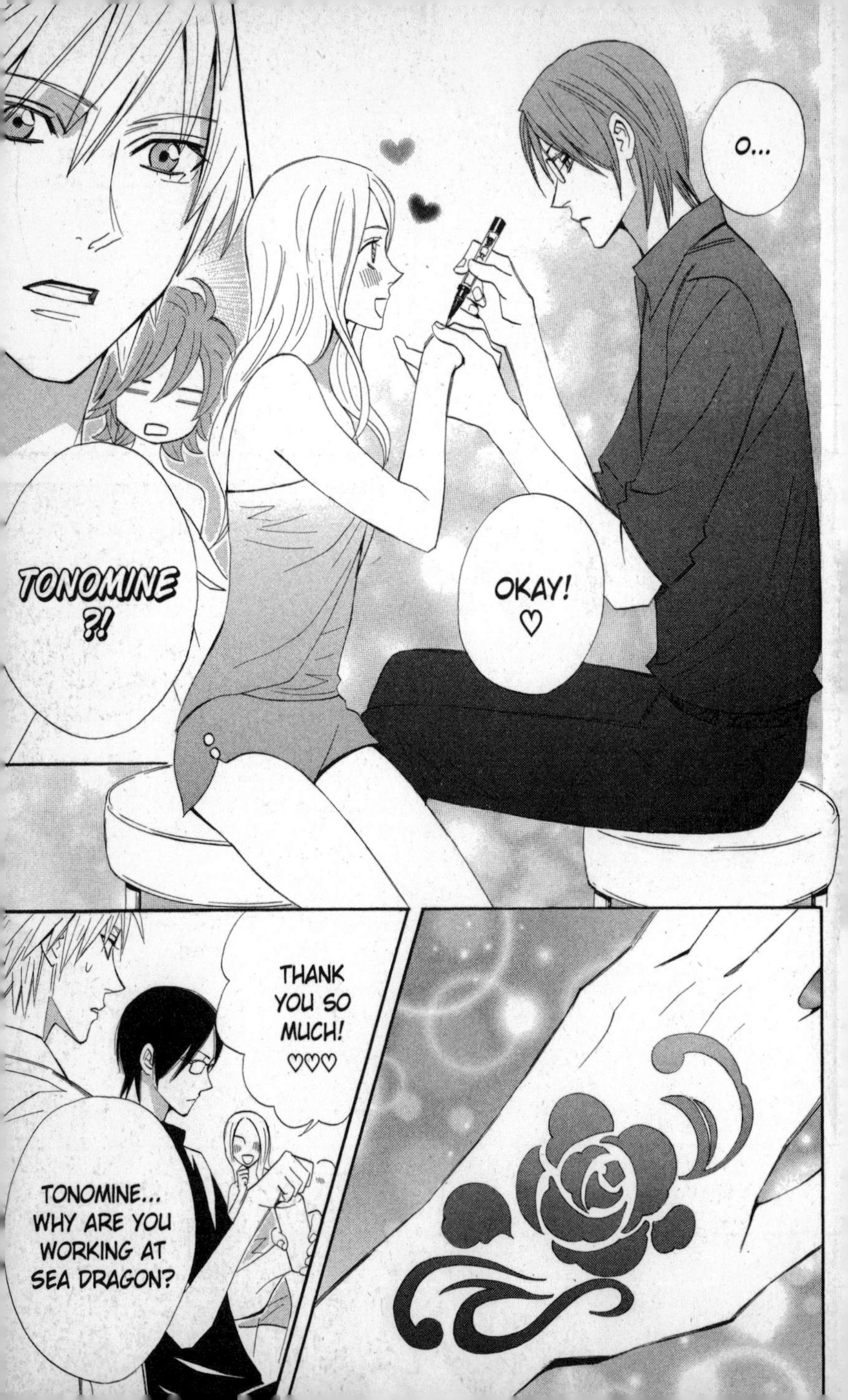
O...
OKAY! ♡
TONOMINE ?!
THANK YOU SO MUCH! ♡♡♡
TONOMINE... WHY ARE YOU WORKING AT SEA DRAGON?

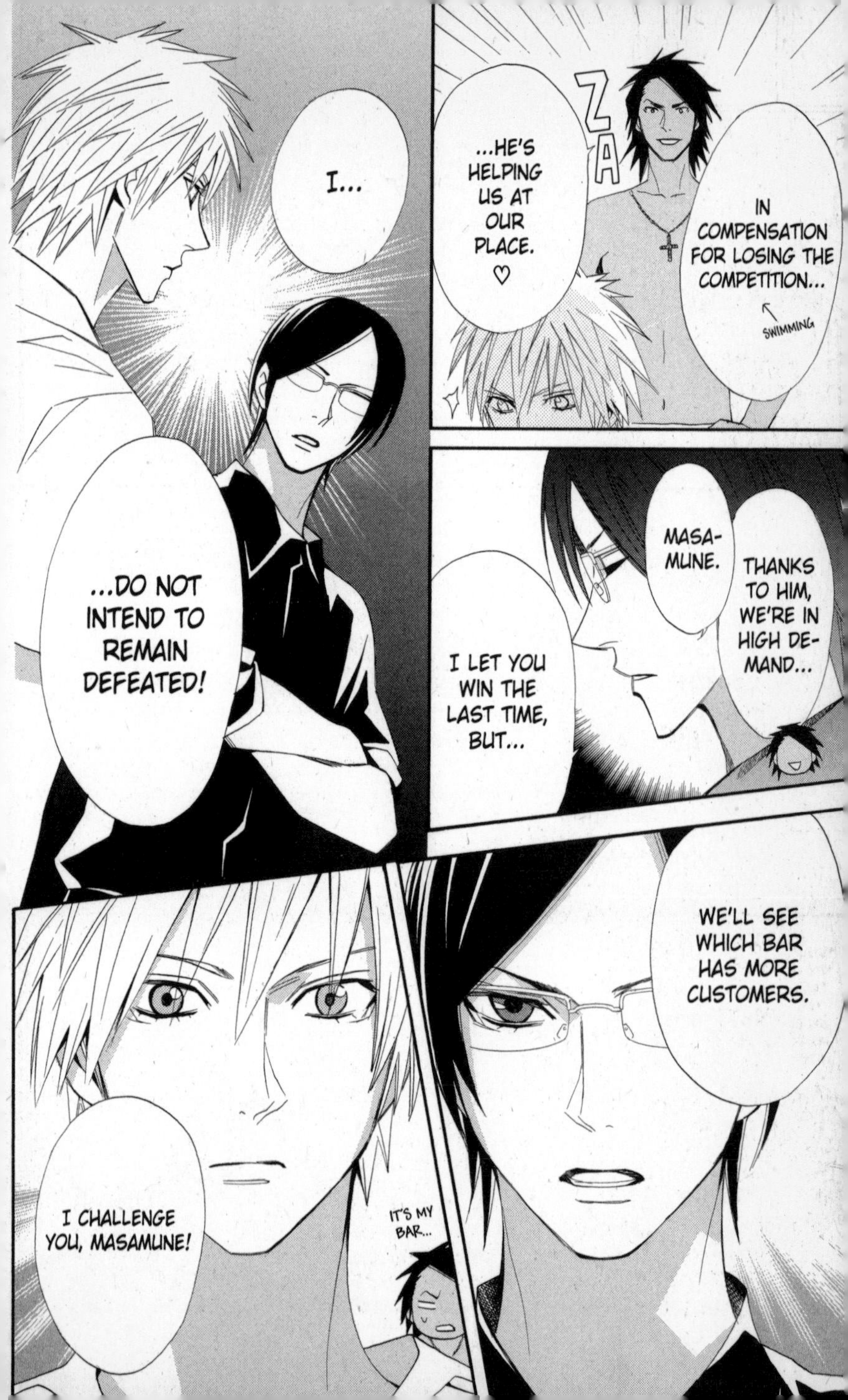
IN COMPENSATION FOR LOSING THE COMPETITION...
SWIMMING
ZA
...HE'S HELPING US AT OUR PLACE. ♡
MASA-MUNE.
THANKS TO HIM, WE'RE IN HIGH DE-MAND...
I LET YOU WIN THE LAST TIME, BUT...
I...
...DO NOT INTEND TO REMAIN DEFEATED!
WE'LL SEE WHICH BAR HAS MORE CUSTOMERS.
IT'S MY BAR...
I CHALLENGE YOU, MASAMUNE!

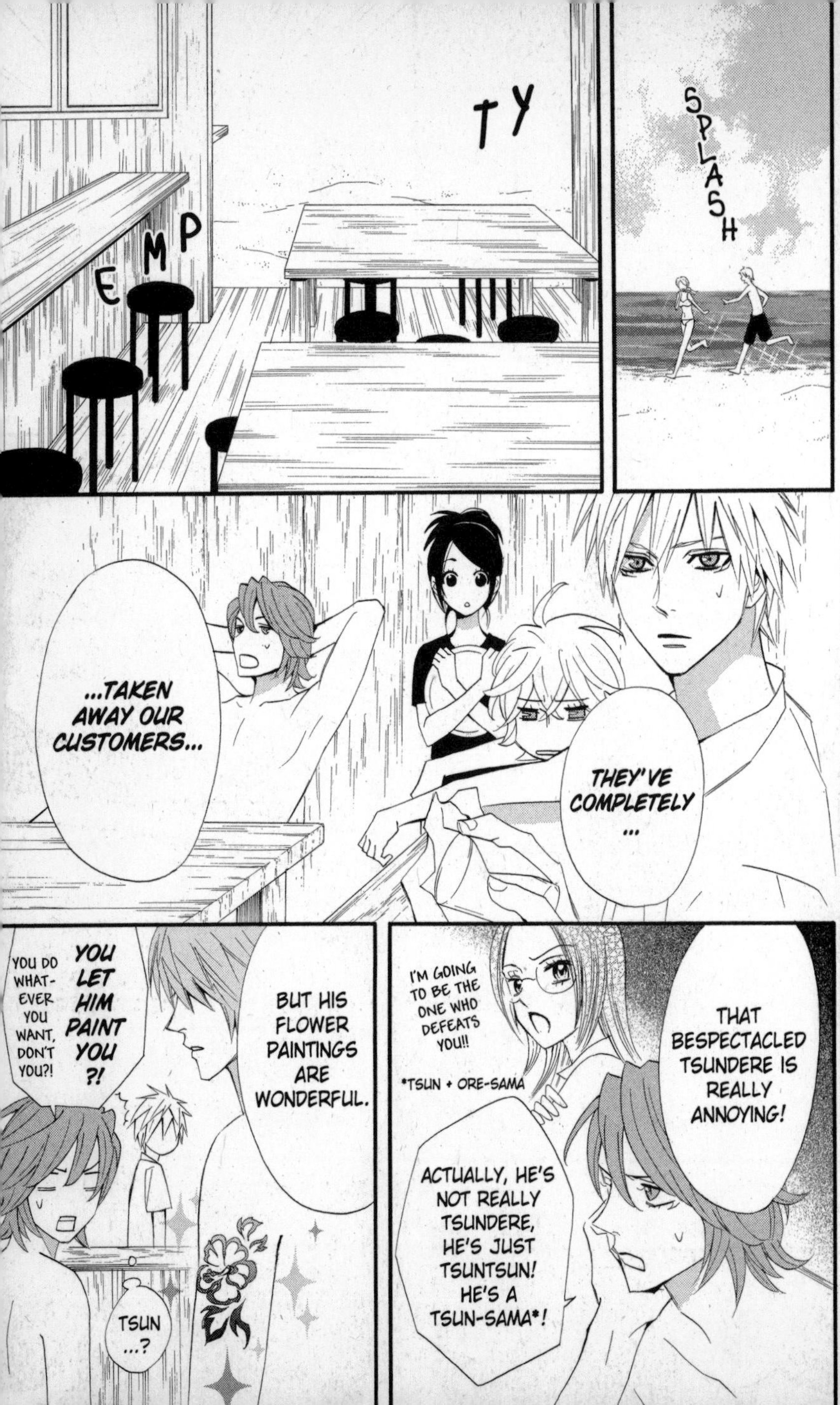
SPLASH
EMPTY
THEY'VE COMPLETELY ...
...TAKEN AWAY OUR CUSTOMERS...
THAT BESPECTACLED TSUNDERE IS REALLY ANNOYING!
I'M GOING TO BE THE ONE WHO DEFEATS YOU!!
ACTUALLY, HE'S NOT REALLY TSUNDERE, HE'S JUST TSUNTSUN! HE'S A TSUN-SAMA*!
*TSUN + ORE-SAMA
BUT HIS FLOWER PAINTINGS ARE WONDERFUL.
YOU LET HIM PAINT YOU?!
YOU DO WHAT-EVER YOU WANT, DON'T YOU?!
TSUN ...?

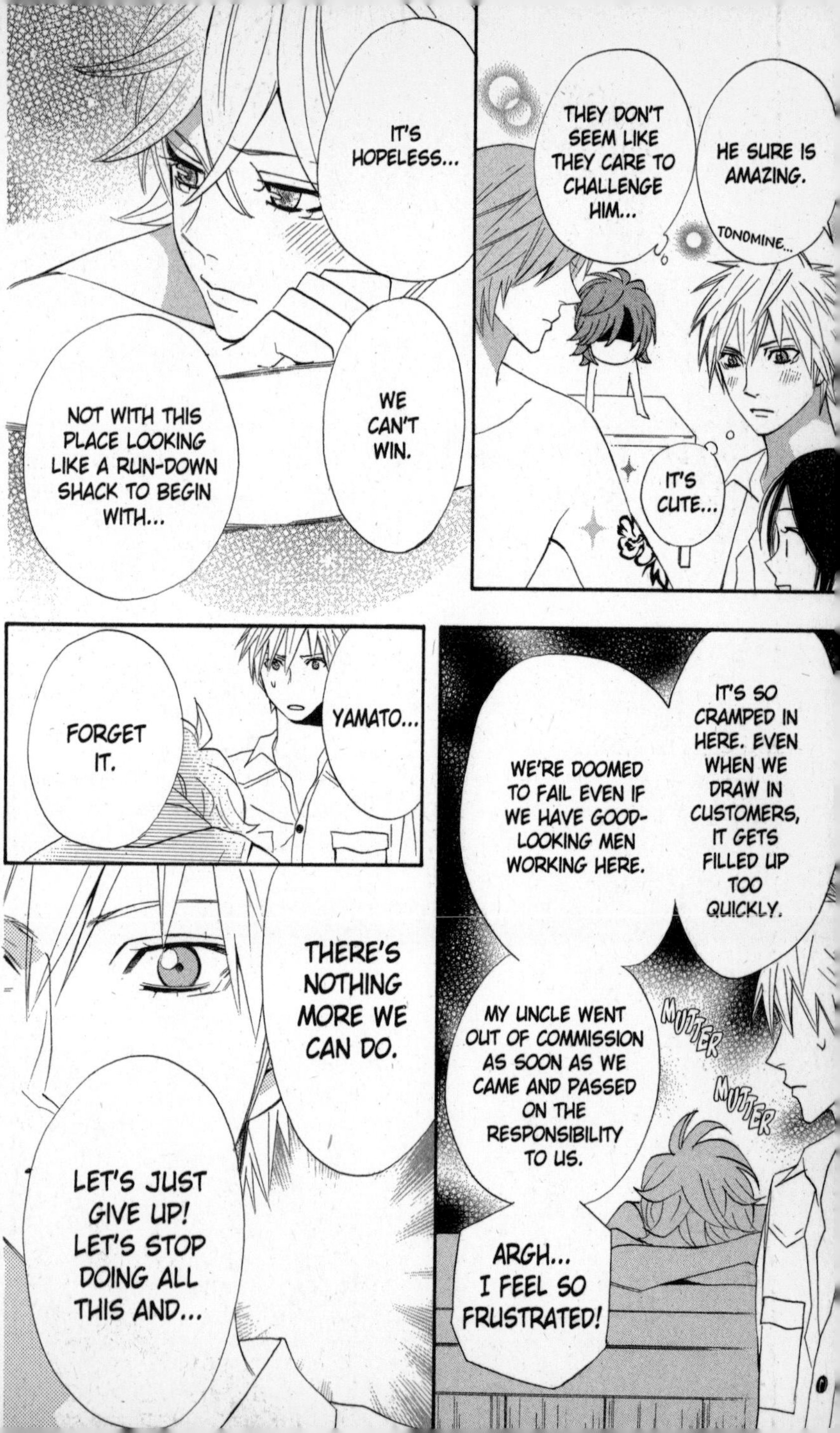
HE SURE IS AMAZING.
TONOMINE...
THEY DON'T SEEM LIKE THEY CARE TO CHALLENGE HIM...
IT'S CUTE...
IT'S HOPELESS...
WE CAN'T WIN.
NOT WITH THIS PLACE LOOKING LIKE A RUN-DOWN SHACK TO BEGIN WITH...
IT'S SO CRAMPED IN HERE. EVEN WHEN WE DRAW IN CUSTOMERS, IT GETS FILLED UP TOO QUICKLY.
WE'RE DOOMED TO FAIL EVEN IF WE HAVE GOOD-LOOKING MEN WORKING HERE.
MY UNCLE WENT OUT OF COMMISSION AS SOON AS WE CAME AND PASSED ON THE RESPONSIBILITY TO US.
MUTTER
MUTTER
ARGH... I FEEL SO FRUSTRATED!
YAMATO...
FORGET IT.
THERE'S NOTHING MORE WE CAN DO.
LET'S JUST GIVE UP! LET'S STOP DOING ALL THIS AND...

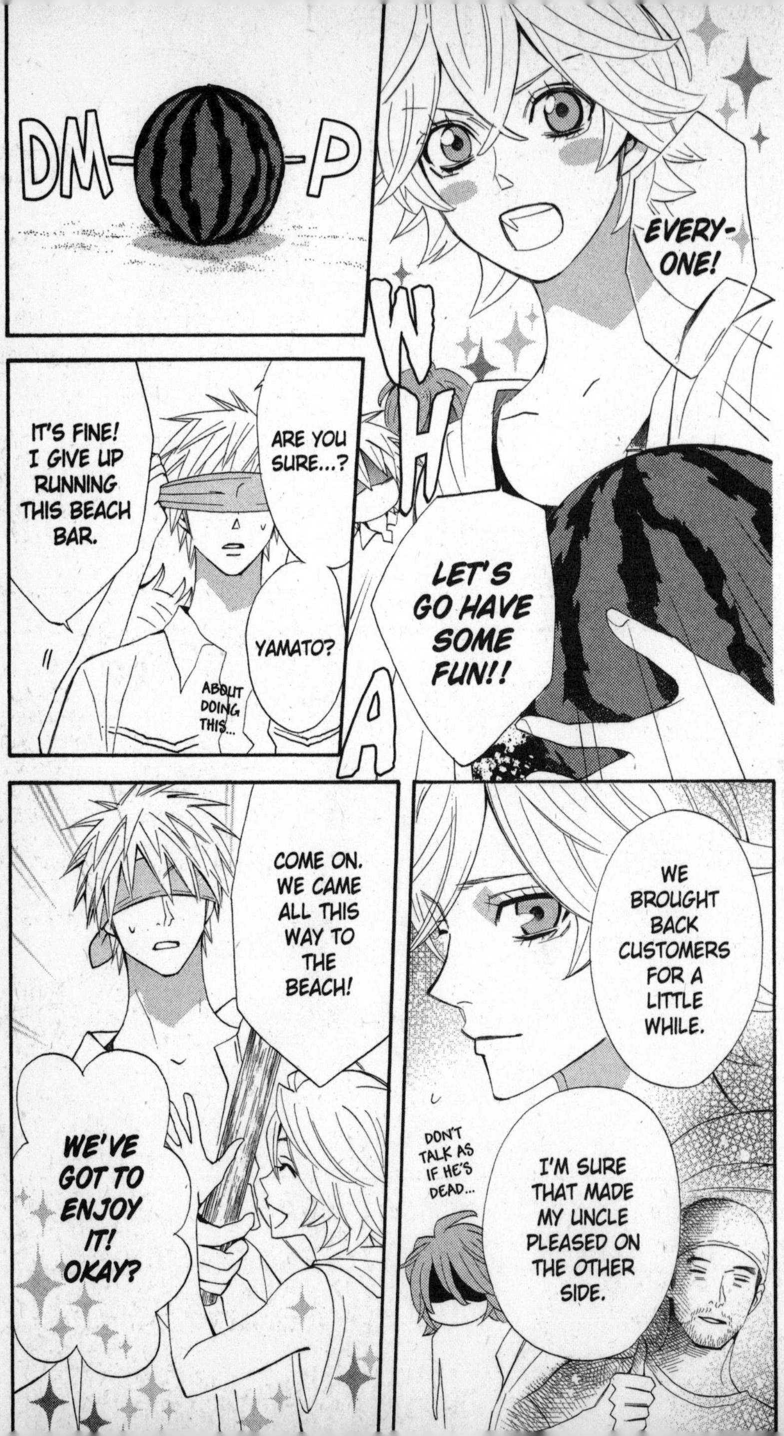
EVERY-ONE!
WHA
LET'S GO HAVE SOME FUN!!
DM-P
ARE YOU SURE...?
YAMATO?
IT'S FINE! I GIVE UP RUNNING THIS BEACH BAR.
ABOUT DOING THIS...
WE BROUGHT BACK CUSTOMERS FOR A LITTLE WHILE.
I'M SURE THAT MADE MY UNCLE PLEASED ON THE OTHER SIDE.
DON'T TALK AS IF HE'S DEAD...
COME ON. WE CAME ALL THIS WAY TO THE BEACH!
WE'VE GOT TO ENJOY IT! OKAY?

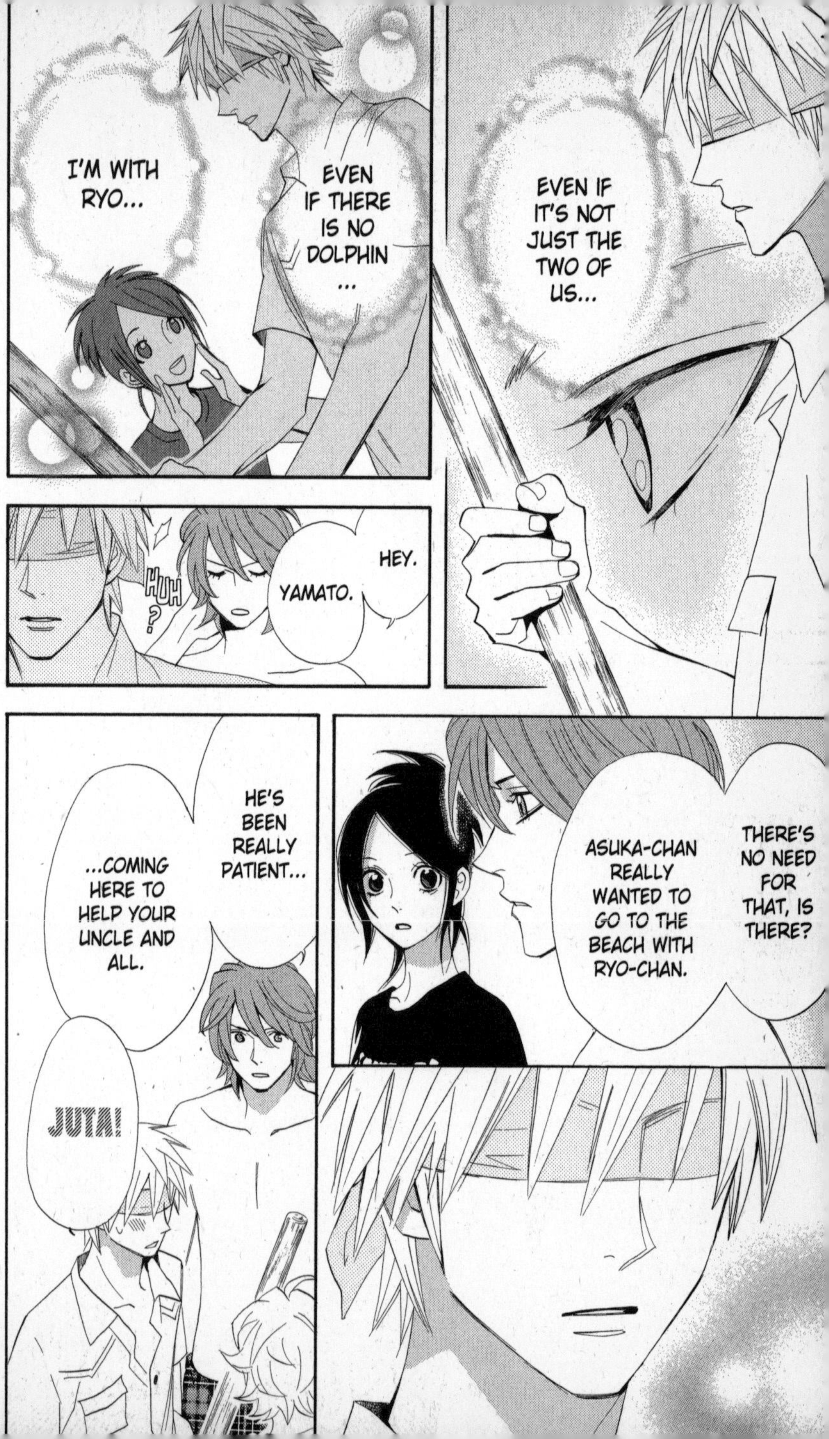
EVEN IF THERE IS NO DOLPHIN ...
I'M WITH RYO...
EVEN IF IT'S NOT JUST THE TWO OF US...
HEY.
YAMATO.
HUH?
THERE'S NO NEED FOR THAT, IS THERE?
ASUKA-CHAN REALLY WANTED TO GO TO THE BEACH WITH RYO-CHAN.
HE'S BEEN REALLY PATIENT...
...COMING HERE TO HELP YOUR UNCLE AND ALL.
JUTA!

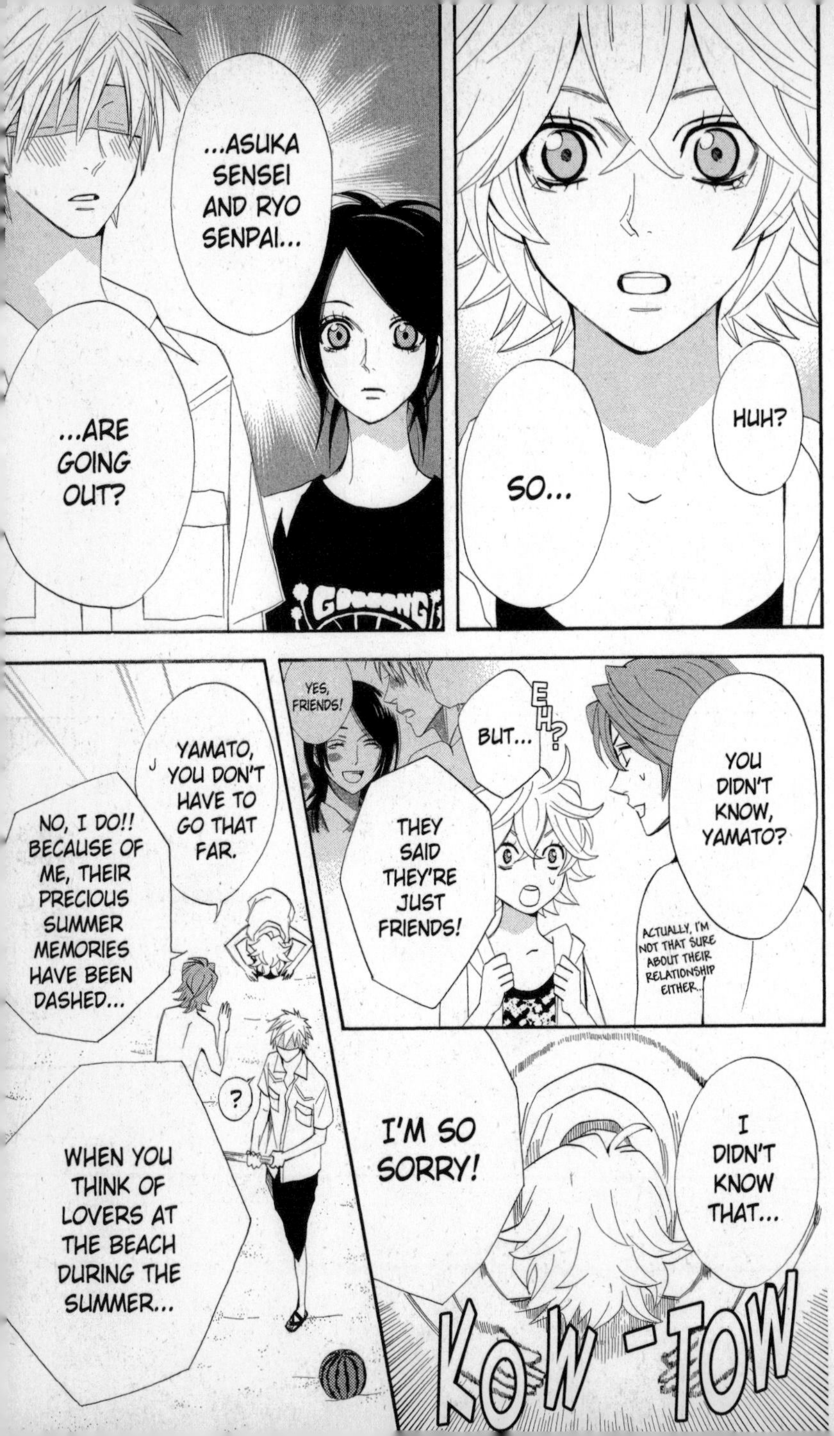
HUH?
SO...
...ASUKA SENSEI AND RYO SENPAI...
...ARE GOING OUT?
YOU DIDN'T KNOW, YAMATO?
EH?
BUT...
THEY SAID THEY'RE JUST FRIENDS!
YES, FRIENDS!
ACTUALLY, I'M NOT THAT SURE ABOUT THEIR RELATIONSHIP EITHER...
I DIDN'T KNOW THAT...
I'M SO SORRY!
KOW-TOW
YAMATO, YOU DON'T HAVE TO GO THAT FAR.
NO, I DO!! BECAUSE OF ME, THEIR PRECIOUS SUMMER MEMORIES HAVE BEEN DASHED...
?
WHEN YOU THINK OF LOVERS AT THE BEACH DURING THE SUMMER...

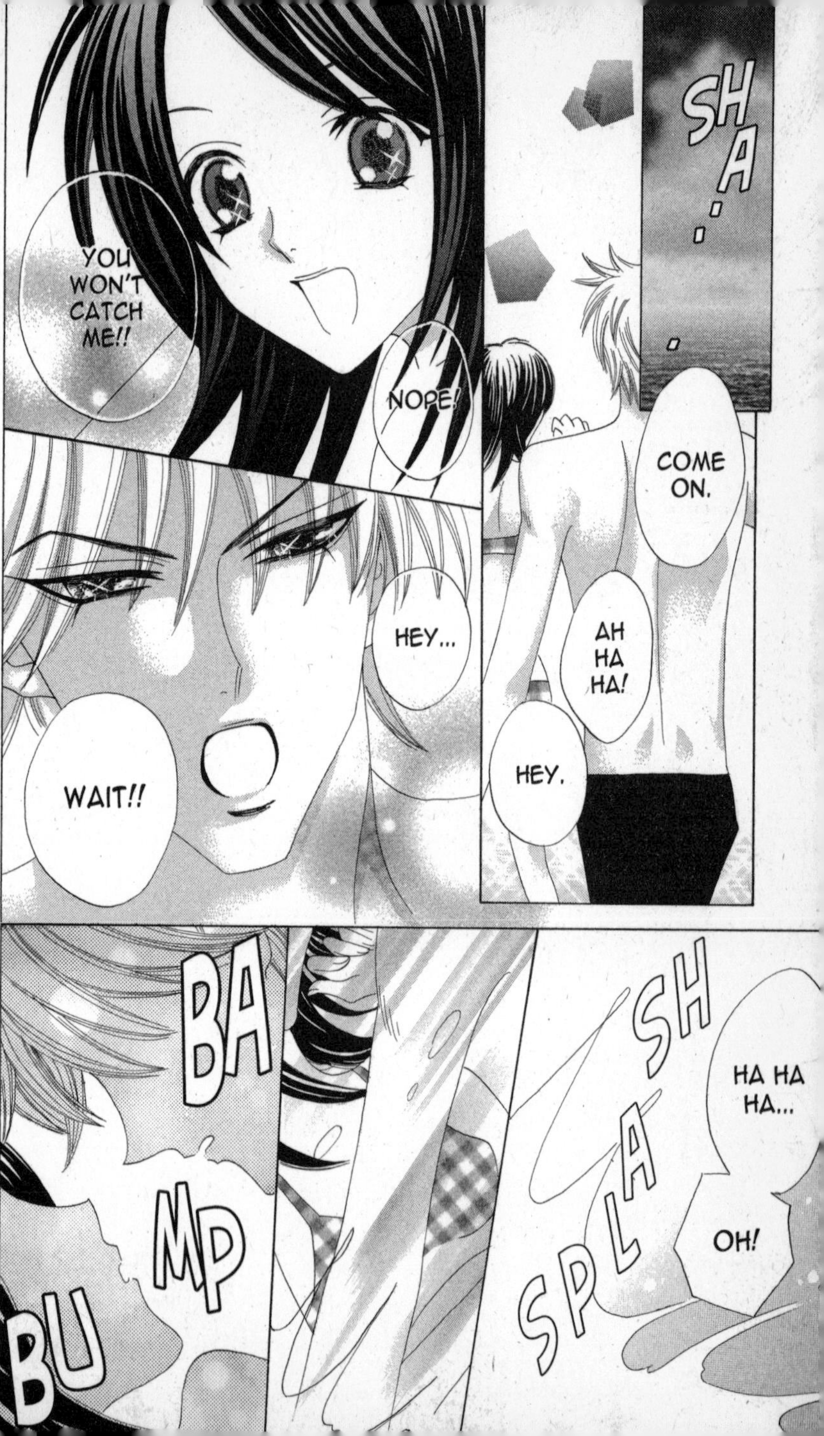
SHA...
COME ON.
AH HA HA!
HEY.
YOU WON'T CATCH ME!!
NOPE!
HEY...
WAIT!!
HA HA HA...
OH!
SPLASH
BA
BUMP

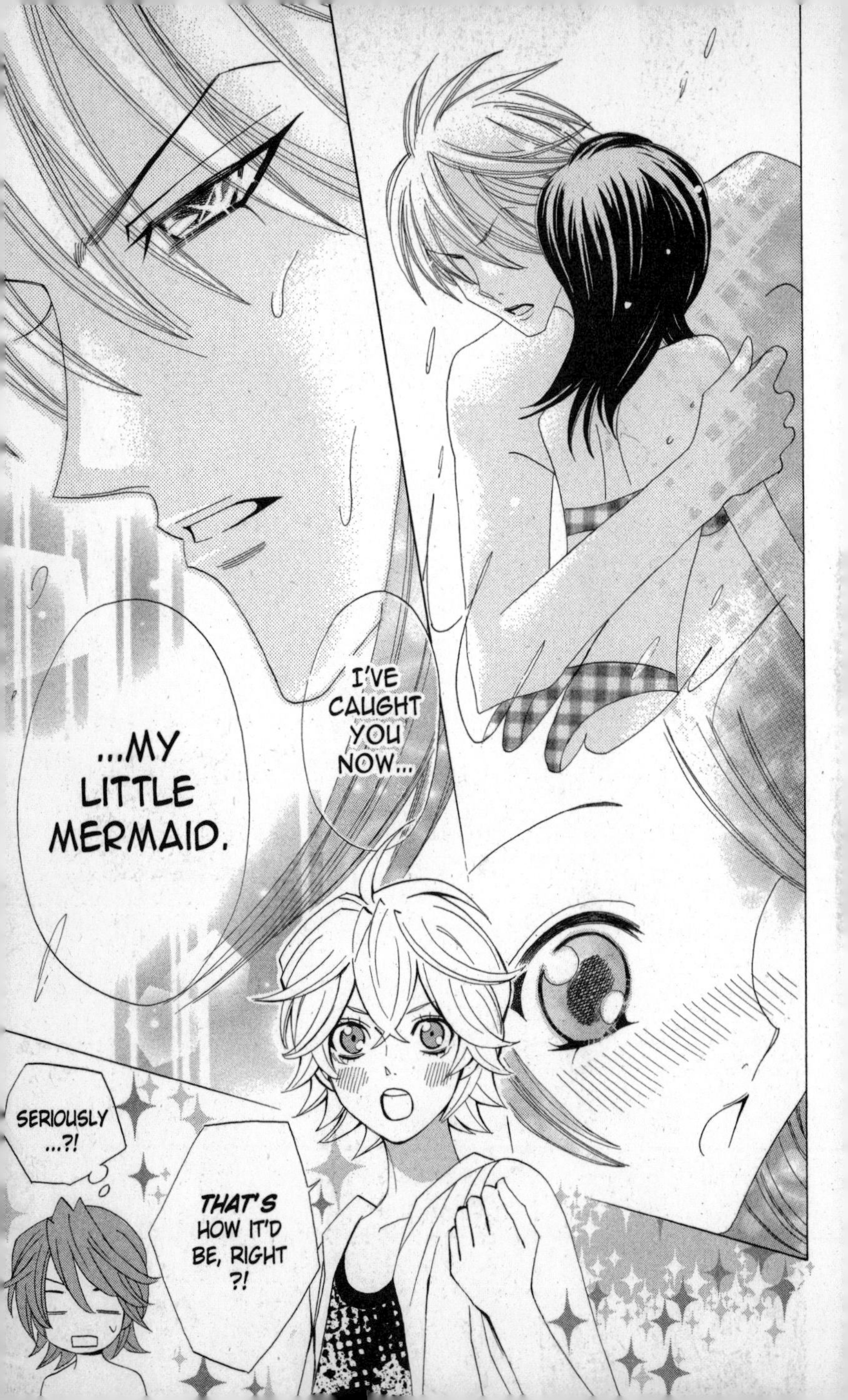
I'VE CAUGHT YOU NOW...
...MY LITTLE MERMAID.
THAT'S HOW IT'D BE, RIGHT?!
SERIOUSLY...?!

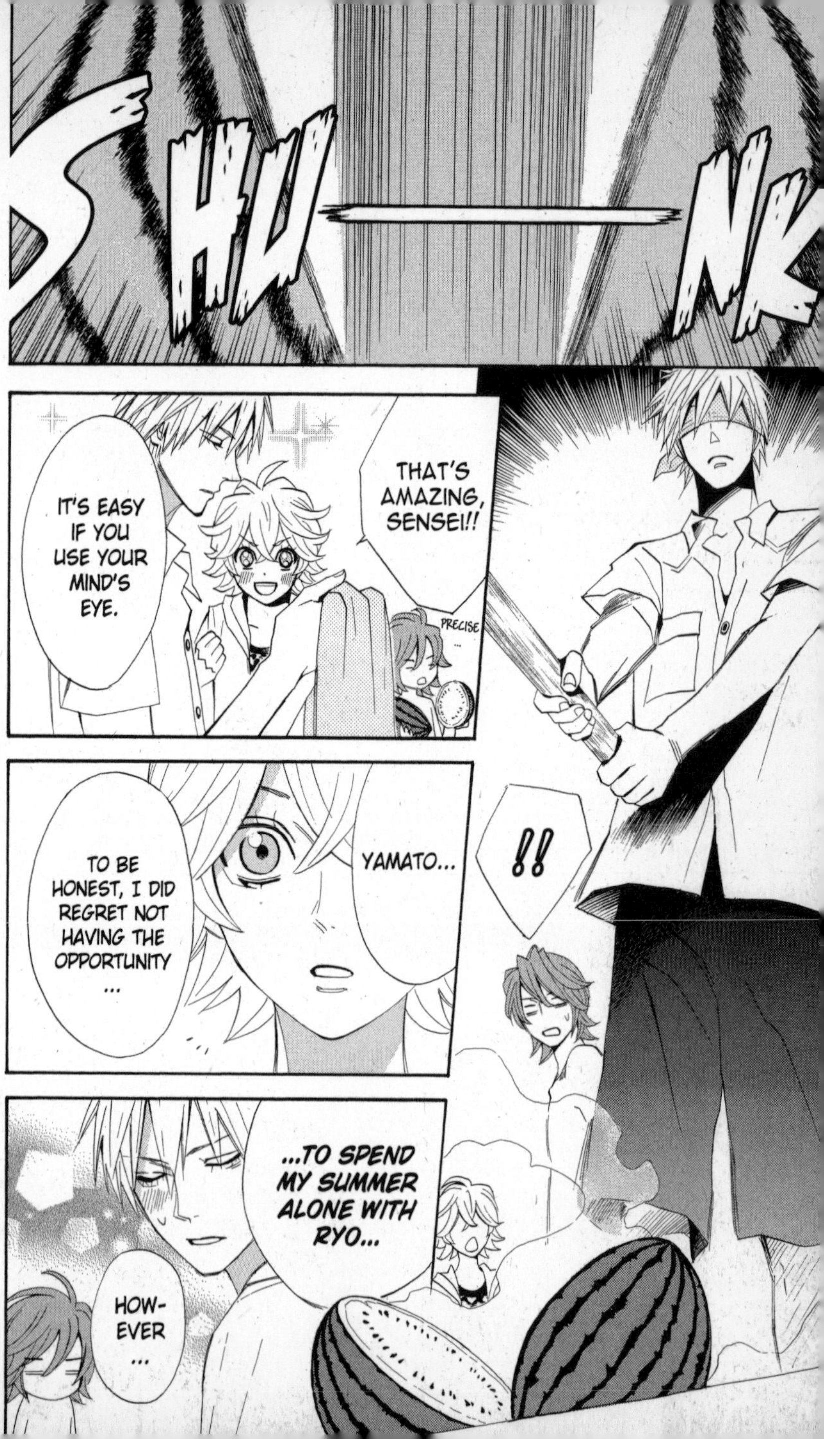
SHU—NK
!!
THAT'S AMAZING, SENSEI!!
PRECISE...
IT'S EASY IF YOU USE YOUR MIND'S EYE.
YAMATO...
TO BE HONEST, I DID REGRET NOT HAVING THE OPPORTUNITY...
...TO SPEND MY SUMMER ALONE WITH RYO...
HOW-EVER...

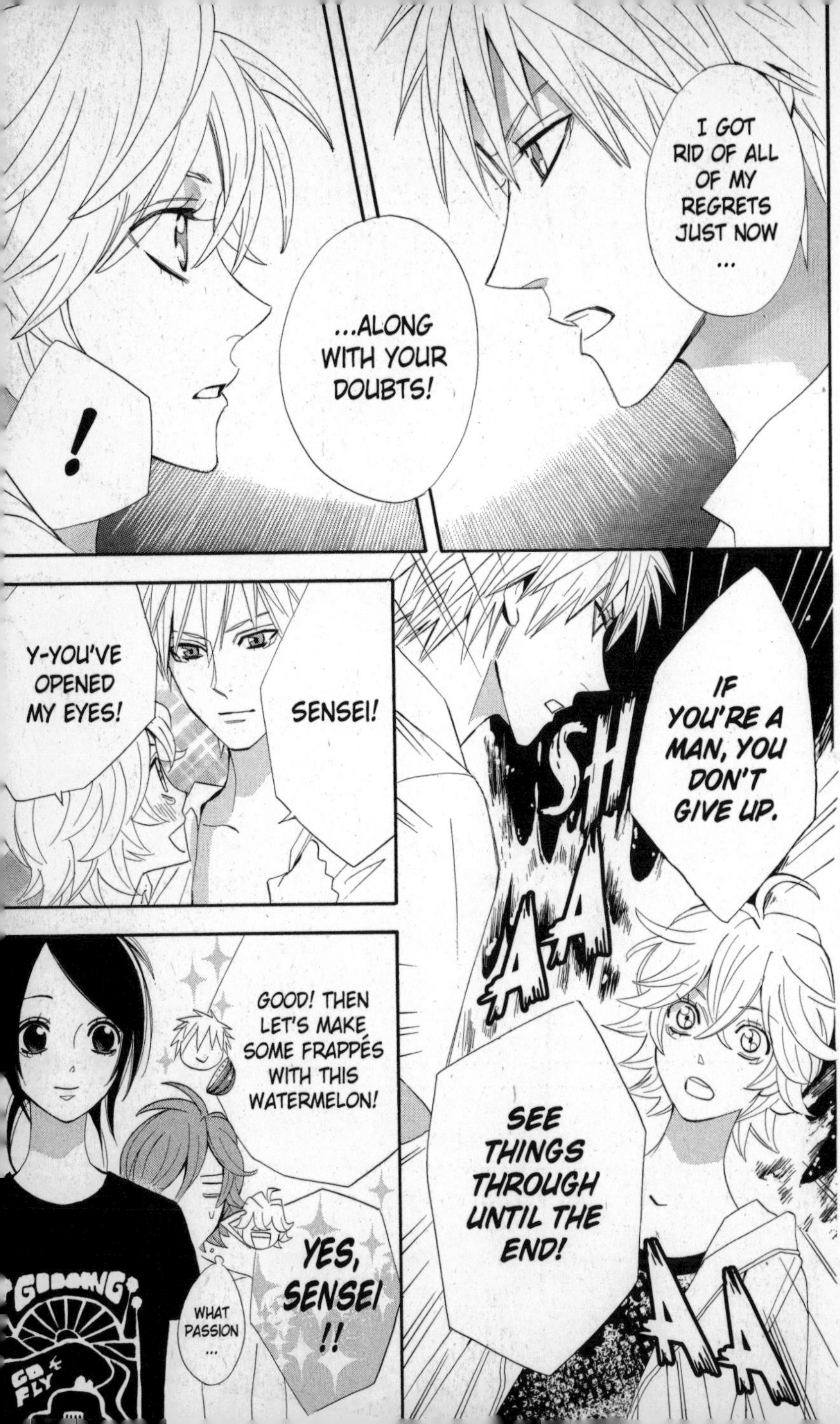
I GOT RID OF ALL OF MY REGRETS JUST NOW ...
...ALONG WITH YOUR DOUBTS!
!
IF YOU'RE A MAN, YOU DON'T GIVE UP.
SHAAA
SEE THINGS THROUGH UNTIL THE END!
AA
SENSEI!
Y-YOU'VE OPENED MY EYES!
GOOD! THEN LET'S MAKE SOME FRAPPÉS WITH THIS WATERMELON!
YES, SENSEI !!
WHAT PASSION ...

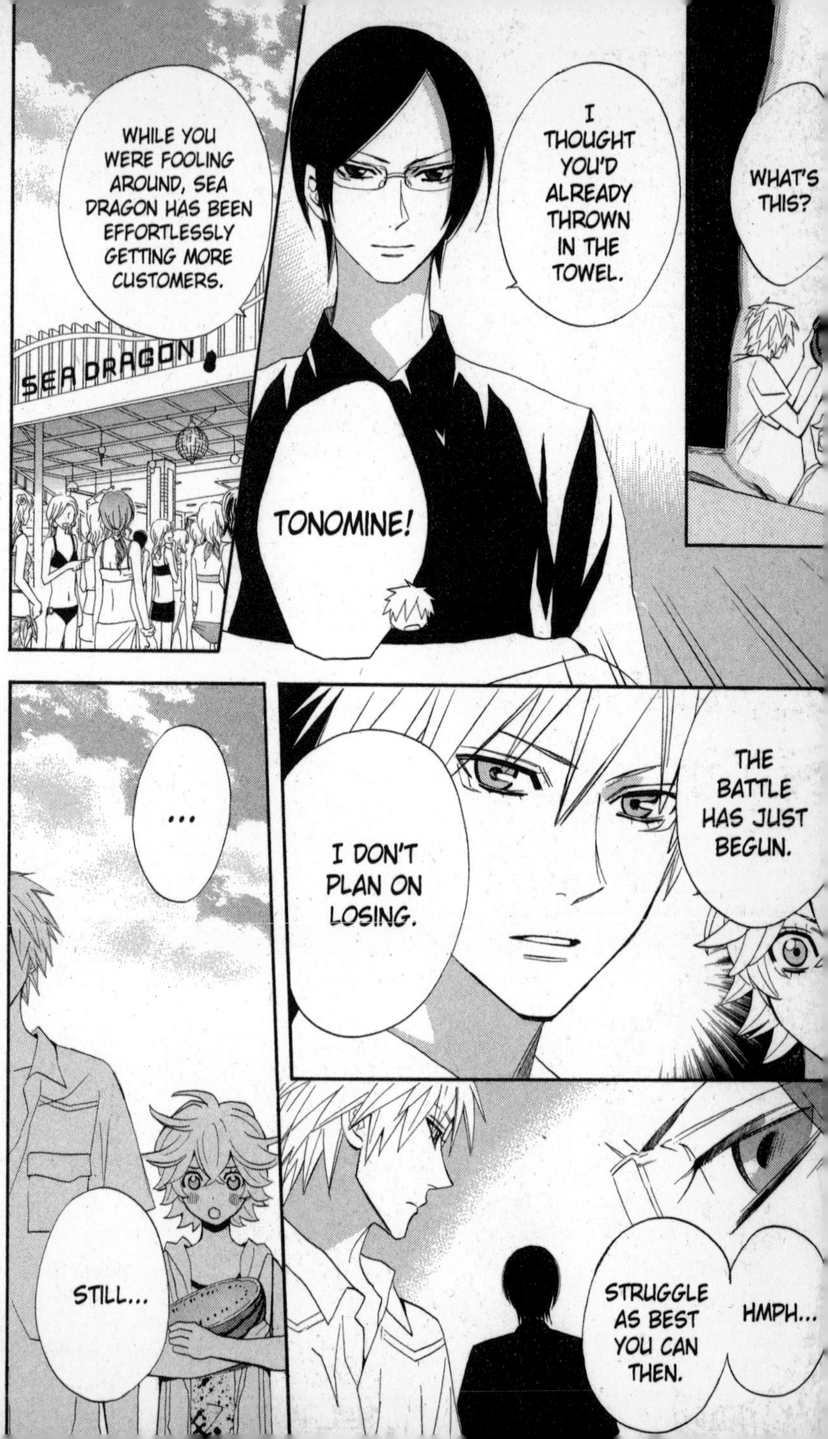
WHAT'S THIS?
I THOUGHT YOU'D ALREADY THROWN IN THE TOWEL.
TONOMINE!
WHILE YOU WERE FOOLING AROUND, SEA DRAGON HAS BEEN EFFORTLESSLY GETTING MORE CUSTOMERS.
SEA DRAGON
THE BATTLE HAS JUST BEGUN.
I DON'T PLAN ON LOSING.
...
HMPH...
STRUGGLE AS BEST YOU CAN THEN.
STILL...

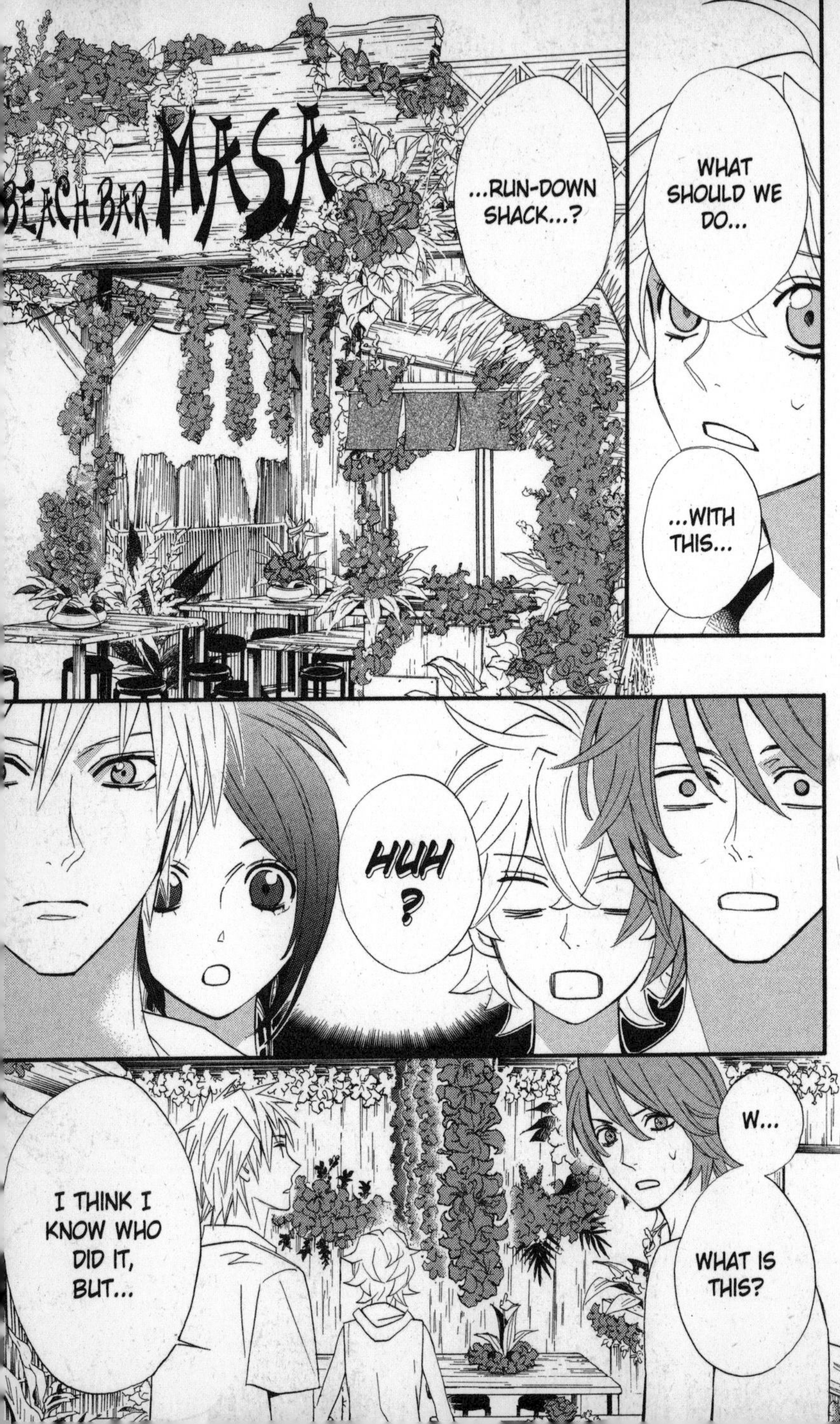
WHAT SHOULD WE DO...
...WITH THIS...
...RUN-DOWN SHACK...?
BEACH BAR MASA
HUH?
W...
WHAT IS THIS?
I THINK I KNOW WHO DID IT, BUT...

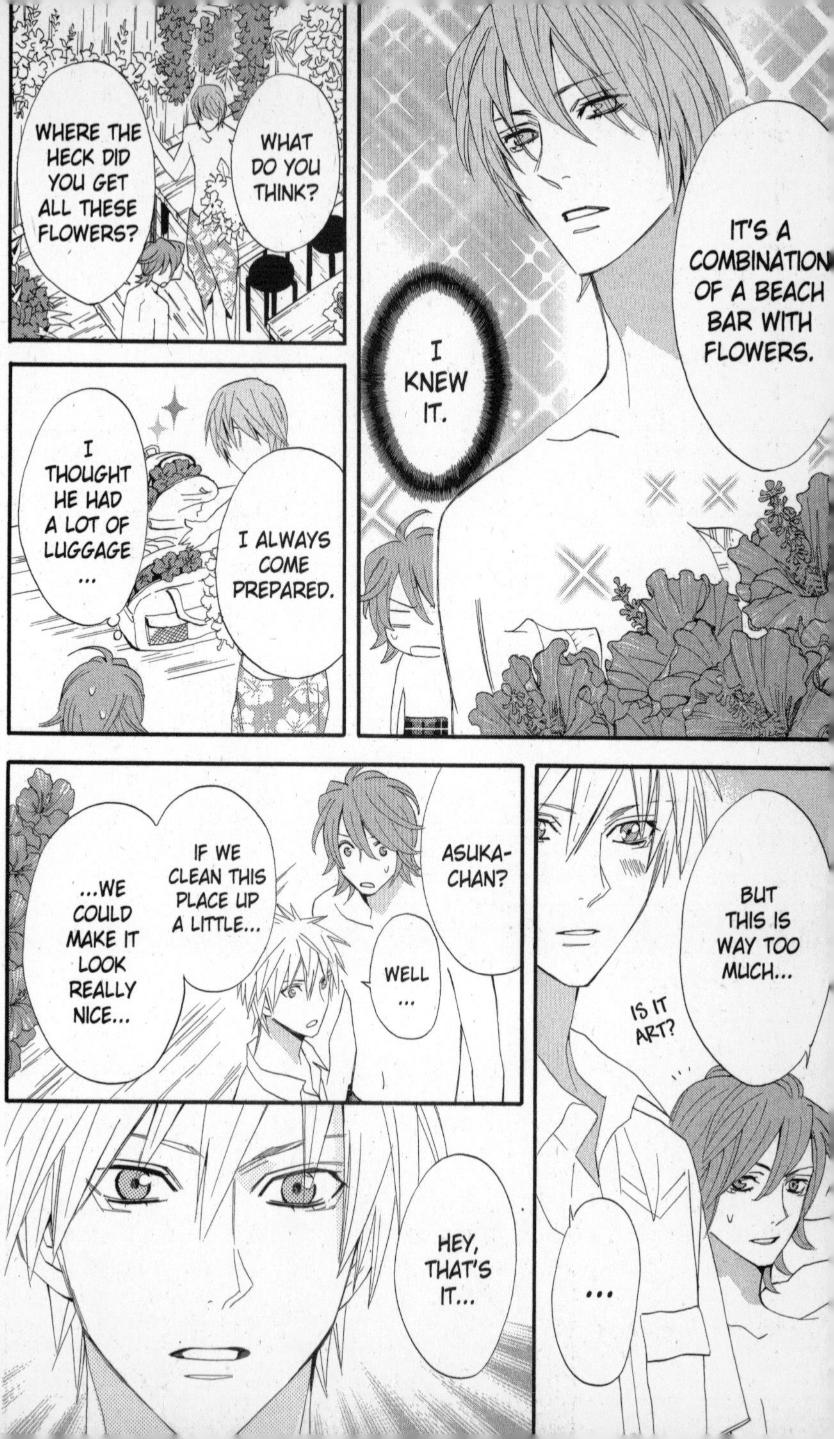
IT'S A COMBINATION OF A BEACH BAR WITH FLOWERS.
I KNEW IT.
WHAT DO YOU THINK?
WHERE THE HECK DID YOU GET ALL THESE FLOWERS?
I ALWAYS COME PREPARED.
I THOUGHT HE HAD A LOT OF LUGGAGE...
BUT THIS IS WAY TOO MUCH...
IS IT ART?
...
ASUKA-CHAN?
WELL...
IF WE CLEAN THIS PLACE UP A LITTLE...
...WE COULD MAKE IT LOOK REALLY NICE...
HEY, THAT'S IT...

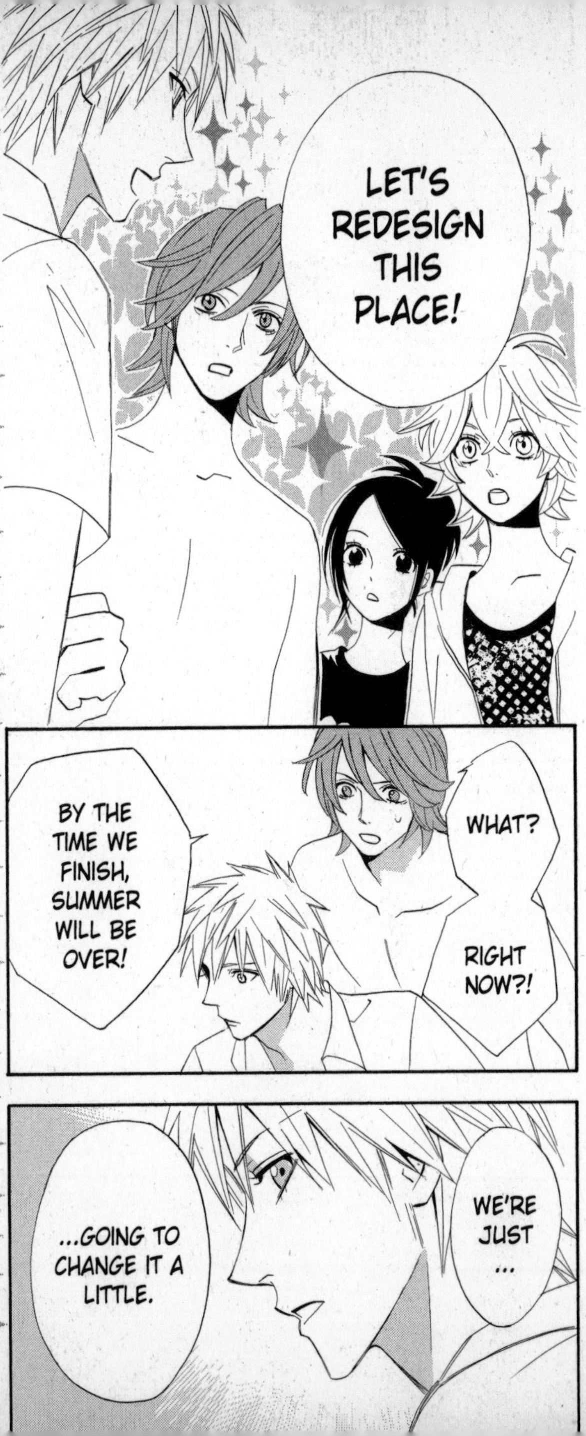
LET'S REDESIGN THIS PLACE!
WHAT?
RIGHT NOW?!
BY THE TIME WE FINISH, SUMMER WILL BE OVER!
WE'RE JUST ...
...GOING TO CHANGE IT A LITTLE.

Production Assistance:

Shimada-san
Takowa-san
Kawashima-san
Sayaka-san
Kuwana-san
Tanaka-san
Nishizawa-san
Yoneyan
Nakazawa-san
Sakurai-san

Special Thanks:

Abe-san
Abewo
Miyajima Fresh Flower Shop
All My Readers

If you have any thoughts or opinions, please write to:

Aya Kanno
C/O Otomen Editor
Viz Media
P.O. Box 77010
San Francisco, CA
94107

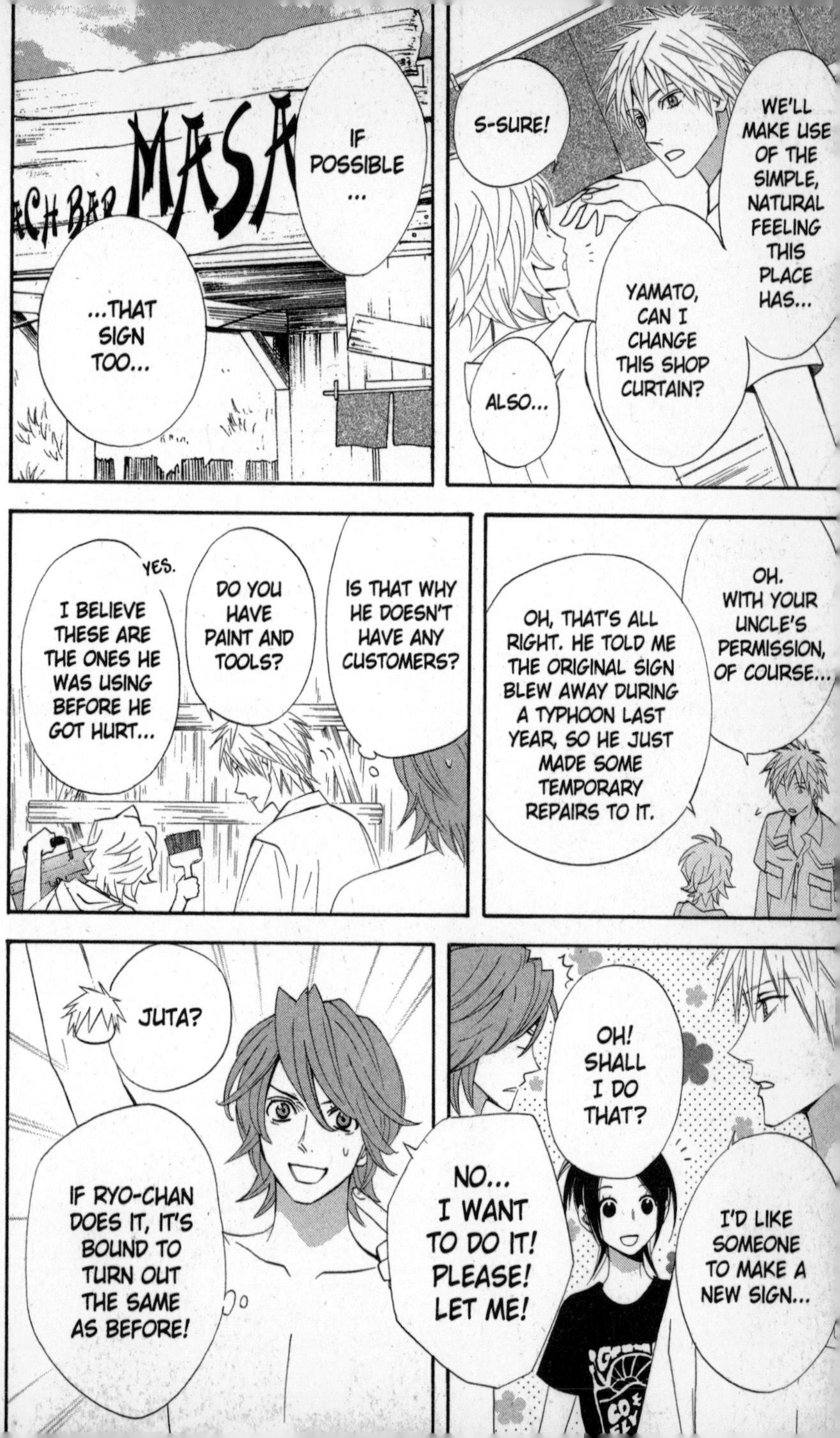
WE'LL MAKE USE OF THE SIMPLE, NATURAL FEELING THIS PLACE HAS...
S-SURE!
YAMATO, CAN I CHANGE THIS SHOP CURTAIN?
ALSO...
IF POSSIBLE...
...THAT SIGN TOO...
OH. WITH YOUR UNCLE'S PERMISSION, OF COURSE...
OH, THAT'S ALL RIGHT. HE TOLD ME THE ORIGINAL SIGN BLEW AWAY DURING A TYPHOON LAST YEAR, SO HE JUST MADE SOME TEMPORARY REPAIRS TO IT.
IS THAT WHY HE DOESN'T HAVE ANY CUSTOMERS?
DO YOU HAVE PAINT AND TOOLS?
YES.
I BELIEVE THESE ARE THE ONES HE WAS USING BEFORE HE GOT HURT...
I'D LIKE SOMEONE TO MAKE A NEW SIGN...
OH! SHALL I DO THAT?
NO... I WANT TO DO IT! PLEASE! LET ME!
JUTA?
IF RYO-CHAN DOES IT, IT'S BOUND TO TURN OUT THE SAME AS BEFORE!

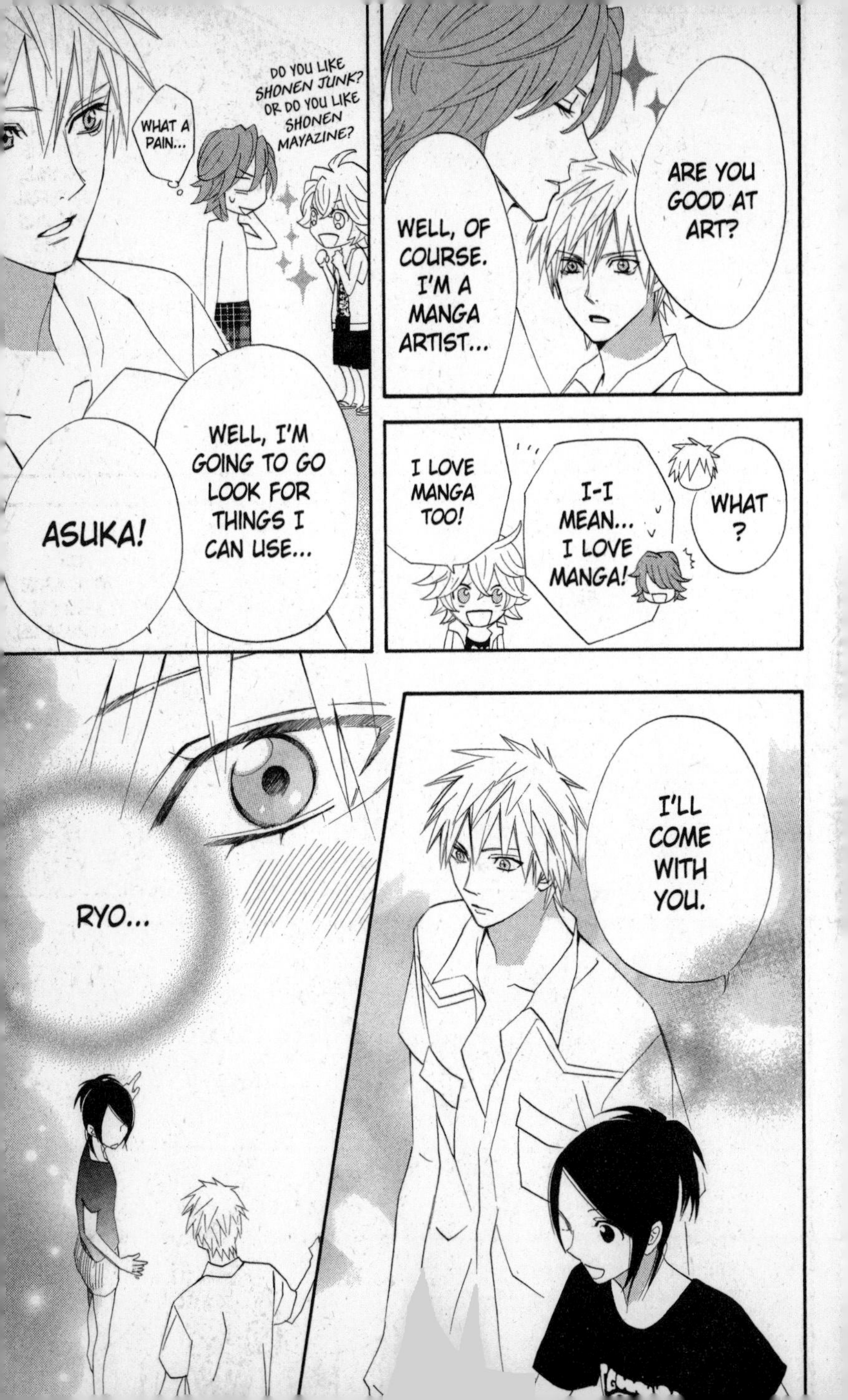
ARE YOU GOOD AT ART?
WELL, OF COURSE. I'M A MANGA ARTIST...
WHAT ?
I-I MEAN... I LOVE MANGA!
I LOVE MANGA TOO!
DO YOU LIKE SHONEN JUNK? OR DO YOU LIKE SHONEN MAYAZINE?
WHAT A PAIN...
WELL, I'M GOING TO GO LOOK FOR THINGS I CAN USE...
ASUKA!
I'LL COME WITH YOU.
RYO...

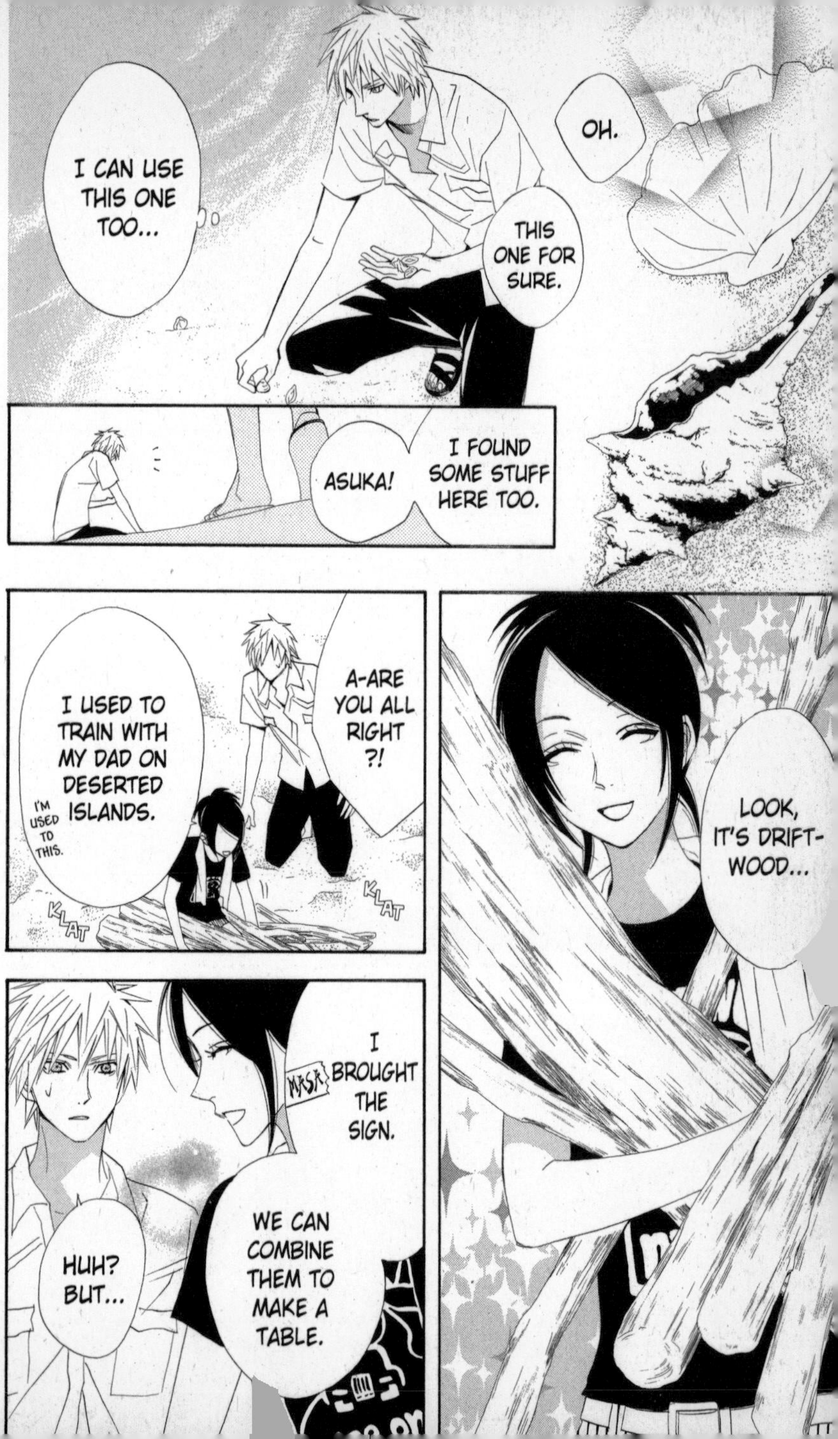
OH.
THIS ONE FOR SURE.
I CAN USE THIS ONE TOO...
I FOUND SOME STUFF HERE TOO.
ASUKA!
LOOK, IT'S DRIFT-WOOD...
A-ARE YOU ALL RIGHT ?!
I USED TO TRAIN WITH MY DAD ON DESERTED ISLANDS.
I'M USED TO THIS.
KLAT
KLAT
I BROUGHT THE SIGN.
MASA
WE CAN COMBINE THEM TO MAKE A TABLE.
HUH? BUT...

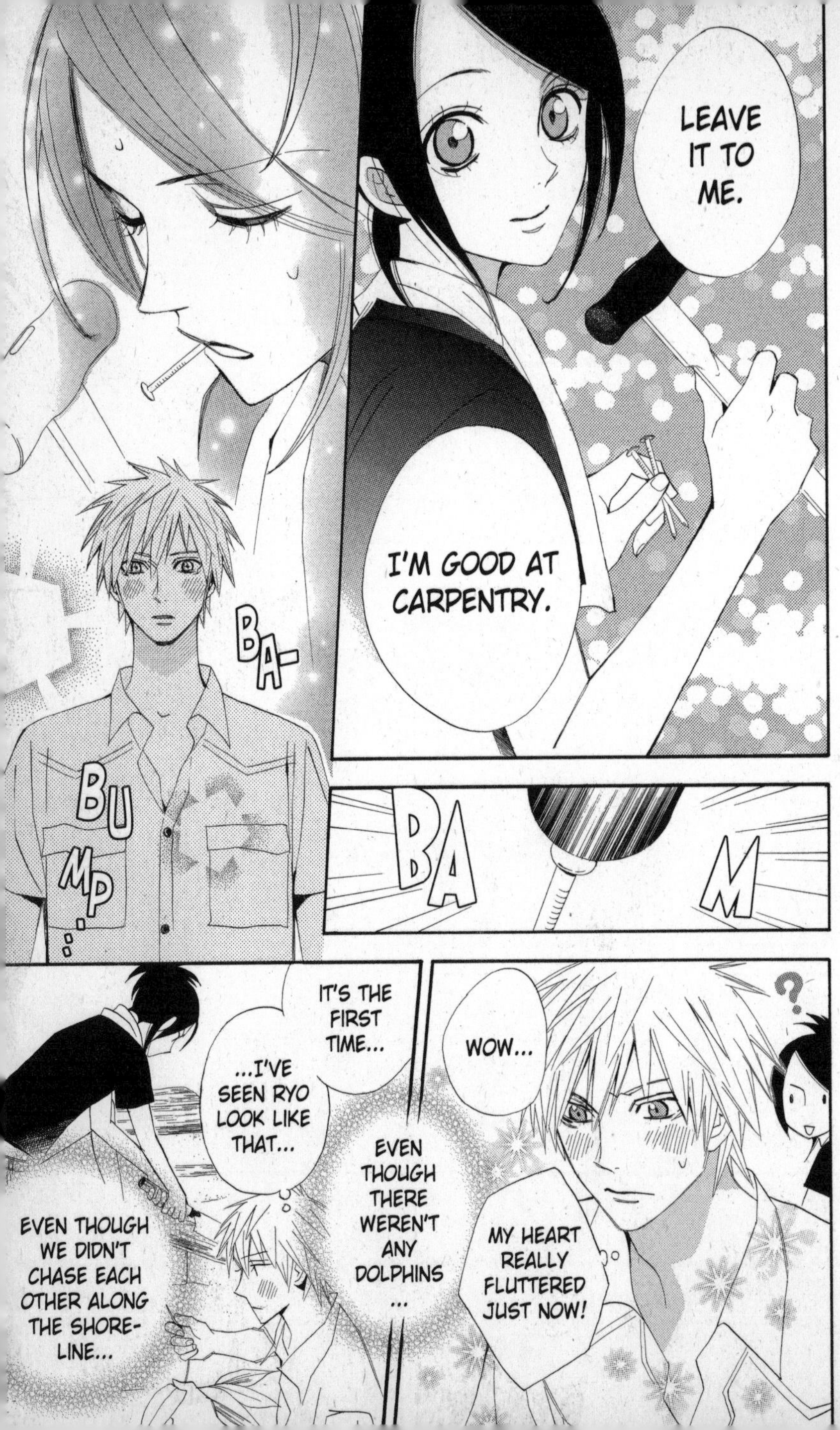
LEAVE IT TO ME.
I'M GOOD AT CARPENTRY.
BAM
BA-BUMP...
?
WOW...
MY HEART REALLY FLUTTERED JUST NOW!
IT'S THE FIRST TIME...
...I'VE SEEN RYO LOOK LIKE THAT...
EVEN THOUGH THERE WEREN'T ANY DOLPHINS...
EVEN THOUGH WE DIDN'T CHASE EACH OTHER ALONG THE SHORE-LINE...

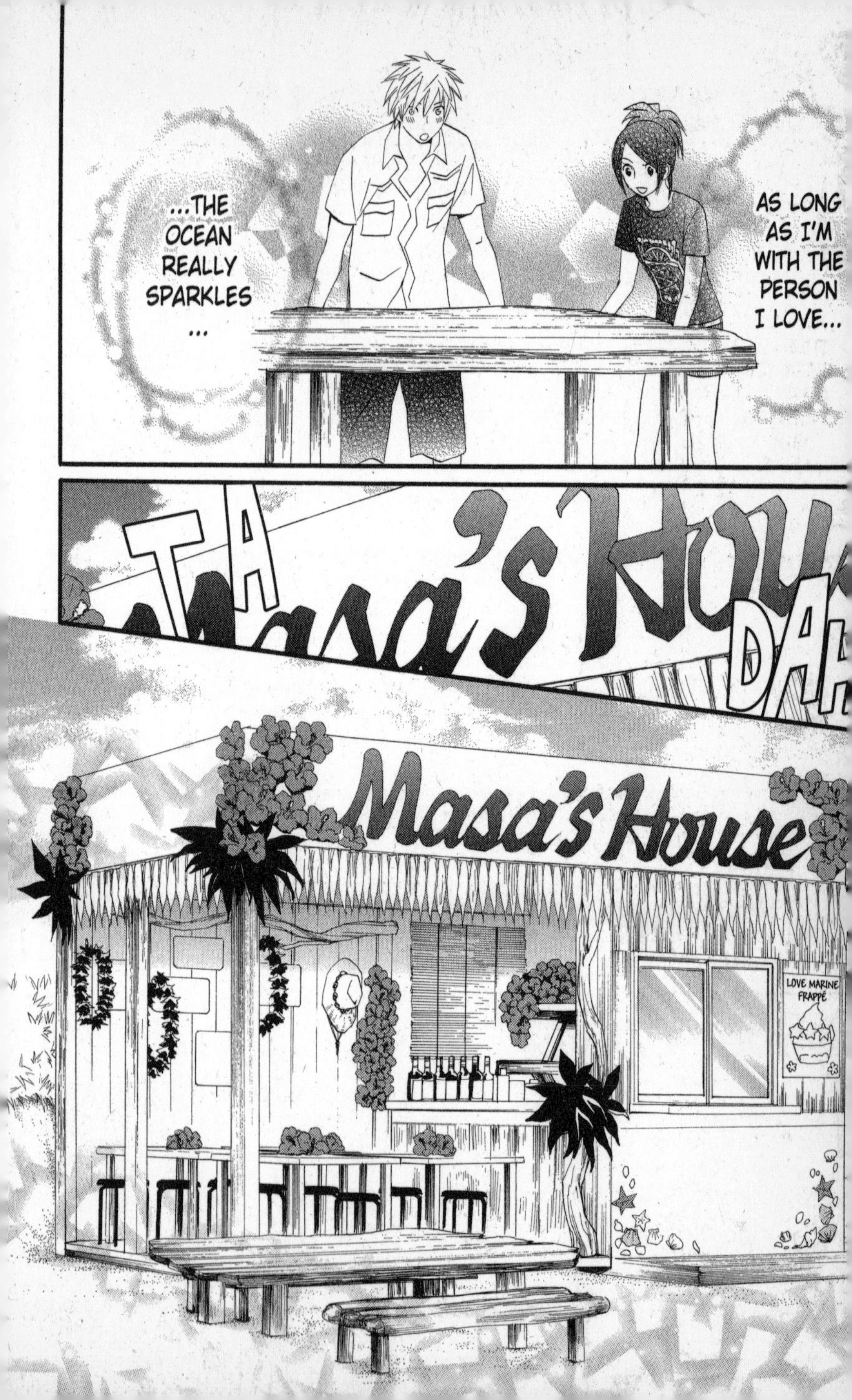

AS LONG AS I'M WITH THE PERSON I LOVE...
...THE OCEAN REALLY SPARKLES...
TA
DA
Masa's House
LOVE MARINE FRAPPÉ

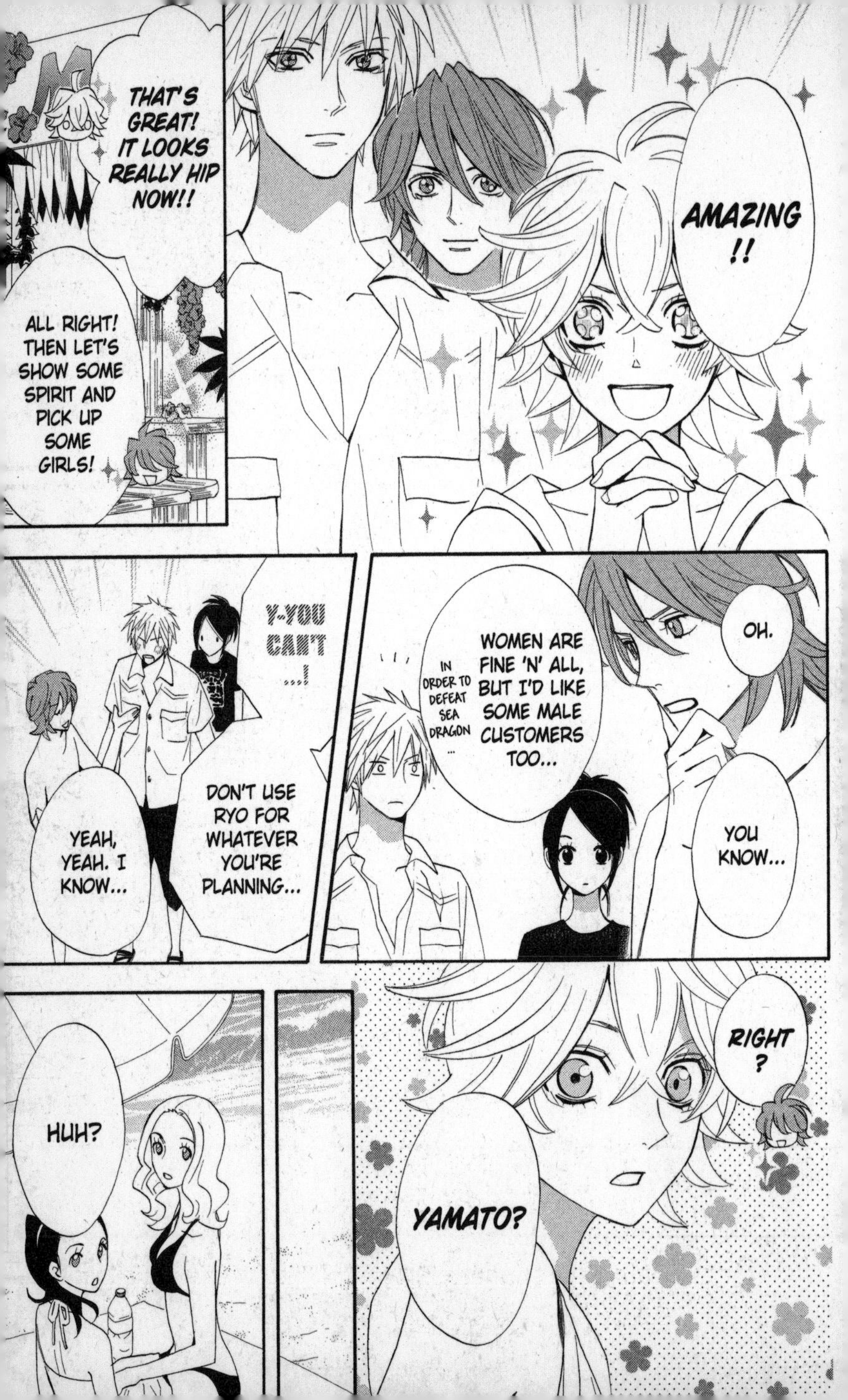
AMAZING!!
THAT'S GREAT! IT LOOKS REALLY HIP NOW!!
ALL RIGHT! THEN LET'S SHOW SOME SPIRIT AND PICK UP SOME GIRLS!
OH.
YOU KNOW...
WOMEN ARE FINE 'N' ALL, BUT I'D LIKE SOME MALE CUSTOMERS TOO...
IN ORDER TO DEFEAT SEA DRAGON...
Y-YOU CAN'T...!
DON'T USE RYO FOR WHATEVER YOU'RE PLANNING...
YEAH, YEAH. I KNOW...
RIGHT?
YAMATO?
HUH?

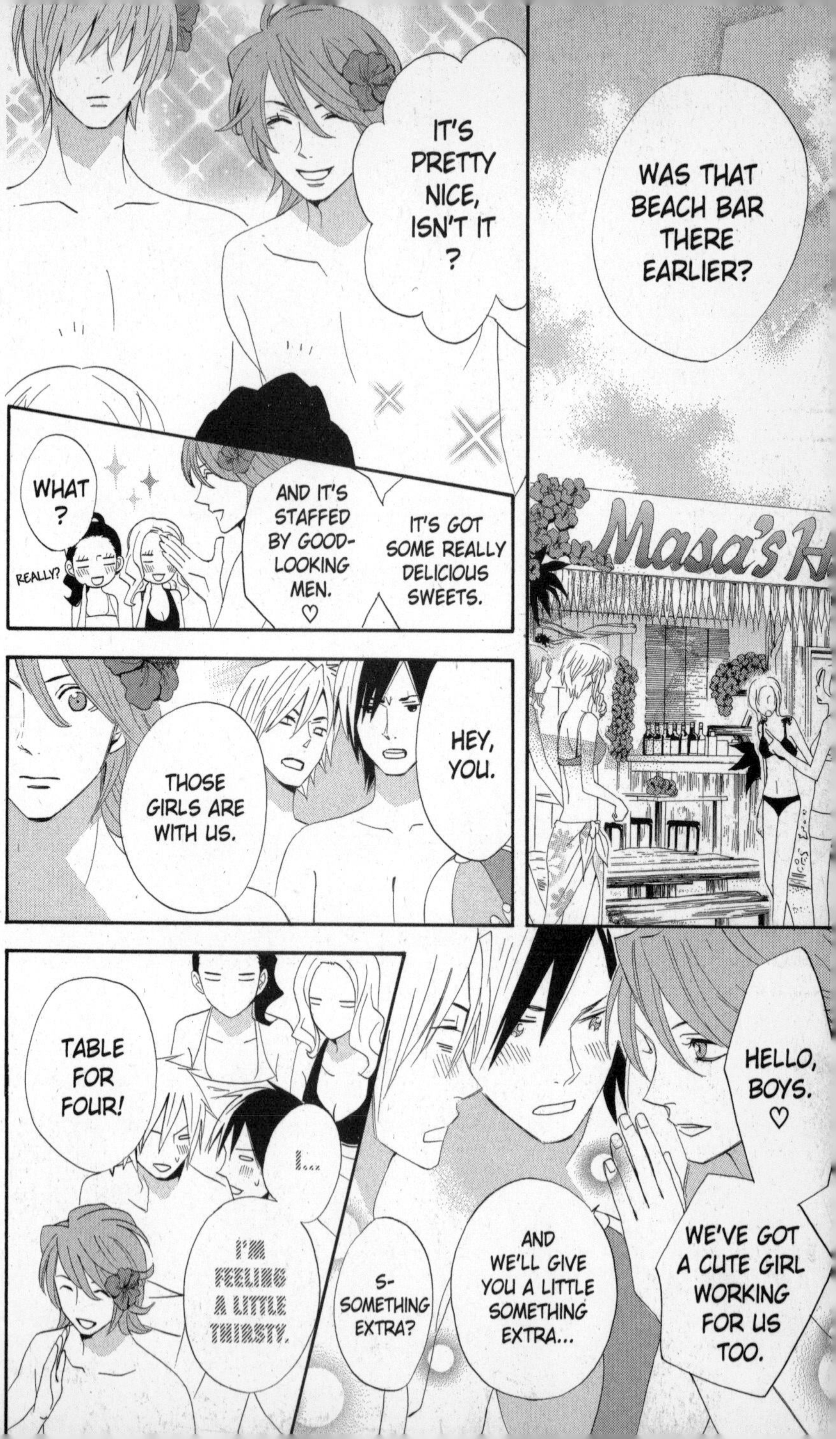
WAS THAT BEACH BAR THERE EARLIER?
IT'S PRETTY NICE, ISN'T IT?
IT'S GOT SOME REALLY DELICIOUS SWEETS.
AND IT'S STAFFED BY GOOD-LOOKING MEN. ♡
WHAT?
REALLY?
HEY, YOU.
THOSE GIRLS ARE WITH US.
HELLO, BOYS. ♡
WE'VE GOT A CUTE GIRL WORKING FOR US TOO.
AND WE'LL GIVE YOU A LITTLE SOMETHING EXTRA...
S-SOMETHING EXTRA?
TABLE FOR FOUR!
I...
I'M FEELING A LITTLE THIRSTY.

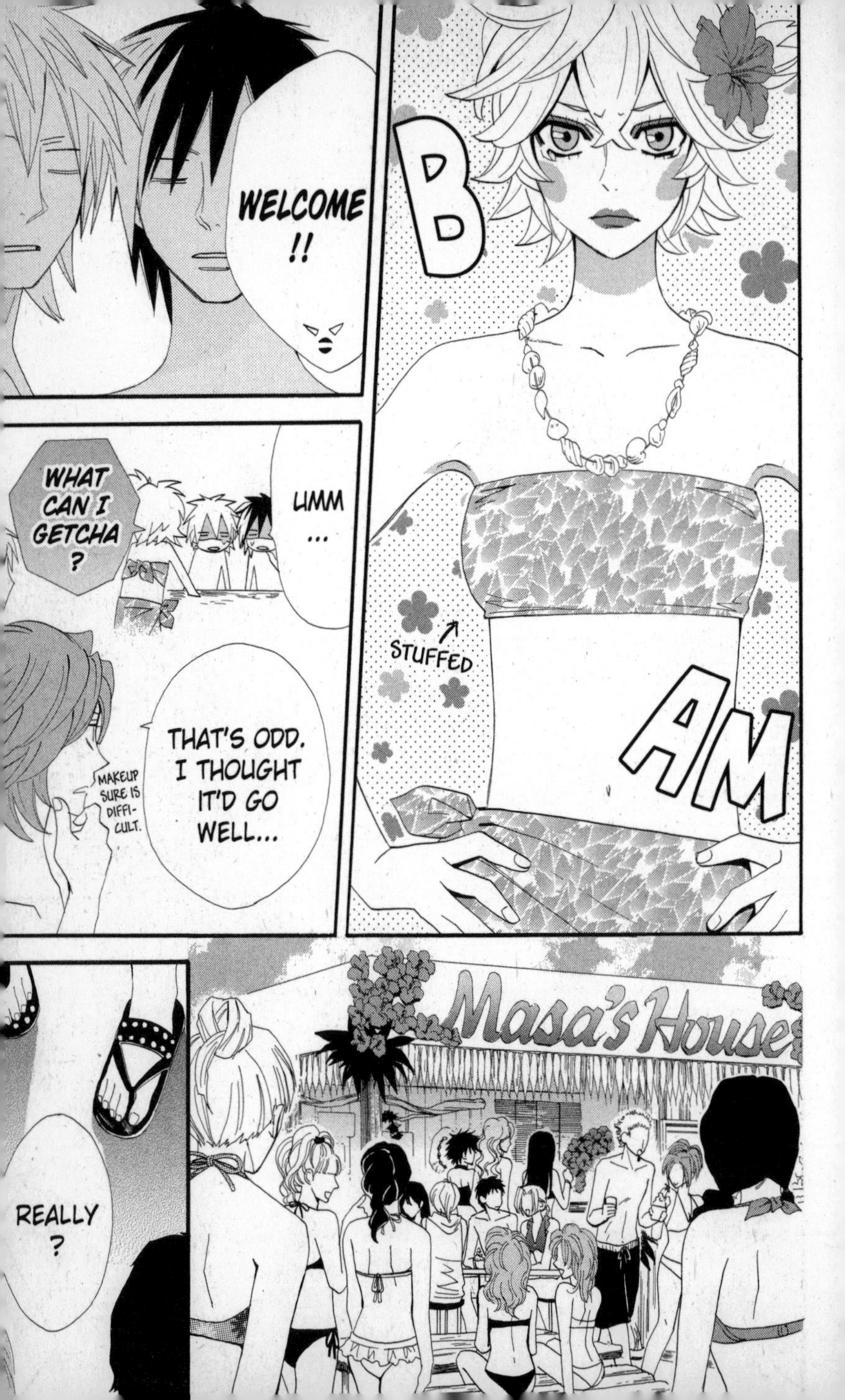
B
STUFFED
AM
WELCOME !!
UMM ...
WHAT CAN I GETCHA ?
THAT'S ODD. I THOUGHT IT'D GO WELL...
MAKEUP SURE IS DIFFICULT.
Masa's House
REALLY ?

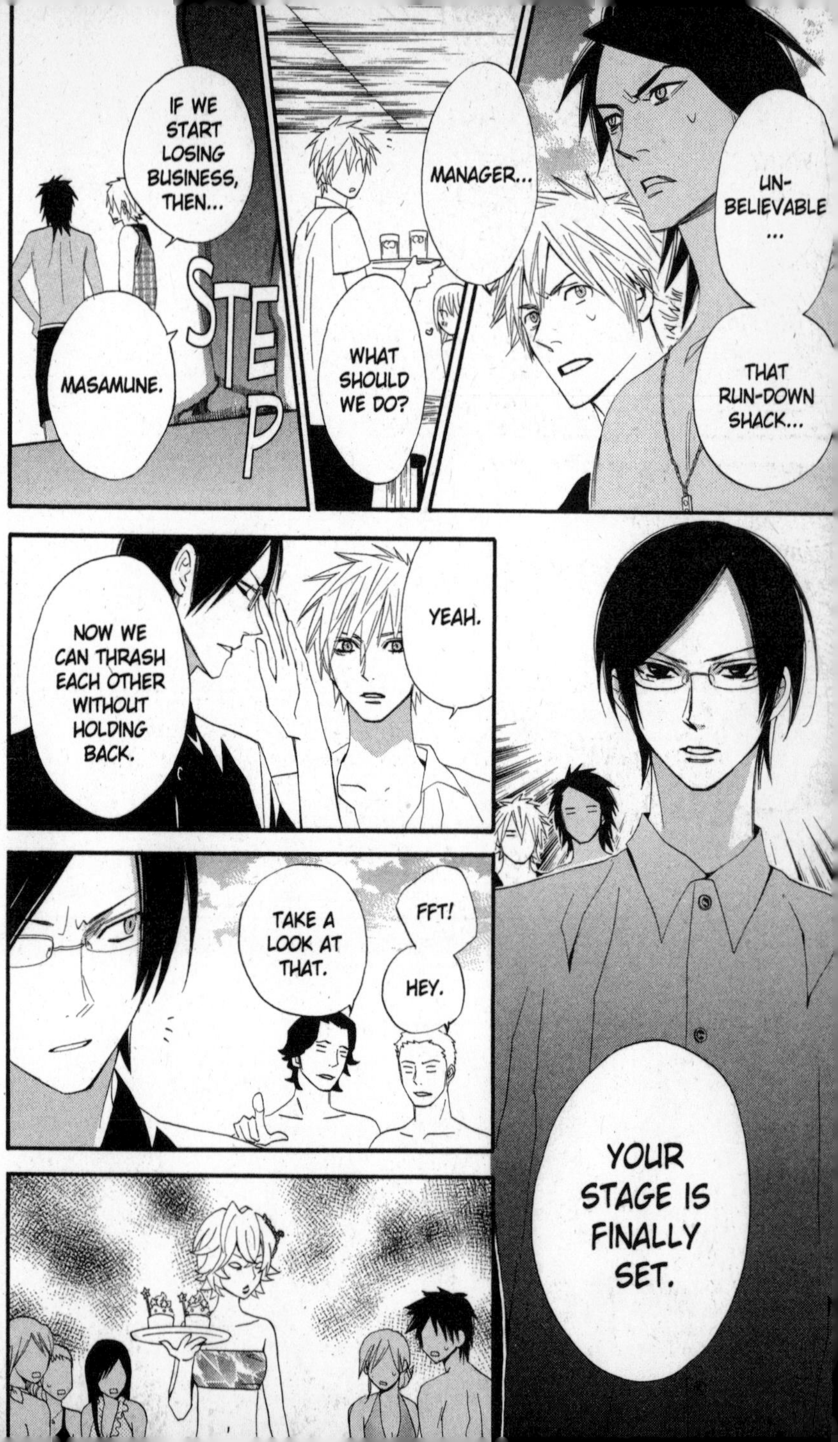
UN-BELIEVABLE...
THAT RUN-DOWN SHACK...
MANAGER...
WHAT SHOULD WE DO?
IF WE START LOSING BUSINESS, THEN...
STEP
MASAMUNE.
YOUR STAGE IS FINALLY SET.
YEAH.
NOW WE CAN THRASH EACH OTHER WITHOUT HOLDING BACK.
FFT!
HEY.
TAKE A LOOK AT THAT.

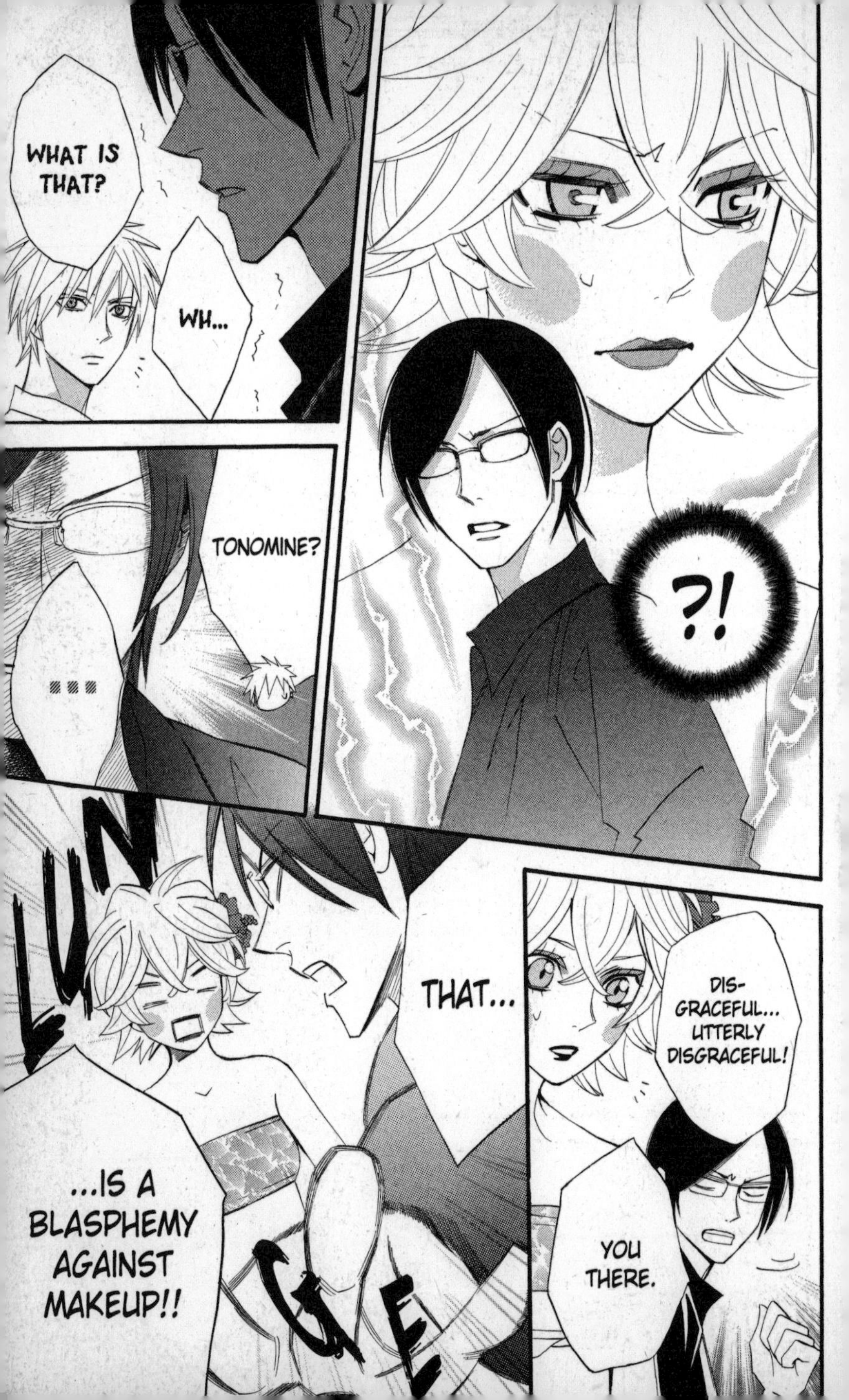
?!
WHAT IS THAT?
WH...
TONOMINE?
...
DIS-GRACEFUL... UTTERLY DISGRACEFUL!
YOU THERE.
THAT...
...IS A BLASPHEMY AGAINST MAKEUP!!
LUNGE

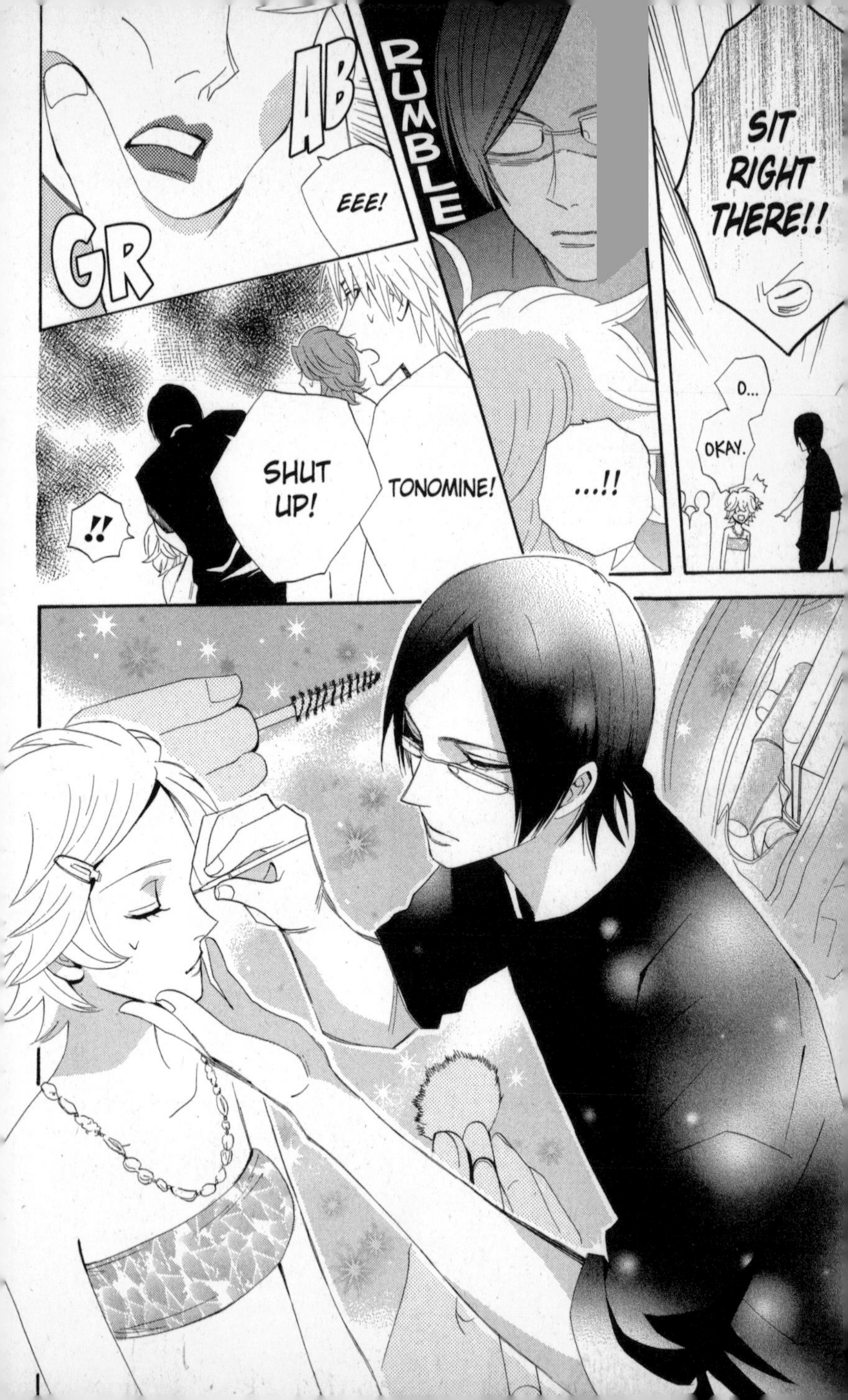
SIT RIGHT THERE!!
O...
OKAY.
RUMBLE
...!!
AB
GR
EEE!
TONOMINE!
SHUT UP!
!!

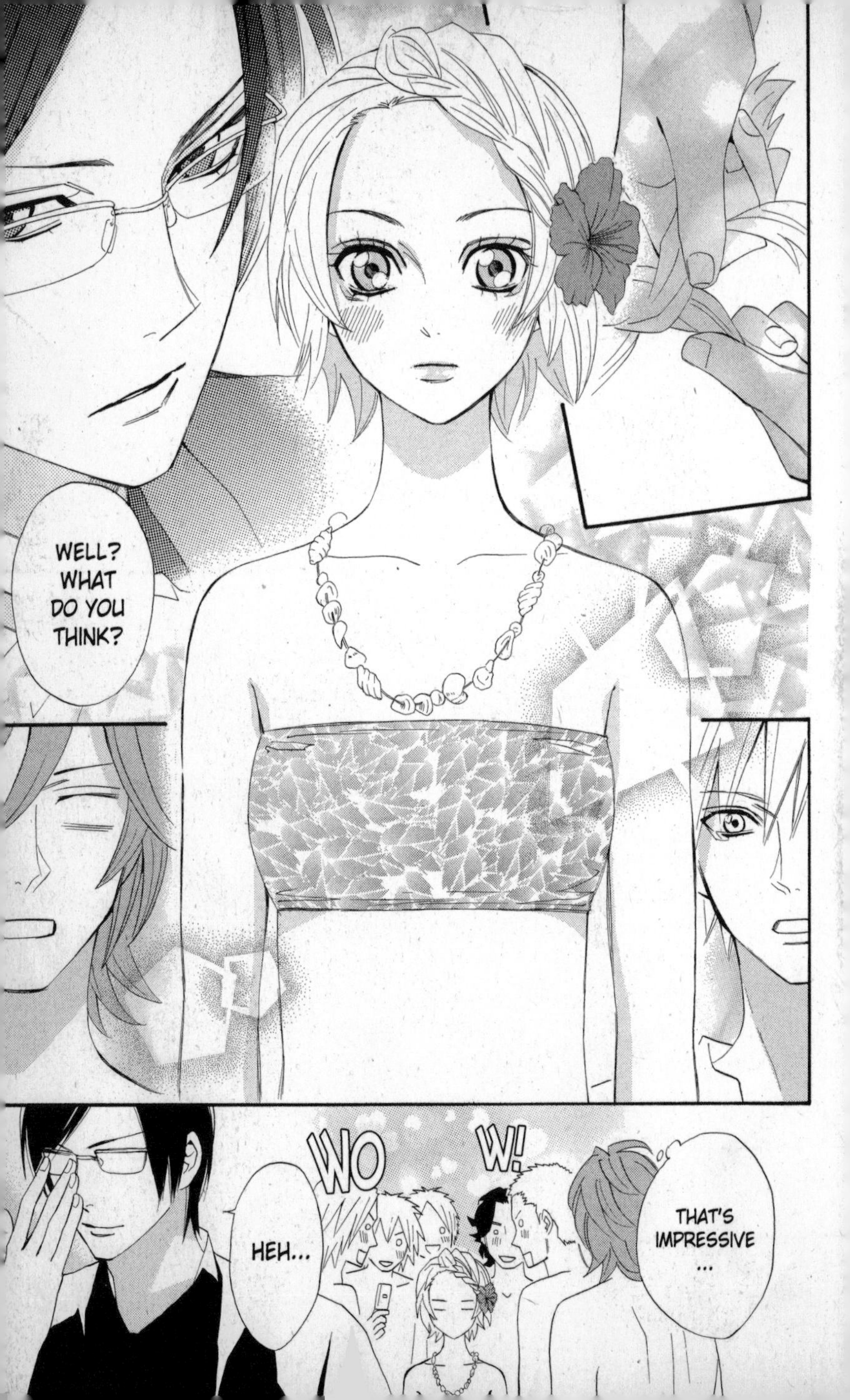
WELL? WHAT DO YOU THINK?
WOW!
THAT'S IMPRESSIVE ...
HEH...

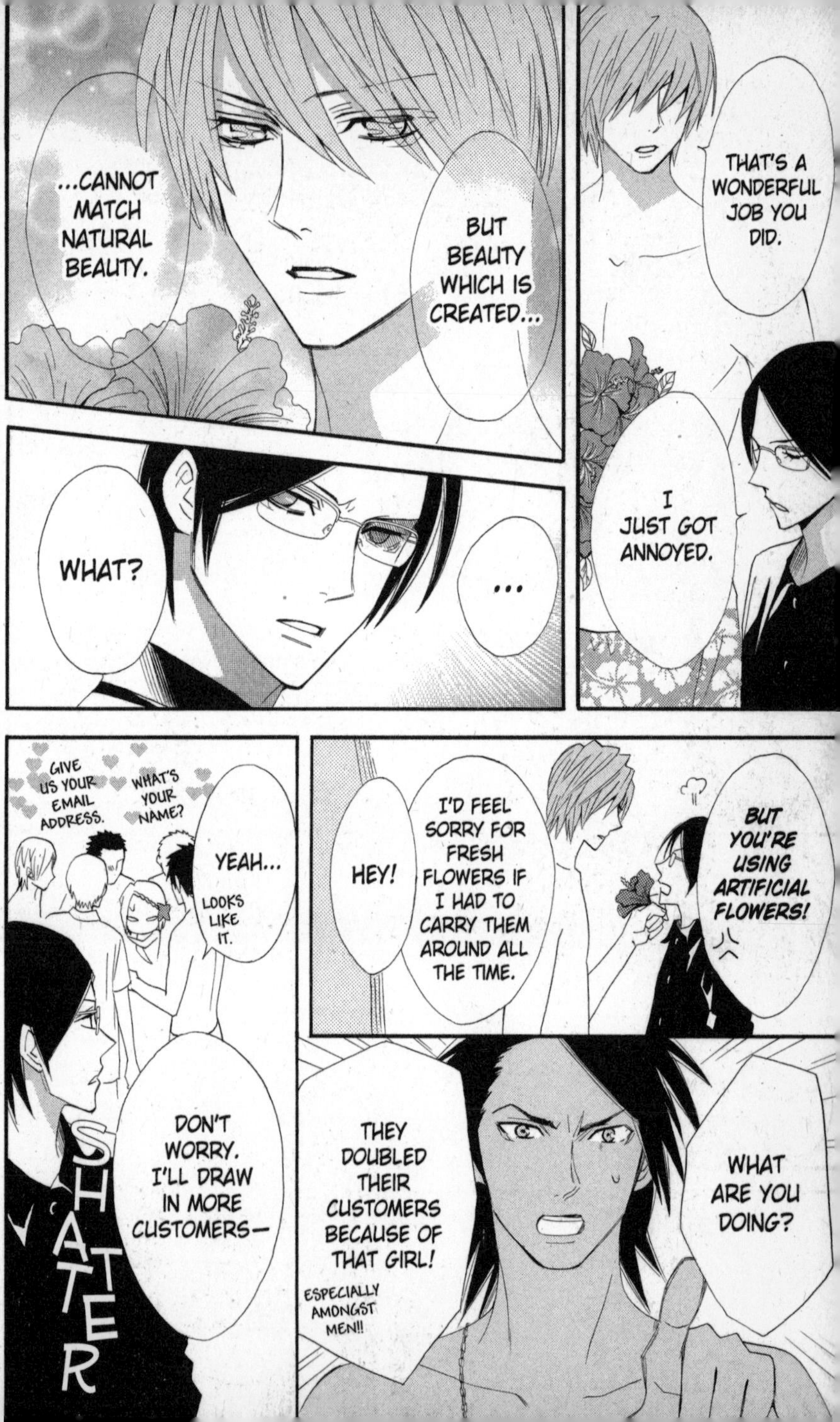
THAT'S A WONDERFUL JOB YOU DID.
I JUST GOT ANNOYED.
BUT BEAUTY WHICH IS CREATED...
...CANNOT MATCH NATURAL BEAUTY.
...
WHAT?
BUT YOU'RE USING ARTIFICIAL FLOWERS!
I'D FEEL SORRY FOR FRESH FLOWERS IF I HAD TO CARRY THEM AROUND ALL THE TIME.
HEY!
YEAH...
LOOKS LIKE IT.
WHAT'S YOUR NAME?
GIVE US YOUR EMAIL ADDRESS.
WHAT ARE YOU DOING?
THEY DOUBLED THEIR CUSTOMERS BECAUSE OF THAT GIRL!
ESPECIALLY AMONGST MEN!!
DON'T WORRY. I'LL DRAW IN MORE CUSTOMERS—
SHATTER

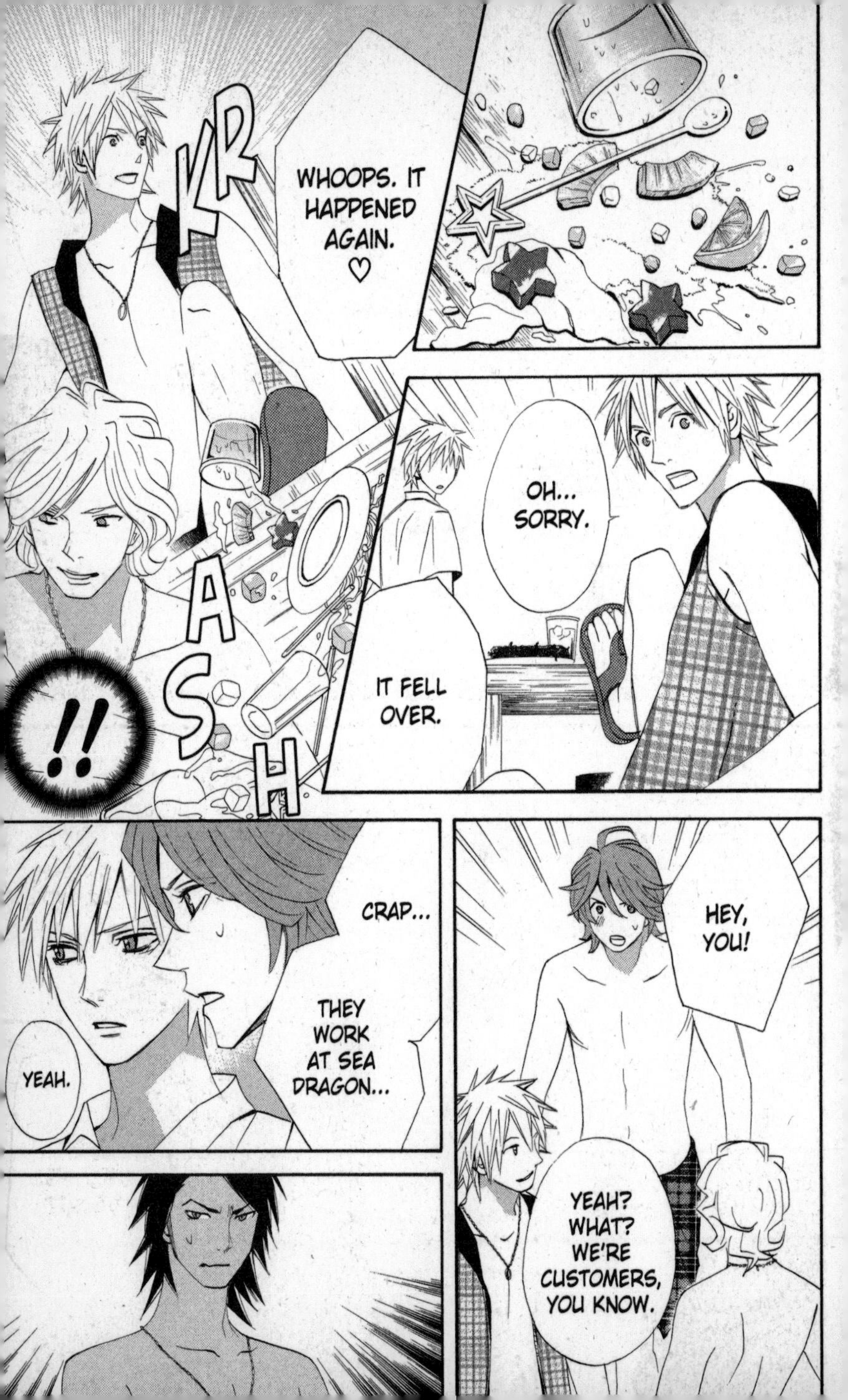
OH... SORRY.
IT FELL OVER.
WHOOPS. IT HAPPENED AGAIN. ♡
KRASH
!!
HEY, YOU!
YEAH? WHAT? WE'RE CUSTOMERS, YOU KNOW.
CRAP...
THEY WORK AT SEA DRAGON...
YEAH.

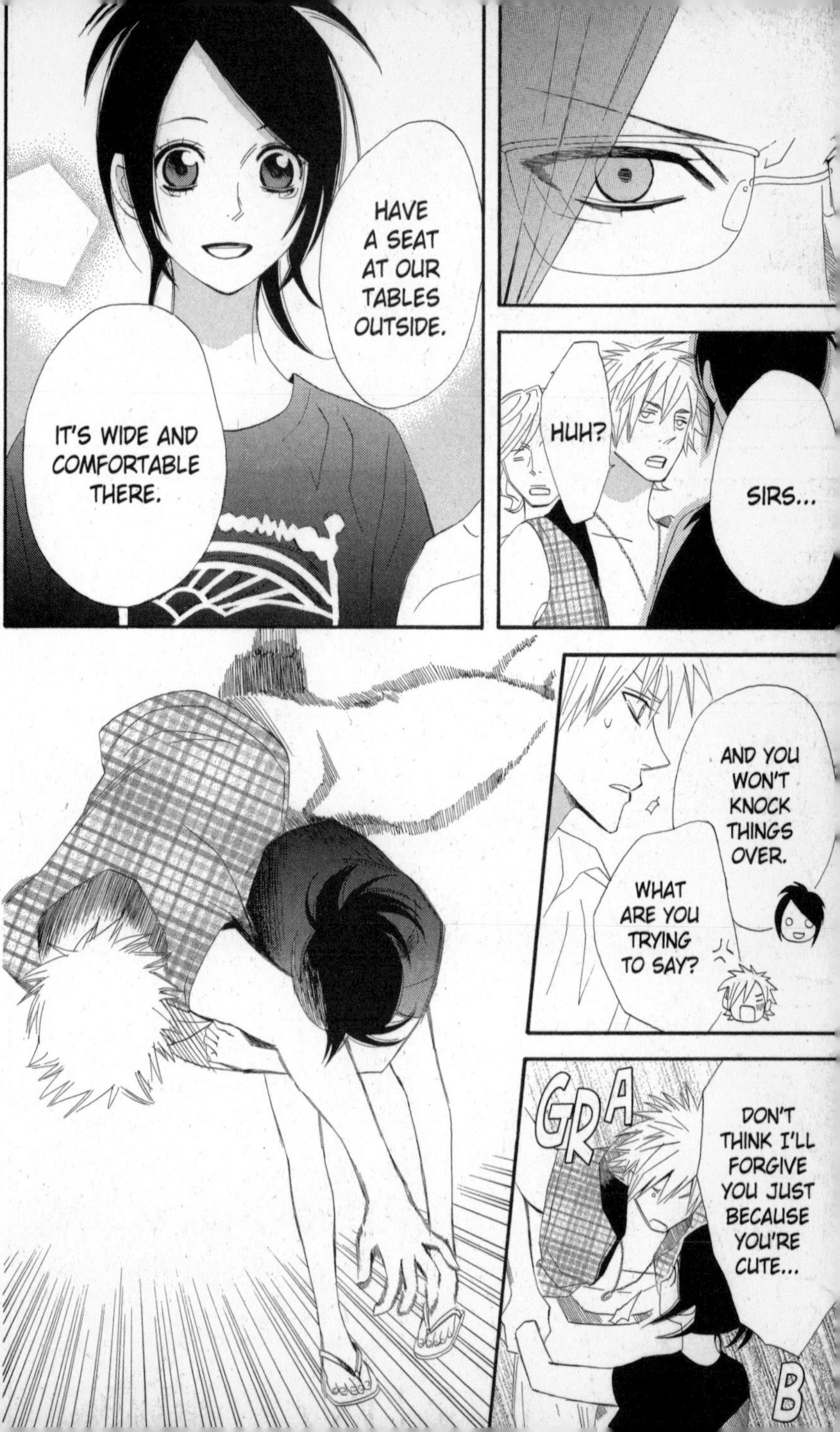
SIRS...
HUH?
HAVE A SEAT AT OUR TABLES OUTSIDE.
IT'S WIDE AND COMFORTABLE THERE.
AND YOU WON'T KNOCK THINGS OVER.
WHAT ARE YOU TRYING TO SAY?
DON'T THINK I'LL FORGIVE YOU JUST BECAUSE YOU'RE CUTE...
GRA
B

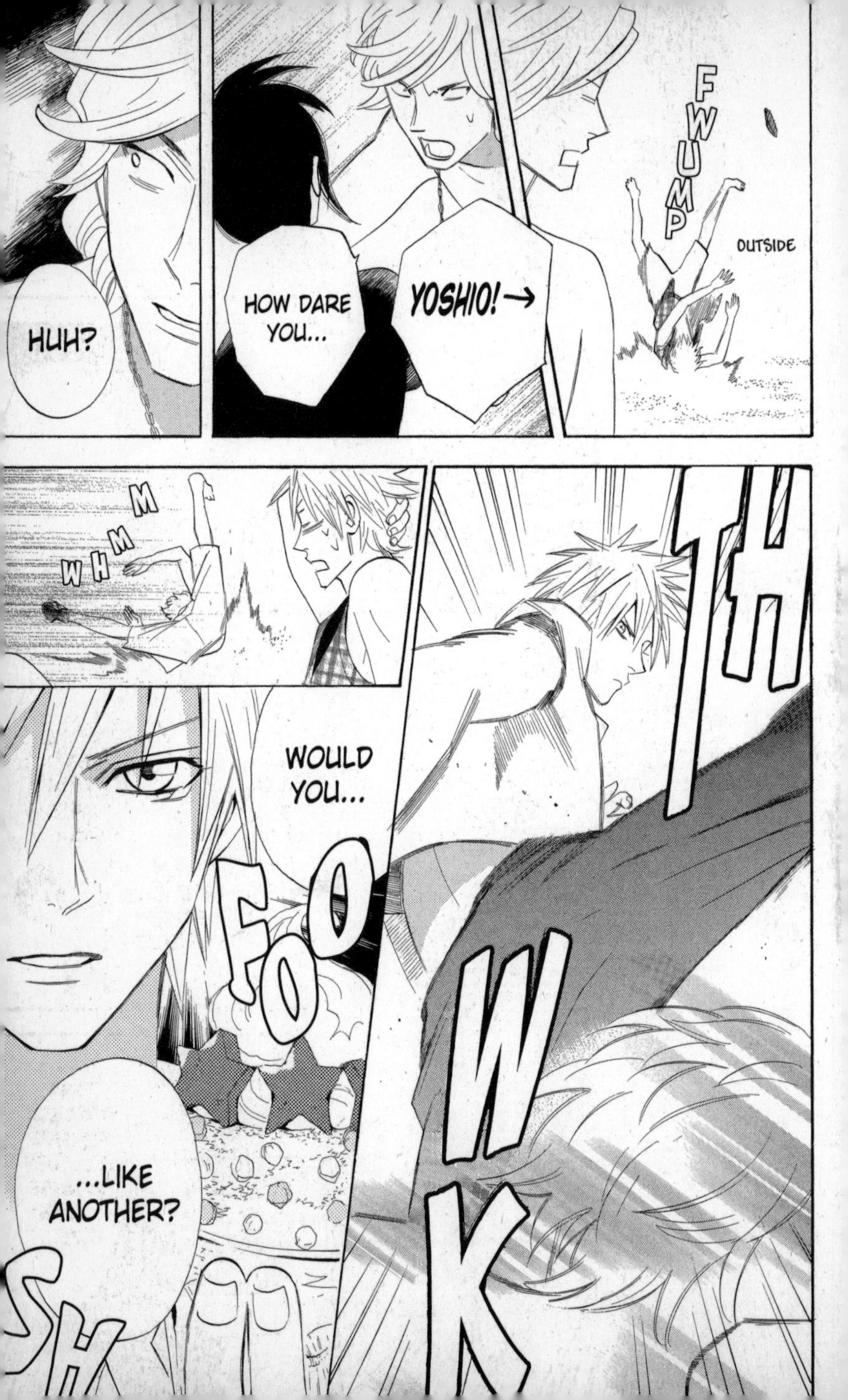
FWUMP
OUTSIDE
YOSHIO! →
HOW DARE YOU...
HUH?
THWK
WHMM
WOULD YOU...
FOOF
...LIKE ANOTHER?
SH

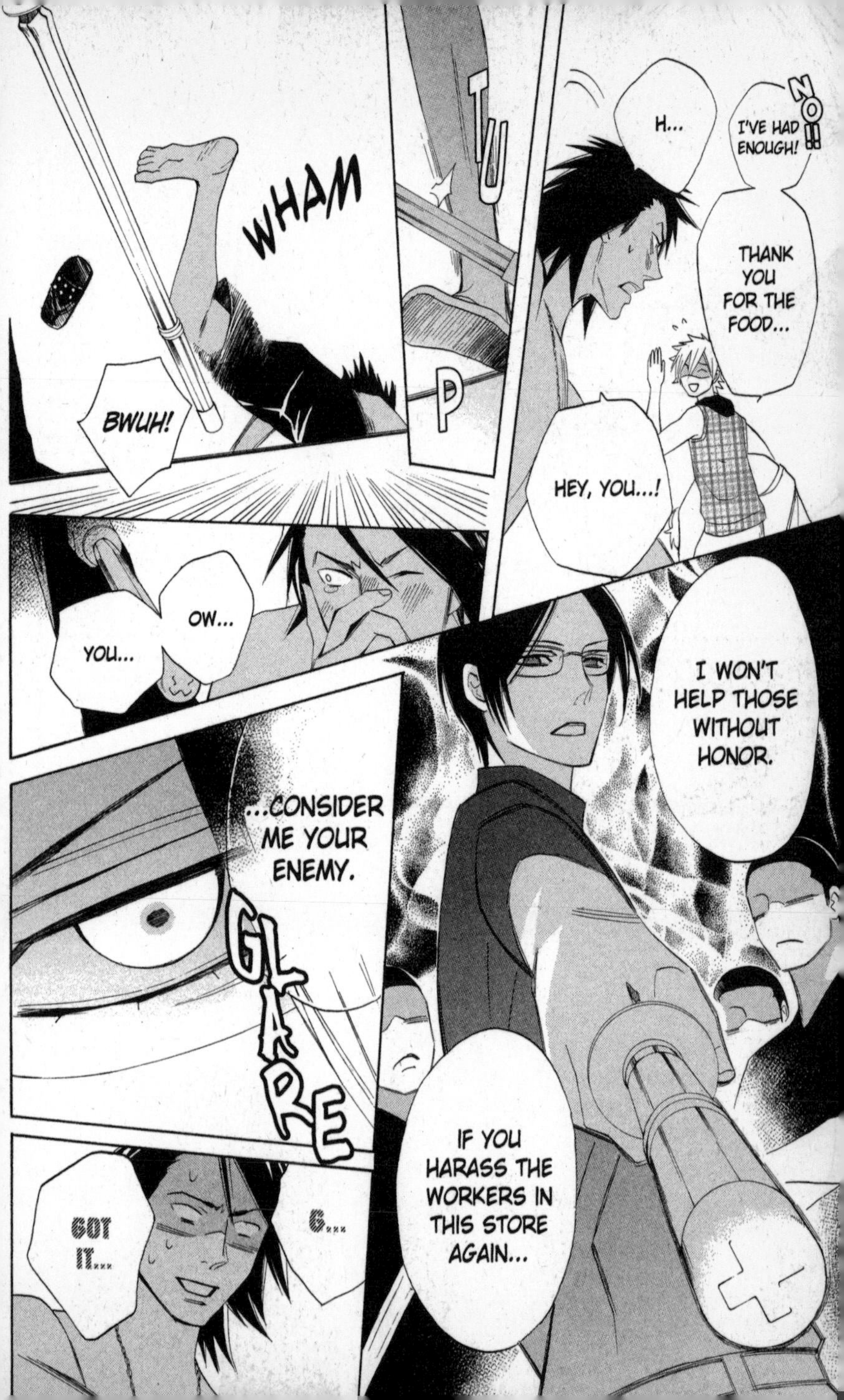
I'VE HAD ENOUGH!
NO!!
H...
THANK YOU FOR THE FOOD...
HEY, YOU...!
TUP
WHAM
BWUH!
OW...
YOU...
I WON'T HELP THOSE WITHOUT HONOR.
IF YOU HARASS THE WORKERS IN THIS STORE AGAIN...
...CONSIDER ME YOUR ENEMY.
GLARE
G...
GOT IT...

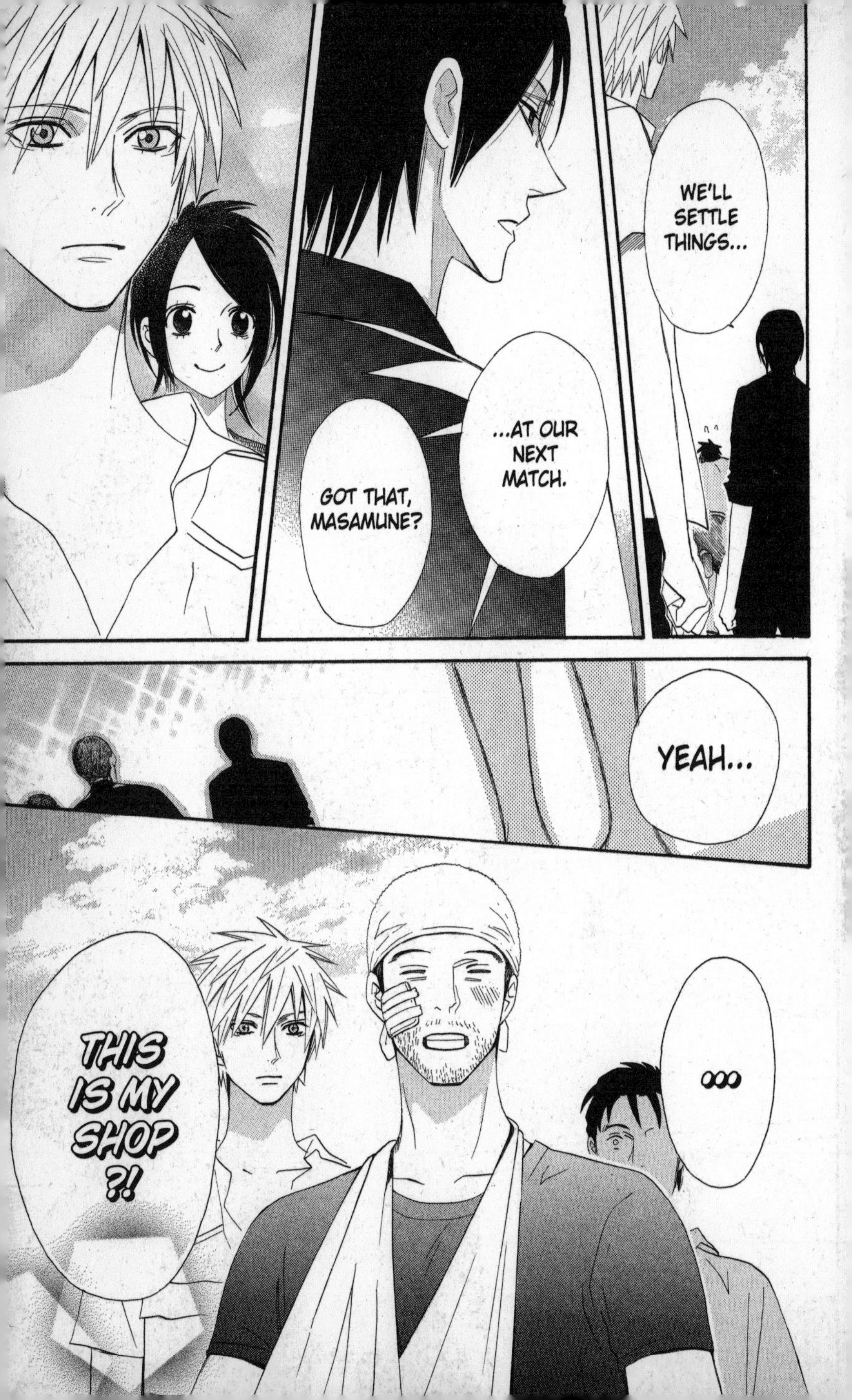
WE'LL SETTLE THINGS...
...AT OUR NEXT MATCH.
GOT THAT, MASAMUNE?
YEAH...
...
THIS IS MY SHOP ?!

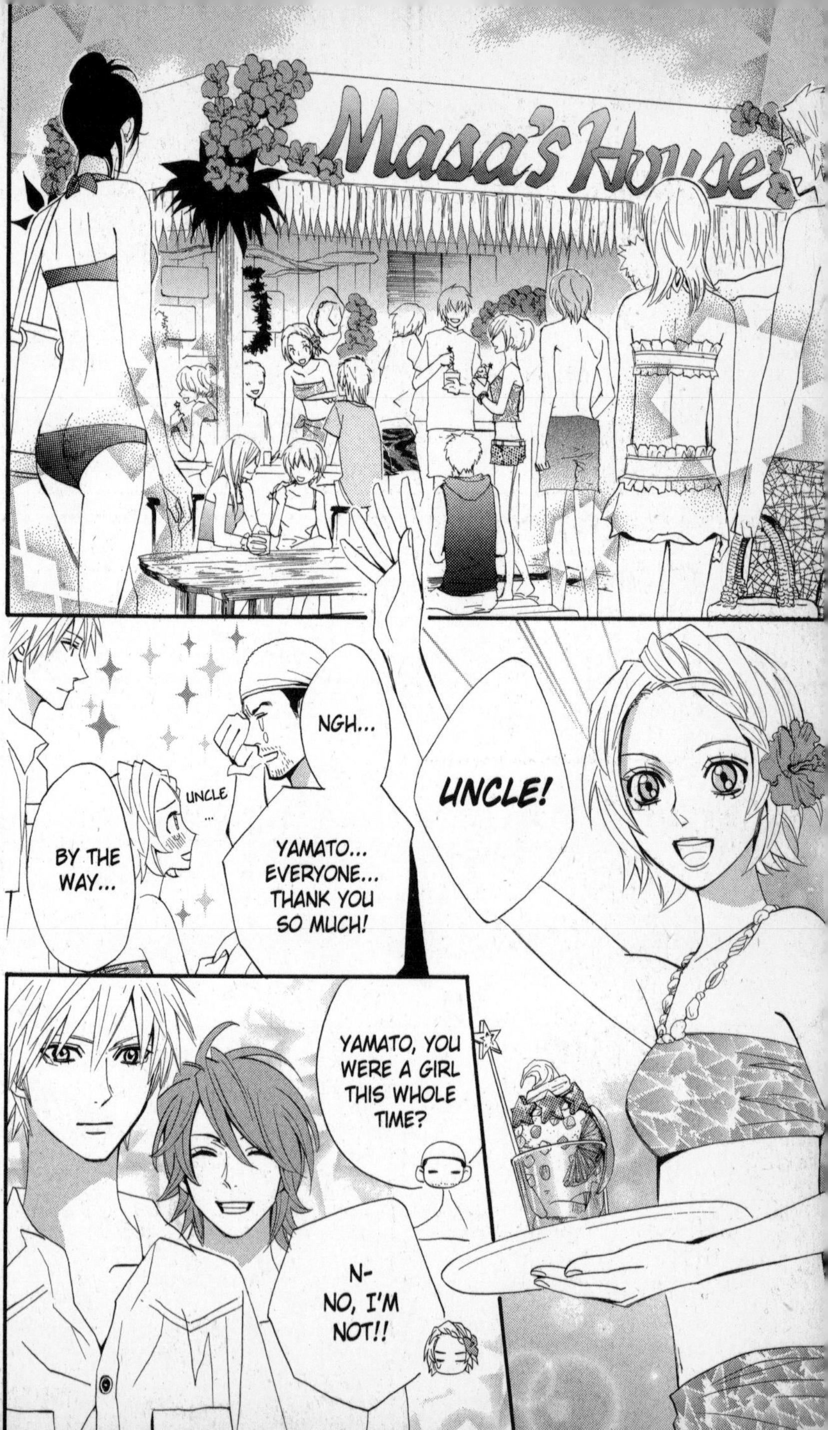

Masa's House
UNCLE!
NGH...
YAMATO... EVERYONE... THANK YOU SO MUCH!
UNCLE ...
BY THE WAY...
YAMATO, YOU WERE A GIRL THIS WHOLE TIME?
N- NO, I'M NOT!!

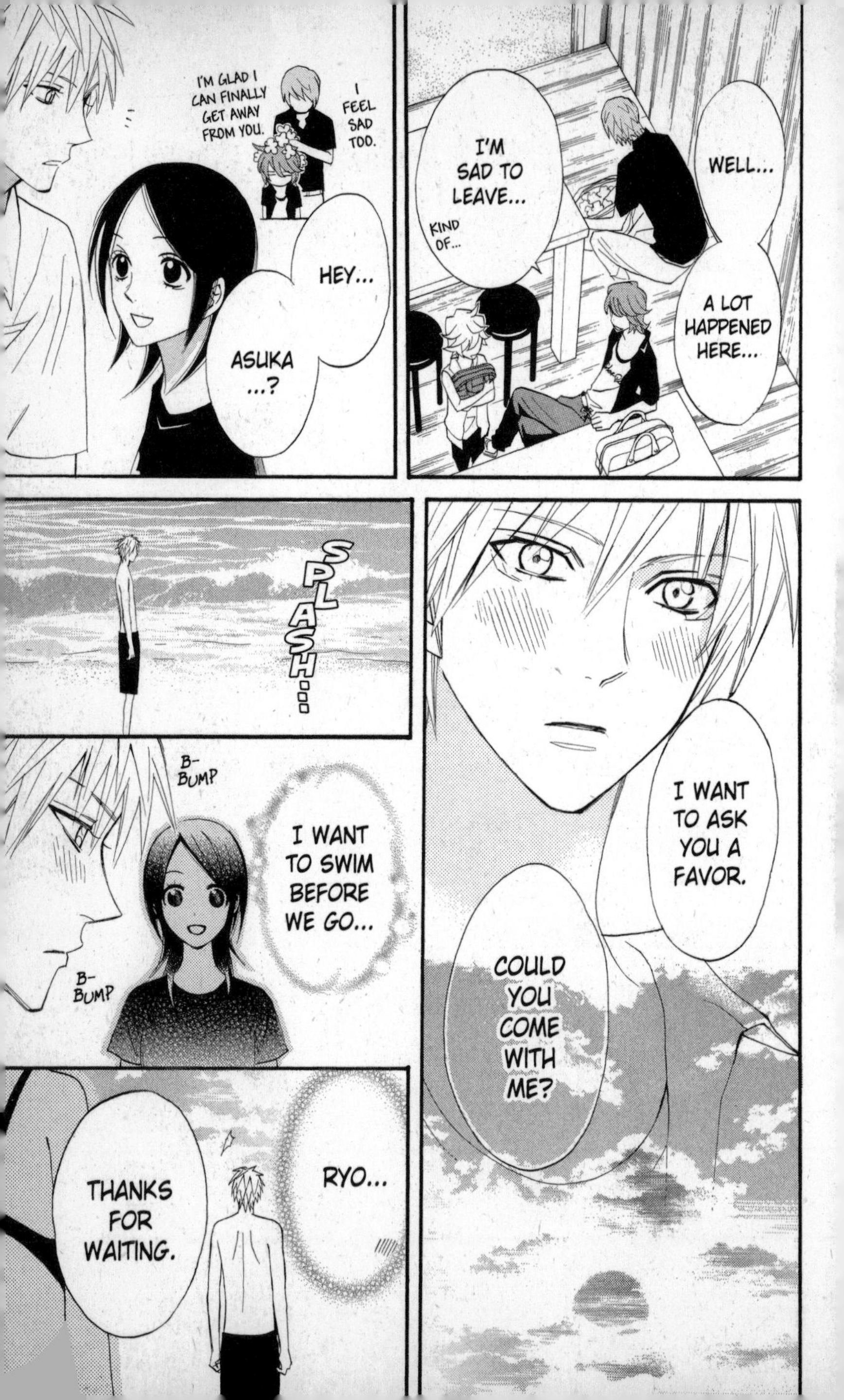
WELL...
A LOT HAPPENED HERE...
I'M SAD TO LEAVE...
KIND OF...
I FEEL SAD TOO.
I'M GLAD I CAN FINALLY GET AWAY FROM YOU.
HEY...
ASUKA ...?
I WANT TO ASK YOU A FAVOR.
COULD YOU COME WITH ME?
SPLASH...
B-BUMP
I WANT TO SWIM BEFORE WE GO...
B-BUMP
RYO...
THANKS FOR WAITING.

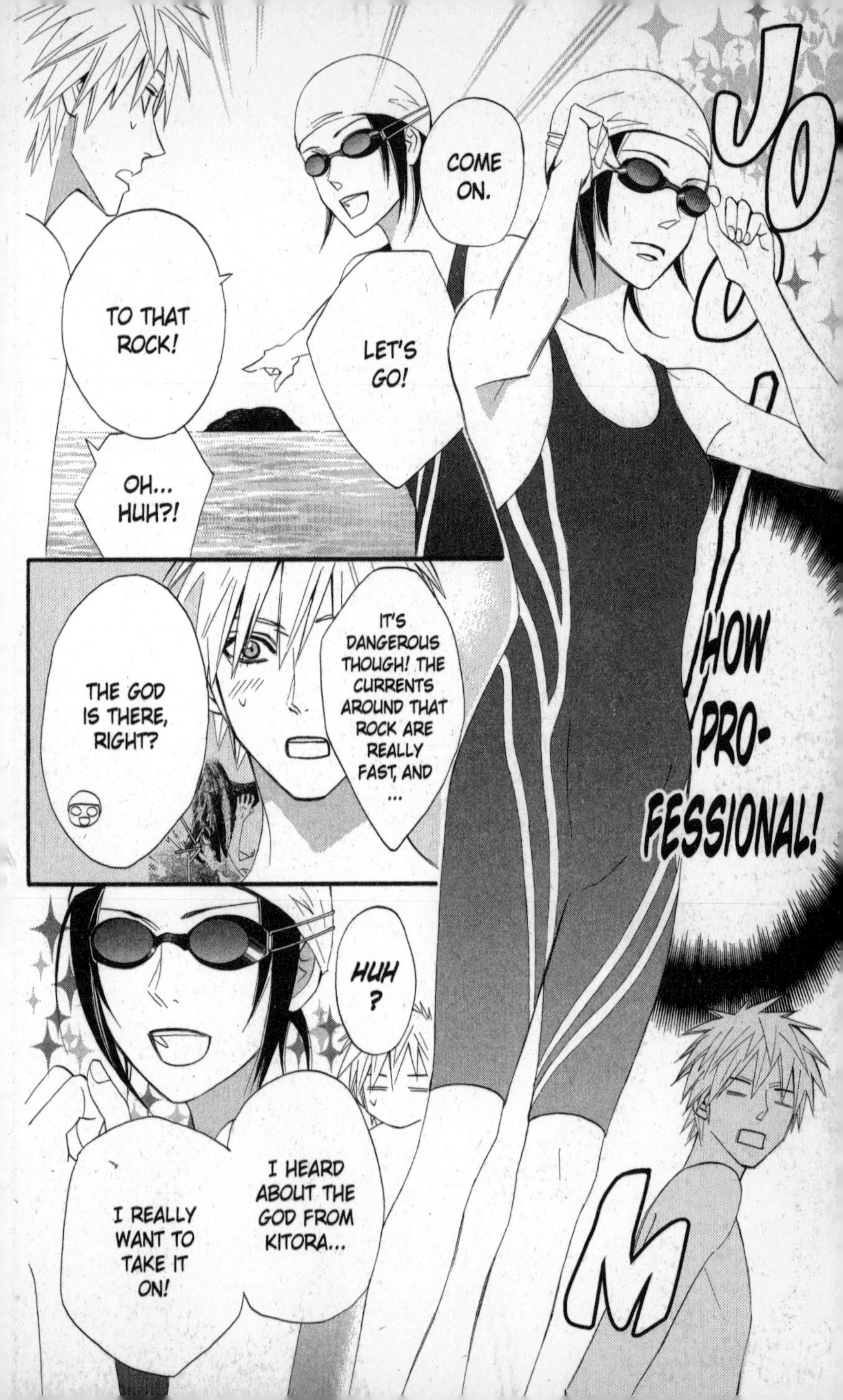
JO
HOW PRO-FESSIONAL!
M
COME ON.
LET'S GO!
TO THAT ROCK!
OH... HUH?!
IT'S DANGEROUS THOUGH! THE CURRENTS AROUND THAT ROCK ARE REALLY FAST, AND ...
THE GOD IS THERE, RIGHT?
HUH ?
I HEARD ABOUT THE GOD FROM KITORA...
I REALLY WANT TO TAKE IT ON!

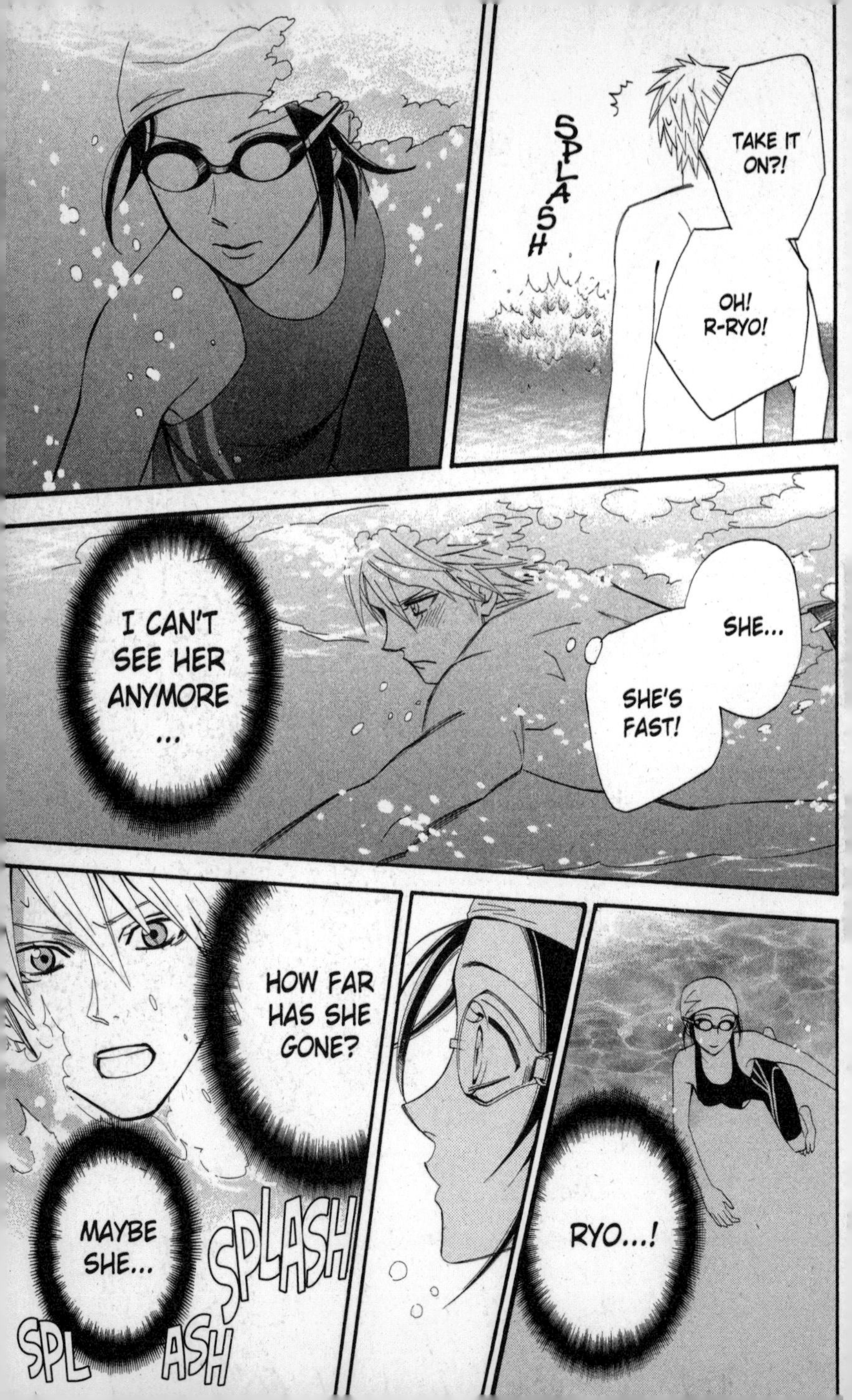
SPLASH
TAKE IT ON?!
OH! R-RYO!
SHE...
SHE'S FAST!
I CAN'T SEE HER ANYMORE ...
RYO...!
HOW FAR HAS SHE GONE?
MAYBE SHE...
SPLASH
SPL ASH

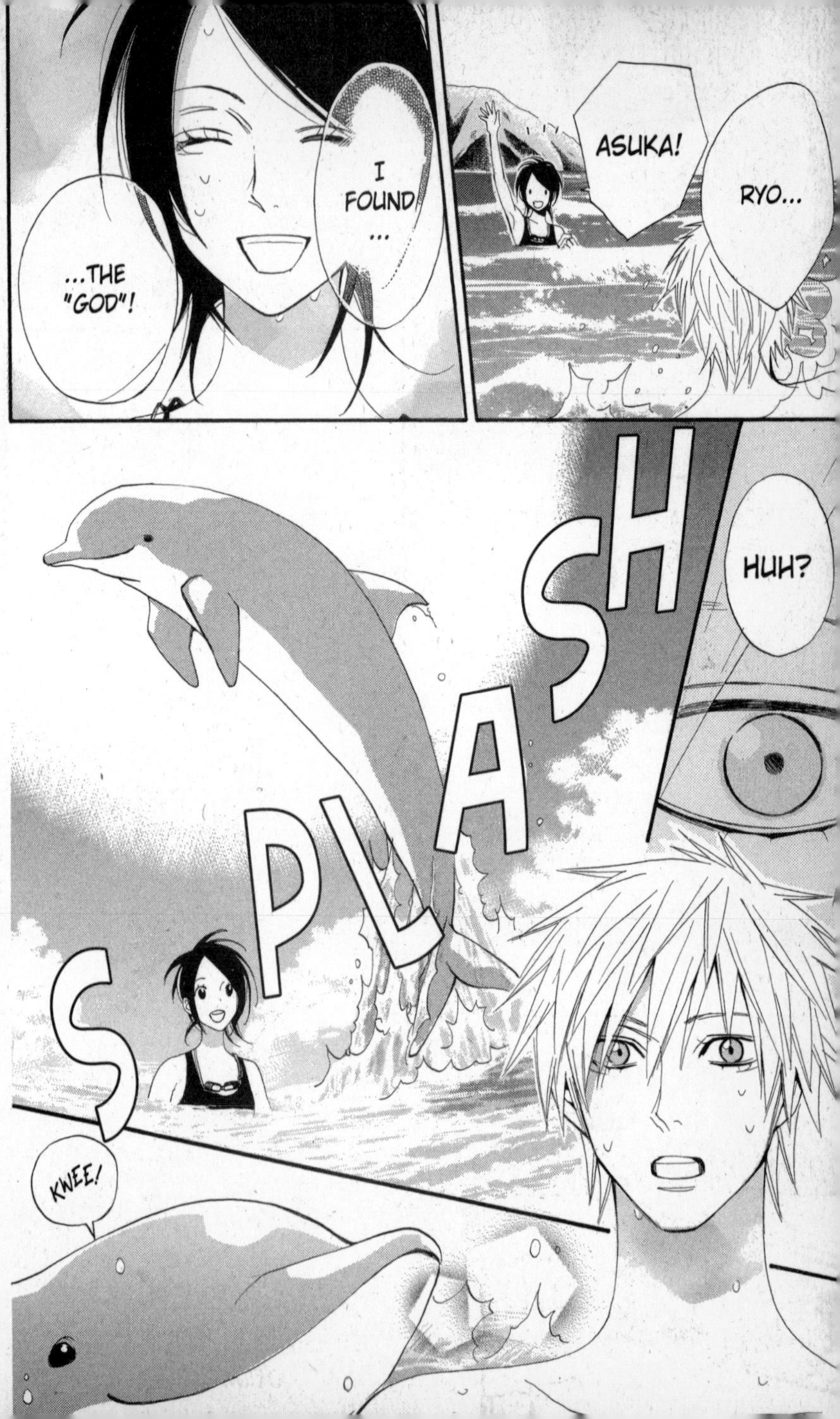
RYO...
ASUKA!
I FOUND ...
...THE "GOD"!
HUH?
SPLASH
KWEE!

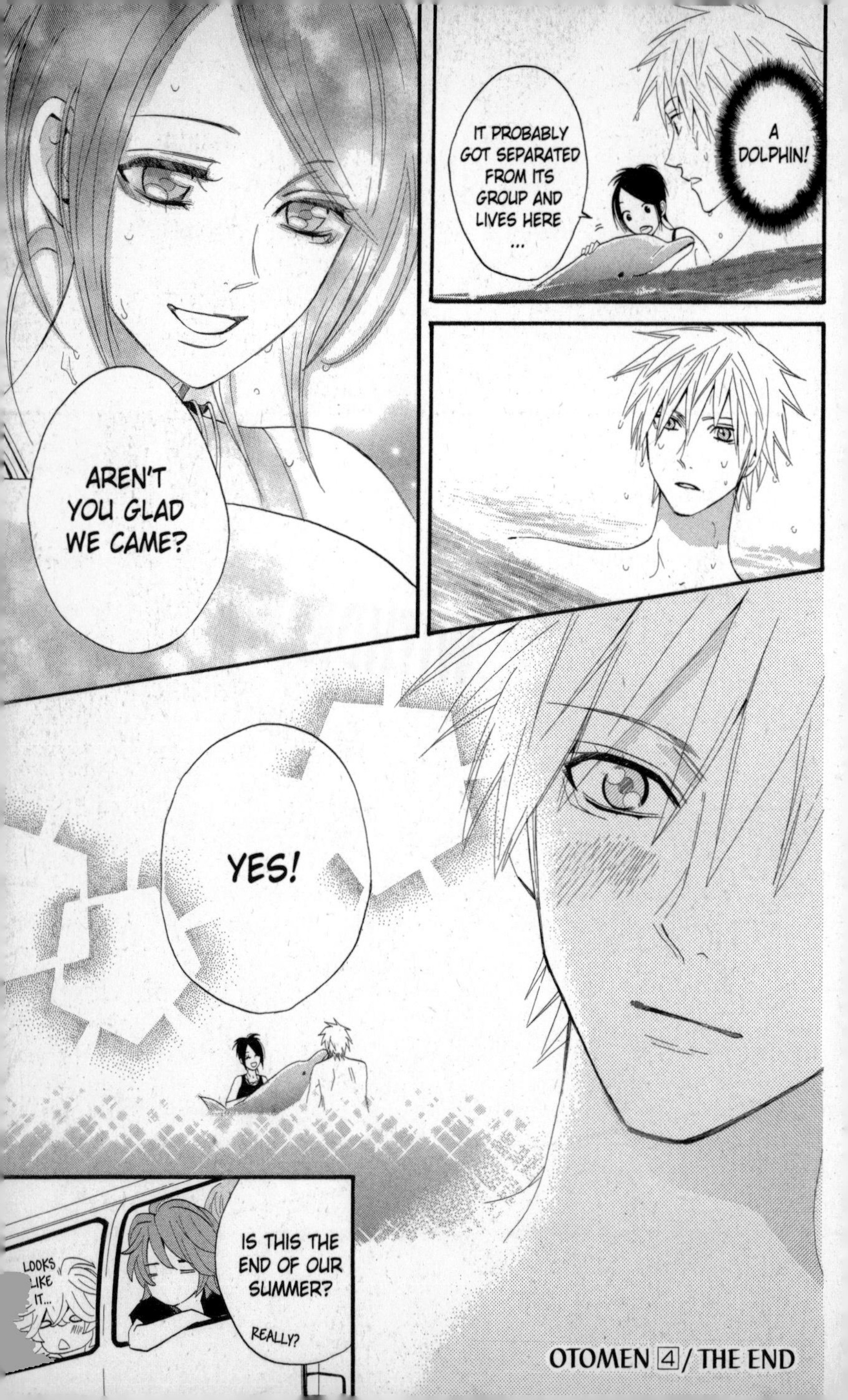
A DOLPHIN!
IT PROBABLY GOT SEPARATED FROM ITS GROUP AND LIVES HERE ...
AREN'T YOU GLAD WE CAME?
YES!
IS THIS THE END OF OUR SUMMER?
REALLY?
LOOKS LIKE IT...

OTOMEN 4 / THE END

OTOMEN

Confused by some of the terms, but too MANLY to ask for help?

Here are some **cultural notes** to assist you!

HONORIFICS

Chan – an informal honorific used to address children and females. *Chan* can also be used toward animals, lovers, intimate friends and people whom one has known since childhood.

Kun – an informal honorific used primarily toward males. It can be used by people of more senior status addressing those junior to them or by anyone addressing boys or young men. Like *chan*, *kun* is often added to nicknames to emphasize friendship or intimacy.

San – the most common honorific title. It is used to address people outside one's immediate family and close circle of friends.

Senpai – used to address one's senior colleagues or mentor figures. It is used when students refer to or address more senior students in their school.

Sensei – honorific title used to address teachers as well as professionals such as doctors, lawyers and artists.

Sama – honorific used to address persons much higher in rank than oneself.

NOTES

Page 3 | **Hana to Mame**
The name *Hana to Mame* (Flowers and Beans) is a
play on the real shojo manga magazine *Hana to Yume*
(Flowers and Dreams) published by Hakusensha.

Page 3 | **Tsun-sama**
Juta makes this word up by combining *tsundere* and
ore-sama. *Tsundere* describes a character who is
tsuntsun (cold or irritable) and later becomes *deredere*
(affectionate or sentimental). *Ore-sama* describes a
pompous and arrogant person, as it combines *ore* (me)
with the honorific *sama*.

Page 8, panel 2 | **Bento**
A lunch box that may contain rice, meat, pickles and an assortment of side dishes.
Sometimes the food is arranged in such a way as to resemble objects like animals,
flowers, leaves, and so forth.

Page 22, panel 1 | **Otōsan**
Otōsan means "father" in Japanese. Asuka is using this term as a sign of respect
rather than actually calling Ryo's father his own.

Page 48, panel 3 | **Sambo and Kalarippayattu**
Sambo is a modern-day martial art developed in the Soviet Union. Kalarippayattu is
a South Indian martial art.

Page 71, panel 3 | **Yo Nihiruda**
A character from the manga *High School! Kimengumi*.

Page 109, panel 4 | **Yakisoba**
Panfried noodles often sold at vendors and grocery stores in Japan. *Kata-yakisoba*
uses deep-fried noodles so it is crunchy.

Page 116, panel 1 | **Splitting Watermelons**
Known as *suika-wari*, splitting watermelons while blindfolded is a classic beach
activity in Japan.

Page 165, panel 3 | **Shonen Junk and Shonen Mayazine**
A play on the names of the shonen manga magazines *Shonen Jump* (published by
Shueisha) and *Shonen Magazine* (published by Kodansha).

Aya Kanno was born in Tokyo, Japan.
She is the creator of *Soul Rescue* and *Blank Slate*
(originally published as *Akusaga* in Japan's
BetsuHana magazine). Her latest work, *Otomen*,
is currently being serialized in *BetsuHana*.

OTOMEN

Vol. 4
Shojo Beat Manga Edition

Story and Art by | **AYA KANNO**

Translation & Adaptation | **JN Productions**
Touch-up Art & Lettering | **Mark McMurray**
Design | **Fawn Lau**
Editor | **Amy Yu**

VP, Production | **Alvin Lu**
VP, Publishing Licensing | **Rika Inouye**
VP, Sales & Product Marketing | **Gonzalo Ferreyra**
VP, Creative | **Linda Espinosa**
Publisher | **Hyoe Narita**

Printed in the U.S.A.

Published by VIZ Media, LLC
P.O. Box 77010
San Francisco, CA 94107

10 9 8 7 6 5 4 3 2 1
First printing, November 2009

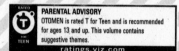

PARENTAL ADVISORY
OTOMEN is rated T for Teen and is recommended
for ages 13 and up. This volume contains
suggestive themes.
ratings.viz.com

www.viz.com

www.shojobeat.com